SHINING THE LIGHT
BOOK III

HUMANITY GETS A SECOND CHANCE

Source Information by
Zoosh through Robert Shapiro
YHWH through Arthur Fanning

Light Technology Research

Cover art by
Robert Lewis Arnold

ISBN 0-929385-71-3

Published by
Light Technology Publishing
P.O. Box 1526
Sedona, AZ 86339

Printed by
MISSION POSSIBLE
Commercial Printing
P.O. Box 1495
Sedona, AZ 86339

Preface

Light Technology has finally published the books that give the background, the history, the purpose and the future of humanity. We recommend:

The Explorer Race – Zoosh through Robert Shapiro

Soul Evolution Father – Jehovah through Arthur Fanning

These books are a prelude to and a preparation for the concepts contained in the *Shining the Light* books.

This third book of the ongoing Shining the Light series covers events in this solar system from March 1995 through October 1995. It ends with the astonishing fact that the Creator, the cosmic councils and many great beings who love humanity shifted our reality from a position about one third of the way up from the third dimension to a position almost halfway between the third and fourth dimensions. Their purpose for taking this unprecedented action was to move humanity beyond the effects of Earth movements, viruses and plagues that were going to happen at humanity's then-level of existence. We would have been wiped out.

This is an awesome fact to contemplate. We woke up on 9 September 1995 not even knowing what had happened, but as we sought answers to questions raised by Zoosh's channelings, we got the story from Zoosh and Jehovah.

We are publishing the history of the end times as we are living it, thanks to Zoosh's and Jehovah's great love and compassion for us, "the pieces of the Creator that got stuck." Great and tremendous thanks go to Robert Shapiro and Arthur Fanning for their courage and skill in bringing this information through so that we can understand our participation in this dramatic event.

Although the "saving humanity" section is a hard act to top, there are many events chronicled here – from the real story of the Oklahoma bombing to cracks in time and documentation of the Council of Nine visiting Earth. But even beyond these stories is the ultimate fact – that we create our reality, and the reality we need to focus on is our "becoming" who we are. We need to be aware of what goes on around us, but not get lost in it. The next step is integrating with the godself of each of us arriving in what is called the "Photon Belt." Stay tuned for more adventures.

O'Ryin Swanson
Publisher

This book is dedicated
to all of the souls
who are attending
the Creator's
Apprentice Creator School
on planet Earth.

Arthur Fanning was born and raised in Providence, Rhode Island. He attended the University of Rhode Island, receiving a B.S. in agriculture. After graduation, he entered the U.S. Marine Corps in the officer candidate program. Upon graduation he earned his navy wings at Pensacola Naval Air Station in Florida. From 1968 to 1969 he was a marine helicopter pilot in Vietnam.

Arthur had many experiences as a little child, leaving his body and talking with beings in the stars at night. As a medivac pilot in Vietnam, the real nature of these experiences began to reveal themselves to him as a guiding and guarding force that all being share.

In 1986 he had what he calls the "Big One" of his spiritual awakening. An entity appeared over his bed while Arthur was still awake. Arthur's body lifted off the bed, bent in half, straightened out horizontally, and then lay back down, all in less than two second. There was no pain involved, nor was it frightening. Arthur says, "It just happened. It felt like white electricity."

Since then, Arthur has been channeling and working with the entity that appeared to him above his bed —Jehovah/YHWH. His first book, *Simon*, was his first attempt to explain some of the phenomena he has experienced in his spiritual awakening. The material was excerpted from both his physical life and his dreaming life. The second book, *Soul, Evolution, Father* was dictated through him by Jehovah.

Arthur Fanning lives with his wife Cheryl and may be contacted for channeling and healing appointments at P.O. Box 684, Cornville, AZ 86325.

Jehovah/YHWH is part of a great group of beings from another universe who created and are responsible for maintaining this part of the galaxy. His sense of adventure and his great love, wisdom and compassion for humanity radiate through the energy and words of his channeling through Arthur.

Other books by Arthur Fanning
Published by Light Technology Publishing
Simon
Soul, Evolution, Father

 **Robert Shapiro** is a man who has grown up with the experience of extra-terrestrial contact. From age twelve he has had a series of personal UFO contacts. Throughout his life there have been communications with beings from several star systems and dimensions. The development of his career and life-style has come as a direct result of this communication. Robert has been a pro-fessional channel for over 15 years, and although he can channel almost anyone of anything with an excep-tionally clear and profound connection, he most often channels Zoosh, who describes himself below. Robert's great contribution to an understanding of the history and purpose of humanity is his epochal work, *The Explorer Race*, and he is one of several channels featured in *Sedona Vortex Guidebook*. When he is not channeling, Robert is a shaman and spiritual teacher in his own right. He lives with his wife Nancy in Sedona, Arizona. He is available for personal appointments and can be reached at (520) 282-5883; P.O. Box 2849, Sedona, AZ 86339.

Zoosh ensouled the first planet that humanity experienced as souls and he has been with us ever since, for "about a trillion years." He is witty, wise and compassionate. He says about himself, "It has been my job and my purpose in life to follow the birth of your souls on your journey to recreating the universe. My job is to be your companion, your guide, occasionally your entertainer. I have to nurture that sense of mystery — it's not as if you're going to have it forever.

"It is my job to help you get there, to help you to understand your experience and to observe everything. And, in time, to remind you of the everything you are in one of my many guises."

Other books by Robert Shapiro
Published by Light Technology Publishing
The Explorer Race
Sedona Vortex Guidebook

Robert Meyer works with Pleiadian beings who tell him where to go, where to aim his camera and when to snap the shutter — sometimes in the middle of the night. The activity in the sky is illuminated by his lightbody so that pictures are developed of beings not seen by the naked eye. His photographs of interdimensional activity have been featured in *Sedona Journal of Emergence* since January 1995. Cards, postcards and prints of his work are available. For more information contact Robert at P.O. Box 2292, Sequim, WA 98382.

Photo Credits

All photographs are by Robert Meyer except the following:

Page 190 by Tom Dongo (P.O. Box 2571, Sedona, AZ 86339). This picture appears in the Tom Dongo/Linda Bradshaw book *Merging Dimensions*.

Pages 251-252 from *Evidencia OVNI*. (P.O. Box 29516, San Juan, PR 00929-0516), no. 5.

Pages 259 and 263 by Jackie McCormick (1532 Pheasant Ridge Dr., Ellisville, MO 63011). Submitted by Richard Dannelley.

Pages 353-355 from *Mañana Del Sur*, August 2, 1995.

Contents

1

Attack on Earth!

Zoosh through Robert Shapiro
March 7, 1995

T his is a red-hot flash for all lightworkers everywhere! Spread this around, please. As commented in the first *Shining the Light* book, the battle has begun. The battle is not between what you see as the forces of light and dark, but rather the battle is within yourself. And the battle is truly between allowing, unconditional love vs. impatience and greed. Now, if you understand – and this is essential – if you can understand that you do not have people who are unconditionally loving all the time, or people who are greedy all the time, then you will be halfway home. This battle that is engaged fully right now is for all to take note within themselves: In order to be allowing and unconditionally loving, this means that *all things, all life, is allowed to be what it is.* Any life that disrupts, corrupts, attacks or otherwise interferes with any other life, when that life is not fully willing, is functioning within the dark side. All of you, because of your society, are necessarily enmeshed with the dark side. You must recognize these characteristics within yourself – primarily impatience and greed. Hate, anger, yes, all of these things that you recognize – but impatience and greed are the most important.

Now, as we speak, areas that have been sacrosanct – totally sacred, set apart – are being attacked. Do I mean people? No, no. I mean that the sacred minerals, that which you think of as products, are being ripped from the Earth without its permission. You are physical beings; you know that you need vitamins and minerals to survive. What does that tell you? Since your bodies are made up physically of Mother Earth's body, she also needs her vitamins and her minerals to survive. You cannot survive well without them and you do not live pleasantly or to an old age. That's why the foods you eat have nutrients in them.

You must look sharp now. It is time to stop taking minerals out of the Earth. As we speak, those forces of greed and impatience are lusting, planning and even grabbing minerals out of a sacrosanct area known as Hopiland. For many years now, the elders of this tribe have been crying that if Hopiland is attacked, what will happen is what has already happened to Tibet. These two sacrosanct areas, which are protecting the pathways to the Inner Earth – both of them will be overrun by the forces of greed, impatience and darkness. The Inner Earth, *which is the reservoir of unconditional love and allowance,* will be shut off and people on the Earth will have to work harder, much harder, to be allowing and unconditionally loving.

So you forces of light out there, you forces of unconditional love – **it is absolutely essential that every day, without a day going by, you spend a few moments broadcasting loving light**. Now, what is loving light? Loving light is light with the colors of the rainbow in it, and/or gold light. Gold light has the capacity to move, it is kinetic. Loving light has the capacity to heal, for it is loving.

So you have your assignment. You must do this now and tell all your friends to do it. Have them send unconditional love, allowance, loving light, gold light, healing energy to Hopiland and Tibet so that the doorways to the Inner Earth are not sealed. If they are sealed by those who reside there, there will be much less radiation of this energy to the surface. And while you will be able to produce allowance and unconditional love, you will have to work very hard to do it.

This emergency means that everyone will have to come together as groups. Not someday, but *right now!* This is a call to arms. Pay attention. Act now.

The Hopi have a prophecy that if their homeland mesa is mined – which we understand the shadow government is attempting to do at this very moment – there will be worldwide floods and earthquakes. Can you discuss that?

I will. People do not understand the strong links. Some times ago, the poles – the North and South poles – were open. Admiral Byrd, who happened to fly into the Inner Earth one day with his group, saw the inner world. It's hard to imagine that a person of his standing was not believed, but he was not; yet he knew what he saw. However, because of excess activity in these areas and because of the forces of impatience and greed – mining, digging, drilling – these poles were closed. The auxiliary poles (meaning the places where the radiance and beauty could exit) in Tibet and in Hopiland were activated more strongly. The auxiliary pole in Tibet is almost totally closed now because of the invasion by China. This closure happens only when there are attacks to the ground as well as to the people. This is what I believe will occur:

In the Southwest there will be widespread flooding on a regular basis. I'm not predicting a great flood; I'm saying that *regular flooding will occur all the time*. The 1% chance per year of a major flood such as a hundred-year flood will increase to 30% per year. Ask your oddsmakers what this means. It is also very possible that if uranium is removed from Hopiland, there will be earthquakes of significant magnitude on the west coast of the United States, the east coast of the United States, and on the opposite side of the world — significantly, China and Tibet. Be on the alert, Afghanistan and Japan! It is especially important for the people of Japan, because much of the magnetic pole and bipolar flotation effects that keep the island of Japan intact have to do with the mineral deposits on the other side of the world. Be aware that mineral deposits are as important to Mother Earth as the minerals you must have in your body; if you do not have them, you get sick and die.

You said earlier that the secret/shadow government was already planning to extract these minerals from old tunnels that already exist. Can you expand on that?

Underground tunnels used by the secret government have intersected certain mine shafts, bringing their attention to the presence of uranium they desperately needed for their nefarious deeds. They did not care that it was near and goes directly under this holy place (for Hopiland is indeed a special place, partly because the Hopis are there, but primarily because of the place itself). The Hopis are there to guard it!

So the secret government decided that they would move quickly, before legal action could be carried out. (Simply taking legal action may not be effective; for example, clear-cutting an entire forest before the law can move.) They could dash underground, get as much as they can get their hands on, and get out before anyone could stop them. That is their intent. The plans are being laid right now, and the initial activities, including the cutting of core samples and the analysis of same, has taken place already.

Certain mining companies that are already in place may be drafted into participation. Mining companies who have long-term contracts and can't say no to some people will be left holding the bag when the lawsuits begin. Be aware.

Okay, what to do right now, besides the light . . .

By all means, demonstrate. Carry signs, but *do not under any circumstances be violent.* Take a lesson from the civil rights demonstrations of the South. Nonviolence did succeed. If you are violent, it will just add to the agitation and will keep you fighting amongst each other. The secret government has fostered this sort of thing for years and years to keep you confused while it pulls the rabbit out of the hat. *This situation is a rabbit that the hat cannot afford to lose!*

Within two and a half weeks, the mining, the drilling, will be happening. If uranium is removed from under Hopiland, it will be a crisis beyond all understanding. Uranium is Mother Earth's brain and nervous system. As you know, much uranium has been removed from the Earth in the southwestern United States as well as other places in the world. The Southwest is important. Your scientists have noticed in recent years that the weather patterns have become chaotic: huge storms, June snowstorms, totally unexpected snow in the South where snow is not usually experienced, earthquakes where they're not expected.

Mother Earth's primitive brain is dense — a very critical mass, uranium. It is correlated to your experience of the upper portions of your spinal cord as it taps into your primitive brain, or your id. If this uranium is taken out from under Hopiland, Mother Earth's nervous system will not be able to function as it has in the past. Weather will not only be unusual, it will be chaotic. Hurricanes may blow straight inland; they'll keep building up strength over, say, Minnesota! Your weather people will say, "Impossible!" but I'll say, not impossible, just not normal.

Maybe you'll have volcanoes erupting like crazy before their time sequence. Do you know that the volcanoes, especially the ones up in the state of Washington, are intended by Mother Earth to erupt about 450 years from now in a spectacular fashion that will essentially unite the upstate coast of what is now Washington State, with Vancouver Island off the coast of Canada. This landmass is expected to extend 450 years from now, when people will have been redistributed.

But suppose this happened now. Can you imagine the level of catastrophe? The signal that would be transmitted through Earth's nervous system would be disrupted! The choice is before you: You can live a healthful life if you just live properly, or you can abuse yourself and come down with a nerve disorder that will cause you to suffer horribly and die a ghastly death. You have your choice right now.

What can stop this?

Public awareness can stop it. Write to your congressmen. Call them, telegraph them. It is true that the secret government, the shadow government, is not apportioned only of the United States. Mining operations can be detected from above the surface. If the mining is not authorized, there is a tremendous amount of pressure your government can bring to bear, to say nothing of what your legitimate military can do if they are told to go in and stop it immediately. Believe me, they have the means to do it. The secret government's attitude will be, "Well, we'll wait." But it can be stopped, and if you stay vigilant, it will keep it stopped. But you will have to stay vigilant.

There was something a few weeks ago about the electric company coming in to put in power poles on Hopi mesa. Is that connected with this, or are they separate situations?

It is connected, you might say. There are certain people there who would like to have the utilities and the support of modern conveniences. However, think about this:

Instead of running a small amp service to Hopi mesa, what would happen if, unbeknownst to the Hopis, a megawatt service was put in? Or even ten times the needed voltage? Do they expect the Hopis to suddenly give birth to ten times as many people and thus need that much? No, it would be to serve the industrial base they hope to build there. Let's understand something about mining companies: They build smelters and processing plants as close as possible to the source of their raw materials for both convenience and economy. They intend to put heavy industrial processing plants as close as possible to the Hopi reservation, possibly on the Navajo reservation, on what they would conveniently refer to as "disputed territory." They would get what they would call a "temporary" lease — which would last a good thirty years, mark my words! — to build what they want, and they would use a tremendous amount of electrical power. You know, there is no dispute between the Navajos and the Hopis that they can't amiably work out themselves. It's happened because other people are interfering and trying to shift people away from certain locations so that they can secretly do things in those places. This is known by many, but it is good to get it out more widely.

You just have to understand that it's no longer the case that the rainforest can be demolished while they mine and dig and drill for portions of Mother Earth's body, and you can still go on about your business. No. When they drill into the heart of Mother Earth, when they remove her brain, this affects everyone equally. You can't just say, "Oh, well, we do what we can," or "We do the best we can." You have to *act!*

Do they plan to go through Williams?

Yes, through Williams.

They want to go underground?

They want to do everything underground! The whole purpose of demonstrations is to create confrontation so there can be publicity. But if everything is going on underground, it eliminates confrontation, you see?

YHWH through Arthur Fanning
March 7, 1995

So you've got a quandary, eh?

Yes. What can we do about it? How should we proceed? Zoosh said two and a half weeks.

You have pushed yourselves to your spiritual edge at this time. Know you what I mean? What has been spoken of is true. It is what has been talked about in what you term your great prophecies, the cataclysms, and we've told you before that it is within the consciousness of mankind to change these things. Did you think we were kidding?

So you are on your spiritual brink. Those of you who have the power will tune into the God forces that you are, will what you call "decide" to play with that united portion of your brain that we've talked of many times, the one brain, eh? And that will assist in ceasing, we say slowing down, because when these things begin, your fears (simply walking in your street) are going to manifest tenfold. Not because of the weather patterns and changes, but because you have lost the opportunity to become the masters of your own destiny any longer, in the manner that you have not been taking the seriousness of any teachings that we turn you to, your power and the power of the individual consciousness; you haven't taken them seriously; you take them for your little chitty-chats until, as I've joked before, you get right to the edge! Then you begin to run.

The point you're going to have to concede, now, unto your own self is, you must connect with what you term — this applies individually, now —with your spiritual portion of your being that is residing in what is termed the Pleiades and residing in what is termed, some of you, Orion and the Sirian system. You are connected to all of these things. You must connect now. We're past the game of playing. Because you must remember now, many of you still reside on some of the councils that are assisting these ones to pull this off.

Many of us have aspects that are of the dark forces?

Let's not use "dark forces," let's simply say [aspects that are] not willing to rush into enlightenment.

So we now begin to petition, put it this way, with the unified brain that you have, know you? What we spoke of in our meditations. There is a purpose for these things being given, a purpose for you to understand that your brain is simply a tool to allow the thought to be sent through the filter, know you? For you choose what you filter, and you can control, you can alter. Because out there, you understand you are God. But you must be able to do that, you see, as you disseminate the information, or spread it out, know you? Put it out there. The ability to change it at this time is going to require an awful lot of what you term the opinion of the public. But the public is not interested in their God forces. It'll take a grouping willing to concentrate in what you term the etheric, in other levels, to create this shifting. Now I will tell you this: there are many things going on this month to alter and to prevent there be the destruction of the planet, the complete destruction. There are going to be these great quakings; we're not going to completely stop what is occurring here. And it is neither good thing nor bad thing, it is however a sad thing this is occurring in the first place.

Are they going to occur whether or not the shadow government mines the uranium?

What you call your quakings?

Yes.

They're going to occur, but this portion . . .

If they pull that uranium out, are they going to accelerate the process?

There will be much acceleration and much greater magnitude. It will create such a destabilization that this will require what you term major surgery. What you term, in a manner, rescue. And if the rescue is required, mankind will not have any say at all what is going on. You have a little bit of free will left (we made a joke about this before), yet you still have some. These forces now are . . . it is, in a manner, the battle has begun.

It is all in a manner also, this system, you are learning to become a unified being within yourself, in your metaphysics, your polarities, unified being within your brain, know you left/right, here? Single brain, indeed; as it goes forward to that sequence [to become unified] it's called, from your perspective, the parts that are left behind, so to speak, have fear. Know you how part of your fears don't want to die? It is the same with any portion of your personality that you have utilized —your personality trait that you have utilized to get this far in your lives, as you think it is in your evolution you think they are needed in the future. That is not so.

In this game being played here now there has already been one visit to those that are participating in this game. And they have been talked to on many levels now. And again the choices. There is the possibility that it can be stopped, or at least the severity lessened. However, the likelihood is very, very small.

That it can be stopped or lessened?

Well, that it can be lessened; it cannot be stopped. We're going to do a portion of this thing anyway. Now, pay attention to this: What is important is that the information does indeed get out, know you? And when the fan is hit by the feces, then those that see what is happening will have an opportunity to see who is causing this thing, and how you can correct. Because when the rescue begins, if it comes to that point, you will still know how to, I will say, once the balance has been set again, you will still need to know how you continue your consciousness here. How you utilize it. Not left/ right. Know what I mean?

How you utilize your consciousness . . .

Not left/right brain.

Oh, yes, integrated, unified.

Indeed. You are going to have to know how to do that. The majority of mankind isn't even aware that that process exists, know you? They think they think in your brain here. Among you metaphysical people you think that thing also.

Will we be working on that in the next intensives?

We have started the process. It is difficult; we have already started it, say, several years ago. You beings quit when you get your headaches. It is a seam growing together here [top of head].

Now about this thing in your mesa. It is indeed a good place. A place of high energy, a place of power. If you will see some of the other happenings that are occurring upon your planet, that some of the records are moving out of what is termed the Tibetan archives,

you term them sanctuaries. So too we will say, some of the energies
are being moved from the Hopi arena, have shifted a bit.

What do you mean by energies? People, things, records?

The energies, I will term; what you have within your mineraliza-
tion on that mesa are records. It has always been mankind's selfish-
ness and greed that has caused his own demise. But what occurs —
don't worry, you'll live forever, yet you can go through your oops in
this time. I'm being a little light and also it is very serious because
your friend is right: great, great destabilization to the planet. You're
watched over here, you're not going to destroy it, even though you
think you can. Now. What is occurring at the end of this month,
know you your equinox?

Yes.

There is great power being raised, great power being set, opened. It be time, if one concentrates on the unification of his consciousness, it will only take what would be termed twelve beings, together,
to alter this thing. But it takes twelve thinking here [points to area
above head], not in here [points to brain].

*Zoosh said two-and-a-half weeks from today [i.e. the 24th of March],
they were going to be mining, and the equinox is the 21st of March.*

Well, I believe we have a Friday night then. That's a coincidence,
eh? [Laughter.] I am involved with the group that sits on the edge of
the cliff and runs when the chasm opens wide! Any other questions?

*We'll get this out to as many people as possible, even though you're
saying we can't stop it?*

Well, let's put it this way: You won't stop it with public opinion
at this time. What you will stop it with is the beings that you have
been . . . Do you think I've been working for nothing down here?
[Laughter.]

*Even though the information won't stop it, it'll still be helpful to get this
out, right?*

Indeed. Because when these things begin to shift — and we're
going to alter as much as we can, you understand —*you* beings are,
you know. As you begin to shift and what you alter, at least you have
put the information out that a lot of the weather changes are indeed
involved with what these beings are doing and not unified in consciousness with the planet; they'll understand. Others will, you understand? Humanity.

*Is there any sense in going to these miners? These miners are going to be
sort of coerced and then Zoosh says they'll be left facing all the lawsuits.*

Well, they're already being talked to, know you what I mean? I and others have been talking to their hearts. And I've been known to create what you would term an attack of the heart, till I get your attention.

Oh. But, I mean, if they're forced by the secret government, no matter what their hearts say, are they going to be strong enough to stand up to it?

I'm also talking to these beings that you term your secret government.

Oh! Not to do this thing.

I talk in my own manner. The greater purpose, however, is that you beings are going to begin to understand that you are loved indeed, consciousness is yourselves about your planet, know you? That you are aware. Then your secret government, as you wish to term it, the military, won't be able to control you anymore, no matter what they do. They are a dying tiger now, you must understand. Don't take it too personally. And you're all doing as best you can, we understand this, we see these things. Well, you're also taking care of this in what is termed those months of six we play with, know you?

When we ask for this unified consciousness . . . what makes our heads hurt? What's resisting it?

Portions of the brain identify themselves as portions of personalities.

And like you said, they don't want to die. But they don't have to die.

Not at all!

They can get expanded into the larger consciousness.

They blend into one. Know you the crystals we put in your head at times? That is to sort of sew this seam in the middle together so it gets used to being one brain. And you need that, because it requires an opening of more circuitry and it allows a lot of thought to come through so you may pay attention to what you want to participate in and what is going on where. It will take time for you beings to understand the miracles that you are and that you are playing with.

Right now your moneys are the most popular things. That's all right. Your Earth and its stability is very popular. Your weather and its predictability is popular. Pretty soon it's all going to become unpopular. Because you don't know who you are. A lot of you think you do; that is almost as dangerous as not knowing. Sometimes more so. But you will learn. There is no other alternative. We are through.

2

Shadow Government's Technology Beyond Science Fiction

Zoosh through Robert Shapiro
March 19, 1995

*H*ave they started drilling under any of the Hopi mesas?

I'm going to tell you something now that I really couldn't tell you before (because, you know, it's in the nature of what I do that certain things have to happen before I can say certain things). Let's just say that everything is now in place: the underground railroad, all the equipment, and the main tunnel. The way it works with mines is that very often there's a main tunnel used to get to where they are going; that's all in place.

And it is not only under Black Mesa, as you know, but there is a branch tunnel that goes directly under Second Mesa; this is the problem. I do not wish to offend Hopi people, but I will obliquely say only this, because now it can be told — that there is a very sacred area which is guarded by spirits and which cherishes spirits and protects them. One of these tunnels is so close to that special place under Second Mesa that the actual energy of that sacred place is being depleted right now. Let me discuss the ramifications of that so that people in other places don't just say, "Oh, isn't that a shame."

That particular sacred area is connected directly to the actual North Pole of this planet, and the intent of what goes on there, in religious rites and prayers and ceremonies of the highest quality, is to keep the Earth intact. Understand that it's hard for a people who have only an intellectual grasp of religion and philosophy to fully realize that science and religion as they are now practiced by much of the Western world are really not associated with the heart, they are not associated with magnetic energy. I know this seems like a long aside, but we need to recognize that the will comes from the mind and the body. And religions based upon the mind and the will tend to be wrathful and vengeful — not totally, but they have those aspects as a strong part of them, so God is seen in some faces as wrathful and vengeful. These religions are based on the scientific — believe it or not — foundation that it is humankind's job and destiny to govern the world. That is part of the reason that the Bible has been rewritten: to make it look like it's humankind's job to govern the world, as it were, whereas humankind's job is really to learn his place in the world.

Now, these kinds of religions and intellectual and scientific pursuits do not really allow an equal place for the feminine energy of the heart, of the emotions, of the feelings, of the instincts. As a result, they have only one part of the equation: the part that involves doing. They do not have the part of the equation that involves allowing. And for that matter since they don't have the allowing, they don't have receiving. You can go out and get something by doing, but you can't attract something to you. If you want to go out and dig gold, you have to go out and dig all over the place for it. You can't just manifest gold, you cannot apport gold, you understand? So, because of that ethic, there is a complete lack of knowledge of what is actually happening under the Hopi mesas. This is not only, as some people might say, a Hopi religion; what is going on under the Hopi mesas, and what's going on in the culture of the Hopi and other ancient tribal cultures, which are barely hanging on, is literally affecting the glue, the fabric, the seams that hold this planet together. As you all know, you must feel continuity to live, to survive, to *be*. A life without continuity is a very nervous life indeed. Take away the continuity, and the planet gets nervous. If she gets nervous, earthquakes, fires and floods will happen. Because as you know, when you as physical individuals get nervous, you are more apt to be jumpy, aggressive, defensive — and you are microcosms of Mother Earth!

So this sacred area that is within about ten meters of the main tunnel is having its energy depleted. The result of this will be, in time, the gradual and almost complete melting of the polar icecaps — and I can assure you, if it happens before its time, you're just going to find land under there; you're not going to find anything magical, as you will later if it melts when it's supposed to melt. If both polar icecaps melt (and almost all the glaciers everywhere would melt as well), your oceans could rise perhaps as much as one-and-a-half or two-

and-a-half inches. That could be catastrophic – ask any weather person. An inch doesn't seem like much, you'd think, but that is compounded not only by the tides but by the forces of weather. Many of you have seen the I Am America and Scallion maps. What I'm saying is that these maps are predicated upon these kinds of atrocities happening to sacred shrines that literally hold the world together. So you might say they are predicated upon a worst-case scenario. And without going into the whole idea of the end of the world, I'd rather say that these things must be stopped because so much damage has been done.

Mineral Deposits Are the Key to Both the Magic and the Greed

You have to understand something now, and not to put too fine a point on it, I can say this now because the secret government and the forces behind this nefarious digging know this; I'm not giving anything away, and I'm not going to be specific. But I will mention that these shrines are in place where they are because of the mineral deposits around them. It's as if a doctor were to put a special instrument into your spine – and someday they'll do this when they understand it better. It's like a neural device put into your spine, into the base of your skull and going into your brain and into your spine – someday people will actually pay money to get these things, because they will essentially stimulate the flow and excretion of serotonin and all the benevolent brain chemicals.

I'm using this example because these shrines are connected to what I'd call threads that go to the spine of Mother Earth, and her magnetic poles would be the spine. As this mining goes on, it cuts those threads. Then the shrine no longer has the effect. The shrine's intent – I'm calling it a shrine just to give it a word that people will understand – is to compliment and to love Mother Earth as much as she loves you.

As you all know, if a child has his source of love and continuity completely cut off, he gets nervous, angry, resentful – and maybe he turns into a delinquent, or worse. Now, you have some means of dealing with youngsters like this. Most of those means are not very good, but you do have means. But what are you going to do if Mother Earth turns into a delinquent? Are you going to say "I'm sorry"? You know, you've come to believe in recent years – even the best environmentalists – that things can be done to make it right. Now, to be perfectly honest, the best environmentalist really knows that once something has been disrupted, corrupted, or otherwise damaged, it can never be put to right again by the hands of human beings. But you try, you know: "Well, there's too many animals over here, so we'll move them over there. Too many predators here, so we'll move them over there." This kind of belief has actually encouraged these mining companies, because they believe they have to "put it back together and make it look nice." People who live in Tennessee understand this, because some of the area that was strip-mined and demolished has been put back together so it looks nice on the surface, but of course, under the surface it's a mess. I can assure you, *you can't put this back together and make it nice.* Once these things are cut, it would be like cutting certain nerves along your spine: things don't work anymore, period – that's the end! And then your body begins to act strange and do strange things.

So this is an emergency situation. I'm not saying go out and start shooting people; I'm saying that you have to nonviolently get the word out. You really do have to encourage people to put this out on the Internet and globally – not only locally – because people must understand that everyone will suffer as a result of this, and that it will take a long, long time to recover. We're not talking about a little government emergency funding; we're talking about the resulting damage being *so extreme that no government,* even those that are the "best," financially speaking, *will be able to recover!* There could be chaos in the world. The economic system that is so painstakingly put into place now to make things work better globally –yes, to some extent it's based on greed, but eventually it'll turn into a world economic order which could be good – in time, the whole thing will be destroyed. You'll have to start all over again.

So what I'm saying here – and I'm talking now to certain power brokers, as you call yourselves, as well as the public – is that this short-sighted, greedy effort to steal (and it is stealing) these minerals under the Hopi mesas will, in the long run, destroy you. So think about it. You may think, Well, the world will fall apart, and then we can grab power. But you know, it doesn't do you much good to grab something that isn't there anymore. Once it's wrecked, you're not going to want it.

Where is the drilling?

I'll tell you this: The main tunnel goes from Williams to Black Mesa. Then you find the point on that line which passes as close to Second Mesa as you can get (because they're not going to tell anyone they don't have to). Then you're going to be pretty close. But we have to be a little discreet and not say "under this place" and "under that place."

I'm going to talk about other places where there's mining going on. There are certain things I can talk about and certain things I can't talk about. As you know, the mines in Jerome are going full-tilt. That's not a secret, and it is a matter of public record, as has been stated. Once they have an opening in the ground and they get to the mine, they can go other places. In the old days, they just tunneled everywhere underground. It's ridiculous. Now there is almost as much construction underground as there is aboveground! Now that they have the means to do it, you know? They didn't develop high-energy lasers primarily for use as death rays in combat; they immediately applied them to mining techniques, obviously not for drilling for oil, but for mining. And they have techniques by which they can go anywhere they want underground —which is a disaster. So the mine in Jerome is almost to Prescott.

It has spread out in other directions: it's well under Cotton-wood, all over under Cottonwood. Part of the problem in Cotton-wood, why people get nervous there sometimes and have ailments sometimes, is that not only are they using laser devices (which aren't going to have much effect unless you're close to them) but worse than that, they're using ultrasonic devices.

Ultrasonic Devices

Years ago the government did a lot of research on ultrasonics to see if they could be used somehow in combat. But they discovered they couldn't be used because their own troops were being affected just as much as the enemy's, so they gave up on it. But others didn't, and they adapted it. It's used now very often instead of dynamite. It can be focused just like a laser and it can be a destructive weapon, essentially, that blows through just about anything. They don't need dynamite much. And dynamite is kind of hazardous anyway, because you never quite know what it's going to do even if you're an artist with it. So what's going on in many places is that people are getting blasted, and even if this is happening forty miles down (and they're never that far down; they're usually not much more than a couple miles down at the most, very often only a half-mile down), people are getting blasted with ultrasonic sound waves, which, I don't have to tell you, can be very destructive.

They're under Cottonwood, under Clarkdale, the whole area, and they've moved out from that point and connected to main shafts. See, there are mine shafts and there are travel shafts, and segmenting off from that, there are places where the workers stay —I mean to tell you, there are underground cities! There is teeming life underground, and I'm not talking about the Inner Earth people – most of whom, I might add, have escaped by now, because they've been invaded – but this whole network is going on down there. And there are ramifications to it. Do you know that there are families living down there? And it isn't all just suffering and slavery; there are people in regular families, people working for the company, as it were, who have had children, and those children have never seen the sun! There are some children down there who have been born in regular American families and families of all different races, who are nine years old, and they have never seen the surface. Oh, they've been able to peek out now and then, and they see films, but they've never really seen the surface. I'm not saying that's bad; I'm just saying that life underground is becoming more complex.

It is so extensive you cannot believe it, all right? But why? Why is it so extensive? After all, you can only acquire so much mineral wealth; after a while you just have it stacked up in safes and places, and all you can do is look at it and run your fingers through it. Is it just greed? Is it lust for wealth? No! What's the motivation of the secret government?

ET Connections: Off-Planet Sales and Secret Government Control Technology

As I've said before, the secret government is in business with certain extraterrestrials. And certain extraterrestrials whom I've referred to before as Xpotaz act as middlemen and deliver through various means things that eventually wind up on the "legitimate" market in other planetary civilizations who don't – by the time it's gone through several hands and been disguised a little bit – have any idea it's from Earth. Some of these ores that are common to your Earth you don't even consider to be of great value, but they are of tremendous value elsewhere – such as quartz crystal, which is used in a great deal of sophisticated technology elsewhere. Also, common table salt is used not as a spice, but as a basis for crystalline technology that is primarily what I would call liquid crystal. That technology is used instead of what you now use in your electronics. The next stage in circuitry, I might add, is liquid-circuitry – but that's another story.

Now, the secret government is using these materials to trade, and they want not only weapons, more exotic weapons, but they want technology they can use to essentially manipulate the human race. They will sometimes disguise this technology, through the influence they have in certain legitimate companies by way of legitimate government contracts, by putting little secret circuits, as it were, into otherwise benign devices, to create the means by which they can literally usurp those devices, take them over from their original intent and use them for their own nefarious purposes. Now we're getting into areas of broadcasting the ELF.

ELF Pulse Technology

As you know, a tremendous amount of research has gone into extra-low frequencies. And it's true that there are certain pulses (we call them frequencies, but that is a bit of a misnomer) that can be broadcast that will make a person feel wonderful, euphoric. There are other pulses that can make you feel sick and, if pulsed at a high enough intensity, can kill. So there are certain devices, one of which is now installed on Mingus Mountain, another of which, though a smaller version, may be installed at Airport Mesa. One is installed in Australia; it is well known and looks rather benign, if you look at it it just looks like a small box, an odd little shape on the ground with a huge aerial, a mast, as it's called, which originally was intended to create an absolutely accurate means of global navigation for all modes of transportation as well as a means of absolute precision accuracy so that they can communicate with all ally vessels (whoever they might be), whether they be undersea, whether they be in space or . . . whether they be underground.

Conventional radio – even high-frequency radio – obviously doesn't work very well when you're trying to transmit a message from the surface through hundreds if not thousands of miles of rock and everything else underground, water and so on; if they get the message at all, it is totally garbled. So they needed to have a means by which they could essentially shoot a signal underground using highly focused ultrasonic compressed beams, not what you could call sonograms but like a sonic laser, though it can't be wired like your cable TV. So that essentially is what they're going to use it for. They've discovered that if they use extra-low frequency, a much better signal comes through. But many times this extra-low frequency broadcast has negative or deleterious effects on other life around you. And here you've got one right up there on Mingus Mountain overlooking the entire Verde Valley!

It's on it or in it?

It's on it, on the surface. It can be photographed. And you *** also got one smaller version that will be a little harder to discern – especially with the antenna force that one finds normally at any airport – up there on Airport Mesa. And another one, albeit smaller, may go up somewhere on top of Schnebly Hill, as it's called, and other high points. You're used to seeing antennas on the highest points, but these antennas are different. They're not intended so much to go up (although yes, they can communicate with space), but they intend to go down. So they might be in places without too much population, they might be high, but not at the tippy-top. In any event, it's having a lot of negative side effects on people.

Are those the only places on the planet where these things are?

There are other places where a lot of this underground mining and these ELF communications devices are being installed. Let's talk about it. Perhaps one of the more significant places is Sydney, Australia, where this underground mining coincides with these antennas that are intended to communicate underground and also broadcast ELF. I might add that this explains some of the "natural" disasters that have occurred recently in Australia — not the least of which was a very bad fire they had there a while back. This was largely the result of an accident in the transmission of a frequency that causes spontaneous combustion. This was not intended, actually; it was an accident. We don't want to say they burned down half of the Australian Outback for fun; they didn't. It was a mistake. But nevertheless, it happened. I know that people can say that it got started because of this and that, but the point of combustion I believe was from this transmission.

And where else? Greenland, of course; we've talked about that before. They tend to have these devices where they have their secret underground bases, but the intent is to create these antennas, as it were, that aim underground all over the planet. But there is more to it.

You know, for a long time now your science fiction writers have been talking about force fields — force fields that you can't penetrate with anything like bullets and so on. The long-range intent is to put enough of these things around the Earth so that communication would be absolute, though everyone would be getting bombarded with ultrasonics and there would be a lot of disasters there, not the least of which is the birth rate — there would be problems with birthing. And you could say, if you were cold-hearted, that that's good because there's too many people. But you know, it can be done in different ways so that people don't have to suffer.

In the long run, not only is the intent to run the energy downward, but there's a secondary level: Once there are enough of these things around on the surface of the Earth (and I can tell you right now they're undersea as well), they will be able to have this energy that they can broadcast. The energy has a couple of purposes. One, the energy will allow the secret government's flying ships, flying saucers, to skip along an artificially created electromagnetic field – not unlike skipping a rock over the water. Now, the secret government knows that with all this mining and tearing the Earth apart, the Earth's electromagnetic field is changing, and she cannot broadcast as much energy as she has before, because she is injured.

So even though they're causing injury, they have decided that they will stimulate their own field. Because the ships they have are the older type of ships that use electromagnetic fields to skip along, and without going into too much else, the reason they use the fields is that the ship uses its motive energy, as it were, to move forward between skips. Picture the rock skipping on the water: Every time it bounces off the water it is propelled by that intermagnetic effect. So it's propelled. And by skipping off of this field, it uses one-tenth as much energy as it would have to use to just move along on its own.

In Process: Earth Shield

The thing they're working furiously on now is being able to perfect what amounts to a shielding device. Now, what is the long-range goal of having a shield? You might say, well, then countries won't have to worry about incoming missiles or weapons or anything – and it's true: with these shielding devices you can literally fire a nuclear missile at one, and the missile will explode without penetrating the shield at all. And even though there will be radiation, that won't get in either.

So what's it about? I'll tell you what it's about. *The shield is intended to shield the Earth from any and all contact with extraterrestrial civilizations that are coming here to help you.* And the shield is designed not only to keep vehicles out, but to actually be used as a means to broadcast an energy that is so destructive to the navigational systems of these ships that they won't be able to come within a light year of Earth. And it will destroy and damage many other things beyond Earth as well.

So this is really, as you say, bad news. If it weren't for the fact that Creator, that benevolent spirits, that higher forces in general will not allow this to be put into place, it would really be a serious problem for you. But what happens is that when people who just want to defend themselves start defending themselves, they can go overboard. Maybe you get yourself a little spray canister of mace, and you say, Well, that's enough. And then the neighborhood gets a little worse, a little more scary, or something happens to your friend and you get worried, and then you start carrying a gun. And things get even worse and maybe you start hanging around with other people who carry guns. And one thing leads to another and before you know it you're driving around in tanks. And before you know it you're putting up force fields. What happens is that these things lead to other things, because these types of defense systems become offense systems. And without going into the whole Luciferian concept, which it is, it's essentially designed as a tool to keep all things away. But eventually, when you get more involved in feminine technology . . . the days of feminine technology are coming, so don't despair.

When I talk of these things, I'm doing this to wake you up, to say, Hey, you have to act now, you have to do something: You have to form groups; you have to start broadcasting unconditional love; you have to start broadcasting gold light; you have to send signals out to the universe saying help; you have to pray; you have to do whatever is in your conscience to change the energy here — and not only send it out and up, but down and in, because things are going on in there that need to be changed. I know that sounds vague, but many of you are practicing your spiritual things, and I can assure you, *no force*, no matter how formidable it looks, *can withstand the power of love.* All right? I'm not saying it's going to save you to shove a flower down the barrel of a rifle. But in a larger sense, that works. I'll say more about that in the future.

Are there any other places besides here in Sedona and in Sydney, Australia, where these devices are already installed?

Yes, they're installed in all the secret government areas, and they're installed all along the deepest trenches in the oceans where casual observers do not notice.

But they don't stick up above the water?

Yes, they do, but not totally. They're somewhat disguised down there. But you can tell where they are because there are not any fish around there. And . . . let's see, let's get some locations. The devices are either located now or will be located soon in the following areas: Madison, Wisconsin; several in the Texas panhandle and one near San Antonio; many of them are along the shorelines, I might add. (I can't mention them all, we'd be here all day.) One in the hills of Tennessee. There are several of them, and there will be more, in the mountains in New York State, the Adirondacks, there's one now and several others planned; in Alberta, Canada, there are quite a few, but they barely stick above ground because they're being done without permission of the Canadian government. So if they stick above ground at all, they're disguised to look like something ordinary, or they're somewhat underground. A couple of them are located near Canadian Air Force bases. And I might simply mention that this puts the Canadian Air Force at significant risk because they can use these devices to utterly destroy all of the navigational capabilities of any plane in flight. So Canadian Air Force, please check it out.

Let's see, there are many of these devices planned for South America: Venezuela already has a few; extreme southern Chile may have one, and Argentina has several. Bolivia and Peru are next. I might add as a sideline that the so-called drug war, having singled out South America and even gone public with it by promoting and encouraging so much popular fiction about so-called South American drug wars, is largely done because the people in South America do not take kindly to having devices put up in their places. So the idea is, well, to keep the drug money flowing they'll just transfer the seat of power in terms of illegal drugs to the Far East, which I've discussed before. And this is because the people in the Far East, from the secret government's point of view, can be more easily controlled. They will riot interfere. But people in South America, if they see something they don't like, they do something about it right away. That's why a lot (not all, but a lot) of the so-called drug war has the underlying purpose of controlling the people of South America. I'm not trying to say that the Drug Enforcement Agency or the FBI or anybody is a pawn of the secret government; I will just say that unbeknownst to them, for the most part, that is the intent from the secret government's point of view: to control and manipulate the people of South America through the use of a clever screen. That's why when these helicopters come in they have all these odd-looking arrays on them. These arrays are not only designed to broadcast electromagnetic energies and ELF, but also to receive them, so they're almost like flying air versions of these devices on the ground.

Disasters Can Galvanize People

You know, I don't want to say too much about this because people are going to get the feeling of "I give up, what can we do?" But I don't need to tell you what you've learned from disasters before: that in a disaster, almost everybody forgets about why they're angry at their neighbors, and they all pitch in and do things, and they feel this tremendous energy, such as in many earthquakes. All ideas of enemies are forgotten; they pitch in and work like crazy to rescue people, and when they're working together they feel this wonderful energy, even though they're upset. And when they find and rescue someone they feel this fantastic energy. That energy is the energy of cosmic creation which includes absolute love and absolute transformation, and can transform all evil intent.

I'm telling you this now because I'm trying to light a fire under you. I'm not trying to create a disaster, I'm trying to light a fire under you. Because if you all just forget about why you're angry at each other, or how someone looks different or smells different or how they have a different culture — if you can just get over that and work together, you will create that energy of cosmic creation, and all this is going to go away. And in the process of doing that, you're going to find out that you like more about these other people than you dislike. So all of this is designed to get you to do that, and I think it'd be a lot easier for you to do it by coming together in groups now, through motion. Some people will broadcast light. Some people will broadcast love. Other people will use motions, certain motions of the hands, certain positions of the hands, that are called mudras — the hands take these positions and then move through the air. Not unlike someone here, eh? [He points to a statue of Shiva on the table.] Not unlike certain motions associated with dance. A lot of people will do that, and that will broadcast it and amplify it. The basis of all martial arts comes from this. Martial arts come from broadcasting transformative, cosmic love energy.

So I want you to start thinking about these things and consider what you can do because one thing you've learned, even if you forget it from time to time: violence inevitably creates other violence. You know this. Also know that love inevitably creates love; that's cosmic transformation. That's what you're going to re-create here, and that's the basis of cocreating with God. God knows that chaos precedes creation. Creation such as created us is love and cosmic transformation. That's what you're learning to do. And the reason you're being squeezed is so that you can do it. And you *will* do it. I know. What else?

Do you want to just talk about the gates up there at the Sedona Airport?

I will say simply that the gates that are being installed, and possibly a fence around the entire area, which right now, as you see, has barbed wire but eventually might have razor wire (although I question whether they'll do that because people will raise a fuss) are really designed to create a means of securing the upper mesa there. It's true that there are tunnels under there, but primarily this is being done because, how can we say, certain political officials, some of whom will go on to become major players in the government of the

United States, *like* this area —just as other presidents have come here and other people of well-known elected and generally recognized political powers will come here, and eventually a certain area here — which we will not mention by name, but a well-known local resort — will be used even more than it is used now as a secure, essentially western White House. And as a result, your airport is simply being made more secure for these visits. As I stated before, people can travel underground to these places. And yet, the fact that the airport is being made more secure tells you that certain things are going to happen on the surface, which means that this area of Sedona is going to become more publicly recognized as a western White House. I might add, however, that it's not designed for the president currently in office.

3

The Council of Nine

Zoosh through Robert Shapiro
March 19, 1995

W hat's good about this *[figure 3.1]* is that after all the talk of
frightening and scary stuff, here we have the smiling lips of the
Goddess in the skies, and she is smiling not only to say that she has
plans for you, since she has been liberated to rise again like the
phoenix, but also because Creator has invited Goddess to come to be
with all women and men on the surface and inside the planet, to help
them to attune to their humor, to their true magic and to their true
relationship with Creator. Maybe someday the photographer will get
a picture of her whole face, but you see her smiling there; you can
almost see lips, can't you, you can see her smiling benevolently in the
sky, saying, "I'm here now!" I just wanted to make that comment to
cheer you.

Inner Earth Delegation Off to Find Posse

Figure 3.2. Here we have a flying disk, fairly large, flying out of
a mountain and caught in midflight, as it were. The disk is on its way
to a distant part of the galaxy. This is a benevolent ship, carrying
some denizens, citizens, of the original Inner Earth who are essentially going off to the deepest part of the galaxy to round up a sheriff's
posse and come back. You know, things are getting hot under the
surface, as they say, and they have done a couple of things. One, they
have placed certain crystals that would look to you very much like
rubies if you saw them, but they're of slightly different chemistry,
near, as close as they can get them, to volcanic vents. The intent is to

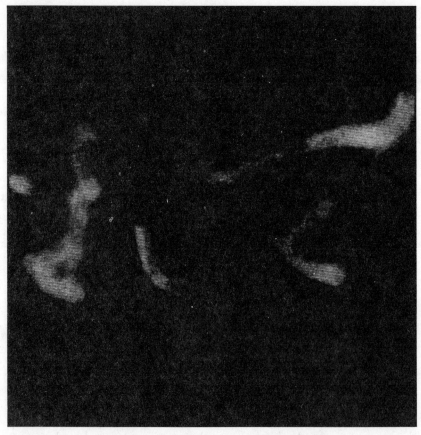

Fig. 3.1 The smiling lips of the Goddess Shakti.

try to encourage Mother Earth, through the emanation of certain broadcast energies that sort of calm Mother Earth, to hold off in her intent — because, you know, if things get bad with Mother Earth, her attitude is very simple: "Well, if I have to take care of myself, if I have to fix myself, if I have to work with my doctor, Dr. Photon Belt, I'm going to just erupt." And these people that are going off to get the sheriff and the posse to come back and help, their mission will take a few years. Because even though the ship travels in light, there is a lot to be done, approvals to be gained, and the ships that will have to come back will have to be very special indeed. Because they will be using certain rays that will help.

Now, they're not going to rescue you. It's kind of interesting: These rays are not like death rays, it's not Buck Rogers. Again, picture the laser technology idea of compressed light; these lasers or rays use compressed emotions. A highly compressed and volatile emotion

Fig. 3.2 Inner Earth delegation leaving to round up posse..

can be compounded and retransmitted to Earth, but the people do not have permission and the ray itself does not have the capacity to broadcast, say, and emotion of love at the Earth, because that would be interference. But if everybody here on Earth and a whole bunch of people who I'm trying to get rounded up to do this — and a bunch of others, too — are broadcasting loving light . . . loving light is what? It's not just white light; loving light is light with colors in it, colors of the rainbow, or gold light, or love — that's right. As much as that is being amplified and broadcast, they can accumulate it, compound it, compress it and aim it toward the places where it's most needed. But you see, *you* have to do it first, and then they can help. But it'll take a little while to get permission.

Where's the sheriff going?

They're going to the farthest reaches of the galaxy, to a planet that is all feminine, and their focus on this planet is love and all of its applications. These people do not actually have ships; they travel in light, in loving light. You might see them sometimes because they travel in bubbles if you saw it, it would look just like a glass bubble, and it would be amazing. You would see people floating through the sky in glass bubbles and you'd say that they look just like human beings. It's astonishing! They do not use machines as you know them, because their technology is so advanced. I'll see if 1 can get a name for their planet; the closest I can get it in sounds that you recognize is Su-shann. There would have to be more than one *n* at the end: Su-shannnnn.

And they've agreed to help, or they have to be asked?

They have to be asked. And because they will not involve themselves in any way with conflict, approval will take time, but those attempting to get this assistance will show them that it is in no way interference, because they will only be reflecting and supporting that which is being sent to them. So it would be an exchange of love, and I feel that would be a pretty good thing.

Yes!

A New Neural Weapon on Mingus Mountain

Figure 3.3. This is a test of a weapon that is broadcast essentially into space and is reflected in any way that the protagonist wishes it to be reflected. It is designed to stimulate the secretion and the velocity, as it were, the flow of spinal fluid. Think about it. The weapon is designed to stimulate so much secretion of spinal fluid that people will essentially have a brain hemorrhage. It's a terrible weapon. It was a test, done within a very small area, and there were no birds in flight so no one was injured there.

Where is its point of origin?

The point of origin was a secret underground facility located in Mingus Mountain that is involved in light-transmission devices used to stimulate neural reactions. Very specific. Their larger grant, however, is to produce light images that are destructive. They started out using laser technology and then they learned how to turn the laser on itself so that the laser essentially implodes and then creates tremendous stress — almost like a dark star effect, a collapsing star so that when any of the energy is beamed out in a specific way, there's tremendous pressure behind it. In any event, I don't want to describe the technology too much, because it could be reproduced without much trouble — all of the technology that you need to reproduce this

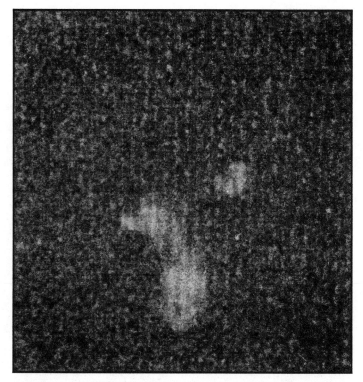

Fig. 3.3. A sinister neural weapon.

weapon is in existence right now! So it's a mischievous weapon, to put it mildly; once before this weapon was developed on this planet, in a different density of this planet, and it was accidentally left on and wiped out most of the surface population. This was not in Atlantis.

Is there a name for this culture?

Their culture was originally referred to as the Tsadi. This culture was a beautiful culture, and they didn't even realize it was a weapon; they just thought it was something that produced, essentially, light shows. They had what amounted to a rheostat control, but it was an automatic rheostat, so they'd press it, and while it's true that at low power it does create a beautiful light effect, the thing would build up, and build up, and build up, and eventually it got to the point (and no one was near the control at the time) where everyone started getting headaches, and by that time they couldn't get back and stop it. Anyway, it was a disaster.

Is there anyone on the planet now who was in that culture?

You mean reincarnated? Yes. Several of the present researchers in the weapons system were involved in that culture at that time.

They may not remember that right now but they will soon - which will be good, because when they do they'll be careful not to install automatic rheostats. I'm calling it a rheostat just so that you can understand increasing energy.

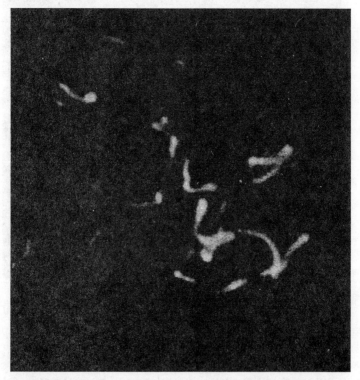

Fig. 3.4. The wake of the visit of the Council of Nine.

A Visit from the Council of Nine

Figure 3.4. This is an interesting factor. This, you see — and I want people to take note — is the wake (as in a ship's wake) of the visit of the Council of Nine, which came here to observe the circumstances firsthand. You know, normally they observe things from a distance. But they came to observe it in such a way that they could actually feel what was going on, because they felt that sometimes their distance keeps them from understanding fully the urgency of situations. Several individuals came to the Council of Nine and said, "This situation is really very urgent, and we would like you to feel the urgency." So they came for a visit to feel the significant urgency of the circumstances, and that's really all they did.

They traveled to several places: to the tip of South America, to Greenland, generally over Sedona, and they also went to Egypt – interestingly enough, not to the Pyramids, but over Cairo. They went to Midway Island. They went to several other places, including under the sea, which we can't talk about. And they felt. That's what they did: They came here and felt the feelings of the people, the feelings of the land, the feelings of the spirits, and they also felt the feelings of the spirits who had departed here, meaning animals who are no longer incarnated on the Earth, such as dinosaurs and other species that are just gone, as well as the feelings of departed civilizations. This is something they needed to do for themselves so that they could act with a little more urgency, which was needed, but also so that they could influence their people – and they do have certain people that they're influential with; the people don't actually do anything, but by their existence the people stimulate certain things to happen in others – so that all of this could happen a little more powerfully and a little quicker. So I thought you'd appreciate seeing the wake of the Council of Nine, something one does not see very often.

Why Midway Island?

There is an energy under Midway Island that taps directly into the heart of Mother Earth, in the very center. When I talk about the heart I'm not talking about her physical heart, but about the heart of which I've spoken to you before: the 90% energy that is being held inside the Earth. This is a can of worms, here. You only have 10% of your real heart energy, now, your real love – the other 90% is being held for you to keep it safe, but it is being somewhat affected by the emotions on the surface. So they're tapping in to see one thing: They want to see if they want to lend their support to making this vessel (which holds your heart energy, preserves it and keeps it safe) impenetrable by anything, or whether they want to let it just emanate gradually up to the surface. Because it may be necessary to hold it and keep it protected for a little while longer – that hasn't been decided yet – or whether it will be allowed to percolate to the surface to be integrated into you. A lot of it has to do with you and your actions, what you do. That's why I'm encouraging you to get together in these groups and broadcast love.

When was the time we would have gotten that 90% back, or has that time schedule changed?

Well, it was really intended for about the year 2005, but now it's a question mark.

Earlier or later?

Yes! The question mark is earlier-or-later.

Why Cairo?

In Cairo the citizens have very strong feelings, and because they are near the pyramids they are constantly radiated by the Great Pyramid, which tends to amplify their emotional feelings. So going to Cairo, one can get like a larger sense of what's happening on Earth.

Cairo's not a good place to be living if you're an emotionally volatile person; you'll be explosive there. On the other hand, if you're a happy person it's a great place to go, at least for a visit.

4

Primal Energies/
Ancient Forces

YHWH through Arthur Fanning
March 24, 1995

Lighten up! Things have not begun to be crazy. We're going to do a little meditation first. Allow your spines to be erect. Center yourself.

Allow a golden pyramid of light above your head to be there, you would say six inches above you. Peace. And feel it spinning what you would term counterclockwise above you. And within the pyramid there is a crystal sphere, brilliant light. Allow a golden beam to come from that sphere through the base of the pyramid into your body. Open the seven chakras. Peace. Now allow it to move to the center of the Earth through the root chakra. Open the heart chakra. Open the heart chakra. Allow. Open the seven wider. Peace. Open the sixth seal wider. Open the crown wider. See your brain, your physical brain, as golden light, feel it, golden color. Allow. Open the root chakra wider. Allow more light. Feel white light returning from the center of the Earth up into your body to the pyramid above you. Allow. Peace. Open the heart chakra wider. Allow. Love. Peace. Allow. Feel a gold light in the heart chakra. Open the chakra at your back. In a gentle manner slowly open your physical eyes.

You are beginning to deal with very primal energies now in your physical body, and it is this arena of the brain that remembers power. This is a very difficult time, mankind, in your phase of loving one another, soon to be, only because you repeat same patterns, don't want to change. That is all right.

The forces now are speeding up. It is time to communicate with your body, *all parts*, from your little toe to the little hairs, all parts. I've told you before, this part here [brain], inside, doesn't get it until last. This part of you [heart chakra/soul] knows. Everyone breathe.

Your meditations are tools to get you to understand prana, force. Your breath is a tool. You should learn to breathe out each chakra when you exhale, open to flower. But you close your chakras down, not because you fear another, but because you don't love another and don't understand power, what is termed *Sacred Power, Law*. That is all right. Everyone breathe.

In your next nine months you're going to be playing with this energy. Some of the old rules will not apply at all. Some of you will have to make up a new one to fit. Some of you will be wise enough to make none up.

You Are Coming to Understand Your Speed-Up

Now, the most important thing to understand in this time are these forces through your bodies, and you do this understanding by paying attention to the wisdom of the love that is inside you here. It is going to be critical.

This speed-up is that your thoughts manifest quicker, what you think will be in front of you in a moment. It is. Look for it. (Everyone breathe out your chakras.) These are nothing new. You knew these things before you were born. You are playing now in that knowing, all of you. It is simply easier to deny this thing. It is easier to, how you say, understand it here with words. *Contemplate a lavender light counterclockwise, it is termed around your brain.* It activates this thing. Around your body and within it. It assists you. The energy forces are going to desire, and they *will* succeed, to blend, bridge both parts of your brain. You are evolving to what is termed a one-brain system. It is your choice where you want to stop *your* evolution.

Now, when you begin to feel those energies in the head doing this thing, allow it, and then allow another and another and another, because it is the ability to utilize thought through your, we'll call it a central channel. That ability becomes you a master, what *you* term master. These are the times when the meditations get more powerful, when you do them yourselves. Strange things will happen, *strange* only because you don't know what you're doing. That is all right, you'll learn.

Now, the turmoil upon the planet will be evidence of your ability to control these forces. Your planet is going to utilize these forces also, for the *becoming* of the planet. Everyone breathe.

Be the First Ball on the String

You have heard that you are all connected, like a little ball with a string to another, and a string to another, and a string to another, and another and another. And it's wound very smoothly. What being is holding this first ball, bubble, that connects to all, that is physical being? It is your planet, and this one is going to do this now [gestures like cracking a whip] to straighten out this coil. It would be wise if you were the first ball. The last one is going to get quite a shaking, and then it will recoil. Your consciousness will tell you where you are along that line. Everyone breathe. Lighten up.

You are always perfectly aligned with your ability within what is termed the light of you. When you are out of line, the great love that you are what you term "out there" and within you, causes what you call a pendulum to swing, to move you toward the center, and many of you enjoy riding that pendulum incredibly. [He laughs.] You have great fun here in looking at the light and swinging through and out the other side, to come back. You're bliss when you swing through the light, and you think it is more fun than this side now because, "I'm moving," and that is true. So enjoy the movement. There was humor there. You're all going to go through it, and it *is* because you want to.

Now, because these are very ancient forces that are being activated you would term it (they've been activated before — don't pick a day), they know not sickness — it does not exist in these forces. These are the forces you utilized long, long ago when you didn't have your, you term them bodies as they are now, that you feel trapped in. So they are very beneficial to you, and they are also the forces that didn't know what they were doing. They were simply applying the movement. Everyone breathe. Breathe you, and as you do, feel the planet breathe a little bit easier.

Now, these are the times of the masters becoming, individually. These are the times to desire to become the master more, when you will be given lessons, instructions, as you would term it. You apply and know, apply and know, apply and know, apply and know, apply and know, and that does not mean your N-O, either. That didn't exist until you beings made it here. It's always Yes, just the way it is always Love.

Now: All of you are already beginning to experience what the term psychic activity is — visions, clairvoyance. Don't try to fit it in. Learn to work with these things, allow it to be more. The moment you judge what you see the tiniest bit, you will have to go through the judgments, clear them up, so you will allow yourself to see it again, and then when you see that one, you'll see another, and more, and more and more. That is how you do it. To judge what you see limits you to get over your judgment. Everyone breathe.

This is not simply metaphysical chitty chat, entities. It is literally leading to your what you say understanding, that *you* manipulate *your* thought forms in *your* drama for *your* pleasure. Are all of you having a good time? Do not enter into these halls of the master that is you, your inner sanctum, your pyramid here, unless you truly desire to become, because it will be *you* who will be experiencing your own training, reading your own inscriptions upon your tablets, so to speak.

Meditation

Allow your eyes to close for a little moment. Now see you ones, yourself, residing within the chest cavity of your heart chakra in the pyramid of the soul there. Feel you there. See you sitting there, feel it. Now allow that pyramid that is at the throat, just a little bit, to push upward to the top of the head and open itself at the apex. Allow. Allow. Peace. And feel the light at the crown chakra. Allow. And feel the light bathing the heart chakra, allow it, allow all of the visions. Allow the feeling in the body, allow it. Peace. Deep within there you are holy and loved forever, and you know it. Be there. Allow. Take a breath and breathe the diamond that is in the heart chakra forward in front of you, diamond light. Allow it. Peace. And above your head allow you to feel what is termed a giant cloud of light, white light. And there's a golden pyramid within that, and from that pyramid, there are strings of light that connect you to the crown chakra. Now look around you and see that all are connected to that light and the pyramid. Allow. Peace. Feel it in the body. Peace. Allow. No competition. Allow. Peace. Now allow that part of you that is connected to this golden pyramid, that part of you being the line of light, allow it to become golden now, brilliant, it shimmers. Feel it connected to your crown chakra. Allow. Peace. Remember. Remember. Peace. Allow your eyes to open gently. Breathe out of the throat chakra. Allow.

One of the adventures or journeys, adventures *you* say, in this time, is not only to know that you are connected here and how. It's to remember that *you are* and *always have been*, and how you utilize the forces of the soul and your physical brain in unison with other beings. *Everyone* is connected to that light. All of your planets, all of your galaxies are. It is the same light. In the joy of the journey, it is sometimes appropriate to petition to develop a more interesting *flavor* to the story that you will tell over, and over again when you return to that light. (Everyone breathe now at what you term the solar plexus, out.) Now if you know this thing, it is no big deal. *You acknowledge you know what you're doing*, and everything around you. If you do not know this thing, you will eventually draw another to you to teach this thing to you. *That* is the difficult part because you don't think you're being taught anything —you know it all already [sarcastically]. Everyone breathe a moment.

The Soul's Desire for Freedom

Now, one of the first arenas, playgrounds, that these forces will be felt will be in the disturbance [of] what you term the electrical forces of this brain here, this unit you term brain, not your great spiritual mind. The electrical within here [brain] is governed by the electrical that is here [soul/heart chakra], that keeps you alive. What some of you are going to find is that the energy within your soul has been repressed, put down, so long that it is building a great desire for freedom, outrageous freedom. That is what's moving. And the soul will achieve its freedom, for that is what you all are. Everyone breathe a moment.

Now, some of you have built outrageous bodies on many levels to hide during these times. And because I've told you before that all of the ancient gods are within you now, who are you hiding from, on any level? You are just asleep. I am not trying to frighten you. I am simply advising you of these times.

Everyone is very powerful now, they think. As they move into these times called of greatness, understanding death, what would be termed contemplating this thing and the movement, *not* "Does this after-life exist?" or "Did my past life be true?" or that "I come from this great star system out there which is better than your star system," and "I'm so grand, I know not the name of my star system, I be such an old being" —your game here is not to worry of those things, or to understand that it's possible. It's to understand your life, your soul forces that you are applying here, and to overcome this thing that is termed play die, *not* to do it again to see if you do live. To awaken. In a manner, *to defeat the fear that keeps you returning.* Everyone breathe.

How do you do this? You do not commit suicide to understand death. That is foolish. You don't see how close you can come to dying and defeat it. You do do it with your meditations, however, and understand how the body feels in different states, and where the controlling board is with all the knobs. You're all into your technology. I communicate better when I talk about your knobs, huh, and your circuits.

Now, being as how you're all connected to this Great Light, and it's around you, as you move into your knowing and those that are ill allow, they will remember simply by feeling your energy. And it would be wise not to talk about it, to be sneaky like I am. Push the energy and allow them to do what they are going to do with it. Know you what I mean? It is not up to you to save the planet. It is up to you to assist in the energy shift here. Indeed, *that* is a truth. It is up to you to save you, in your own wisdom, to *be* the light more and more. And no matter what happens, you are always sacred. Everyone breathe a moment.

The reason I am bringing this up is because there is a lot of fear beginning to develop around the planet with these changes. These are different forces. You have contemplated this thing called Atlantis and what happened, or you think, and your great talkings — how it build big city and destroy. (You're not that technologically advanced yet, and you won't be, either, unless you get your acts together.) Can you imagine the force involved here? It's building again. Can you handle it this time? (Everyone breathe.) I think you can. I know some of you can because I've seen you in the shift.

Now, this journey that you are on here is one of *force*, one of *love*. In each moment, you are going to begin to understand where you are in relationship to love of all things as you walk your day to day, because that is going to be the power that's going to save your bottoms. I did not say it would not be challenging. You all enjoy the challenges.

Meditation

Now, allow your eyes to close gently, gently. Be in the soul and allow you to call the greatest moment of ecstasy you've experienced upon this planet inside your body now. Allow you to recall that memory. It is all right to pull in the event if you need it; call in the memory of that experience. Allow the event to go after you've gotten the feeling. Peace. Push that energy up to the crown chakra now. Allow. Leave it at the crown and allow it to descend over the physical body and blend into each cell so the cells remember also. Allow. Peace. Let the event go. You have the wisdom of this energy now, feel it in the body and allow it to attract the same feeling again. The event does not have to be the same, it is the feeling we speak of now. Allow. In a gentle manner slowly open your physical eyes. Peace.

When you utilize the forces of the soul — we are being very

delicate here because your words limit, so we are purposefully creating great pause to shift your frequencies. Powers of the soul – they were given freely to you so you would remember, to know who you are. You can utilize any of them. They work with the seven chakras, initially, all of the chakras in your feet, the many eyes you have in here [forehead], and your thoughts. Everyone take a breath now in here, what is termed your cranium, and breathe it out the crown chakra. Grand. Allow. Center.

Now, this cycle, this wave that you are in, what you term your '95-'96 arena, '97 here, is again another time of choosing. Choose you you, the light of you here to play, know. Recall you what I've said before of the metaphysical going to be the next great church? It is, it's already starting, and it is being attempted for power – it is all right. Initially the intent is pure. Does anyone have anything they want to chat about?

Can you comment on what happened in the Yucatan this week?

There was a great movement of energy from the center of your planet outward, being met from above, so to speak, to create what is termed a wave. Know you, I say you, energy, as it moves from your planet would have continued outward, you understand – gravity does not apply here, indeed – so as this light was moving forth here, there was another that came and met it, do you understand, to create a wave around your planet. You are beginning to experience that wave now. You have been feeling this for the past three months, little bit. Now it became, from a metaphysical perspective, physical. That is why there is going to be a lot of reaction to these forces. Do you understand?

Now, this force that came to create the wave, this one [from above], is still there to be of assistance to this energy, and it is a guardian. It is more interested in . . . likened unto you humans, you're more interested in the *result* of the one you assisted, what that is working with, and not to care what goes on around. So this light is more interested in this energy that has moved around, in the energy itself, literally that consciousness, evolution and succeeding, that light succeeding in its mission, its journey. Know you what I mean? So this force is not particularly concerned with the result in human understanding.

It's not modulating it, or watching it, or caring if it's too much.

It is not modulating it at this time. It will only modulate it if the force from within the center of the planet is not completing its desire. Are you clear on that thing?

What is the desire of the force coming from the planet?

It is to clean itself. It is to get the job done.

The pains I'm feeling in my body — is this part of this or is it something totally different?

It is part, it is also part of the ability of you to align your thoughts in light.

Is the pain good or bad?

What do you think?

It doesn't feel good.

Indeed, then allow yourself to change it. I understand you say, "Well, how do I do this thing?" You find one that can do this thing, can see this thing, can advise you, know you? The *advise* should be to instruct you how to *not* to do it, you understand, and you can shift your own thought. Know you what I mean? Now, because of your belief systems (we have spoken of this thing before), that your doctors know more of you than you, if that is even *there* to contemplate, to *debate*, then you better go see one of your doctors. This body thing, as you be in it, is part of your journey. Seek those that are loving unto you so you may understand. It is also this body thing, do not say you commit suicide through your ignorance of your own beliefs, do you understand? Don't make yourselves so ill simply to be metaphysical — that is foolish, also. Know you, recognize where your own belief system is, what it is. It will save you a lot of agony. Everyone breathe.

Now, know you your DNA spirals, indeed? [He pauses to drink more water and he comments:] We are giving his throat a workout. I need deeper forces here. We will get them. [His voice throughout the session was very deep and gravelly, sometimes so soft and low that it was a whisper, and was inaudible to many of the participants. This is not usually the case.] *Now, if you would allow yourself to contemplate yourself as spinning spirals in the physical, in your body, you will understand that you're a great rope of same thing, love, and when you allow that spiral to become very tight from about you, about you, about you, about you, about you, so it centers in the center of your spine, you ignite forces.* We've done some exercises to get you ready for this. We're not going to do it tonight, we've already started it. So you incorporate all things here and you're aligned simply by the thought of it.

Because your bodies have not been trained (unless you are what is termed a yogi) in muscular control, it would be advisable to do a little bit of exercise called your walking, or something, to strengthen the muscle fiber. It will assist you in this time. Any other questions? . . . Oh, come on now, you have a whole bunch.

Your Soul Is Your Spaceship

The ships won't be landing for a while. You are on a ship now. (Everyone breathe a moment.) You've been taught about consciousness. You've been taught about the soul. Many of you've read so much you're confused now. Yet the soul exists with-in-side you, it's a pyramidal form, electrical force. It is consciousness. It is your aeroship, your spaceship. Some of you, when you think you're out of your body, running around in other journeys, are united with your friends, what you would say, and others see the shape of your soul joining other souls on the journey, and they think it is a spaceship.

Now be more concerned with you and your soul in this time than with what you term your extraterrestrials. They're in just as much muck as you are. We've told you this before, that's why they're coming back now. You are the ones doing this thing. That's how important it is.

Always desire to know more. It will be there for you. Desire to remember, and desire to love, and love more. Not what you term your mind love, where you get so caught up in if you're doing wrong, that you walk down the street telling everyone you love them even if you're angry at them. (Everyone breathe.) Contemplate it not in the head physical, contemplate the feeling in the body. Allow, because it is *your* journey you will be experiencing in your body, in your physical form.

Yes, it is true, you can ascend. You have to turn your body into a blast of light first, and then you have to bring it back, and blast off and back, and blast off and back, to truly get it. Or you can die and leave your body. That's allowed. And you can contemplate how you manipulate your forces in your body to be you, to exist even. It is through love of you, you do exist —your love. You're that powerful. So you allow yourself to experience more love, more love, more love, and you understand. Indeed?

Indeed.

As you beings play this game called love, you play grab on, know you? You will never understand your body because these are the times you're in now. I am not making light of it. Lighten up! But I am making light of it because that is what you are, light. Oh, you've heard it before, but you're in it now.

In this movement now, you're going to be taken through steps, literally in your physical form. One of the first steps that's going to be felt in the body is what you term your levitation, know you, float up, and when you do, you're going to get frightened. It has already happened. But you'll do it again and overcome, and then you'll be bumping into each other in the air, and that'll be fun. And then you must go beyond that, because that is one of the first steps to blast off.

"I Arise the Vibration I Am"

You must allow your body to vibrate faster. You simply tell it to, and you use these words, in a manner — not ritual, but in an understanding that I (being you, individually), *arise* (that is a command, not a pleading) *the vibration that I am* (that you already know that you are). So you *arise the vibration I am.* You contemplate this as you sleep and upon your waking moment. Body heals as you understand. Things alter within you, because you're tired of the lower density and you command this, and the soul forces spin within you and around you when you are in gentleness. And each time you move further, and further and further, and it's a lot of fun.

Know you humor? I think some of you are having just about as much humor as you can stand, out of your knowing. You must understand this part, that it is *fun* to be human, it's fun to touch, and it's fun, in this limited understanding, to fantasize, [as] if it were a different journey, to understand energies in a different manner, how they play. How I am god here in this journey, which dreamer am I, which one? How do I play in this force that touches everything?

The phase that you're moving through now is very powerful. It is being initiated because you wanted more. This force that is moving now has been here before, and one utilized it with great intent, know you, great purpose, initially. Then the power overcame this one. You call this one Hitler. So too another is feeling this force. The intent is beauteous *this* time. Pay attention to you. Everyone breathe.

Know you when we did our meditation, prior, to send peace to certain lands, some of you that were here? It was because we knew this was coming. So we activate you willingly out of love, another also, that will what you term have a journey with this one. Do not be caught up in the drama. Indeed, be caught up in your drama, in your mastership and your desire to know more.

Now let me tell you a thing here. It'll be likened unto a little story. As you move through this great cloud of light, there is what you would term, from your perspective, a top to it, and it rests against a grand mountain. And there are beings sitting on the ledge of this mountain, watching this cloud of light — it's very thick, can't see through it — and they have great excitement when one moves up through the cloud and floats over to the ledge. And the one that has the most excitement in this thing, the most ecstasy, is the one you call Sananda, know you Jesus? And Buddha is there, also, by the way. Sananda has great ecstasy, because he thinks of those times, the pain he went through, even in what you call the reality shifting, not that he was on the cross, it's the ignorance overcoming that his pain, his ridicule, was with it, that someone listened. And there are other masters, same, as they watch this cloud of light.

When one becomes a master on the planet from any teaching, it doesn't matter, the master that spoke it has ecstasy that another utilized a tool that he left to move through this cloud of light. Everyone breathe.

Your journey is to not only move through within, but above this cloud of light, and sit with whichever master you desire — it doesn't matter, and you must acknowledge the tool you utilized, however, because that is within you and that's the master you begin to understand is the same. So you know. And it is great humor, because I've seen some of you, I be watch, also, so I can understand, and I've seen some of you come to the top and put your hand through, but decide not to. "One more time in density, Father," you say. And I've seen some of you fly out of there and land and talk to the master that taught you, some of you centuries ago, and be in such ecstasy that you jump right back in — you're not going to forget this time, you say. But that is all right, you've experienced the ecstasy, and you know how it's done.

Now it is time to remember and to go further. To go further is this thing: that you become the master here in physical, and leave a tool for anyone, doesn't matter, and then you blast off, and you purposely upset beings in a manner so that a religion cannot be established out of it. That is part of what is going on now in these changes. Each one simply has to be reminded how to do this thing, say you, drive car. Each one. That is the process that is evolving now. These are outrageous times, entities, in what you would term the denial of who you are, because the Father, what you term the force of life that began you, is still there. It has fun in the body, for the body is an outrageous toy, tool. Anyone have any other questions?

Meditation

Allow your eyes to close for a little moment. Now we want to activate a force that is within you here. We'll call it a little tablet. It is about the size of your silver dollar, and in a manner, you're sitting on it now. On this coin you are sitting on, see an inscription — it doesn't matter what it is, feel it at your base. Allow. Now allow this to move up the spine, up the center of the body, to sit at the top of your head, the crown chakra. Allow. Allow it to move. There is no judgment here. Allow. Peace. Let it begin to what you would term melt from the heat of the crown chakra, and as it does it descends into the body. Peace. Peace. Allow. Grand.

Now in the palms of each hand feel a large clear crystal sphere. It is what is termed eight inches across in each hand. Let that sphere move up the arms to the shoulders. Peace. And let that sphere join between your shoulder blades. Allow. Open the heart chakra. Open the heart chakra. Peace. Feel yourself surrounded by a pyramid of white light now, the entire physical body. Peace. You are in safety. Allow your guides to come forth. Allow your guides to come forth. Allow. Now allow the energy that is what you term your guides to be placed over your heart chakra — these are your entities now. Allow. Now allow the guides to very gently assist in opening the heart chakra wider. Feel a little pressure, not too much. Allow it to open and allow more light in there. Feel it. Allow. Open the throat chakra. Peace. Allow. There are two vortices at your temples, open them. Breathe gently. Peace. Peace. In a gentle manner slowly open your physical eyes. Peace. Peace. Peace. Allow. Peace. Allow your eyes to close slowly a moment and feel about you, look at your body now, your physical form, very gently. Allow. Peace. Do not judge a thing. Allow. Peace. Center. Open your physical eyes.

As your consciousness begins to shift more and more, you will understand that it's not necessary to move rapidly. You've trained your vision to be this, that, click, clack. When you've gone through your meditations, allow yourself slow movement here. Slow movement. Some of you we are working with to get you up to what is termed a three-hour meditation. It is necessary, because then you'll understand you don't have to do ritual or play with what you term your drugs, your peyote, that you know it here in your body, and you know how to do it. It takes discipline within the body and what you term the mind, and your willingness to do this thing for yourself.

You are living in a time of great change. You're going to read and hear of many things, many. Some of you are going to get caught emotionally in this thing, and then we will have a great meeting. We will pull the emotion in and then we will understand it, and then we will let it go, and things will change.

There is a thing called this *divinity* — it exists within each one of you, and all things upon your planet. You have pretended it does not because that is part of the game here. The game is shifting now. The experiences you're going to begin to be involved in have to do with very psychic power; that is a very spiritual power. And the domain is your physical form, that is the arena. You're going to understand, entities, within your reality called physical body, your truths, your light, your fun, and your not-so-fun. In greater humor, all things are fun.

Now, over these two what is termed week time, contemplate you in your form physical a red light at your root chakra, moving up through you, very thin. Contemplate I arise the vibration that I am, that is you. And contemplate peace.

One of the things that you're not aware of, because of this great power being opened, released in a manner, it is going to be very important to be gentle, to be what is termed, your words, kind. Know you kind, gentle? To others, ultimately unto yourself, and yourself, kind. Know how some of you enjoy what is termed beating your-selves up? Hmm? Not at all? You've gotten over it? Grand! And then some of you enjoy beating others up. Better have a good idea who you are before you begin these two things. Anyone have any questions they want to bring up?

I want to do another meditation, indeed. They don't take long. They take short time, because it is the thought that will align. They are simply tools to get you.

Meditation

Contemplate a brilliant gold pyramid. Its apex is at the top of your head. It is four-sided and it descends around your physical body. You can stand up in it. Peace. Allow this pyramid to spin counterclockwise around you. As it does, center the energy in what you term the sixth seal, your consciousness is called the energy. Peace. Power. Peace. Now allow the pyramid to expand, apex upward, base downward. Further. Allow. Allow the vortex at the sixth seal to open wider, grand. Allow the base to extend further. Power. You are safe. Allow. Open. Open the sixth seal. Allow the apex to extend further. Do not be concerned where it's going, it is out of sight. Allow the base to go further, it is through the planet and it's out of sight. Open the sixth seal. Peace. Open the heart chakra. Allow you. Now from you heart chakra in this pyramid see you a flash of white light go out through the sides of the pyramid, that is you, out the sides. Allow. Open the sixth seal. Peace. Grand. Allow. Love. Gently. Love. Now in your heart chakra (do not say a thing, do not repeat what I say) contemplate these words, Light in the heart chakra, I know! Let it vibrate up to the head and to your perineum. I know! I remember! I remember! Let it vibrate up. Allow. Open the throat chakra. Feel I know in the throat chakra, and then feel the energy move up into what you term your ears. Allow. I know! Allow the brain to hear it, gently. I know! I remember!

The pyramid is still spinning. Allow. I remember! Peace. Now you can't see the apex of this pyramid, but sense, have the feeling in the body that it has opened. Allow. Peace. I remember. Throat chakra: I remember! In a gentle manner slowly open your physical eyes. Be gentle. Allow. Open the seven wider now. Open. Open the throat. Allow.

This force that is moving is expecting, though there has been what is termed a delay, to eventually join upward from the center into all living things, its light to start a journey. It is expecting the lower chakras to be opened. It is expecting to anchor here in what you term your solar plexus. It's expecting clarity in these arenas. It is not going to worry about clarity. It is expecting this thing to be done. Everyone breathe.

The Emotion Is the Wisdom

It is your body and it is part of your journey now. You're going to find many of your friends having difficulty in these chakra areas, not only emotional, you're going to go further with this thing because the emotion is the wisdom. The physical pain is not understanding the wisdom. When it begins its pressure here it's going to desire for the soul to know how to leave the body, not that it's going to kick itself out, what you call kick it out. It's going to make adjustments. That's why the requirement of mastership is necessary now, to know what the soul is, to have played the game called love and apply it, not mental gymnastics — that will not cut it. Later on it will be very important.

We are now in the cycle of love now again, mental love. Some of you have heard me before, what is termed your three years [prior]. I told you in order to make it to this time, "You must expand the soul, to have the understanding that it can expand or it will never be able to support the great light that comes down upon it. It'll crush." You are in another one of those phases. Be kind. Your thoughts are beginning to what is termed be applied gently now. Be . . . know you filter? Slow pour of the water. Pretty soon, very much. So you be aware. As your decade completes, this force that is joining with you is expecting clarity here and here and within. So it is a lot of fun, eh? It is all energy.

If one has completely merged with the Divine Mother and finds oneself back in a personality, how does one tell whether God has kept that personality in a provisional state, or if one has decided to come back from an ego perspective and to be an ego again?

It is necessary to have an ego in this reality, and these journeys are all allowed to be participated within by anyone, and they are signposts more than labels. You beings utilize your labels and your words to create, from this perspective, places you have been upon this great map, know you? "I have been here, here, here." They must be all traveled to be understood. Do you understand? In other words, you *all* must become the Christ, and go beyond that. And you must become the Buddha and go beyond in order to reunite with your Father, and you must meet Lucifer and understand who be he to get back. So you identify your own mirrors, so to speak, in your terms. Did that explain it?

One of the purposes of metaphysical teaching is to get you to a level, and then once you're at that level, you're willing to practice and participate within those understandings, not verbally, within the powers of the soul that you are, being willing to go further. The experiences you beings play with are yours. Some of you should be sharing them. Some of you should not, because they are your power and when you put a label upon your power, you have trapped yourself, because it is a definition, and you fit into the box. Anyone have anything else they want to chat about? We'll move more into this next thing.

New Activations: In the Temples and Above You

You've all heard of this what is termed your sixth seal, third eye. Everyone wants it to open. Well, there are many more than just one in there, and they're termed vortices. They too now desire to open. One of the requirements is that these vortices [temples] should be open also or you will get great headache. It will release what is termed vapor, what you would say, vortex, as it opens. There is force involved – it has to go somewhere, so you let it out of the temples.

There is another portion of your being now that is being activated, or is going to be shortly, and it resides right about here [approximately six inches] above you. It is not your soul, yet it is part of your being. Your soul is in your body. It's a force and a pulse there that is keeping you alive. This, we're going to call it a vector, know you vector? This vector is about to be, we're going to say, realigned in you. As it does, some of you are going to feel sort of tippy. Your light now desires to connect on another hook, and you thought you had it all right at the same time. "I've got my stuff together!" The one that knows the answer of which way to turn this thing, and it must be turned, is in here [soul]. And as the light [from center of Earth] is moving now up here [above the head/crown chakra] and expects clarity, so too this one expects upon the turning a connection. And if this one [within the soul] desires in its knowing, it will get the connection.

5

Ancient Visitors in Mexico

Zoosh through Robert Shapiro
April 18, 1995

Hmm. This *[figure 5.1]* will shake a few people up, because it's *white* light, you know. I gave it to you top side up, and if you hold it at a distance you can see a face there. That is the current representation of Lucifer.

Oh, great!

You had the face of God before; now you've got the face of Lucifer. This is not Lucifer as he actually looks, but Lucifer in the guise that is necessary for him to broadcast, inasmuch as he must be responsive to those who have attachments and expectations of him. So, that is his face. He is —well, how can we put this delicately? The photographer was not touched by the energy because the energy was sent in another direction, but if the photographer had been asked to remember when he took that picture (if he could identify that picture), he would have had a strange tingle in the back of his legs and the bottom of his feet. That's the tingle you sometimes get when you know it's time to turn around and run. I will say that if that energy had been facing toward the photographer, he would have done just that. But the beings that sent him there knew that he would be safe.

Now, we must understand that Lucifer is only evil insofar as fear and evil energy is portrayed as portions of his being. He reflects, just like all energies; he reflects. But I'm calling him Lucifer in this case because I'm differentiating between Lucifer and Satan.

These are two words meaning essentially the same thing, but I'm going to differentiate Satan as Lucifer's dark side. People might find that amusing, considering the fact that Lucifer himself perpetuates the idea of the dark side. However, the more corrupted, the more extreme side of Lucifer I'm going to call Satan. Now, that is not what is pictured; that is Lucifer. One might wonder in terms of the light, but you must remember that white light is absolutely unconditionally loving and does not

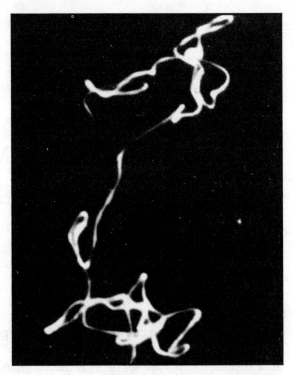

Fig. 5.1. Lucifer.

have any means or desire to change that which it joins with. It is just unconditionally loving and takes you as you come; it does not expect you to change in any way. So we must understand, then, that the white light is love, but it is not discernment, nor is it associated with transformation, from the Earth point of view. It is associated with transformation when you're in the stars, but when you're on Earth, white light can protect you only if you are protected. That means it can protect you if it radiates, so if you have another means of protection anyway, that's a sidelight.

One might ask, "Well, what was Lucifer doing there at that time?" I will say that he had been called in by certain individuals — not in Sedona, but not very far away, within a 50-mile radius of Sedona —who were performing, perhaps irresponsibly, a ceremony that I cannot say was a satanic ceremony; I would rather say it was an ill-advised, irresponsible attempt to call up the power of Lucifer to support them —almost what I would call a childish attempt. Sometimes these childish attempts will be answered, so let this be a warning to those of you out there who might fool around with this kind of thing: It's not the sort of thing to fool around with! I might add that those who brought this energy into a version of materialization were affected somewhat by it. They did not get the power they asked for because, after all, Lucifer can only reflect; he cannot grant. But they did get a certain amount of discomfort associated with guilt. So on the one hand that's good, because that suggests they knew they were doing something they shouldn't; and on the other hand it showed that there wasn't much gained, either positive or negative.

I thought Lucifer had turned toward the light!

Yes! But as long as people attempt to bring him forward in the role of the dark; as long as there is a certain amount of evil running around on Earth; as long as people are attached to utilizing him and the world being polarized that way, he is being dragged back into his role. However, I will say this: He will no longer give more energy than he gets. In other words, he is not an amplifying energy anymore. So that's a plus. He's managed to escape that much of it. He's turned toward the light, yes, but even if you turn toward something, that doesn't mean everyone will accept that, do you understand?

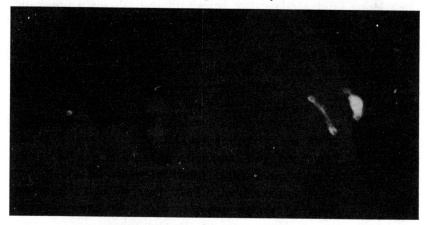

Fig. 5.2. Floating portal tethered to a ship of light.

Figure 5.2 This one's pretty difficult to see, but we have a light here and we have a vague light over here. I'm going to allude to that vague light, but I doubt very much whether it will duplicate. This is a floating portal, a portal that is tethered. This might cause you to wonder, tethered to what? It's actually tethered to a vehicle. One might ask how this is possible. There are circumstances in which very highly evolved beings who travel in ships of light (which do not take substantive form, but remain as light) can manufacture their own portals. They will sometimes tether a portal to their vehicle with a cord of light, providing that portal with only a certain frequency of energy that will allow it to be activated only by certain individuals, ships or lightbeings, and remain safe for others who have to fly near or through it.

So this is a tethered portal. That slightly vague light that is almost invisible on the picture is the vehicle waiting to fly through it. We're just seeing it begin to emerge into a form of light. It might be hard to pick up, but it's there. Anyway, the tethered portal is designed to transfer a vehicle and/or lightbeings to the center of your galaxy. The purpose here was to move certain forms of light, certain rays of colors, into the center of your galaxy from which planets and various forms of mass spew out, and where the recycling of this matter to the center of your galaxy is designed to slow down the process of creation in the center of your galaxy.

Your galaxy actually needs to stop its creative process while Earth goes through its transformation from dimension to dimension. This way there will be no possibility of producing another polarized planet. When one has what is essentially a polarized planet within one's being (and a galaxy is a being), there is always a possibility (albeit an astronomical possibility) that one might produce another polarized planet, long odds though they may be. So this matter is being sent to the center of the galaxy to slow down and then stop the creative process in this galaxy only.

For how long a period?

Probably for no more than 25 to 35 experiential years. This will not really harm anything.

And where are the beings in the lightship from?

They are from the spiritual — oh, I don't like to use this word — how can we say . . . they are the guides and spiritual teachers who help the Arcturian beings. They are from about the 18th dimension, which is a dimension, by the way, that does not exactly play into being in this galaxy or in the space this galaxy occupies. So they have to come from some distance to perform this job. Even traveling at the speed of time, meaning traveling in time, it took them approximately two weeks' experiential time to get here.

Why here? Why are they doing it here?

Because they need to gather material; it's like an inoculation. You might say that you have a disease; in this case, polarity is being referred to as the disease. You know, this planet is way out on the outer boundaries of this galaxy. They need to gather material from a polarized planet and remind the point of creation from the center of your galaxy that this planet exists and that it is not desirable to reproduce another one even remotely like it. So it's essentially an inoculation of this planet's material matter. It can't be done by inoculating dark energy, but it can be done by inoculating the actual matter of the planet equal to about . . . well, I suppose if you were to hold it in your hands (theoretically, if you were the strongest person in the galaxy), it would be about the size of a modern portable computer, weighing approximately 35 or 40 tons. So it's very dense, but it's actually matter associated with your planet. It has been removed from about two-thirds of the way down to the core so it would not be polluted by anything. It is not anything that was then concentrated. It was volunteered by Mother Earth; it was not taken without her permission.

An Opening from the Fifth Dimension

Figure 5.3. Here's an interesting one. We have here a door that is opened up from inside an etheric mountain, we could say. You can almost see by that light the shape that looks like a mountain in the background. But this is a mountain that is associated with the fifth dimension (not to be confused with the musical group by the same name). It is actively opening there to allow beings, individuals of the fifth dimension, to emigrate, though temporarily, into the experience of your dimension. It is their job — and we see here the portal being opened, the light shining out here — to gather the last bits of mental matter that can be gathered for what amounts to a museum. You know that you're going from the third to the fourth, but you won't stay in the fourth very long. From there you're going to the fifth, and you'll stay there for a while — at least Earth, you know, your experience there and so on. Your life will become much more involved with study.

So these are essentially future lives associated with people who are now alive in the third dimension; they are coming back in the fifth dimension to gather, how can we say — if you were sitting and thinking, you would have a lot of neural activity in your brain. They are going to their past lives (fifth-dimensional people going to their third-dimensional past lives) to hang around with them for a while. They'll gather the radiation that comes off the skull's auric field (roughly, a little behind the crown chakra) as a result of intense thought. They will gather this energy and place it in a crystal to be viewed prismatically, not directly, because it is the only way in which third-dimensional reality can be studied in the fifth dimension, where people cannot deal with extreme negativity.

Now people who are in their third-dimensional being, the third-

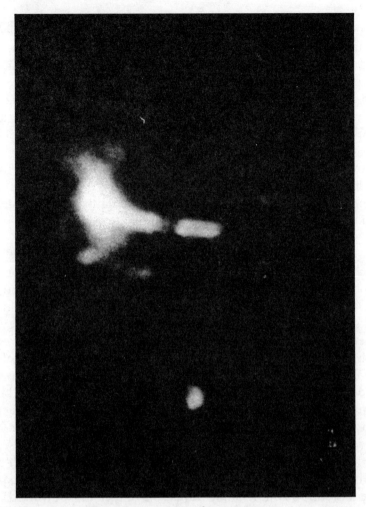

Fig. 5.3 Doorway to etheric mountain.

dimensional past life, might conceivably have a thought about something abstract (maybe mathematics, maybe language, who knows).
But because they are human beings in these times, those thoughts
will be colored by their feelings, by their past, by their history, by
their imagination and so on. So there will be a certain amount of
polarity or discomfort (negative energy, as you call it).

In the fifth dimension, where this kind of experience is studied,
it cannot be studied directly, so the crystal will have a condensed
form of light passed through it which is associated with sound rather
than light. It can't be seen, it's not a real laser, but it would be
associated with condensed sound and can be seen only through
certain lenses. Other than that, you can't see it, and you have to be

careful with it. It will stimulate the image which will reflect, essentially, into a larger crystal which will display the multiple facets of potential thought, imagination, feeling, and all of the various processes of the thought of the third-dimensional beings onto this display crystal. This crystal is very organized: any thought reflected into it using this method of condensed sound will display all its different facets from the inside out onto the facets of this crystal. The display crystal is set up to show no more than about 128 facets. It's probable that the thought will have more than that, but that's as far advanced as they are in that kind of crystal research to observe, calculate and measure third-dimensional thoughts in a way that will not affect them. That's a little more scientific than you probably had in mind, but that's what they're doing.

Next?

Fig. 5.4. A vehicle from a civilization in Earth's past that predates Atlantis and Lemuria. (Chichen Itza, Yucatan, Mexico.)

The Obelisk-Builder Civilization

Figure 5.4. The foreground is obvious; I will comment on the vehicle in the sky. At this particular gathering in Mexico, many extraterrestrial vehicles came to observe and celebrate and support. This particular vehicle is from the past of this planet. It is from a civilization that predates Atlantis and Lemuria and even Mu, for that matter (which, from my point of view, is not the same as Lemuria). It is a civilization in which the founders of the civilization that evolved into those that built the pyramids were interacting with time travel.

To put a time line on it, they existed on Earth roughly a million and a half years ago. They did not look exactly like what you would now call Earth people.

Can you sketch?

A little bit. [He sketches something, chuckling.] I am not the greatest artist. But the idea here is that the people looked somewhat like that. They were human beings and not animals — kindly do not confuse them with that. They had an extended jawline. This was probably associated with their distant past in which they were significant meat-eaters, but by the time they had arrived on what you now know as Earth, they had evolved past the need for that, and, I might add, their work was no longer sufficiently strenuous that it required them to eat meat.

This civilization was one of the more profound civilizations that has ever occupied this planet. It was their job essentially to set up obelisks all over Earth. You know the meaning of that word? Obelisks that would welcome all of the different civilizations, all of the different cultures, including some which still exist today in areas that have managed to remain fairly isolated, associated for the most part with native peoples. These obelisks would not only welcome but guide these races and cultures to Earth. They are no longer on the surface of the Earth, but they're still on Earth. They started out on the surface when there was no reason to disguise them or hide them, but by now they've been sunk to a depth of about 65 miles in solid rock. Of course, that can only by done through the use of energy-motion, changing the alternates of the matter so they could move through molecular structure. But these obelisks were very important; they not only attracted these cultures, they sort of created a "this is the place" navigational system. They also established the form and function of the obelisk as your planet's functional physical symbol.

If one were to study Earth from another civilization, one would say that the obelisk (although in this case the obelisk would be free-floating and would have two points, not unlike a double-terminated crystal) is associated with this planet's spiritual and cultural heritage. These beings lived on this planet really only for about . . . well, their years were different, but roughly about seven or eight hundred years. Not very long, but long enough to invite cultures, long enough to train some of the people that were here at that time (referring in this case I think to the Andazi, whom I've spoken about at length before). We're talking about beings that did not walk around too much on the surface of the Earth. They were under the

Earth; they were in the skies above the Earth; and they have everything to do with the diversity of cultures here. We really ought to talk
about them at length some other time.

Why were the obelisks put under the Earth?

Once there became more curious and technologically advanced
civilizations here, including Atlantis, then the obelisks came somewhat under assault and were no longer fully able to broadcast their
signals, some of which were, in Atlantean times, picked up. And then
as civilizations of technology continued to flourish, other obelisks,
which were under the sea, were gradually detected. So they've all
been moved into the Earth. At this time they are no longer broadcasting or receiving information; they are dormant and in places where
they cannot be found. This civilization moved them.

This civilization?

Yes, this civilization moved them.

So they came back, then, because that was much . . .

That's right. They can travel through time, though, you have to
remember.

Where do they hang out when they're not traveling through time?

Right now they're situated in the ninth dimension, in the neth-
erworld between the place of personality-only and the place where
personality manifests into form. That is about the lowest dimension
where they could activate here for any length of time. They have
recombined as a single personality. In this case they came to visit
from that past time, when they were here for 500 years. They just
knew what was coming. So you might say that the point of origin of
that ship was Earth, about a million and a half years ago.

Is there a name associated with them that we've ever heard?

Let's see if we can get that into your language. I'd call them the
Kier-anis, with a kind of rolled *r* there. These are not be confused
with the Kier-anubis, which is associated with a later time, with the
Egyptian culture, which is primarily a feminine civilization. This
civilization we're talking about is one of masculine and feminine
polarity. Onward?

Onward.

Figure 5.5. This photograph, I believe, shows vehicles in the sky
here, does it not?

Yes, right above the horizon.

I'm only bringing this one to the fore here because people love

Fig. 5.5. A Pleiadian ship here to observe from the recent past.
A friend of Semjase is aboard. (Uxmal, Yucatan.)

this. We have a Pleiadian ship, okay? That's the only reason I'm mentioning this, and I really don't have to wax on about that.

From the present time?

It is Pleiadians from the recent past. Not wanting to rain on anybody's parade (you can choose to print it or not, it is up to you), I will add that the person aboard the ship is Semjase's friend, all right? Now, Semjase's become well-known through the Billy Meier contacts.

What's the friend's name?

I'm not allowed to give the name, I'm sorry. I'm not allowed to give the name because the person is a direct relative to Semjase. I'm calling it a "friend" (in quotes), who is here strictly to observe. I only bring it up because I know that many of your readers identify with the Pleiades, but there's really nothing else to say about it.

Liaison Mothership from Orion

Figure 5.6. Here we have again a vehicle in the sky, yes?

Yes.

This vehicle, interestingly enough, has been on television before. A few years ago it was seen rotating in the sky and was put on TV. It is a vehicle from Orion. Many different sources visited this place. It's in the area on assignment. Many of the vehicles that were there are

Fig. 5.6. A Vehicle from Orion that has previously been on television rotating in the sky. (Uxmal.)

Fig. 5.6a. Close-up.

associated with your direct cousins, as it were, and that Orion vehicle is present. They're not doing anything in particular, they're just observing. The reason so many ships were here is that they were choosing to be observed. In many cases they were observed not just by people who could see these things, but by regular, normal people, not sensitive people. So they were there to be seen as well as to observe.

What is their function normally?

Normally they are liaisons between the Inner Earth beings (who have largely evacuated your planet, by the way) and the Pleiadians. I hate to use the term "mothership" because it's been used to death, but it is that. It comes fairly close to your planet from time to time, but they don't come as close as they used to. It comes, it dodges in and out in time, and it comes only as close as its defense systems and your offense systems allow.

Does it have a name? Have we heard of it before, this mothership?

I don't think it has a name. I think it's strictly one that is here to observe and has been here for many years.

How many, like hundreds? Thousands?

Thousands.

So this Orion ship is a benevolent mothership?

Yes.

Now that the Inner Earth beings are gone, how is it going to liaison, what is it going to do?

It's probably going to withdraw. The beings are not totally gone, but there are not many of them left. And the ship is probably going to withdraw because it's no longer needed. The rest of the Inner Earth beings, if they need to get off, will be transported off by lightships. That is the usual method, anyway; the Orion ship was primarily there to act as a go-between, because they have tremendous defensive potential. They can defend almost anything. They have almost the ultimate defensive weapon. Actual defensive weapons do not harm anyone, understand? True defense is simply a reaction to an attack. Their defensive "weapons" — I'm using "weapons" in quotes here — are simply the ultimate masking devices, so that you cannot tell if it is a physical reality or an illusion. Thus you might say that this ship has an extremely advanced capacity for illusions.

Did some of your not-so-benevolent friends give that technology to the Earth?

No, their technology is not now available on the Earth. We're not talking here about a rudimentary invisibility or anything like that. Here's an example: They have the ability to stand off at a distance of several million miles if they choose, and to broadcast a signal that would allow something to be seen or not seen, or, more likely, allow an apparition to be seen that would be taken for something else. They have a device that allows them to simply aim a sampling device at what they would call a sample subject, a person from a culture, and know everything about the culture from that person without harming that person at all. They can be a million miles away and do this, and then they will know not only what causes that culture to be frightened, but what causes them to feel reverence. Therefore they could manifest something that would cause the threatening culture to stop threatening, either for religious reasons or for fearful reasons, but in any event not cause any harm.

What dimension are they from?

They're from the sixth or seventh.

Fig. 5.7. A lightbeing emerging from building at bottom. (Uxmal.)

A Sirian Race Here to Help
the Evolution of Human Thought

Figure 5.7. We save the best for last. This one is light on the bottom, and inside the light there is more. Here we see a purple light, I believe, surrounding a roughly blue, sort of turquoise — aqua if you would — lightbeing who is emerging from the building upon which people are standing.

Yes! I didn't see that before; it was just a blob.

Yes. This is almost cover material. This is a lightbeing that is associated with the culture that urged the building of these edifices to be used not only for landing ships, but for creating underground facilities to support, sustain and otherwise assist Mother Earth's acceleration. These times you're living in, as I've said many times, are not really your natural times. If, say, 40 or 50 years ago you contin-

Fig. 5.7a. A lightbeing emerging, close-up.

ued forward on your natural progress, you wouldn't be that far yet. But devices such as those placed underneath these buildings, these structures, have caused a certain acceleration, in a sense, of Mother Earth so that those who live upon her (you) can get to where you're going faster.

You know, your favorite thing is how you can get there faster. So, this lightbeing is essentially emerging to walk with the people up the steps, to participate in the ceremony. I'm seeing them coming up from the back; this is their back. This being is associated with a very spiritual place; they are from a very high level of Sirius, about the twelfth dimension. They are from a race that's involved in teaching. They're involved in artificial as well as natural evolution. They're involved with the creation of thought as you know it. It was this race's job to abstract (meaning obtain) the Andromedan as well as the Alpha Centauri thought process, mix it all up and create what you have now as a form of condensed thought – alien thought actually, your thought process – and make it not only compatible with human bodies but with the souls or immortal personalities you possess. These beings can create, they can uncreate. If we were to say that the Creator had neural synapses, these beings would be the synaptic relays of the Creator's brain. They are absolute experts on every form of conceivable thought, including that which can manifest and that which is rudimentary.

Have we ever heard about them in myth or legend? Do they have a name? Were they here when the Explorer Race was formed?

They visited here long before that time in order to prepare the thought patterns as well as the thought forms and even the wave forms of your brain's measurable electrical patterns. They are as close as you can get to the Creator of thought.

So how did they do that before we were here? Were they here in one of our predecessor bodies?

No, no. You have to remember that they are so closely associated with the Creator, they can work on that which did not yet physically exist. One might say (and some people believe this) that thought exists before form. These beings might support that.

@QUESTION = What's the light at the top, then?

The reflection of the sun.

So are they here, how are they here . . . ?

They are here because they are working with the Founders who live inside the Earth. They are helping you because you are literally changing your thought from this old version of thought that you've had for a time, which isn't yours, into your natural thought process, which is more of what I've called vertical thought, or instantaneous knowledge, knowing what you need to know when you need to know it.

So they're helping us make this change, then.

They are involved with making the change, yes. They still choose to live in that general area, even though the machines, the devices, are no longer active there. The access that they choose to use to the center of the Earth is available there, but only through the upper dimensions. It is not available physically.

Okay, is this particular one in the Yucatan or Palenque?

I would just like to say it's in Mexico.

Okay, what really happened in Mexico? How can you describe what really happened on the day of those ceremonies?

Well, of course the ceremonies were not complete, because the intent was to reveal a certain amount of the knowledge of the Mayan people to a large group of people, and that didn't happen. So then people simply had to sort of fend for themselves in their own groups. It became more of a coming together of different peoples, but because the day was dedicated to revelations, it became a day in which individuals, if they really desired it, could see the truth for themselves. Some individuals who continued on with their spiritual work there did support that and sustain that, and many people did have personal revelations.

Why didn't what they thought would happen, happen?

Well, there are physical explanations, but the main explanation is that this was all supposed to happen several years ago. It would have been best if the spokespeople for various tribes — Mayan, Hopi, certain African tribes — were to get together along with certain members of certain religions, the most significant of which would be the LDS Church (the Latter Day Saints), who were intended to come together years ago and reveal what they know, cosmically speaking. We sort of have to wait now for certain planets to line up again for this to happen again in its own sequence. When people try to reveal these things out of sequence (it was supposed to happen about six or seven years ago), it just doesn't work. That's because the people have to be receptive, okay? Now, this might happen again because the United Nations is going to become a significant factor. If this information were revealed at the United Nations, I think it could be done within the next five years.

Why wasn't it done six or seven years ago? Was it because the tribes wouldn't give the information then?

No. Certain individuals did not show up who needed to show up. The tribes' representatives felt that those who needed to understand this (which were not individuals in those tribes but individuals in the outer world or the world which you simply occupy here) would have to consider it valid. Certain individuals from certain religions did not show up to do this. This is probably because these religions did not wish to be viewed as something other than normal. Even today there is significant prejudice against the Mormon Church, so that's why they didn't show up. They felt that had they come forth six or seven years ago and reveal some of the cosmic knowledge they have, they and their people would have been treated badly. I must admit that that is true, to a degree. So they chose to hang back and wait for a second chance, when they feel there will be a better reception for this, and they may be right.

So they have cosmic knowledge that no one except the elders in the inner circle know?

The elders of the LDS Church have cosmic knowledge not unlike that of the elders of other religions that go back a ways. It is more likely that the LDS Church will reveal it, because they have been living it for a time in their initiations, which I will not talk about because I do not wish to step on their toes or offend them. I will simply say that with a few minor changes, their religion is probably the only Christian religion that will survive into the 2500s. They need to make a few changes; probably the younger members will make those changes as time goes on.

So a group of people got together to have this ceremony in the Yucatan. I thought that perhaps it was without being aware of the astronomical energies that needed to be set up, or was it something with the various other churches?

This thing that went on in the Yucatan that has nothing to do with the event of five or six or seven years ago; it is not the same thing.

But they attempted to bring information out . . .

The attempt, but it wasn't a receptive enough time for it to be brought out, so circumstances prevailed that did not allow the Mayan elders to speak to large groups of people.

But what about the Tibetans bringing the energy from Tibet? There was tremendous energy there.

Yes! You can have a lot of energy, but you can't use energy to force anything on anybody, do you understand that? That's essential. The people have to want it. If they don't want it, that's it. And there were many people there who didn't want it, or who just were enjoying the day off, the festival aspect of it.

Right, in addition to the people that came for this there were thousands of people who were there on holiday, ordinary, everyday people.

Yes! And this tended to dilute the intent.

6

You Are in the Process of Living Your Book Called Revelations

YHWH through Arthur Fanning
April 21, 1995

Y ou are all having a grand time on your planet, eh? [He laughs.]

Allow your eyes to close for a little moment. Open your heart chakra. Command white light to be around you and within your being. Now, let the white light that is within your being and around you spread outward through your community, push it outward through your state, through your country, and clear the consciousness now, and white light around your planet. Peace. Center your thoughts in your heart chakra. Peace. Allow. Love. In a gentle manner slowly open your physical eyes. Everyone breathe lightly.

You are in that phase, entities, where consciousness can become confused, not knowing what it is, who it is. Not knowing the Father. Your religions have separated you, and you're going through the process of unification and it is difficult. All the fears will come and they will be faced. We have spoken of this before. You are in the process of understanding you and your relationship to All That Is — whether you term it God or Source, it doesn't matter — it's to the Great Creative Force, and your place within it. Everyone's place is sacred within this understanding. (Everyone breathe a moment.) You're just *beginning* to see the confusion as it begins to move, we will say. Now, that is all I'll say on that thing. Everyone breathe again now, a breath, and breathe it out the throat chakra.

You all are divine beings, everyone is. And it is your divinity that is important now, each one's, and understanding that divinity, that life force that is you, that you're playing with now. It is time to learn to share your divinity. Not to be a victim, but to share the divineness in yourself with another. That is going to happen. The steps may seem a little difficult, but we'll get there.

One of the things that is going to begin to accelerate within your week coming, your dream activity is going to change in this manner: you term them lucid dreams. They are realities, and they're part of your realities that you're going to learn to blend. What this truly is, is that you are now moving into a phase where your consciousness desires to become unified within the left and right portions of your brain, desires to think, in a manner, whole. You remember this from what would be termed past lives, some of you. You have been untrained in this lifetime. That portion of untraining will not support these new systems that are going to be going on within your being. Say your thought processes are going to appear to be accelerated within you. You're going to *feel* them in your body. You're going to feel them rather quickly in your body. Say you thought of love, you will feel it in your body, and you will feel it in the appropriate arena, what you term organ. Thought of anger will be felt also. Jealousy will be felt. All of the emotional energies you beings enjoy playing with, that you don't think you are responsible for, are going to be, you would term, allowed to be showed to you in your body, what your thoughts do. Not only what they do to another, but what they do unto you, your divine self. That is why it's going to be appropriate now to love all beings, bless them, even if they don't know what they're doing. Don't judge them, it is not your place at this time to judge. It is your place now to have compassion for the ignorance that is going to manifest. Have compassion, entities. Be kind to one another. It is very important now. Everyone breathe.

This year, your '95, you have heard from many sources, it is going to be very interesting. You have heard speed-up and all of this. This is truth. In one manner, it is very exciting because your divinity is blooming, believe it or not. In another manner it can be very threatening if you don't know where your divinity is, where it resides within you. You will be running all over looking for your divinity outside of you. Can get confusing, eh? Does anyone have any questions?

Many people that I've been talking to have been experiencing nausea, dizziness and headaches. Can you explain why?

It is different for different people. There is an energy shift going on. There is what you term a bug that is being activated in the bodies for, you say, flu. It lasts a short time. And it is because of the increase in frequency now that is happening. You define yourself as your personality in this one body. You are much more than that. And as you become rigid in your structure that this is all of who you are, this one persona, as the greater portion of you begins to activate itself within you, the resistance to hold on is going to create an energy vortex that will be termed sickness, it'll be termed the flu, it'll be termed many things. You have within your form physical, dormant within you, every disease that can exist on the planet. What you're beginning to understand, it is your choice to activate it or not. (Everyone breathe.) You already have that you term it wisdom, that resides in your body. As this greater frequency begins to increase itself, the ability to shift will lessen the discomfort or disorientation. I've told you before that as these times approach, it's going to be not a bad idea to be a little crazy, know you? I don't mean crazy what you call run amok, I mean *feel* disoriented, allow yourself to see the other realities. Allow yourself to *know* these things do exist. Allow yourself to know more, more than what you've read. Begin to define your own books now as you live here.

The physical body, your physical form, is changing. It's being altered, and that alteration is being done from within you. There *is* a force that resides in you, entities, it's called the soul. It is a real force. It is part of your journey here. And the forces within the soul have been with you forever, through all of your journeys, and the forces about you in some manner have been with you forever, also. You've forgotten the connection. You begin to understand now that you are simply a membrane, body human, between these two forces. (Everyone breathe.) So there are changes moving.

There is this thing called life forever. You have this word you play with what is termed ascension. The way a master ascends is that he commands and quickens his body physical into light, to vibrate faster. That means the brain vibrates faster. That means thoughts don't crystallize within the physical brain — they flow through. Because around you is all thought, and you vibrate with all thought and you become lighter and lighter and lighter, and lighter. And you manipulate what will be termed the sieve that is the brain to pick a density, very simply, pick a density you want to play in. It is a manner of adjusting your sieve in here in conjunction with the desires of the soul for its journey.

Know you how at times you have not done a thing and you want to do it? It is something you haven't done. That is what propels you on your journey. When you are bored, you have done these things before.

They don't bring any excitement to you, so it is time to seek another journey. [He laughs and says:] Did that answer your question?
Yes.

A little bit.
A little bit.

Lighten up, entities. Part of what is working in the body is an increase in, at one phase, thought; at another phase, light; at another phase, electrical current. Electrical force that exists in the body may be termed God manifested. It is simply thought lowered, and you are that thought, all existing, each one of you, along a line of light out of a greater light, by thought lowered. You are participating in a divine play, and each is working a part of the Father's scheme we will call it, along their own line of light. Soon you're going to figure that out, but it will take you a number of years, from your present point what you call six. It is a sacred journey, and divine. And each being on the planet, whether you like to think so or not, is living their divinity as best they can, as best they can, with what they understand, and the tools, and what you call their spiritual chromosomes, if you will. They are doing the best they can. The only way you can assist is to have compassion and love them through their journey, as other beings have loved you through your journeys, those that you don't want to remember, those past lives that you say you could not have lived and been so cruel. You all have done it. That's why you react to it so much in this lifetime, you remember. It is all right. Everyone breathe a moment. Let's get to some magic, huh? [To a participant:] Do you have a question?
Not at this moment, no. . . . I do, I have many.

Not one that you think others don't know about. How will I rephrase this thing? You are all beings of light, connected along a line of light to this great light here, indeed? And out here everyone knows everything. It's fun to be in this form to pretend you don't know, know you what I mean? Do you understand? And each one is doing the same thing, they're all agreeing with you. That's what keeps this game going. Wait till ten of you masters wake up at once, then everyone realizes, "I knew that! No big deal," and the game called die ends. Know you what I mean? [To the same participant:] How many chakras do you have?
Twelve.

Well, in the main physical form?
Seven.

The main seven, we'll just go seven, indeed? Let's not get metaphysical here. You have what is termed millions of chakras, actually. What is this one saying to you here [navel chakra]? When was the last time you talked to this being that is in there (and I don't mean in bossy manner, either)? Will you allow yourself in your dreams this evening to go into this chakra and hug this being that is in there? To hug the being, embrace the being, indeed? And tell it everything will be all right. Bargain?

Bargain.

Now, your journey in the physical (we'll keep this very simple) is through the seven chakras. Within those forces there is an identity called you. These are termed the seven seals in your Bible. There is a persona you that is in there, looks just like you. As you would treat it as a child, you would say you store memories, you term them, there in your body (you do in a manner), of what happened to you and how you reacted to your parents and this being and that being and the other. The memory is stored in the vortices here, this one. And as you grew up, your fears at times you didn't want to acknowledge or whatever, you played with them within the chakra forces, left them there. So it's now time to become the adult that you are and love all of these things that are there, indeed, and bless it, because it provided you wisdom. Believe it or not, all of your experiences, regardless of what they are or what they were in your terms, were required to get you to where you are now. See you? So once you can understand that, you bless all of the experiences. Do not take them personally. Understand the treasure within this thing. Indeed? There is a treasure there within all of you, and that treasure is your divinity. It was never taken away, you're simply playing hide-'n-seek with it. [He laughs.]

If we are all one, we must all be feeling what has happened in Oklahoma City. It must have caused all of us sorrow and stress.

Well, you're all judging it, that's for sure. That's why we did this meditation. Allow this peace to be there. As these changes happen all over — this is not only occurring in your country —you are dealing with an evolution of consciousness now, and there will be some that do not have wisdom, you understand, and they are what you would term ignorant, little boys and girls playing game. As difficult as it is, because you are divine, if you allow what would be termed a judgment of you to be placed there, then part of your being is going to be placed there and you will learn to be in that arena, to not judge it. Send light through you out, and bless. The consciousness that is there, the consciousness that shifted in that experience, understand, needs the light, know you, so they can see where it is going. Do you understand? So you send light the minute you hear of these things. No matter where it is on your planet, you send it through the planet, indeed? You do that thing, and let the consciousness that's leaving the body see the light. It will find its way home. You understand? You're going to have many opportunities to judge. This is a baby one, by the way. And you're even having interference what you call from your beings of light out there to prevent some of these other things from occurring. They are *too* outrageous. Won't be allowed to be done. You're not going to blow your planet up. You might think you're coming close, however. Everyone breathe.

The important thing to remember as you walk through this time, that you are dealing with your divinity. And you are all aware that you're dealing with an entity that is termed the Antichrist now that is present. He be working here, and there be another working, the opposite, yet it's difficult at this time for you to understand who is who. What is important is not to figure out who is who, it's to learn to discover your own divinity daily, and that will take you right through this muck without what you call any problem —well, little bit of problem, not much. It'll only be a problem because you judge it, know you? You have been taught even in your book, [your Bible] to condemn not another, know you? That didn't mean simply 2000 years ago, know you? Everyone breathe, lighten up now. Gently. Now I want you to do this:

Know you your bottom, your buttocks? Your perineum? It sits right in the center there. Squeeze it tight, just squeeze it. Relax it. Relax. Squeeze it again. Relax. Now you have a hole at the top of your head called the crown chakra, soft spot [on] little baby. This time when you squeeze your perineum and your bottoms, visualize what you would term a little white marble, ball. As you squeeze, that ball goes up and shoots right out of the top of your head and sort of sits there. Indeed? Now squeeze and send the ball up. Allow. Relax, allow the ball to come down. Center your being. Squeeze the ball and let it down. Relax. Squeeze. Relax. And take a breath in and fill what you term your pelvic area with this breath. Simply breathe it down, hold it there, and push it up and out. Allow. Gently, gently in your being here. You're moving energies.

This little ball trick, you may change the color. Start you off white and then move into gold. Don't want you comparing. And you can do that what you term driving your auto or anywhere you sit. That will align your chakras, and it brings excitement to the seven. It also has a great healing effect upon those that reside in here [within the chakras]. It'll help the energy move. It also assists your kundalini, know you? And I know some of you want your kundalini to move dramatically. Don't make that ball too big, not at the present time. You'll have more excitement than you can stand. Won't feel comfortable in the body, either. Everyone lighten up a bit here. Everyone breathe a little bit.

Now, one of the things that is difficult now is this thing I've spoken of before, this fear thought form. I know how all of you beings in your metaphysical understanding are very powerful here [brain], you've got it all figured out. This [soul] is where the power is, and it must be large enough to support the great thinking capacity as it expands, because if it is not, the great weight from the thoughts as they come forth unto you will crush the soul, and the soul will leave the body. (Everyone breathe.) That is why it's important to expand the heart chakra. That's why it's important to love and be in love. You can be in love with a flower – that will save you. You can be in love with an ant – that will save you. But you must have that energy of being in love moving inside you or you will face great difficulty in these times coming. That is simply the way it is. Now, give me a moment. I don't want to disorient you too much here.

Now, as you beings are made up of light, you're light beings, brilliant light. As you allow your consciousness to shift within your physical body, the light color, the frequency, changes and you begin displaying different colors. In one manner the colors identify who you are in relationship to, we'll call it the great light, where you are. Soon to come, as you beings see more of these lights you are going to get into comparing again. I will tell you at this time, don't do it, but you will. Have a grand time. All of my favorite words. Remember what you did to get there. You increased your vibration, you allowed your consciousness to shift, to consider that you are more than simply physical form, that you are connected to divinity, forever. And there will be those that don't want you to be divine, it makes them uncomfortable, but it is your choice now.

Some of the meditations that you have been given were purposeful in exciting your physical body, exciting the organs of you. Now, this is where I get to be funny. I enjoy my humor. Some of you aren't going to think this is very funny, but it won't matter. You are made up of light, and I've told you before that your appendages have consciousness – your fingers, your toes. They're part of you, they are part of your being. Your organs are too, your eyes. They are entities, a collection of consciousness doing a job, so to speak, and you have considered them slaves. So it is time now to see parts of your body as persona. You may even indulge in the little whimsy and see faces on them so you can communicate, talk to those consciousness units that are involved in your form. The difficult part will be, however, to listen to the return conversation. You beings are so interested in having your own way all of the time. Everyone breathe. Lighten up here.

As I look at your form from another level, and as I peer from inside you outward, I see you made up of many different shapes, many different beings. Some of you enjoy what is termed the limbs of animals, because it's part of your experience, you remember. So from my perspective at times, you beings are sitting there with leg of crocodile or leg of lion. Different body parts forming what, you term from your perspective, is your physical form. You've forgotten how to communicate with you, and what thought processes you use to build you. That is all right. You're now simply beginning to learn that it is okay to talk to your food before eat it, and to listen to the food to see if it is appropriate. You have had cultures that knew that a long time ago. Now you're getting back there. It is time to communicate not only with your neighbor, but with parts of your beings here, and allow the changes.

There is a spark of life in you, your original light that exists in here [soul], and when that light is quickened and allowed to quicken, it'll flash through you in an instant and can heal anything in a moment, even broken bones, because the light remembers how easy it is. You've been trained out of it. That is all right, part of the joke.

Part of the game down here is forgetting, and it is fun to forget because then you can blame someone. And it lets you enjoy the game more fully: you don't judge yourself because you forgot, until you get to the next level. Then you play, as you all do, judge yourself for judging. It is time for the lot of you to remember now, all of you. It is not that difficult.

Now, there is an energy pattern, as it moves, that is going to begin to affect the rear portion of your brain here, particularly this side [left rear]. It wants to spread to unify all around. You may consider this as seven concentric rings existing in here [within the head], and the energy will want to go around the bottom ring, which will excite the one above it. (You've heard of the term *resonance*?) So as it does, it's going to do it all the way up within the physical, and it's going to be a counterclockwise energy. Clockwise creates third dimension. Counterclockwise allows you to accelerate the physical form within the body. Now, I will do this little meditation here, as you would term it, for your physical form.

Meditation

Allow your spines to be erect. At this time it's going to be particularly important to be sure that the throat chakra is aligned, that your neck is straight, and you feel comfortable in that position. Peace. Now contemplate your feet enveloped with golden spheres. Simply feel your feet within these golden spheres, and they are two feet across, each one. Allow the energy that is within those spheres to begin to move up the soles of your feet and up your legs.

Take a breath in down to your perineum and tighten it. Hold the breath and breathe it out, and allow that energy to move up the legs, up to the thighs, up to the pelvic area. Allow. Golden light, allow it. Now take another breath and hold it at the perineum. Focus on the perineum, tighten your buttocks, and exhale out allowing the energy to move up to your stomach. Gently now. You're moving Shiva. I want you to tighten your perineum, take a breath and tighten your stomach, hold it, tighter, and let the breath out. Allow the energy to move up the spine. Allow. Peace. Peace. Allow the energy to move up to the solar plexus very gently here, move up to the heart chakra, move up to the throat.

As it moves behind your jaw, allow it to envelop that first ring and see that first ring within your head become golden. Allow. Peace. Peace. Take a breath in and tighten the perineum, tighter, tighten the stomach, and breathe out the top of your head. See the six above, those rings, become golden. They all vibrate golden. Allow. And feel the energy around the inside of your brain, golden light. Allow. Allow. And allow that gold light to enter your physical form, your physical brain form, and pass through it to the other side. Allow. Peace. And see the energy within the seven rings spinning, allow it. Feel the gold in your head physically, allow. Peace. Open the throat chakra. Peace. Above your head six inches there is another chakra – tell it to open, and allow it to spin counterclockwise now. Open it. Allow. Peace. At that chakra what would be termed see you and feel an eye there. It is part of your being. Allow. In a gentle manner slowly open your physical eyes. Peace. Open the heart chakra in the body.

Allow yourselves compassion, entities, in these times. Allow compassion for yourself and for others. That certainly does not mean you must be a victim. In a definitive sense, compassion in the manner even for the male entities, and especially for the male energies, the manner of love that a mama has for a baby, and the manner of love that your mama had for you when you were first born, moment first born, that energy, that love. Compassion. Everyone breathe.

As you begin to accept your divinity more, there is a responsibility to understand and know the use of these forces, to understand the within and without, these energies. Many of you are sitting on what you would term concrete slabs, standing there thinking you're anchored to this thing. You are not. You are much more than the concrete, yet you're part of it. You are your life. You are energy and light. You have been told you are a belief system. You are going to find out differently, because you are each individually in your own evolutionary spiral, understanding as much as you want to at any moment, and knowing as much light as you want to at any moment. Yet light is all that you are. So you see, it is a fun game. Indeed.

Now everyone take a breath, and when you hold it in your belly this time, I want you to breathe it out of your heart chakra. Take a breath in. Hold it in your belly and love your belly, and breathe it out the heart chakra. Allow.

What is important in your journey is truly the love that you show. That is what is important. In the ecstasy you're willing to share, and the beauty of things around you, that is what you cherish most as you leave this plane and move to another. That is what is important here. For those of you that desire, we are going to open on your palms what you call the chakras of compassion. There are many there.

For your understanding, simply allow you to see a rectangle in here [palms], long way this way [wrist to fingers], tilted a little bit, and allow your palms to be upwards upon your knees, your thighs. Allow. You may allow your eyes to open. Some of you that can see will see the energy blast out, so to speak. And focus here, what is termed in the heart, and contemplate all love that you've ever experienced in this lifetime for anything, and all the love that you've ever experienced in any lifetime for anything. Contemplate it within your heart chakra, and contemplate the love of the Father that allowed you to play in this arena. It is there also. Allow. Feel that love in the body that is there with you now, and allow that love to move down the arms and out of those vortices — they will open. Allow that love to come out. Display it, indeed as you see. Allow. Peace.

In a greater understanding, your thoughts and your energy, what you term feelings, move through the vortices that you have, and there are many in your hands, and they're at the soles of your feet. That's why the Earth knows who you are when you walk, when you display your energy to the Earth. The Earth recognizes who you are when you recognize who you are. It is that loving. Any questions? Anything you want to chat about?

You said the Ring of Fire was going to open up in May, and there would

be a lot of earth activity. Is it something in particular that triggers it?

What particularly triggers this thing is the consciousness involved on the planet — that is the initial trigger — and how you utilize the energies that are being released and presented here. As you understand that you are light, so too the Earth understands that it is light. And as you understand you have diseasement in your body that you want to release or get rid of, so too the Earth has that same understanding. You are in for exciting times in your May in what you term your earth activity. I know many of you play in this thing called this pole-shift thing — that it what is termed come about, and I have told you before, it is not truly a shift of the poles. It is a shift of the magnetics. And what is magnetics?

Magnetics is light lowered and consciousness adjusting itself as it plays to become electricity in the physical form. So it is your consciousness shifting. It is your consciousness. Now, you think it is just you persona, just you soul, but you have *petitioned* within the soul to the greater lights that you are to get this thing fixed, so to speak. And the greater lights that you are, are coming together with you to participate in this fixing. So it is not what you term your ego identity so much; it is more if you can remember the petitioning that you did when you were little one and as you grew up, that God would be here to fix this thing. They have, and you better get working on it, because you are the gods here that are going to do it. And your friend Sananda, what you term Jesus, he be around assisting and watching. Some of you what you term have little chats with this one in your sleep at night. It is a good thing. There are many other beings assisting you. *That* is a good thing.

We understand how you say, "It is my persona that is most important." It *is* important in this lifetime, for you could not be physical without it. But now it is time to shift and allow the persona to shift. That is difficult because you think the persona is what has kept you *alive* all of this little bitty lifetime. It is not that at all. It's the life force that exists within you, that spark that keeps the heart beating. Your persona had nothing to do with it. It is a good thing, would have mucked it up. Can you imagine trying to stay awake all night telling your heart to beat?

Changes in your month come May exciting, through July, exciting. Little calm down for what is termed one month. September exciting more. How high can you jump? [Laughter.] It is nothing to be what is termed afraid of. It is to be understood that you are all connected here in these times. And it seems that the closer you get to the edge of this big cavity, big chasm, as it opens, the more fun you have. And you can run away from it. Many of you beings like the excitement of the adventure, to see how close you can get into it and still get out. Well, you're really into it now in more ways than one. And many of you, some beings on your planet think you're more powerful than the Antichrist. Don't muck with this being, you don't know what you're doing. It is part of the scenario that must be played out. Why? Because you wanted it that way. Everyone breathe.

When will he become more visible?

Very shortly. Be you say, he's already made one appearance. It'll be understood July and more to the end of your year. It is part of the play. I have advised you not to begin to figure it out which one this be. There be two beings come forth. Initially, you're going to gravitate to what would be termed the Antichrist. You won't realize it. Give me a moment here.

Is this person in the physical?

This one is physical. He will be come from what you call the European continent. And there will be another from what you term the Middle East that is his balance. Anything else?

Is it important for our physical bodies to have the amalgam in our teeth removed because of the mercury?

At this stage, your body has become accustomed to it. By *accustomed* I mean you have already done the damage; and by *damage* I should say you have adjusted these forces. For little ones it should be avoided completely, know you, even what you term in your twenties.

What about the effect of the electrical activity which is increasing through the metal in one's mouth?

It'll give you some exciting visions, take advantage of it. If you feel discomfort or what you'd term threatened by this thing, then it is appropriate to be removed, you understand? If your belief system is that it is damaging you, then do it. Know you what I mean? It is the same way with what you call your medicines. In the body called health, you have all been given your wisdoms. And if you know what you're doing and you apply it in what you would term it spiritual — but it's called the wisdom of the gods — you *know* how to fix things; do it. And if you don't know and your belief system has entrained you in such a way that you have a doubt about what you're doing, it is best to go along with the belief system because that is where your rescuer is. Don't think you know it all unless you can prove that you do.

These are outrageous times, entities. You do not prove you're god by jumping off a cliff. You do not prove you live forever by standing in front of a truck or a train. You will find out that you're still alive, but the beings witnessing the act will think you're dead. This is the phase where you're learning to manipulate the physical body, to bring it more light. It is not a phase where you are questioning the fact that you're going to live again — you already understand that, you've done it before. That is kindergarten. You're in the phase where you understand you're light, you've lived life before, you're manipulating the light within the being, and you're manifesting your body each moment, and you're understanding your shift in consciousness, how you do it. You're learning these things. That is what this is about. There will be many levels, especially as you approach your year 2000, where it gets really exciting in this expansion of consciousness. Many beings in your religious community call it Christ consciousness, the returning of Christ coming to the planet. Well, in one manner it *is* the returning of Christ coming to the planet, and that is the Christ within each one remembering it is the Christ, remembering the lessons that this one you call Jesus taught, that you are to do the same thing. That is what is going on, so don't go sitting on a rock waiting to be rescued. It won't happen. You're into it. Any other questions?

You had said a couple of years ago that it would help get us out of the hypnosis of the third dimension to consider the 13-month calendar. But did you mean just working with the phases of the Moon? We don't have to learn the Mayan symbology, right?

What I referred to, to get you a step, what would be termed, if you would understand the Mayan calendar, know you? That would be an outrageous thing to understand, indeed it would. What I told you, you would do best for you, is to understand that your calendar was altered, indeed, and the first month is what would be termed your Aries, know you? And you play your Aries part March, part April. Yet that is — the part March, part April — really an Aries month, know you? You understand? And there is a cycle there. And so too with what you call your Taurus — it is a Taurus month. Then you would understand how you were born, know you, because your light moves through your constellations to be present here.

Your constellations don't affect you. You have assumed and been told that they do. But in your great light, you chose your constellation to go through because you knew it was a great lens that you could focus specifically upon the planet with that energy, to complete your job, so to speak. So you *use* these forces, you *plan* to use them, do you understand? You have been taught that this affects you this way, that way. This planet be retrograde, everything go amok. If that is the god's belief system, so be it! You've been taught even in what you term your Bible that you are the ruler of the stars. How did you forget that? What be termed "loose the bands of Orion," know you? You exist on the other side also; not trapped here.

How do you get twelve signs into thirteen periods?

I've told you before, I'm not going to give you cookbook, know you? Now you have an entity [Jose Argüelles] that has shared some great information with you —what would be termed the Mayan thing. It is a difficult teaching. People become confused. They don't want to understand it. This [the Mayan calendar referred to above] was simply a very little template to get you to even shift out of the old structure a little bit. Know you what I mean? This one [Argüelles] is correct in what you term the cycles of energies that work. It is very commonsensical, know you? You beings have frequencies within your body; you don't rely upon them because you have to be at work at 8 o'clock and leave at 5; have one hour for lunch. It is what you would term a training that told you that you are hungry at 12 o'clock, to feed the body.

Sometimes I just want to get out of there.

Indeed, but you see my point. You beings, if you would allow yourself —what you would term, you take your vacations to rest, and you're still so uptight that by the time you get back to work, *that* is when you feel like resting. If you allow your body to figure itself out, you would figure your body out. It has a natural cycle. It requires little bit of sleep; wake up, play a little bit; little bit of sleep; wake up, play little bit; little bit of food, not tons of food. It likes delicate foods, is what it *likes*, because it knows the light moves faster through the body when you eat delicately. And then you would learn that you are light; you wouldn't be so trapped in all of your foods, which is where a lot of you get stuck. But that is all right.

You need the physical form to complete your journey of becoming the Christ. If you don't do it this time, you'll do it another time. Doesn't matter. No big deal! It's like getting new suit of clothes. You are each being here because you wanted to be here at this time, and you're in what you would term Christ school, or Buddha school, or Mohammed school —whatever you want to call it. You thought it was outrageous that some beings could come down here and succeed in becoming masters, as you term it here.

There are many beings that have never walked this planet. You term them Brotherhood of Light, etc., etc. They don't *want* to! Because once you set foot on this place, you're going to have to get it! You're *stuck* until you become the master of this place. They are not that dumb! They don't have that much courage, either. You beings are courageous . . . or lack brains — we're not sure which yet. [Laughter.]

When do you think you'll know?

Those are simply your words to explain an idea. That is why the entity you term Buddha, the one you term Mohammed, the one you term the Christ, and a lot of the other ascended masters love you so much, because they know the difficulties that *they* went through to succeed. And they want you to succeed! They don't want a bunch of rules down here to control you. They're excited when one being succeeds in this thing called ascension, as you play it. Not die the body; takes the body away, appears the body. That creates a great camaraderie, know you? Like another being won the game, and there's great cheering, great blessings, great joy? You see you? They be sitting not there judging you at all. You're having too much fun doing that yourself. They don't want to take your fun away. So you're in your Christedness, your Buddhaness, and your Mohammedness — you're in it! Pick your own name when you do it.

There have been a lot of rumors about three waves of ascension. Is that still holding true?

I use the word "ascension." Indeed, there indeed are [three waves]. But this word, ascension, is incorrect the way you beings interpret it. There are three we will call it time cycles, know you, and you are in the middle of the second one [he laughs] or approaching it very rapidly.

When was the first one?

It was what you would term your 1993. How many of you made it? You have two more, what is termed your '96 and your '99, if you want to term them cycles. But don't concentrate on this thing. Concentrate on you understanding the vibration. Don't put it off till your '99 — that's going to be very critical. That'll be the real bug-a-boo. How you say here, you think people are beginning to lose it *now*? Know you lose it? (Everyone breathe a moment.) Remember this light thing, send light along. Be all right.

In one manner you are very fortunate, because your greater light being desires you to succeed in this thing, it desires *itself* to succeed be even more appropriate. So it's going to force the light that it is to its persona — that is you here — that is upon the planet so it can identify with itself, and you identify with it. So you identify that you're a much larger being, much grander being, much lighter being, and you don't identify with belief systems any longer. You identify with the beauty and the compassion and the love that you are; and you identify with your success in doing this thing. Belief systems have always been used to trap you, this, that and the other.

In your year I will say you '97, many of you are literally begin to see the physical grid system that exists, what you term your meridians, around your body. You'll see others walking with their meridians looking like skeleton, so to speak, meridianally. Don't let it upset you, because you must quicken those meridians. They need to become thicker for you to do these things. (Everyone breathe a moment.)

As you quicken your body, it becomes lighter, and there will be a time when you know that you can pass your hand through your hand, because you're passing light through light. There you are not your hand unless you want to be your hand. That is your ability to love and be in love with this game. And you'll understand that when you do that, you're affecting all consciousness. Not simply around you, but all consciousness upon the planet. You're affecting all things when you move in that manner. And then you will begin to understand what a joy it is to be in the physical body, how the light has ecstasy as it enters the body, [because] it can feel itself and it can feel the other gods here. And you'll understand that the light loves density, because it can play here and communicate and touch. I know you've been taught that your orgasms are going to be much greater when you're light beings passing through everyone. Well, they do accelerate in a manner, but you must remember how much you enjoy touching. A lot of you beings, as you entered into this time, have been told it's inappropriate to touch this being, that being, this, that, the other. It's one of the reasons – one – that you are physical and have a physical form, because it is fun to touch. It is fun for your light being to touch itself, to feel itself as physical form. It's fun for your light. That has always been the case.

Will the meridians be merging, will the meridianal lines become so wide that they become one?

Indeed. It will appear that way; you'll flash. Like your chakras are becoming one chakra. That needs to happen also. And you'll be one light, and then you separate your . . . see your divinity, your chakras seven here is your game to play here. This is not the rule. Out there you're one light ball, so to speak, and out of that light ball you create the seven chakras to be physical, and held within the meridian and soul; it's the way it works. So to get one, you be one, and you *think* the form you want to be. You're it.

Now, give me a moment. As you are light, you are love. You vibrate it. It is felt. It is enjoyed. It perpetuates life, light does, the light that you are. It allows life all of its journeys. It does not tell life not to be. It allows life. So allow yourselves to become the gods that you are, to remember, indeed, and remember your own divinity. Remember all the divine beings that you think you know that have made it here — they're rooting for you. They're not judging you at all. They can't wait for you to make it to begin another party. Indeed. Anyone have anything else they want to chat about?

Last night, I feel as though in my . . . I'll call it the dream state, I was reading or being given this information in written form about what felt like coming through the star systems, and I was kind of rejecting it and saying, "That doesn't apply to me," and then getting the message that it did apply to me. I felt it had something to do with my male energy and how I was using it in a connection with my father, but I can't quite grasp beyond that. Can you help me with that?

As you are born, each one, you are in love. Female baby in love with papa on more than one level. We'll say it starts off in the root chakra, know you? Male baby in love with mama, what we would term great sexual attraction, know you? Do you understand? Now, as you be in your world, this sexual attraction that attracted baby, we'll say female baby to daddy, is understood in the feelings of the bodies, know you? Baby loves daddy, daddy loves baby, sexually even. But in your society, and it's appropriate from what you term your level of understanding, it is taboo. You understand? As you grow, you be taught you don't love the being. As times play in reincarnation, that "don't love" begins to be overwhelming, create judgment. You carry it forth, you term it karma, know you what I mean? (Everyone breathe a moment.)

That does not mean if you have a baby to molest it, that's not what I'm saying here. I'm telling you the way the energy is and the ways you beings interpret these things. So there's a great attraction. Another reason that you beings born yourselves is to do something that you haven't done here. Know you what I mean? That creates part of the excitement.

Now, this realm of activity, what you call in third-dimensional form planet Earth here, has laws. And there are laws prior to coming here also, that have to do with the understanding of what love is, and it is not only root chakra. So that is part of the energy that you're learning to understand. Know you what I mean? "Out there" there is no judgment. The law out there, to put it simply, is that once you incarnate upon this plane, you are to complete it. That is, to become the master; to become, and become, and become; to understand all of the energies, to understand love completely, without a focus in a particular vortex. That is the law.

Your churches have told you, or kept from you, part of them. Some of them have told you, called it karma, good/bad. It is that you have this desire to complete that is built in, and it will complete. It is simply your timing, how you want to do this thing. One of the easiest ways to overcome the judgment that you beings have regarding sexuality, and all of this and that nonsense, is to allow a little one to sleep with the parents up until what you call three to four, to five, to six; to be in same energy bed, sleep with. The baby [is] borned to touch, be touched. You, in your society, take it away from mama and papa, stick it in own room, shut door. Put a little box there so in case it cries you can run in and touch. Your technology is going to destroy your spirituality, entities, and even the purpose of being born, some forms here. Doesn't matter.

The families you are born in you are connected to what you term in a very loving journey. And some of the lessons that you said you would learn prior to you forgot, so you play back with same energies, same entities, switch roles even, to understand in this dimension polarity, and understand the center. Know you polarity, opposite? Know you your DNA, it sort of goes like this also, indeed? If you want to straighten your DNA out, you center the light in your being and the DNA will come right into the light. Knows what it is. It's doing you a favor, however, out here. Part of your play, part of your fun. Everyone breathe. You're not being judged, you're all having fun.

Why is it more gentle when it spirals? Is that what you're saying?

I will say it this way: Know when you dive to bottom of ocean, indeed, and you wear your weights to keep you down so you can see the bottom of the ocean? So too as you spiral, your DNA puts it out there, know you, its bands. It keeps you grounded in a manner, your weights. So allow your light, and allow it to come. Your DNA desires and knows the light. You get that part and you'll be shooting out of here in a moment. Just remember how to shift it out again. You begin to manipulate the lights with the thoughts — how you do it, how you remember. So it becomes fun. The memory is fun. You're doing it automatically, so to speak. The memory is the fun. Anything else?

When you shift into Christedness, does the persona all go away and you're just god in your thought now?

Not at all. You remember your persona, you love your persona because it helped you get there.

Sure, I'm just curious if you forget it all.

Not at all, it was part of your wisdom. You must remember your persona or you wouldn't become. You remember all of your personas; they achieved a purpose for you advancing, you understand?

So you get to be Christ and still hold some of your thoughts of this.

You hold them all because you're not going to judge them. Know you what I mean? You're going to acknowledge each one because it took you to become, each thought, indeed. When you judge them you're not going to become. You're going to have to love all of your personas, entities, even the ones that committed murder and rape, all of your heinous things. That is why you forget them now, however. You don't want to remember. That does not mean that you say, "This must be done in order to accomplish." You understand the wisdom of what it means. This is the game of *not;* that is the game down here at this time. "Let's see what's not God." Well, you're finding out soon, everything is. We can't wait to get you into the shower to clean you all up, get all this not-notness off of you. Humor. Is there anything else?

Could you talk about the merkabah breathing?

What do you want to know about it?

Everything you care to comment on.

How do you think it works? Where does this exist in your body?

Along the spine, through the feet.

Are you a three- or fourth-dimensional being when you are breathing, physically? As you become, you learn little steps to do more, and they take you to [a] point. There are symbols, signs that tell you how to do this what you term breathe. There is a hole here [middle of the small of back]. Know you whale and dolphin? Know you the hole at top of head there? There's one there [a hole similar to the blowhole of dolphin and whale, but in the small of the back]. Now there are beings playing with this thing; they're not getting the power of the energy. There is also here and here holes [front of each shoulder, just below clavicle], and you're required to concentrate out here and here [front of shoulders] to get the first activation. You learn to breathe in here [small of back] and out here [front of shoulders], and then you'll breathe out here [front of shoulders] and two other vortices that we're not going to talk of yet. But it is a form, what you term a shape, a design, that is doing the breathing, that coordinates with your physical body and the light that you are. So it is not the body breathing, it is the form of light that is breathing, in your words. Do you understand what I am speaking about? Are you sure? In a manner, it is a pulse, not a breath. It is a pulse from the thought of you to activate. It'll feel like breathing. Everyone breathe a moment, gently.

Know you how at times beings have many teachings on kundalini, how to activate it — this, that, and the other, indeed?

Indeed!

You have ancient deities that are in charge here of this kundalini within physical form. Shiva is involved, Agni (the god of fire) is involved, [and] Shakti. I have spoken at times to you that Shiva is female, and you beings went into your labels. But in order to experience Shiva in your body, creates an activation of movement, and that movement is female that you define as Shakti. So your labels will get you stuck. It is all movement of energy within your being, how you do it.

We even had to create a play in order to get what you term your label Shiva to move. Agni being within here had to create an excitement, what you call a challenge for Shiva, how you would term it. So Agni had sort of a dance with Shakti, and Shiva got all upset. So he decided to move and get a little battle with Agni. But that created the movement.

Because in this density you beings create your physical form out of seven chakras, you think there are seven levels, basically. You don't understand that you're one; you've forgotten. So you're learning, and you use your labels, you use Buddha, Mohammed and Jesus as examples of succeeding. And you use the ancient deities as examples of movement in those arenas — not that they did it or they're the ones to judge, but you can do what they did. Definitions have caught you.

So this merkabah everyone's into here is a breathing of form in your body as light pulses, and you recognize it, you pulse it by the thought. You can open these points with what you call your acupressure, your acupuncture. The two primary ones to open is the one on your back and the two here [front of shoulders]. The next one be here [third eye], and then there are more around your shoulder blades, but that will create some difficulty for you if you're not ready to let go of your judgments or your karma. Create great pain in the body. But have a grand time with it.

When kundalini started moving, many of you had little back pains and you couldn't figure it out. In fact, you couldn't believe it was kundalini. Thought it was something else. And you were told to bring the energy to the center of the spine and let it move. And you didn't and your backs hurt. And then it moved up higher, and your back hurt; and then your head hurt. You're dealing with much more energy when you deal with what you term the merkabah here. It is part of your divinity.

All of these teachings, as they come forth, are designed to get you to remember that you are light being within the physical form, and you're utilizing the thought of you, all around you, as light within your physical form. Be gentle with your physical form as you work with these frequencies, very loving, because *you have not told your physical form you love it.* You think it simply exists as a toy. It is a toy, it's a grand toy. It's a grand tool. It's a palace that your light is within. And the light within the center here and the light about you is going to understand that there is communication required between this membrane that is between the two of you. And the physical form will communicate, it will love to. Anything else? Didn't like my answer?

It's going to become important to . . . as you start playing with this thing, there are temple vortices here that must be opened, all of the time, for fun, to release pressure in the head. You've got to remember, you're dealing with the fluid that is around the brain now. As it becomes excited and quickened, it wants more. But there is not often times that you sit in meditation and allow the more within the body. You define the experience and limit it. Give not a label to your experiences, they will simply slow you down.

Did the bombing in Oklahoma City have some cosmic purpose? Is it bringing what's going on in the rest of the world to our attention? Is there something we need to learn from this, or was it just a senseless act?

What I told you before, in what you term the country called Russia, know you Russia? The same thing that is going on there is going to go on here, because you're mirrors of each other. Know you what I mean?

Yeah, the U.S. will fall apart into little groupings.

And the struggle is going on. Be not caught into this thing. It is an outrageous manner ignorance, of the occurrences. You humans react in a very clumsy way with your divinity. Eventually you will learn you're one planet, but that frightens many beings, know you? You must have your enemies, and you must have your flags and this, that and the other. If you saluted the god that you were and the Father that exists in all things as much as you salute your flags, things would be a lot better around here. That applies to all countries, not just this one. You're in the midst of it. You are missing some things in your wisdoms, but you're going to get them.

You are in the process of living your book called Revelations and others now. You've heard that before. You're right there. You can almost pick out your timetable. If you would allow your consciousness to shift, you could change it, however. Everyone wants to get *off* the planet so they don't experience this thing. Not too many are having success. And the way some are choosing to get out of here doesn't look very attractive to the others.

This portion here [brain] gets it last, know you? This is the sieve. This portion [soul/heart chakra] knows. This portion [brain] tells you what others will think and say — can't do that, this, that, the other. You must allow your manifestations as they come forth to you, and are presented unto you for you to acknowledge them. Know you what I mean? Too often you beings think a thing and want it to happen, and as it comes up to you, you say, "No, I don't want that to happen." Well, what are you doing? You are training yourself *not* to manifest. *You must acknowledge all things you manifest.* That teaches you how to manifest. It's really very simple. We are through.

7

Midwest Bombers
Manipulated through Time

Zoosh through Robert Shapiro
April 28, 1995

Now, this recent circumstance in the Midwest [the Oklahoma City bombing] was a direct outgrowth of a secret government plan to activate and delude your duly elected government. I do not wish to say that there was not a conspiracy amongst men to create this destructive and heinous activity. However, I would like to support one thing that is believed by the perpetrator who is in custody: that this person has had injected into his body an enzymatic suffusion of material that reforms itself and attaches itself to the aortic muscle, to the thymus gland and to the endocrine system within his body. This material prompts this person to become overly suggestible to motivations transmitted to him through time. The reason it is not passed to him from any input device in your time is that he is being directed from the past so that those who direct him cannot be detected or punished in any way. You might call it a technological possession.

By this I do not wish to suggest that this young man is free from responsibility for his actions. However, if this material had not been placed in his body, he would have been able to resist the impulse and it would have taken its natural form as a fantasy in his mind. You all have fantasies about many different things, and (with some exceptions) they are not particularly harmful to the bodies and souls of others. This privilege has been granted to you so that you can feel the creative ability you have in other dimensions, but you are not encouraged to bring these fantasies into reality most of the time, because you are here to learn about the responsibility of creation rather than to become creators of chaos.

So this young man was directed by a force not of his own creation. This is not going to save his life, because he will be found guilty and will most likely be executed, though it is possible that various maneuverings for stays of execution might cause him to survive many years into the future. However, it is not going to be a pleasant life, and he would probably just as soon pass over, which is why he has not cooperated, on the one hand, but also not objected to the punishment.

When this material was injected into him, he was in the military service. However, I wish to make it abundantly clear that the military had absolutely no awareness that this was being done to him; there was not a conspiracy by your duly appointed military authorities. The whole thing happened in a short amount of time, when he was supposedly on leave. This material was injected, and he received what amounted to an inculcated indoctrination, meaning that a great deal of pressure, force and suggestion were applied to him in a short amount of time, essentially allowing him to become a blank slate (tabula rasa, as it's referred to legally) manipulable by those who would prompt him to have this thought of anger against the federal government and to take it out against innocent people who were simply employees.

Now, for the sake of the families, I do not wish for you to think that I am exploiting your misery. Know that no one dies without giving permission, that all who passed over passed over in the time that was expected for them. Know that before the explosion took place, about five seconds before, the area was flooded with angels and divine beings who received the spirits and stayed with those who suffered — even those who suffered and passed over later had angels with them the whole time. And even some who are grieving their losses have angels with them now. God is not vindictive, and when mass suffering like this takes place, the angelic kingdom rises to the occasion.

Understand that this deed was stimulated by your archenemy, the secret government, to usurp your abilities to respond — to essentially grab for power and to put the tenets of this power in place legally, giving them the means to temporarily suspend the Constitution and the Bill of Rights in order to establish a control that will usurp all authority. The one great advantage you have is that the people in the military who might be called on to establish a temporary martial law are all from your ranks, and they are not going to go along with any orders to take a wholesale action against the civilian population. They identify more with you than they do with their temporary military assignment, so know that there is that safety check.

Also, I want to say something that's very important. The patriotic organizations that have been formed are primarily an outgrowth of a desire to preserve the Constitution and the Bill of Rights. But know this: All training toward this preservation should include the loving law of allowance and an appreciation for the sacredness of all life. Speaking to all parties on all sides of the issue, just remember that life is sacred. Let's remember that if you're angry at the government, you can always burn a flag, if it makes you feel better — or better yet, fly it upside down. This gets the point across. You don't have to destroy life and limb of innocent beings, okay? I know you're not planning on doing that; I know that these patriotic organizations have no intention of doing that. But don't forget, the government is people. Never forget that.

The secret government wants to gradually usurp your rights, yes, but this is done primarily to give them a way to control you, and to create within that legacy of control the means by which they can take power legally, rather than illegally, as they have done. There are certain individuals within your elected or appointed bureaucracy who are right now totally controlled by the secret government; they are outer-ring participants. The secret government is set up in rings — inner and outer rings — and there are outer-ring participants in the bureaucracy of your country.

How does that work? Are elected and appointed officials part of the outer ring before they come to Washington, or do they join after they get there?

Here is an example of how it works. One newly elected or appointed person (I won't give the name) was given an injection. When he arrived in Washington, the first evening he slept, he was given an injection in the base of his spine, not with a needle, but with a technique I call compressed sound. This material, not unlike the material injected into this young man, was injected into the base of his spine and traveled to various areas of his brain as well as his nervous system, making him susceptible to secret government control to such a great extent that he is an outer-ring member now. When as a result of a new election such officials are no longer in their positions, there is a very good chance that their lives will be foreshortened. They will die before their time. You might say, then, that in the long run, they are being murdered. I don't like that.

What a crime — these innocent souls, advocates of great and wonderful things . . .

They are good souls. These souls are right now struggling in the bodies, and would just as soon pass over because of the control placed upon them.

This does not mean these people are evil; some are simply being influenced by an inner-ring member who they think is a friend. This is why sometimes they will do things that are not good for them personally.

The outer ring of the secret government is the most important to understand, because that is the group of people who are still functioning in positions of influence and can have reasonably functional lives. Inner-ring members cannot do anything but be full-time active in the secret government. Outer-ring members can conduct another aspect of life and be somewhat unconscious of who they are in the secret government, as some do not know they are in the secret government.

Good People in Government

Vice President Gore is not affected at all by the secret government, nor are any members of his family. He is a shining light in the White House. When his son had a near-death experience, the Vice President connected with the angelic kingdom. He is a force for the angelic kingdom within the government. And while he may never become President, he will probably be very active — someday, hopefully, within the United Nations. So know that there are not only forces of control in Washington, there are forces of good.

Some powerful people have within them what I call a light bud (like a plant bud) that does not allow them to be overly influenced. They can go along, but they cannot be pushed too far in either direction, or pushed too hard. They are protected.

This grab for power by the secret government is important to pay attention to now because there is an opportunity for people to do something. Not only can you write to your representatives, as I've suggested before in other cases, but now is the time for all people — whether you be oriented to the New Age or to shamanic ways, whether you be oriented to angelic energies or to organized religion. Ask that the gold and the purple flames combine together. See it within the Earth, expanding all around as a ray; see the gold-and-purple flame come in to influence all that exists. I will tell you this right now: If one hundred thousand people ask for, visualize, pray for and try to feel the gold-and-purple flame within, all around and about

Earth, things will get better. I'd like some of you to make this homework. If you have circles, do meditations. See the flame on the inside. See it coming out as rays of light through the planet, all around and about it, infusing the people, the plants, the animals, everything. It will help.

Right now the Photon Belt is here. The Photon Belt is here to help Earth, but it will have side effects on you. You can protect yourself with the gold-and-purple flame, and you can also create a more benevolent atmosphere for the Photon Belt to help Earth.

The Montauk Connection

Now I will say a little more. The young man currently in prison for this terrible deed done in the Midwest is not the same soul that was born into the body. The soul that is in his body now has been infused with a trinary soul — a soul that has been combined artificially by individuals involved in the Montauk experiment. For those of you who wish to know more about that, there are several books available. Preston B. Nichols is one of the authors. The Montauk people are directly involved with the secret government and they have gone into the past to anchor their means to control the present and the future, because in the past they not only have less danger of being detected, but less danger of even being noticed.

When they did this, they rounded up through various nefarious means many young boys and men, extracted soul energy from them, combined three souls and injected them into this young man's body who is currently under arrest for this heinous misdeed done in the Midwest. (Of course, they can only do this on a temporary basis because they are not functioning in the light; but they can do it for a short time.) As a result, this young man is currently experiencing total confusion about who he is.

If any people who have spoken with him read or hear about this material, you'll notice that one of the things this young man has trouble with is talking rationally. This is because the soul that he is, that was first in his body, is confused by the other three souls that have been programmed to encourage him to do things not of his own motivation. So he is not directly a Montauk child, but he is being influenced by them.

Influence Anchored in A.D. 1451

Who specifically inculcated McVeigh, and at what point in the past? You said on his leave, but at what point in the past? Where are they operating?

Oh, where are they anchored in the past? They're anchored in the year 1451.

That far back?

Yes. Well you know, there's not much fear of detection by the local population, and they are located about 300 miles beneath what's now the city of Milan, Italy. They are in a natural formation that is not exactly a cave, but is something akin to a cave, like a bubble. And they are directing their means to control from there. One crimp in their activities is that they must project from the present into the past, and then back into the present or the future. So there's a certain amount of signal loss that takes place. And because of the curvature of time, there is also a crimp. So they are using a huge amount of power to direct into the past — about ten times what they might normally need — because by the time the signal comes back into the present, it has already lost about 90% of its effectiveness.

Where are they aiming this power from, in the present time?

I am constrained but I will try and give you a vague idea. I will say that they are in the Northeast, but they are not in the United States . . .

Iceland?

Yes. But please, people of Iceland, if you read this, do not fear: You will have plenty of advance notice so you can move if you need to. Fortunately, in the current time, Iceland is becoming a little warmer and might become a little more volcanic. This warmth and volcanism will further decrease their ability to function, because it will create a certain amount of underground tremors as well as heat, which will affect the equipment used. But that will not take place in terms of an effect for about another year and a half. As you may already know, you are in a global warming stage now, so they will probably at some point need to move their bases under the sea and operate in vehicles not unlike large submarines; these are not so much designed to move about like submarines, but can be moved about, almost like an underwater barge, if you would. In any event, this will further reduce their capacity to be influential in terms of time work, as in the Montauk work. This doesn't reduce their effect in the present, if beamed from the present. But when they move they will become detectable, and the purple-and-gold ray, especially if supported and called forth — invoked, if you would, by those of the light — will be able to offset much of what they do.

All right. Is there a group of people permanently there under Milan in

1451 who have to refocus this back?

Not permanently.

They go back when they do this?

That's right. They can't stay permanently because it's too much strain. A tremendous amount of energy comes in, but because of the curvature of time you're now in, it necessarily comes back distorted. So they usually don't have many more than two or three individuals who refine the energy — or redefine it, if you like — smooth it out and send it back. Then they have to do it again in the present, or it gets distorted. In any event, people cannot survive this circumstance for more than three weeks, so they generally get cycled about every ten days. However, there have been deaths. That's why the people sent back to do this are usually the ones known as the Montauk children. I don't have to tell you how evil this is; nevertheless I report it to you as I see it.

Sound Is the Weapon

The machinery is simple. It basically amounts to using a sound oscillator so that the signal is read as sound, and attuning that oscillation through the use of crystal attunement refinement. But of course, after six or seven days one's hearing tends to become decreased, and after ten days an individual would have a significant hearing loss.

So how broad is the extent of this control of people, from this past? Are there many, many beings being controlled right now in all walks of life?

No. The young man who was captured, as it were, for the use of this work and is currently in prison, is one of only about ten.

And who are the others?

One of them is still on the loose, as you know, but he may be captured soon — or he may be projected into the past, in which case he will never be captured, although it's hard to say; they might get someone they think is the person but isn't. In any event, that's not set in stone at the moment. I would say that of the other eight, about six are in positions of influence, meaning in government circles or in significant positions of influence in corporate circles ("corporate" in this case referring to, essentially, international Fortune 500 companies, major corporations). And the other two are just ordinary folks, invisible people, as it were, who can come and go without being noticed — not spies, but people who are designed to be, how can we say, onlookers; the sort of people who for example are known to become involved in assassinations.

RFK Assassination

Let's give an example. As you know, when Robert Kennedy was running for President years ago, he was supposedly assassinated by a young man. This young man had not been fully influenced by this technique, but he had been partially influenced by it, to take something that was basically a fantasy and turn it into a physical reality. However, the true individuals who actually performed the murder on Robert Kennedy were not influenced in this particular way. There were two other people present who looked rather like any two people you'd normally see. The young man called Sirhan, while he fired at Mr. Kennedy, did not deliver a death bullet to that man, and these other individuals performed the actual assassination, leaving this young man Sirhan to essentially take the blame. And again we have a circumstance in which a young man who, because of his nationality, felt rightly (to him) that his people were being mistreated, and he had a fantasy about something which in its own right is not particularly harmful, but he was prompted to actually take a gun and go do it. But, not to put too fine a point on it, he was not a crack shot. And while he fired the gun many times, most of the bullets he fired missed or hit the wrong people, as often happens in attacks such as this. But the actual assassins did the job and walked off and left him holding the bag, as they say.

Where are they now, the actual assassins of Robert Kennedy?

They are no longer amongst the living. I don't wish to sound callous, but as many people in this kind of activity know, if you wish to have something like this done and go undetected, very often the people who pull the trigger later have the trigger pulled on them to remove all traces. This is what happened; the actual assassins are no longer alive.

So all the shots he fired missed . . .

They missed the senator. One, I believe, hit him, but in a place that would not have killed him. But he did manage to hit several other people, as one might expect in a room or hall crowded full of people.

Okay. So the two people designed to be assassins, these two people out of the ten, are still walking around out there right now. Are they going to be used to assassinate somebody?

They can be. It's not that they're going to be; they can be. And again, there will be people who have certain political thoughts who might fantasize against or even *for* certain individuals, and that in its own right is not a crime. You understand, everyone gets mad and says, "Oh, I'd like to kill him" or "I'd like to kill her," and then five minutes later you know you don't really mean it and you'd never do it. It's just a thought. But these people are walking time bombs because they can be activated in their political fantasies.

And they don't know . . .

They do not know. Again, they are like this young man who has been captured. That's part of the reason those who've been talking to him think he's insane. Because if you had four souls in you, three of which were desperately struggling because they're being incorporated in a plot, they were usurped from normal youngsters and don't want to be doing what they're doing in the first place (not to mention that the man's actual original soul doesn't enjoy being a participant in this activity), you too would exhibit all of the symptoms of a person who's mentally ill. He will be tried as a sane person, but many people on the inner circle of those who try him will say that this man is not fit to stand trial.

What about the implant in his hip? He said he had something in his buttocks.

This was a result of a contact he had that was unrelated to the actual means by which he is being controlled. It was a residual effect of an examination he received that is not unlike that which one has aboard a craft, okay? And he was told at the time that he'd been taken aboard a ship and mistreated by ETs, which was not the case. This was the means used to motivate him to submit to other things being done to him. In other words, it was a story utilized to manipulate him. But it is true that a device was placed up in his body, though it did not discharge something into his body.

It was placed by the same secret government, then they gave him screen memories of an ET, then they told him they were going to help him?

That's right.

I understand. My God!

It is a terrible thing. Not only were all these innocent people maimed, injured and killed in this terrible blast, but the people involved in the bombing in the first place were totally manipulated and upset and confused — especially the one who has not been captured as of the moment of our conversation. This person is totally confused and nervous and upset, and is struggling desperately against doing what he has been doing. So it is just a terrible thing altogether. And I am hopeful that in time all parties, everyone, will see that this is a terrible drama that has been played out.

You know, you're all in material mastery school, as I've said. And the true purpose of material mastery school on Earth is to experience all aspects of creativity that produce consequences, in order not only to achieve the status of the Explorer Race, but to replace the Creator. And I must say that this current drama is basically an exercise in impatience. Those who would control are impatient to have their control, and even those who would prevent control by manipulative and evil sources are impatient for the ones who are exhibiting this evil to come to the light and love. So I must say, being equal here, and balanced, that even those who would like the evil ones to become loving are impatient with them. That's why the best thing you can do right now is to meditate on the gold-and-purple ray. It will help. Because it doesn't rush anybody, and yet it does tend to influence them. And purple and gold cannot influence in a harmful way.

A Messiah for the U.S.

So everything has changed since 1990 when the secret government first went back into the past and moved the time track of the Peace President. Now they just go back and forth with impunity? They're not afraid of what they do, they have perfected it?

Yes, they've done enough work with it that, as you say, they just move back and forth at will. There have been several attempts to prevent messiahs from being born. I will say, however, that there are three people right now living on various parts of the surface of the Earth who would qualify quite nicely as messiahs. However, these people are primarily focusing, as well as being encouraged to focus, on radiating energy from them so that all people will become messiahs for themselves; they do not intend to come out and be charismatic leaders and save you. I will say, however, that the secret government is still intending to create enough chaos, at least on a temporary basis, so that people will increasingly feel that their duly elected officials and government and process cannot be trusted, with the aim that eventually the secret government will put forth a charismatic leader who will say, "Follow me, have I got a way of life for you! Let's get rid of this Constitution and Bill of Rights because it's just making things dangerous for people." You understand that many other governments currently in action on the surface of the planet have loosely patterned their manifestoes after the Constitution and Bill of Rights of the United States, which was created by people of vision.

Are you saying we're going to have a charismatic leader, an Antichrist type, here in the United States?

Yes, it's very possible that this person will be put forth. You will be able to recognize him quite clearly, because he will, to put not too fine a point on it, drape himself in the flag and in religion. He will sound very much like a religious, patriotic, charismatic leader – sort of a religious version of Hitler.

Now, this is in the United States – this isn't the Antichrist we've got over in the Middle East?

This is the United States. I want you to watch out for this to come upon you before the year 2000. You have to be very alert to this. This doesn't mean to just say, "Oh, this person must be the Antichrist, let's shoot him." Don't do that. The only thing you can do with someone you suspect is the Antichrist, if you're religious, is to pray for his redemption; if you are involved in benevolent magic, to perform spells that will tie him to the light; or if you are New Age-oriented, to do meditations within your group to bring loving gold and purple light to him. Be cautious about white light; as wonderful as white light is, it is absolutely unconditionally loving, which means that it will give energy to any and all. Even if they are evil, it will give them energy, because white-light particles are unconditionally loving. So try and send them gold and purple light, because that tends to be conditional in the sense that it tends to bring them toward the heart. Please remember: In order to have love prevail, you must be loving. Impatience and force will never make it so.

Earth Changes

What about the next few months – earthquakes or anything?

You might see some difficulties developing in May. This is because this global warming, you know, is a real factor. You've got glaciers melting back farther than people can remember. You've got significant melting at the poles – just the change of weight of the ice in given places creates more buoyancy for the land, meaning upward movement. Also, the redistribution of this weight in the form of water just creates different pressures for the Earth. So I would say that land motion, but more likely floods, drought and winds are going to be the big factor. I do not see as yet catastrophic earthquakes, but of course I could be mistaken on this – this is not my strong suit. But I still feel strongly that land motion (which is different from earthquakes) and wind and water are the primary changes. So in the United States I do not expect freak storms quite yet – you know, hurricanes in Minnesota – but I do expect high winds, sometimes unexpectedly high. Even recently you've had reports from certain mountain stations of winds that are shockingly high. The weather bureau does not report to you how stunned they are at some of these high winds, but they are stunned. It has given them pause.

I'd say that it might be a time of a certain amount of weather disasters in Africa. Africa has been besieged in recent years by different political forces wishing to control it and really take over the land . . .

And the minerals?

And the minerals, and get rid of the people. This might cause a significant amount of raining. When Mother Earth doesn't like what's going on, she rains. So we'll see, but I don't want to make too many predictions here.

Changing Perceptions among the Great Teachers

So what's happening right now? We haven't had any reports lately about the war in the heavens – do we have any cosmic traffic cops here, any shooting going on?

There's not a lot going on right now. I will say the biggest struggle right now is between the spiritual goals of the past and the spiritual goals of the future, which changed as a result of even the most benevolent beings from the past having a certain given idea of what would occur in your future, compared to their advanced selves, which I've talked about. For example, Jehovah from the past and Jehovah's future self, you understand, have totally different points of view over what is the best thing to do. You might say a lot of the struggle is internal.

You mean all the great teachers, like Buddha and Shiva and Krishna and Christ, have future selves that see things differently now?

Yes. Because, for example, Buddha's idea was originally to create a world of pure thought where people did not give in to their emotional urgings. Buddha perceived the world (understandably in his time) as a world that was overly influenced by people who were being emotional in destructive ways. He believed if you could rise above that, you'd achieve a certain state of being in which pure mentality would create a benevolent state. Now Buddha's future self sees this entirely differently – as pure feeling, heart-centered. But that is in conflict with the Buddha of the past. I mention this only because it creates sort of a tension between the past and the future that will, as you move through time (and as time curves more dramatically), be more easily anchored in the future – which is appropriate, since that is where you are going.

That's interesting. How did the pasts and future ideas of, say, Krishna and Brahma and Vishnu and Shiva change?

Many of these individuals, as you've mentioned, have always seen from the past, and you know what they've seen from the past. Let's discuss what they're seeing from the future. What they're seeing from the future is certain motions, certain mudras that accentuate and amplify feelings that are benevolent and, as a result of motions or dance, can create —more effectively than the spoken word —a benevolent flow of energy to people.

For example, picture people doing tai chi. It creates a certain harmony and a flow of energy. Now picture people doing tai chi aimed at a large group of uninitiated individuals where pure feeling is coming through; pure love is what one would normally experience after the end of a cycle or after death, but this comes through in life. This creates a different focus of the work that they evolved. So the whole thing is geared in the future toward feeling the focus through the heart and broadcasting that to others, to initiate them into their own feelings and into their own natural motions. Certain motions, as well as certain shapes that come about as a result of people making motions or dance in the air, or just forming these shapes, such as circles of humans, will create a degree of benevolence that cannot be resisted by even the most truculent individuals who wish to remain rooted in some negative aspect.

Like Gurdjieff's sacred movements?

That's right. So the futures selves are geared toward the refocusing of shape and form through motion and heart-focus.

So when they tried to do it physically . . . well, even the old yoga was motion!

Yes, but it was also geared toward thought.

So it's progressing from physical and mental into feeling and spirit and the integration of love.

Yes. But the physical is still used. It is just moving from thought, which was once perceived (and understandably so) as the refuge from chaos, into heart, which transforms chaos. Instead of seeking refuge, now, instead of escaping, we are going straight into transforming —not only for the individual but for the mass. This is sort of like taking prayer past the point of asking for something into literally doing it, and influencing others. Yes, it is a wonderful means by which to influence and initiate.

Okay. Thank you. Anything else you want to say?

I just want to say that I have every confidence in everyone's ability to get through these times. I want to again remind people who have misgivings about the government that the best thing to do is to write to your representatives, your senators, and let them know how you feel. Become heart-centered, spiritual politicians. Understand that everybody all over the world has infinitely more in common than they have different. Remember that buildings are not the government; remember that people who work for the government are not trying to control your lives. Remember that it is primarily your fear of having your freedom taken away that prompts actions that are destructive — or self-destructive, in many cases. But when people get together, they find out what they have in common. Work toward underlining and underscoring what you have in common, and resolve your differences this way. Remember, no one's mind has ever been changed as a result of being shot; violence inevitably leads to further violence. It is truly love and common ground that makes permanent benevolent transformations, and I have every confidence in your abilities to come to this.

Hopiland Still in Danger

Okay. The uranium is long gone from Hopiland? All that's over and done with, right?

They're through with that. As a result of mining activities, one tends to notice what other things are there. So they might continue to look for various precious ores and other precious elements underground there. So don't let the issue go; write to your congressmen, senators, try and keep it from happening. Support Native Americans and their need to have the land considered sacred. Support all of these causes in a benevolent, nurturing way. Never become violent about it, and remember, if enough people write to congressmen and senators and presidents and so on — and involve the United Nations, if you can — then things do get done. You may not be able to stop the secret government from desiring things, but you can stop them at least temporarily from doing things.

8

Underground Military Resistance Forming against Secret Government Manipulation

Zoosh through Robert Shapiro
May 11, 1995

All right. An important thing is happening now; I must talk about it. There is an ongoing test being conducted by the secret government of your world in which they are essentially reaching out to test a new weapons technology they have that is almost impossible to detect. It works only on electronics, so it falls under the heading of electronic warfare. There was a recent crash of a highly exotic Air Force fighter jet in northern New Mexico caused by a compressed-sound beacon. Encoded within this compressed-sound beacon is a means by which commands from any electronic source, including one in flight, can not only be countermanded but can be made to essentially mess up the avionics of the flying machine. This technology is being tested in remote places where the vehicles, should they crash (which is the intention of the secret government), will cause as little public attention as possible; hence some of the more remote areas of New Mexico, Arizona and, at some point, perhaps Texas. This represents a new level of aggression.

I'll tell you why this is going on. Right now there are individuals within your legitimate military (all over the world, I might add) who are forming a distinct underground to resist against areas of command directed toward them. These appear to be legitimate commands, but these underground military activists realize that these commands could not possibly be carried out with any sense of morals, so they are resisting. You might ask what kind of commands are coming in. The main one is for training to utilize the military forces of the United States – as well as those of France, Germany, and even countries like Switzerland and Norway that are known for a somewhat more mature evolution – to usurp power within the government; not to take over, but to essentially be in a more controlling situation.

The secret government, through its toadies, is attempting to grab for power. Since the secret government now perceives that the resistors within the legitimate military are not going to go along with being used and abused, they (the secret government) are utilizing advanced weapons technology such as I have mentioned to prove to themselves that with no loss whatsoever on their side, they can knock out America's most advanced technology. This represents an escalation, which is most important to comment on, because this escalation is not only causing loss of life but is truly a confrontation, a form, you might say, of discipline.

The secret government is essentially attempting to go public – not public in the sense of the general public, but attempting, through the use of those they manipulate or control, to take over as the authority within your legitimate military institutions.

Message to Military Personnel
Who Resist Secret Government

I speak now to those who resist, including people from all ranks, but I will not say any more about that. I will just say this: It is better for you to resist in ways that are not violent, and if you can, try to get the information of what you are experiencing out to the general public in some way. I know you cannot go directly to the public, but you might be able to very discreetly go to certain members of the press, even if it is a matter of putting out books or going to the radio talk shows. In this way you might be able to influence the general public so that they will support your position and, most beneficially, create an open debate in Congress about these circumstances. If you can have an open debate in Congress that is encouraged by the press and supported by those within the military who do not want to go along with orders that are obviously attempting to corrupt you, then you might truly achieve the true purpose, which is to go public with grievances and get them out there. I know that you do not have much confidence in your political system, because the political system is made up of people, but doing this will lead to the ultimate benefit. You don't see it now, but there are people within your elected government who are ready to follow your lead and to support significant changes of purification. In this sense purification means clear minds and strong bodies, not anything done to any members of the population. So I support you in your resistance to corruption and I ask that you follow the nonviolent way, if you would. Know that the secret government cannot control you in any way if you go public with this nonviolently. On the other hand, if you attempt to resist in violent ways, even in self-defense, they will be able to manipulate you and public opinion. Public opinion is your best ally now; never forget that.

I had to say that because that is an important escalation that the secret government is performing right now. I might add that with this weapons technology they used to essentially topple this fighter jet (I'm using the term *topple* even though it's usually ascribed to missiles), they intercepted the coded transmissions from one portion of the computer in the jet to another portion, which is not unlike forms of sabotage done in the past with missile systems.

What kind of plane was it?

I'll just say it was part of the legitimate military of the United States, and it was the most advanced jet aircraft that your military force has at this time flying in the skies.

How many people were killed?

I really don't wish to say; I'll just say at least one.

You said once that if they did aggressive acts, the Pleiadian warship would respond. Is it still here?

They are here. The trouble is that the Pleiadian warship, while it is nearby, is really set up to confront — it is a visible enemy, as it were — but this is a technology that is so sophisticated that it is not really located on this planet. It is focused through technological windows. The technology itself is on the Moon, and by usurping signals and breaking down codes, it uses parts of the Star Wars defense system and skips off of it. It doesn't use lasers, as does the Star Wars defense system. It essentially uses what I'd like to call space mirrors (to be somewhat discreet) to bounce the signal off a very precise area. And it is the secret government's way of saying, "Look, we can be as far away as the Moon and knock a single jet fighter out of the sky; what chance have you got?" You know, it's that kind of thing.

How long ago did you say this happened?

This has just happened.

In the last day or so?

Yes. I would like to console the families involved.

The only thing I'm truly concerned about with the secret government right now is that, feeling their backs against the wall, they're having somewhat of a propensity to use weapons technology that they've had for a while. It's kind of like when an animal is backed up into a corner; it fights like crazy. Right now the secret government is experiencing losses among its innermost circles because these people's consciousnesses are beginning to raise a bit.

You or Jehovah said once that of the thirteen innermost players, all but one will eventually see the light.

This is something I believe the other being has said. I will say this: There is hope. They are going to see the light, but meanwhile it has created conflict within the secret government itself, which is in the long run a good thing, but in the short run a little dangerous, because they are beginning to do things that are a little hazardous. So the next few years will be touch-and-go. There may need to be a little interference from benevolent outside sources that will come and make themselves known and interfere in a positive way with the secret government. This might happen in the form of the support of an attitudinal change in the general population that will support (not accelerate, just support) a rise in the consciousness of the general population. Should this take place, it will happen very soon — certainly within the next few months.

How will this benevolent interference change the attitude of the planet?

It will change it by essentially sustaining and supporting within each individual human being a distinct set of feelings by which they will be able to tell immediately whether something is good for themselves and good for others or whether it's the opposite. In other words, it will heighten people's instinctual awareness of what is good and what isn't.

How will they do this?

Well, it will essentially be done functioning through time. I can't say too much. It will function through time, the future, soul, spirit and the angelic kingdom — or queendom, if you like.

What about the Xpotaz and the Orions? What are they doing right now with the shadow government?

Right now there is a serious problem for the Xpotaz people. They're experiencing within their groups a breaking of the ranks. About half of the people — maybe better than half — wish to leave this area and go to another area quite a distance away; it probably will take them several years to get there. They believe that this Earth is a place where there is going to be a serious conflict. I don't think that's true, but they might be perceiving dimensional aspects other than the ones you are going to be in. I believe that they will have a breakdown in their ranks, and it will create an inner struggle. So the Xpotaz might not be so much of a threat, because they're going to move out.

What about their manufacturing ship – will they take that with them?

They'll take all of their equipment with them.

That's a major part of the power of the secret government.

It is, but the secret government – how can we say. They have . . .

They have everything built now, right?

They're built up, that's right. As for the negative Orions, as modern-day Orion culture continues to evolve and spread its light, as you say, I believe this will continue to impact (from our point of view) beneficially on the negative Orion influence. As far as I can tell, there is no longer any negative Orion influence coming here from any other time. That which is here is here; but it is being transformed.

What about the core of evil? There was a sixteen-sided crystal . . .

This crystal is in transition. It is moving right now into the second dimension in an attempt to hide. You know, the best way to hide is to be unseen and to be untouchable. Now, I believe that that crystal will hide out in the second dimension for a while and return when individuals from the secret government attempt to invoke it. I believe, however, that in the process of the invocation, the crystal itself will be affected by the spiritual upliftment on Earth, so when it is called to come to the secret government to support and sustain them, it will not give them the sustenance they like, but will sustain them in ways which we would like.

Outbreaks in Zaire and Northern Arizona

I wish to comment on the outbreak of infectious disease in Zaire, in Africa. This infectious disease *is not*, I repeat, *is not* caused by experimentation in chemical and biological warfare by the secret government or anybody else. Not at this time. I will say, however, that the secret government has placed what amount to time capsules containing microorganisms which they can essentially spread at a moment's notice. Having placed them underground, they could very easily disseminate these biologicals in a lethal way. I do not think they will do it, however, because even as we speak, elements of the secret government are being elevated a little bit in their comprehension and consciousness. So I am hopeful. But I will say again, this outbreak in Zaire is not caused by manipulation or corruption.

Now I will go on and answer the question about the sheep up in Navajo country, even before it is asked. Many sheep have been getting sick, some dying. I might add that many people are getting sick and not doing too well. I am not going to support something that the public health agency will put out; they will say that this is a bacterial disease carried by what they would call a varmint, an animal. It is not that — although it will lead to that, understand? The medical trail will be placed to make public health officials think this is what it is, but it is not, just like the hantavirus was *not* caused by that mouse. Even though the mouse *could* carry the organism, the original outbreak of the hantavirus which killed many people up on the reservation was caused by people.

Now the current outbreak amongst the sheep is essentially being caused by a form of radiation. This is not radiation poisoning, but a radionic effect of certain underground instruments being used. Most of this is going on in the so-called disputed zone between the Hopi and the Navajo reservations. This instrumentation is essentially associated with very high-powered microwave transmission. Now, many people know that if human beings or animals are exposed to extreme microwave transmission, many illnesses can occur. I recommend that if the sheep herders can move their flocks away from that area called the disputed area, it would be safer. Also, if you're living in this disputed area, it would be good if you could go and stay with your relatives away from that area for about three or four months. I know this represents a hardship — and I don't know if you'll even hear or read anything I'm saying — but I'm feeling that due to underground exploration and mining techniques utilizing very high-powered microwave and ultrasonic equipment, the ultrasonic equipment is performing the function of a carrier wave, amplifying the microwave transmission and bringing it to the surface, which is causing this sickness.

Is it a byproduct of their activity, or a deliberate attempt to get people off this land so they can have it?

I think it is a by-product; I don't think they are attempting to make people sick. I think that they really don't care. In some respects I'd have to admit that the people using the machines do care, but those who are behind the program of mining under the reservations do not care that much.

So the people using the machines are protected, I take it?

No! No, the protection is minimal. There is some protection about the head, but you have to understand that those . . . how can we put this discreetly? — those who manufacture, sell and distribute this type of technology (which, I might add, is not in general use, even in mining areas) will not promote the idea that the technology is hazardous. Imagine if you will, with all the microwave transmission towers that are used to broadcast telephone signals and other various forms of communications, if they were to admit that these transmission towers actually caused people and animals to become ill if they came close. Well, I can assure you, there would be a lawyer's field day.

There has been some acknowledgment in order to keep people away, and it is not an accident that the transmission part of a microwave tower is situated well above the landscape. The towers are as tall as they are so the transmitters can be at the top, which is, for the people who manufacture the technology, their way of saying that this stuff isn't safe. If it were safe, the towers would be ten feet tall. And I would say that the operators of the equipment underground are not sufficiently protected to keep them from losing about 30% of their otherwise natural lifespan.

How are they using this microwave? To blast away into mines?

It's a compressed signal that essentially causes the material to break down and crumble, which makes mining significantly easier and reduces the need for blasting techniques. It is well known in mining circles that the most dangerous aspect of mining is explosives. So technology that does not use explosives is highly sought after.

But if the people who manufacture this technology really cared, they could do it in a way that didn't use explosives and was much safer, right?

No, I do not think so. I think that microwave and ultrasonic technology for the purpose of mining is basically harmful. It would have to be reduced to about one-ten-thousandth of its current level of energy to be safe to the user. I don't think it's safe.

Also I must say that it is important for all tribal governments to be absolutely clear in their liaisons with the government of the United States. Be clear by way of "knowing who your friends are." It is better to stick with political friends, and even adversaries, if you know who they are, than to plunge forward and embrace friends about whom you do not know anything. Use your hearts and your spirits to know who to trust. This is most important for tribal governments, because right now there are many well-meaning people who will not do much harm, who will try to support tribal governments, but there are also a few — not many, but a few — who will act like well-meaning people but will attempt to create divisiveness within the tribal governments. If people come from the outside and their effect within the tribal government is divisive, best to settle it amongst yourselves.

Are we talking specifically now to these tribes in Arizona?

Yes. Arizona and New Mexico. And as far as the area of Wounded Knee, I will say that the people up there are very well organized and I support their efforts and wish them well.

9

The Forming of Ninth-Dimensional Mars

Zoosh through Robert Shapiro
May 11 and 26, 1995

Now, even if we don't talk about anything else, we'll want to talk about this one *[figure 9.1]*. Here is a constellation referred to as the Bear. If you look in the sky, there's a bear. This vehicle tracking a light, which your photographer friend obtained, is directly from that constellation. They are bringing with them on this particular visit a highly evolved panel of about fifty of their most illuminated spiritual teachers to discover, at the exact moment the picture was taken, the synapse (in the larger sense of the word, meaning the explosion of light) that turns the consciousness of all human beings away from self-destruction. The biggest problem having faced your species, human beings, has been your natural tendency toward self-destructiveness.

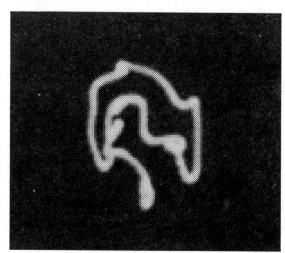

Fig. 9.1. Vehicle from the Bear constellation.

And as you know, anything that causes you to hurt yourself or hurt another is self-destructive. The moment this picture was taken, there was a transfer of light (which is why the ship was there — to observe it) that moved about two percent of your stored light energy, about one percent of your stored cosmic energy and about one percent of your stored heart energy within to the function of all souls on your planet. That is part of the reason why certain elements of the secret government could not help but get more light. No one can resist that kind of a transfer, which was created by Creator Itself. They were here to observe.

So one percent of the ninety percent of our heart energy was given to us. Have they decided now, after the Council of Nine was here, how they're going to handle that return to us?

Yes, it's going to be doled out incrementally like that, and it's probably going to be doled out at a time when people are the most receptive to it, meaning that there will be some sort of a universal feeling of compassion or love or friendliness or good feelings. When that energy is passed out, then, people will be more receptive to it and will be able to integrate it very quickly and assimilate it as well.

So they're going to do like ninety blasts of this in the next how many years? Or will there be different percentages?

There will be different percentages. It'll just be as much as they can squeeze in — here a little, there a little.

So we're going to get it early — we don't have to wait till 2005?

You ought to have it by 2005; then you'll have some time to integrate it.

Figure 9.2. This represents a religious ceremony of a universal religion having to do with the flight of the phoenix. Here you see, at least partially, the light signature of the phoenix bird — which, by the way, is a real bird, besides being light and being symbolic; it's a real bird that used to fly around on your planet a long time ago. The actual vision of this bird had come to glow, as you see, soon after which it will achieve the glowing of white light, and thence will commence the rebirth. I think it is a pleasant sight.

Rebirth of what?

The rebirth of your true consciousness.

This is a universal religion? Do you have people here, do you have a ship?

That is the bird itself, and the light signature.

And who's doing the ceremony? Where are they from? Who are they?

The ceremony is being conducted on fifth-dimensional Earth by

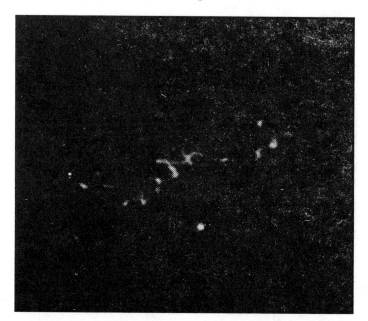

Fig. 9.2. A religious ceremony; the flight of the phoenix.

your future selves, and since they don't know exactly where you are, they have sent out what we can call holographic images of the ceremonial bird to the second, third and fourth dimensions; they're not exactly sure where or when you are.

The Removal of the Compromised Female Energy

Figure 9.3. This is the trail of a vehicle originating in the Sirius star system, having to do with an extraction from your planet of the compromised feminine energy. The true feminine energy is in balance at all times, but in recent years (in terms of linear time, the past three to five thousand years), feminine energy has become compromised so that masculine energy can have its opportunity to show that it has value — or to stumble, depending upon your point of view. This explains the rise of primarily masculine-oriented religions and philosophies in the past three to five thousand years.

The compromised energy model was removed during a synchronistic operation. Part of the operation was pictured here: there was a light vessel here, a light vessel on Sirius, and a light vessel traveling through time performing essentially an operation within time (this is very subtle, but it has to be done very precisely). It was all done at the same time in order to remove that energy of compromise.

Now the feminine energy will be able to reassert itself in its true focus. Feminine beings might notice, certainly within the next three

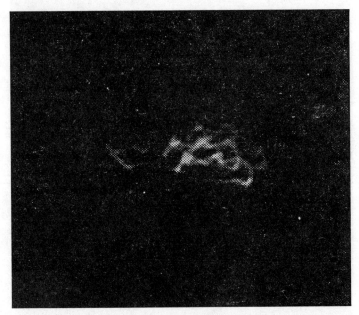

Fig. 9.3. Trail of vehicle from the Sirius star system.

to four-and-a-half months, a greater sense of self-assurance, of power, of certainty in the value of one's own self. In addition, all masculine beings will within this time frame begin to feel a greater sense of value in women and will begin to seek out women more as teachers. Women will become a greater point of philosophical value. They have been devalued in the past three to five thousand years, but they will now begin to regain their true place in the philosophical and religious senses of orientation.

Whose idea was this, who did this? Who carried it out? They're from Sirius, but . . .

The feminine prototype for the human race was developed on Sirius, and they utilized a calendar that is not exactly like your own. It is of course more of a lunar calendar — based upon the Moon (a trinary moon for this particular planet) and due to certain astronomical and, from their perspective, astrological time sequences that overlaid your own astrology, this specific date was picked.

Do we in our mythology or history have names for this feminine prototype?

I suppose the closest thing would be Isis.

And that [the Sirian prototype] was long before Egypt, wasn't it?

Of course. Between you and me, the figure dancing on the desk here, Shiva, is the true feminine prototype.

Shiva is feminine?

Yes! From my perspective. True feminine wisdom is based upon the eternal practical. This means that which is done. Feminine wisdom has to do with that which is done, as compared to masculine wisdom, which is based on that which could be. A very suggestive point.

Which we won't go into now, but it's going on the record.

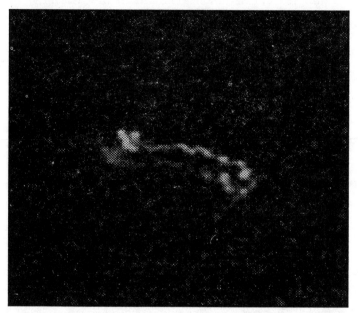

Fig. 9.4. Convergence of two vehicles exchanging light energy.

Figure 9.4. Here we have the convergence of two vehicles allowing their light energy to move back and forth between them. This is an interesting function going on here. We have here a ship from the past and a ship from the future, but they're both based on their own dimensions of Earth. The ship from the past is based in fourth-dimensional Earth and the ship from the future is based in sixth-dimensional Earth. They are essentially in your skies in your now dimension because they are attempting to seed the speeding up of your concentric time — you know, time is no longer linear — in order to help you support and sustain your reemergence as your true selves. Sometimes — as you understand in the study of physics — when you have greater magnetism in a certain place, you can support and sustain greater velocity. Without getting into too many formulas, I will just say that this is an attempt to seed something.

Now I want to add something humorous here. This seeding was *not* authorized by any council. They managed to slip through. They were cousins, if you will – the one in the fourth and the one in the sixth dimension; the one in the past and the one in the future. They managed to slip through and, almost like juvenile delinquents of light, attempted to speed something up that is moving at a slow pace on purpose. And in this case they were reprimanded upon return home to their respective dimensions, and are now learning about the value of third-dimensional studies in school. The attempt to create this seeding was not effective – and that is fortunate, because sometimes when you speed things up they don't get done right. So you might have here essentially two light-based juvenile delinquents.

Fig. 9.5. Partial facial feature of a keeper of time.

Figure 9.5. Here we have a partial feature associated with that which is referred to as a mythological keeper of time. A keeper of time is not a thought – I'm not talking about different means of measuring time that are legitimate within your own timescape, such as the Sun and the Moon, or light and dark. We have here this keeper of time, seen in a contemplative mood (though you can't really see that). He is involved in the restructuring of your time even as we speak about it. As we said, your time is no longer linear, it's concentric. But this being is essentially reformulating the level of concentric time so that instead of looking like a tightly wound coil, it now looks like an elongated coil. This gives you a little longer to do what you need to do experientially so that things are done right.

Was he before or after the juvenile delinquents?

Well, he was there before *and* after. He was necessary for obvious reasons, in light of the light delinquents.

Fig. 9.6. Two clouds of light, vehicles observing humanity.

Figure 9.6. Here we have two factions. These are essentially vehicles, but they're vehicles only insofar as anything that flies is a vehicle. This is really two clouds of light. If we can define life as that which performs some function under its own choosing, then I'm going to use that as a loose definition to define these lightbeings.

These lightbeings were present in your skies, during the time this picture was taken, to observe you, in a sense, but not the way you identify yourself. As you know, there is a tendency in your culture and in all cultures for that matter, to identify and describe all other life within the context of one's own understanding of life. An example is when your culture applies anthropomorphic descriptions to things done by various animals. In this case we have lightbeings looking at individuals within your culture and not seeing you as you look at all, but seeing you as you look in your lightbodies only. If they were here in the room now (which they are not) they would not see your physical bodies at all. They would see only your lightbodies.

The reason they were here was to study you — essentially because they are curious. They know that your lightbodies, when you are here on Earth, are basically humanoid in shape — a body with two arms, two legs and a head. What fascinates them is that, as you float about your physical body, various portions of your lightbody are obscured by being in your physical body and engaged in full activities within the physical body, or by being partway out. When your physical body and your lightbody are somewhat disjointed, this is usually because you are not being focused directly into some physical function. These lightbeings are curious about that. To them, they would see your lightbody, when you're asleep and dreaming; then they would see parts of your lightbody, when you are partly in your physical body and partly out; then other times, when you are completely in your lightbody in your physical body, they wouldn't see the lightbody at all. So they were studying the curious phenomenon of the disappearing lightbodies. Hope this doesn't sound too much like a mystery story!

They were curious about this. So I think that it is reassuring to know that no matter how advanced we might think a particular race of beings is, they're only advanced within the scope of their own understanding. And if they do not see something, even though you know it is there, as far as they are concerned it isn't there. That's good to know, because it's important for you to remember that you have the capacity, if you're trained, and certainly when you are very young and very old, to see not only the physical world but also the light world. These lightbeings, as benevolent and beloved as they are, do not have that capacity.

Are they from a dimension or place or . . .

They are from the seventh-dimensional aspect of the planet you know as Pluto.

Pluto!

They're here exploring the mysteries of the missing light.

A Planet Forming

Figure 9.7. Here is an example of something most unusual. Ofttimes, when a planet is beginning to form, it becomes a collection of what people might call *thoughts*, or ideas — meaning a focus, what the planet is known for. But before it begins to form, it forms its lightbody. We know that planets become physical as a result of a physicalization of their creative effort; they become mass. And yet, what about planets before and after? You know that you have light-

Fig. 9.7. Ninth-dimensional Mars forming.

bodies, immortal personalities —what about planets? Planets also have these.

Here you see a planet forming. This light represents the nucleus of a planet as it is beginning to form its concept of itself, before it actually takes the form of something that you could identify as a physical planet. Right now it is what we can call a predisposition. We can use certain words in your language and say that we have there right now, so far, though it's not complete in that picture, a disposition (or a conceptual derivative) of a desire to focus within the realm of sound and all of sound's various expressions. This planet will eventually emerge in a ninth-dimensional area of space, and it will be the ninth-dimensional version of the planet you now know as Mars. It was here, actually here in spirit form, where it could be photographed in order to consult, as planets consult with each other, with its neighbor.

You have to understand that a planet is a living being in its own sense —a larger sense, but its own sense. It tends to consult with other-dimensional versions of itself before it forms itself into some substance, but it also tends to consult with its neighbors. So right there is the setup for ninth-dimensional Mars.

Does it consult with ninth-dimensional Earth?

No, no. It was here to consult with the aspect of Earth that is shifting from the third to the fourth dimension, which you are on now.

Was there no ninth-dimensional Mars before?

Not in a form that living beings could visit. It was there, within the context of your time, as a dream. But one could only visit it within a dream; you could not visit it and touch it.

So does it work as with people – the third-dimensional Mars is expanding into becoming aware of its ninth-dimensional aspect?

It is not so much *becoming* aware of it – it can dream it right now; but it is making its ninth-dimensional self available to be touched by beings who can either visit the ninth dimension or who are at home in it.

Is there a ninth-dimensional Earth?

Not yet.

How high does Earth go?

Well, you have to understand that the steps aren't necessarily all covered. You might have a second-, third-, fourth-, fifth-, sixth- and seventh-dimensional Earth, then you might have a tenth-dimensional Earth, then maybe a twelfth-dimensional Earth. But a planet will only have a certain dimensional aspect insofar as the planet is needed there. If she is not needed by anybody within that dimension – if she is not needed by anybody external to the planet herself, and if the planet herself does not need that aspect of herself – she does not form it.

How does that work with people? Do we have one aspect on every dimension?

Exactly the same way. You might practically never have a first-dimensional self – the first dimension is essentially occupied by the essence of your immortal personality, so it is not a formative substance. But you might have, for example, second- through fifth-dimensional versions of yourself. It's possible that you've never needed a sixth-dimensional self, so you don't have one. You've never created a sixth-dimensional self – it is there as a dream, in a sense, and it can be visited as a dream, but it would not be substantive, even if you're in the sixth dimension. So right now very few people on Earth know any physical Earth people who have a sixth-dimensional self, as far as I can tell.

As you move to the fourth dimension, then a sixth-dimensional self might become more viable. Because when you are locked into the fourth dimension, you will tend to dream in areas within a certain range of dimensions. Right now, you're in the third dimension totally; then you would tend to dream in the fourth and fifth dimensions. When you're in the fourth dimension you'll tend to dream in the fourth, fifth, sixth and seventh dimensions, okay? It isn't a totally rational setup of predictables.

But dreams are real, so when you say "dream," you mean "visit spiritually?"

Yes.

I've never heard these words before – "the essence of our immortal personality." Say more about that.

The essence of your immortal personality is basically what your religious documents refer to as your soul. But I find the term *soul* to be vague and too integrated with religious archetypes. So I refer to that which you know as your immortal self as your immortal personality, and the essence of your immortal personality is founded in your first-dimensional self.

The Creator is all dimensions, all things. Once you leave the Creator, you must anchor something which is not exactly separate – you're never separate from the Creator – but something which is refocused away from All That Is and into some singular thing. Generally, the essence of your immortal personality is anchored in the first dimension, giving you a means by which you can access Creator, interdimensionally speaking, but not a place where people live and have societies. Variety does not really occur until the second dimension, and it occurs in increasing magnitude as we go up in the dimensions. Very often it is considered that there's a greater spirituality in the higher dimensions, but really it's a greater sense of *variety*. In the first dimension, one must have a very distinct focus, so variety is not a factor of the first dimension.

So if a human has embodiments in many different dimensions and constellations, would he or she have those parts here on Earth? If we're on some planet in the Pleiades in the sixth dimension, would we have a first-dimensional essence anchored there, too, on that planet?

Not really. Your first-dimensional essence is not associated with Earth; it is associated with your immortal personality, your soul.

Oh, it's not the first dimension of Earth.

No. It's just the first dimension, period.

Now, you said in something that I was just looking through this weekend (while getting The Explorer Race *ready) that you had embodied two planets. I had only remembered one, which was the first one before Earth. What was the other one?*

Well, let's see if I can say it. Understand that when I talk about having done something, it's outside the context of your time. So I could have done something in the future, from where you are. But anchoring it in your now time, I will probably be seventh-dimensional Earth, when you are there. I will essentially walk in and hold the dream together, inhabit the molecules of your image of how you would like seventh-dimensional Earth to be as you visit it. You will probably, as a race of souls right now, not inhabit seventh-dimensional Earth, but you will visit it. It will be almost like a park.

I will, as a pleasure — perhaps you could think of it as a reward — inhabit seventh-dimensional Earth as the spirit of the planet, and I will essentially make it possible for any immortal personality who visits there to experience a full range of all they could be, sequentially. This means that you could come to the planet, say for a vacation — but you'd have to be very focused spiritually — and say out loud, or even think, or pray, What could I be that I have not yet been, that I would like to be? And then you could become it, sequentially, one thing after another, and discover expressions of your immortal personality in a form that you may wish to accommodate in a future chain of lives. In this way, people will discover that many of the so-called members of the animal kingdom on your planet now have essences in other planetary areas; they appear and act differently on their home planets, and represent true means of delightful creations of one's immortal personality.

That's wonderful. How did you choose that?

Well, I've always been interested in your potential. And I've always wanted to support means by which you could express your potential that you hadn't seriously considered. And when I heard that seventh-dimensional Earth was going to be a place where this could be experimented with, and where beings from all over the universe would come to see what they could be that would be compatible with them . . .

Open to everybody?

Oh yes — I felt that would be quite wonderful. It would make it a happening!

So would you form the planets similar to this prototype that we're looking at here?

I think it would be a little larger, maybe about one-and-a-half times this size, which will help to support individuality as I see it. I think that there will be a lot of water on the surface, creating a lot of separate areas of land. There would be no great oceans as you know them, but rivers that might be two or three miles wide in places, creating the effect of an island. So when one came, either through projection or on a vehicle, one could land somewhere and essentially have a space to oneself, on which to become all of these different things without having to run across anybody else in that place. And I think as a result we could probably accommodate at any given moment several hundred thousand individual immortal personalities exploring a full range of their true potentials.

Do we have to make a reservation?

Well, I think that would be appropriate!

Fig. 9.8. Pseudo black helicopter.

Figure 9.8. Here we have a pseudo black helicopter. If you look closely, there is a black disk at the bottom of the helicopter. Can you see that, kind of an oval? Look at it closely. What you have there is a helicopter beginning to mask itself. But it is not really a helicopter. This is a vehicle associated with the secret government that does have the capacity to appear as a helicopter, as a commercial jet plane, or even as a biplane, you know, a vintage biplane . . .

By broadcasting some sort of hologram around it?

It broadcasts — how can we say — a receptive image that, using highly amplified circuits which the people inside the vehicle must be thinking about (but most of the time they're simply looking at a picture so they don't have to tax their brains too much, a picture of what it is they want to represent themselves to be). Then their imaging – and they have connections not only to their brains but to their personal optics – amplifies this image, and it creates something like a videogram of this image. So it *appears* to be this.

Now, this tells you that these people are obviously not flying the device, because one could not pay attention to flying something while focusing on this. So here we have a vehicle, which tells you you've got at least three or four individuals in there. These individuals are not human beings. They are humanoids – they have two arms, two legs and a body, and if they were wearing uniforms and had their helmets on, and their smoky plastic shields down over their faces, you would guess that they were people. But they are not.

Is this the pilot that Robert channeled? [See Chapter 10.]

Yes. They are associated with what amounts to a slave race that has been created and is being utilized by the secret government forces. So here we have, as I say, something that appears to be a legitimate helicopter but is not.

And what was it doing over Sedona? Going to Secret Canyon? Getting ready to fly into a docking area or something?

It was, in fact, actually leaving that area, flying north on a mission to gather some organs from sheep, which are being used in an attempt to synthesize artificial human skin.

Where were they going? Up to the Indian reservations?

They were going to southeastern Colorado.

After they take the organs, does the result look like those cattle and sheep mutilations?

Yes, it does. In the case of sheep, they've now discovered a way to do it very quickly, and if it's done within, say, five seconds – a skillful hand can do it within five seconds – it is possible that coyotes will consume the sheep, and the evidence will be lost. But if the hand is not so skillful and it takes anything more than nine seconds, then coyotes will sense the presence of the alien energy. It leaves an electronic signature, which affects the smell so that the sheep carcass does not smell like a sheep or any other animal, and since it is foreign to them, they have the sense to avoid it. But you see, they're attempting to improve their technology because they want to encourage coyotes to consume the evidence.

But these are based in Secret Canyon?

Yes.

Fig. 9.9. A floating aperture.

Emissary from the Stone People

Figure 9.9 As amusing as this looks, it is not a floating bow tie in space. It is not a cartoon, either. It is an aperture, which is different from a portal. The figure-eight portion of it is the obvious aperture. The trailing edge, that which hangs down from it in multiple colors, looks like a tunnel, reaching for something. One might call to a floating aperture and ask for it to extend to oneself. Apertures are different, because they appear briefly, unlike portals; portals will move around or they might stay in the same place; tunnels, doorways and windows are all of a certain ilk, as I've discussed before. But apertures are different. They are very brief, there for a moment and gone the next.

This aperture was called for by a being that was coming to check on the status of that which you call mountains — some people call them stone people. It is hard for you to conceive, but there are those who consider mountains to be real life, and human beings to be like ants in comparison. This being, an emissary who comes from the place where rock is created — it is like the birthing place for crystal life — came here because the stone in this area feels highly threatened. As this is an essential, important place to Mother Earth, they came. They checked on things, and they will report back to the creation place for crystal and, allowing for the slow motion of crystals and rock in general, they will return and they will rebuild all of the mountains in their original condition. They will not rebuild the way humans might construct something — slowly, a wall here, a nail here, a board there. They will rebuild it faster than the time it takes to snap your fingers. This tells all of you who might be nefariously living underground in some mountain that when this takes place, there will not be a moment to escape.

Now, this does not include tunnels that were allowed by various decrees from ancient times; I'm not talking about tunnels and spaces that have existed for thousands or even hundreds of thousands of years under the surface of your planet. I'm talking about recently mined areas, and areas where there are underground places — in other words, areas associated largely with the secret government and to some extent those areas associated with your own Defense Department, which has discovered the value of hiding military bases inside natural structures. It makes it very hard to tell that a military base is in there, obviously.

This is not going to happen immediately, so no need to panic. But this being will be back in about 870 years of your experiential time. I must tell you, that does not mean 870 years from now. Because your time is speeding up at a faster and faster rate all the time, my best guess is that the mountains will be re-created in about 35 years. And that tells all of you who are underground that that's about as much time as you have to either move your bases to some other place and put them on the surface, or you might try moving to the Moon if you can, or to the surface of Mars, if you're willing to go along with the rules and regulations of Mars — which is a whole other can of worms. If you do not have the capacity, then, military folks, you're going to have to bring it back to the surface. So that's what's going on there.

That emissary, if you could see it . . . I don't think you could do so. I'm not sure if this instrument exists in your terminology, but it detects magnetically, using x-rays. Well, I don't think you have the technology — you have the pieces but you haven't put it together. In any event, it's not something that's in your visual light spectrum. It's quite small. As they like to say, even though there's only one of these beings, a hundred thousand of them could dance on the head of a pin. This has been used to describe angels, of course.

Who at this moment is setting up rules and regulations on Mars?

Oh, they're not setting them up at this moment. Rules and regulations on Mars have been in effect for at least a quarter of a million years.

But I thought the secret government went there and then they had to leave, didn't they? They set up a base there, didn't they?

They set up a base, but you notice it didn't last. That's because there is a vast underground civilization on Mars that had to move as the result of a massive disaster on the surface. But their culture, including some subcultures, exists with a significant amount of the populace at a slightly higher dimension than your third-dimensional reality, but not so high above it that they're willing to allow third-dimensional mining and exploring; because it's just a little too close to their dimension to allow it. They might allow this in the second dimension. But second-dimensional people do not generally find that of interest.

So it wasn't the safekeepers around the planet from everywhere – the technocrats with the spaceships – it was Mars itself that forced the secret government to leave?

Yes. You know, you can force someone to leave by just using – essentially to the nth power –various degrees of discomfort. You do not have to do something horrible.

Didn't their crops fail? Weren't there things like that?

Well, let's just say this. One might make a scientific observation of Mars and say this and this will work and this and this will not work because we've done the science and we can tell you what happens. But suppose you're establishing a colony, or at least you have a surveying group digging here and there. And suppose for example (this is one of my favorites, I might add) that you wake up in the morning and you find that you cannot move the way you'd moved before. You find that it takes a significant amount of effort just to bring your fingers up to your mouth. It's as if suddenly you weigh a thousand pounds, but you know you don't. In other words, they have the capacity to change the physics of reality there. And when you change the physics of reality, a lot of things can happen. Suppose, on another occasion, after they go through several hours of that – because a person cannot be expected to go through much more than several hours of that – all of a sudden, gravity is almost nonexistent. And your body feels like "Oh, I feel so good, I don't know what happened" and you take one step out the door and as you take a step you fly about fifty feet up in the air! This makes exploring exceedingly difficult. They do things like that, which do not really hurt anyone, but just make working there impossible.

Could they walk the planet without our knowing? Do the Martians look like us?

Some of them could maybe get away with it for a short amount of time, but I don't think they could deal with the energies here. In the old days they used to come here, of course, fly here and interact with other extraterrestrials who lived below the surface, but those days are not here at the moment. Still, they are humanoid.

But not our height or weight? They don't look like us?

Well, if you put a uniform and a helmet on both of you and all that business, you'd be hard pressed to tell that they look different from you. The differences are minor, physically, but they are not comfortable with the polarity. I might say, however, that they have individuals that protect them. They have what would amount to an automated police force, so that their civilization is not having to deal with or become stressed by the idea that someone is coming to dig on their planet for various minerals. They have this automated force that goes to work and it decides on the most benevolent way to discourage these people from being here.

We're going to talk about that another time. What year was that – the colony?

The secret government colonies? I think it was in the sixties. Yes, people were marching in the streets, and the secret government was on Mars – a little more involved. Can you imagine how they would've been marching if they knew about that? But that's another story.

Figure 9.10. This is basically the Creator winking. I include this picture for your amusement. That's the gist of the story: a wink from the Creator. I might add, for the sake of the photographer, that the wink was directed to him. I might also add, for the sake of the photographer, that before the photographer's life, the Creator had a discussion with the photographer. They had a few jokes about this, and the Creator said, "At some point during this picture-taking, I'm going to come and give you a little wink and a smile." There's the wink. The smile might come later.

Figure 9.11. Here we have two vehicles that are engaged in something that is quite common on other planets: They're engaged in a dance. Very often, as you know on your planet, people dance together and so on, but on other planets, where art has become integrated into life, someone might go aboard a vehicle and, allowing for color, which can be flowing from the vehicle, perform a sequential dance, like two good dancers on Earth dancing together, dancing the rumba or something, and they're quite beautiful together. Here we have people inside two vehicles doing the same thing with color.

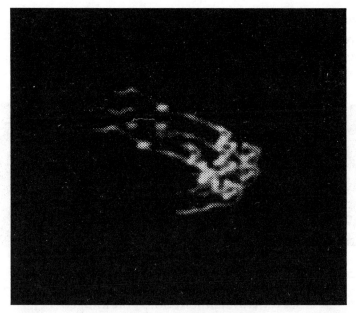

Fig. 9.10. The Creator winking.

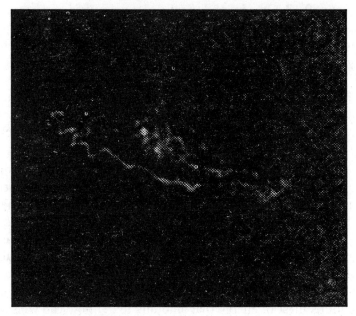

Fig. 9.11. Two vehicles engaged in a dance.

Where are they from?

An interesting question, that. I will surprise you by saying that they are from the distant past, a time when Venus had a significant civilization.

A third-dimensional civilization?

Yes. They are from inside the planet. They were traveling in time, dancing through the universe, if you like.

Fig. 9.12. Pleiadian vehicle pursuing secret government vehicle.

Secret Government Ship "Sabotaged" with Help of Creator Energy

Figure 9.12. On a more dramatic note we have down here in the lower-left corner a vehicle that is an ally to that Pleiadian lightship, in hot pursuit of, in the upper-right corner, a secret government vehicle. And you might ask, why is the secret government vehicle running so hard? Is there going to be a ray-gun fight, are they going to shoot each other out of the sky? No. The Pleiadian vehicle is in hot pursuit because somebody aboard the secret government craft has disabled the secret government craft and enabled the Pleiadian vehicle to make an effort to rescue the disabler.

All the time we talk, the planet is being bombarded, you might say, by a lot of loving energy. And this has effects. Eventually people within the secret government who can reach their hearts, whether they be inner-ring or outer-ring, or simply hirelings or slaves, are being converted. Here we have, then, a vehicle that has had its capacity to move at a high speed, or move through time, disabled, and the Pleiadian ship did catch up. They were able to rescue that individual off the ship, and they caused those within to experience a tremendous blast of energy that amounts to . . . how can we say? — the ultimate tool of conversion (wouldn't the many religions that pursue conversion love that?) and it is essentially an energy from the heart of the Creator. They were able to ask and receive this energy, and it is through the moment of that energy that they transferred the other person off the ship with the help of the angelic realm; in the process, everyone aboard that ship was touched by the energy. As a result, they could not go back to their base, because they would not be welcome there — it would not be safe for them to go there. So they were escorted to a neutral area where they will simply wait until the secret government are no longer disrupters and corrupters and have taken their proper place in an area where they will be able to adjudicate to their hearts' desires and cause no mischief.

Is that that holographic universe you're talking about?

Yes.

That's been the decision — that's going to happen?

Yes. They're going to be able to go someplace where they'll be able to pursue what they've always pursued, but without causing any harm to unwilling participants.

Well, on one level that's what this is, because they're not harming the souls . . .

Yes, you might say in a way that this is a training ground.

More like a holodeck?

Yes, but because you are learning material mastery in order to become teaching masters so that you might give the Creator a coffee break, you are allowed to interact with these people, because it gives you the opportunity to experience "consequences."

10

An ET "Helicopter" Pilot Speaks

Zoosh and Monad through Robert Shapiro
May 6, 1995

Zoosh speaking. I will be the host, as it were, for today's conversation with ETs. We will make an attempt to hear from one of the nonhuman beings that sometimes fly these black helicopters.

These helicopters are not what you would call ordinary helicopters. They have the ability, technologically, to mask their appearance. They can be truly, literally invisible, and they can mask their sound so that only a sensitive instrument or perhaps a sensitive animal might pick it up. They are not associated with your legitimate military or with any legitimate policing organization associated with your government in any way. You might say these particular machines are not even helicopters. They look like helicopters, for all intents and purposes, because if they were to look like UFOs, they'd draw a lot of attention. But as they look like helicopters and give all appearances of being helicopters, they can just fly around pretty much unmolested — or at least they can pass scrutiny.

There are people that fly these machines — not all of them are nonhumans, but many of them are. These individuals are what we could call a variation on beings. They're not exactly true extraterrestrials; there is a rudimentary process of cloning that creates them. They are therefore not very intelligent. They're not stupid, but they have the capacity to do only certain functions. They are never allowed to walk about amongst the people on the surface of the Earth, even wearing their uniforms, which look fairly military: a flying outfit and a helmet with a full face shield. This suit is an environmental suit not unlike that which your own astronauts use to explore the Moon and so on, except that this suit is almost skintight and is advanced beyond the degree of your own space program by several thousand years. They could theoretically walk around in these and be mistaken for any other pilot, but they are not allowed to do this.

These beings are not created on Earth but in a laboratory on a ship near Earth. This ship is associated with a group of individuals I refer to as Xpotaz. Xpotaz is a planet that is essentially not functioning anymore, and these survivors, these linear ancestors, cannot return home because home is really not there anymore. They have had to survive as best they could. Since they are not an advanced race spiritually, they have just drifted around in space and made do as best they could. Some of them are more spiritually advanced than others, so there is hope that they will come to the light, but for right now most of them, certainly those in positions of influence, are primarily, well, space pirates. They do not represent a true threat to the people on Earth directly, because they do not contact you. They have made attempts to influence your legitimate governments but they were deflected by other extraterrestrial races. They are in contact, however, with the secret government. Because the secret government desired what they had to offer — technology, transfers, trades and so on — there was no real way to prevent this interchange. And so it was allowed. Because even those who are in the secret government need to evolve. They are not what you'd call evil, they're not satanic — greedy, yes, but not satanic. There's an important point there, because if we call them satanic we give them some power beyond what is natural, and they do not have that. I would say that this is an unholy alliance, yes, but it will change within a few very short years, and all will come to the light. So do not be concerned.

However, there are things going on that you have a right to know. And that is why we're going to hear pretty soon from one of these beings directly — so you can understand their plight. These beings, as I say, are not allowed to just run around on the surface of the Earth. Of course, if they did so without their gear on, they'd have a hard time breathing because they really can't take your atmosphere, but in addition, if they were allowed to mingle with you even a little bit, they would transform. They would no longer be willing to fly these vehicles. To put not too fine a point on it, these beings who are flying these black helicopters for the secret government — not all of them, but the ones we're going to get in touch with, the ones who are not human — are slaves. So they are not happy doing what they do. On the other hand, they don't know any better. It is as if they were drafted into military action for life. And when they get to the point where they are no longer willing to do the deed, they are eliminated. I have to put it to you like that so you don't think of them as monsters or beasts. They are not that. They are stuck, and later on we're going to do something whereby you can help them. They need help, and they would like it.

These are the beings who are primarily involved in the cattle mutilations, which are really a means of gathering certain material from animals by using very fine surgical techniques so that the organs are not damaged. This material is gathered so that it can be used in attempting to create a perfect soldier that looks human. Now, that was a total disaster, but they're still working on it a little bit. So the cattle mutilations aren't happening as much as they once did, though if you talk to the ranchers you might hear a different story. They were global before, but now they're happening only in the United States, Canada and Australia. It's beginning to shut down as a project. As any scientist knows, you can exhaust your research — at some point you've done everything. They're coming to the point where they've exhausted their research, so that's a good thing.

Now I'm going to stand between Robert and one of these beings, and we're going to hear from him. I'll tell you what this being is doing right now. He is on a mission, in a ship. One of his fellow beings is with him and they are scouting the terrain. I can tell you what state he is in — Wyoming. They're scouting the terrain, not only scoping out certain cattle they need, but looking for cattle that are anomalies — either crossbreeds or simply those having been born different. This gives you an idea of how far down the line they are in their research: the cattle that are normal are not picked up as much as they used to be, because they've almost exhausted that research.

What they're flying in would look very much like an Apache helicopter, which is a type used by your military, so the average person looking at it wouldn't think twice about it. And when I pass on what he has to say, you will just have to understand that you're dealing with a being that is very unsophisticated. He may not understand your ways at all. Also, because this method is happening the way it is and because it's intensely private — it has to be set up in such a way as it's intensely private — there might be times when I have to stop, because every so often, unexpectedly and unpredictably, they get checked by those that monitor them. They're constantly monitored in certain ways, but one of these methods occasionally interferes and it can pick up what we're doing, so I need to protect them.

One or both of the people on the vehicle, flying it, will come through and speak. Probably it will be one, the pilot, while the other person, the copilot or the special weapons and tactics person who actually operates the instruments and so on, will be aware of what's going on. I've been setting this up for quite a while — in terms of your linear time, about three-and-a-half months for this afternoon's talk. I've been preparing them, and I'm going to leave them with a little gift. They know they're going to get this gift, so they're looking forward to it, and you're going to get to participate in the gift. We're going to attach to both of the beings on this vehicle a stream of gold light, right about at the point of the solar plexus. We're going to attach it in such a way as it cannot be detected, which is highly complex, so I won't go into all of the algorithms involved in it. But for your part, when we're done with this channeling with these individuals, I want you to imagine, just imagine and picture that gold light there, all right? Don't picture the ship, don't picture the beings too much; just picture the gold light right there on the two people flying this helicopter, all right? That will help.

In a moment we're going to hear from them. They'll talk a little bit about what they do. They might take questions. If they do, you know, it might not flow smoothly, but we'll make it flow as well as possible. They don't have broad-spectrum knowledge, so don't bother asking them anything about that. All they know about is what they do, and that's it.

All right, this is Zoosh. I am still here but I am in touch now with these individuals. I've had to increase the level of energy a little bit to protect Robert and you and, in my own way, to protect them, to shield them. The pilot will speak. Their names are not like yours — they tend to be associated with things. Now I'm going to repeat what he says.

Message from the Pilot

My name is Monad. It is my job to gather, to research and to acquire materials needed by my masters. They send us out on these missions to do this. I have been functioning (this means, in your terms, "alive") for about two-and-a-half years of your time. I will probably function for no more than one more year, and then Zoosh has told me that upon my death I will become a full soul and I can incarnate in a true life. I cannot wait for this, and my partner feels the same way. He has been in life — if this is life! — for about a year and a half, so he has a little longer to go than I do. (We have to wait a moment now — they're being scanned. All right.)

The work that we do is a corruption of life. This we know. I am not by nature a corrupter, but we work for the corrupters, who wish to hold power that they've never had. Zoosh has taken great time to explain this to us, and we, living in it, can understand the cycle of it all. What keeps us going as a group of beings is that we know our masters' days are numbered. They are human beings like you, and I have even seen them once, in a meeting at which most of them were present.

It was at a very large table, by your standards – an oval table, not a perfect oval but almost. The table was bigger than this room, and the participants sat around the table. There were at that meeting maybe 140 of them present. They came from all over the world, but some places on your surface world were not represented – places that have sparse populations are very often not represented, such as the north and south poles, Greenland, places like that.

They travel through underground conduits to get to these meetings. Most of these people, these humans, do not mingle with surface people at all. They spend most of their time underground, as far as I can tell, and there is an unhealthy aura about them, probably because the human being was designed to be on the surface, not underground. My people can be underground and it does not bother us. I am not sure what they were discussing. I was brought in to be shown, as one might show a pet. They did not smile or frown – they were expressionless from my understanding of human expressions. And even though there were lights on in the room, there was a dark pallor that I could see. I think maybe this was a dark energy that was present. I'm telling you this because it's important for you to know that these people are not superhuman in any way. I could not see anything different about their bodies from what I see in yours through Zoosh's perceptions.

We could take a question.

What sorts of things do you gather?

We gather primarily living organic matter. The people who are experimenting to create artificial life have discovered that if the organic matter removed from certain animals is no longer alive, it cannot be utilized to its maximum potential. I will tell you this: the animals do not suffer. In the beginning, I believe they did. But nowadays they die instantaneously. And then we remove various organs from their bodies in a very special way so that they remain attached to something that keeps them alive. And they go back to the lab very fast.

We will remove sometimes the reproductive systems, sometimes the digestive systems and sometimes the glandular systems, depending on what they want. Occasionally tissue samples will be taken for the purpose of analyzing the genetic structure of the animal, just in case they find one that is right for them. It is an evil thing, I believe, because not only is the innocent animal killed, but the body is left with this particular energy. This energy is unearthly, yes, but it is like an electrostatic energy. This is probably why your animals that would normally consume creatures after death will not approach these carcasses. Sometimes the electrostatic energy even causes the animals' bodies to decompose in an unnatural way, so it will look strange even a week or two afterward. It ought to decompose in a week or two, but it doesn't.

This work, I am sorry to say, is planned by my masters to go on for another 40 years. Fortunately, Zoosh has told me that it won't, but my masters seem to think it will. I think there must be another means to change them. Any other questions?

Do they take humans?

No. I know that it has been reported that they gather human beings, but no. Occasionally I have seen ships from other planets come down and disguise themselves as airplanes or helicopters or balloons or even as conventional aircraft that fly passengers, and take people on board. And sometimes, if the person wants to, and there is no reason not to, the person will stay on board and go back to the planet with these other people. (I wish I could do that. I wish they'd come and get me, but they haven't.) But, no, we do not take human beings. I believe my masters know that if we were assigned to do that, we would be detected very quickly. While we have weapons systems that can evade detection by most of your military forces, and we also have weapons systems that can destroy anything they send to destroy us, it would still draw attention to what we are doing. This is a clandestine operation, and we try our hardest to go undetected – thus the elaborate hoax of the helicopter.

Now and then, our units have participated in other military exercises or even exercises associated with some of your policing organizations. And human pilots have seen one of us. I remember one of my people told me that he had landed on assignment to see if he could pass for a human; he told me this two days before he was terminated. He landed, he didn't talk, but he got out and walked around amongst the human pilots. He did not remove his helmet or face shield, so they could not see he was not one of them. He was spoken to but he did not speak back; he nodded or shook his head. If people spoke to him he would back away. And since it was a military operation, your legitimate military people seemed to, well, if someone doesn't talk to them, they don't pursue it.

So he was telling me that after just that exposure, even fully shielded, he felt an upliftment. He heard the men laughing and joking, and he didn't understand why, but it felt good. And when he got back he talked to as many of us as he could before he was killed (terminated, as they call it) to let us know that life was different other places. There is an underground movement amongst my people . . . (All right, this is Zoosh. They're being scanned again.) *. . . and I am one of the underground participants, as is my partner. I feel that right now almost 35% of our people being used in this evil way are members of the underground. So there is hope.*

I'm going to ask you to pray for us and to send us gold light. Just picture us like this: We look like human beings except for our . . . well, don't picture us the way we look. Picture us in uniform. We wear a black uniform. It is made of some synthetic material – I don't know what – it feels kind of stiff and like plastic or rubber, and it has piping along the seams, which controls the atmosphere and pressure and provides us with what we breathe, because we cannot breathe your oxygen. It would kill us. We have on helmets not unlike motorcycle helmets but all black, with a tinted face shield. And if you can picture us this way, send us gold light if you would. It is hard to come by here, and we cannot meditate to create it. I would ask that.

All right, this is Zoosh. They cannot talk anymore. But I believe they are safe. Now just for a moment, picture gold light in their solar plexus. This is their reward.

11

Opportunity to Go
Home or Not

YHWH through Arthur Fanning
May 26, 1995

Indeed! Everyone take a little water. I won't expose any of your secrets, unless, of course, you give permission. So you must be in tune with all of your being, not just what you term your physical self, [to a participant] know you what I mean?

Yes.

How be you?

Not very good.

Not very good, why is that?

Well, when we left here after the intensive, we went to Texas and we were very sick. We seemed to have quite a release (I believe that's what it was), and just two days before leaving, coming back, I guess I got a bite by . . . I don't know if it was a brown recluse spider or just what.

Mmm, they're hungry beings, eh?

Right. Is that what I got bit by?

No.

No?

Have you heard the expression *Father,* what is termed *God, All That Is?* What do you think He does for you?

Well, teaches us and tries to wake us up.

He doesn't try to waken you, I'll tell you that much.

He does wake us up; is that what He does?

Not really. There are other beings, that's their job. What do you think He does? He allows you to do whatever you want to do, indeed?

Indeed. I wasn't aware I wanted to do this.

So you were *attacked*, unknowingly, by this being?

Yes.

What part of you knew? It is a little bitty being, know you, and you're a great big being, indeed?

Indeed.

And you're becoming a master here, indeed, so what purpose did you call this little being for?

Hmm . . . I'm not aware of why. I guess to try and see what I could do, see what power I had against it.

Part of comparing. How are you doing now?

Not so good.

Not so good. Is that better than not so bad, or it's worse than, which is it?

It's still there and I've tried a number of ways to try and gain my own power to work against it, for one thing, and I'm declaring and demanding my own power. This is what I've been doing.

You don't demand your power, you command it. Have you been to a physician?

No, I've been in contact with a homeopathic, which I would much rather do than go to a physician.

When you're playing in these games now, these becoming forces we will say, your belief systems are going to be tested to the ultimate. Know you what I mean? So you no longer become, in your, what you say your good health, you metaphysically say, "I can defeat any disease," and then portions of illness come to you, and your belief system is challenged, know you what I mean? So if you're not successful, I will say in a three-day period, if you're not successful in overcoming this exposure we will call it, any exposure, if you're not successful in the three, then it be wise for you to reevaluate your belief systems and seek the masters that know, you understand, so you don't play games with your physical being metaphysically anymore. Know you what I mean?

Your metaphysical system has given your medical profession a bad rap, so to speak. Everyone in your medical profession is not evil or stupid, know you, and you can see within this system now there are changes, know you? There are awakenings going on. So at times it is wise to check with these beings. You know, one belief system can be just as limiting as another, know you what I mean? And you're here to experience *everything* on the planet; it's up to you to choose wisely. Know you what I mean? And then you will find out there are no choices. [He laughs.] That's a little joke.

Know you this thing called fear of death, what do you think that is?

Not knowing or not believing in what really is beyond.

That is portion. The other portion is not remembering how you did it last time, so it's more of a not remembering. Know you what I mean? So allow you to get over this not remembering, bargain?

Bargain.

[To another participant] How be you, my little rascal one?

Oh, okay, pretty good, thank you.

Anything you want to chat about?

Yeah, my face is swollen.

You're retaining a little too much fluids. Your legs are a little swollen, too, indeed?

Yeah, they always are. Hmm, I didn't [retain water] before, until this week. What's the reason behind that?

Letting go. All of the bodies are changing now, physically, what you term in your physical form, and because of your belief system that this is the way you must look, the resistance to this change becomes pain in the body, know you what I mean? You're handling it grandly, however. Know you grapefruit? Little bit. I don't mean for you to eat ten grapefruits a day. A little half be good. And raspberry [leaf] tea, you know how I like that one. Everyone breathe a moment.

Now, the way the energies are moving now, they will be played out within the soul that is within the body, and that is within here [heart chakra]. You may say this is a call to come home that will be felt physically. That does not mean you have to leave the body. That means you awaken within you and know, and dwell within the body because it is a joyful experience.

Time is Meeting Itself

Humanity is going to become bombarded, in a manner, with a lot of thought that would appear to be not yours, yet they are; because there has been an awakening within portion of grid systems, other ones, and it has to do with, from your perspective, time beginning to meet itself, you term collapse in time, etc., etc. It is really we say time meeting itself because that is your concept here, linearly. The awakening is causing an alignment within here [heart chakra/soul] and all of your selves: past, present, and future. There is a lot of information there. Some of you played forgive yourself in your past and that's why you do not remember your past life. You have difficulty forgiving yourself in your present, and few contemplate forgiving themselves in the future. It would be important now to forgive yourself in your present moment, and in all of your past moments, and all of your future. And that entails, one manner (and I have to use your words here because it is the only thing you have here) forgetting. Knowing you now. Forgetting is forgiving, and that's why you forgot your past lives: you didn't want to remember. If you want to remember your future lives, then forgive yourself so you can see them.

In the greater context you understand this is all an illusion anyway. Metaphysically you understand that. But the illusion becomes very difficult when you have pain in the human form. Everyone breathe a moment here.

You have each taken this journey, not because you were foolish, not because you desired mastership in this dimension, and if you decide to leave the body now you will simply choose another dimension, or this one again, to complete to remember you, because there is no greater journey than the one you are working in right now. You are at your greatest level of your spiritual power, each one of you. No matter if you've been kings or queens in past lifetimes, or great barbarians.

There is a great movement now within the councils, many councils. Several of the councils, we will term them what you term councils that have jurisdiction over this arena and a few others, are in confusion, because the beings that they are overseeing, so to speak, aren't paying attention. We will say driving the council members nuts, know you? So there have been greater beings assigned to, in a manner, calm these councils down and get things done, from your perspective now. Because there has been a stabilization, so to speak, within the council forces, there is going to become a destabilization here. Everyone breathe.

Things are going to seem to be wreaking havoc with your belief systems. It would be wise to align to your higher self, what you term your great spirit that is within and about you, and l-i-s-t-e-n! Listen for a change. Shut your mind up for a change. Be humble and understand you don't know it all yet. You don't! And listen to what your great light is telling you. It will tell you to move gently, to become aware of this great impinging of thoughts that are coming to you, this great column of your past and future thoughts. So this is a time needed great balance here. It is another auspicious event, however. It is one of the steps that you're going to go through that is going to increase your telepathy.

A lot of you, from one perspective, came to this place to hide out. You thought you couldn't be found here. Why didn't you want to be found? Well, you were part of Lucifer's rebellion, and when he became, we will say, lectured to, straightened out a little bit, there was no more champion for you. Oops! Everyone take a breath and get rid of that guilt. It was great fun. No one is judging you but yourselves now in this thing, and there is a lot of humor going on.

Allow you your right hand to be placed here on your heart chakra, and contemplate the serenity that you are in there, your power, your love. Contemplate your I-Amness here. Contemplate your Father waiting for you to come home. And contemplate you being home. Allow you to move your hand. And when you get home, you can say to Father, "I'm sorry I borrowed the car so long, but it was a great trip! I had fun what you term joy riding!" [He laughs.] Indeed. [To a participant] How be you?

Just fine. Getting over a cold or something similar.

Colds are caused by fear, are you aware of this? They are. How is your tummy?

Okay.

Indeed, you're doing grandly there. You're really whirling around in here.

Well, I thought that since I got sick right after our last meeting in the intensive, maybe I was getting rid of a lot of poisons or toxins.

There was a lot of releasing going on. If you release, however, you don't get sick. It is the holding on that creates the illness. It is not the first time I've been blamed. [Laughter.] The energies created movement, and when you beings play in your metaphysics and you don't *listen* to what I say, you reinterpret, in one manner, the words, to fit your systems, and you allow the energy to move in your being, the energy *will* clean, and you simply put the string out to pull it back. It's all right.

You have your masters here in your physical form that are great healers, and that is their job. My job is to bring you home — that involves the soul, not your ego. That involves the lavender fire that's within you here [heart chakra/soul]. That is *all* I care about. The physical form is *your* form. These teachings are not for everyone, yet these teachings *will* affect everyone. Lot of changes happening about your planet, all over. Everyone wants to see the Father, yet when He gets a little close they say, "Wait a minute, Dad. Not just yet." Well, the movement has started. Daddy's coming! [Laughter.] And you can't run fast enough — no need to run, at any rate.

This [the brain] is the part that gets it last, know you what I mean? This part [heart chakra/soul] knows, this is the power here. [To participant] How are things in Egypt?

Fine, fine.

Everything okay back there?

Yep, yep.

How's the temple construction coming on?

Right on schedule.

Indeed.

I wanted to ask you a question. Do you think that in this new world order that's coming about, and with the new light that's going to resurrect the planet and all that, Arthur and I could get a new head of hair?

You don't have hair out there.

Well, I would like it here, the hair. It used to be curly.

Would it make you feel better to have hair?

Yeah, it shades your head, and the girls can run their fingers through it.

Usually I leave the sexual issues up to [this entity]. [Laughter.] You're hanging out with him now, I see. How do you . . . know you this pyramid you're building in Egypt? Know you this thing? What is its purpose?

To keep the records of past history of humanity.

What else?

And to enlighten the people in the coming age.

Well, what is it termed? Initiation, right?

Yes. The sarcophagus is just for the initiate.

What do you do in there?

Well, they have ceremonies that the individual candidate wants to go through, to enlighten on his way back to the Father, so to speak.

Indeed, and what do you do?

What do I do? I'm just like an officer, a guide and a friend to the candidate.

Indeed, so you've already been through there?

Many times.

And what is one of the things you learn when you're in there? How to rejuvenate the body, indeed? Now, what color do you use to rejuvenate the body from your memory?

Mm, I would say gold.

That is it, you picked it up very well. That be grand. What do you do with the gold? You see the inside of the body golden. You assimilate the gold, allow it to come around each organ, indeed, know you, and you allow the gold to see each organ completely healthy, indeed? Now, what organ grows hair, what you term hair? The hair comes out of the follicles in the skin, indeed? So you flood these things with gold light, indeed, because the memory of how to grow hair is still there, indeed? So you flood it and let it move, and tell the hair to grow. And you can do that with any organ, you understand? Gold light, indeed. You remember these things from the past, and they're going to come more and more. So you don't simply remember and chitchat about them, you *use* this knowledge now.

Apply it.

Indeed, apply.

Like you said before, thought applied.

Well, you are thought.

Unfortunately, we don't apply it.

One of the reasons you don't have hair in this time, know you, you were confused a little bit, you couldn't figure out which hairstyle the women liked the best, so you decided [to] just get rid of it. So stop the confusion. You beings are outrageously creative here.

. . . I think you're right.

Could be the first time, you're saying, indeed? Everyone take a breath.

Now, there is an outrageous amount of light, white light, brilliant light, coming to the planet. Your light inside you, in here [soul], is going to react because it remembers this light. It's going to resonate one unto the same with it. It is the memory. Likened unto you say you have two tuning forks and you bang one and the other begins to vibrate.

Part of this light (it involves many beings) is Lucifer's light, part of it is mine, and several others' that you know. You're going to have to get over your judgment of these things. You will vibrate with it and you will move beyond it. If you don't, there is going to become a mental disturbance in your system. These forces are coming now to remind you of who you are, it is part of the awakening you call it, part of the shifting, part of the divine aspect of you opening up. Lucifer and his game has no influence on you whatsoever unless you are in physical body, because within the physical you forget. This vibration you're all going to begin to feel is going to be very frightening for some. Most of humanity will think there is something wrong with their heart. In some instances that could be because this is an electrical force and it'll affect you. It will be appropriate to be *in* love, in that feeling of love. It will create an outrageous ecstasy in your body. You can say, "Oh boy, here comes that love feeling again!" Some of you are going to see it. The prana in the air will quicken, it will thicken in front of you, and just get ready for the experience. These are outrageous times.

Your thoughts do build your body. Yet at a greater level, deep within here, you're playing: you take thought, know you clay, and play with it in here. It is simply current inside you. Some of you are going to play with the current now and go beyond the limitation of these labels and these words that you need, you're going to play. It will create great force within your being. It will allow you the opportunity to know all things. It'll allow you the opportunity of freedom, and you'll understand this concept that everyone gets all caught up in called ascension, know what it is. And you'll be willing to play a little bit more and a little bit more with these forces, and you'll find that the play occurs in your moments of solitude, we'll say you the play becomes more interesting in your moments of solitude because you're getting it. You're getting it in your quiet moments. But then some of you will run off and begin to show others what you can do and you can't do it. So polish your lights, your brilliant light in here very brightly before you attempt to show others, and know that you must do it, because when you alter your frequency in order to communicate with another at their level, you're allowing portion of your being to be separate from you, and you can't remember. Does anyone have any questions at this time?

I have a question for a friend. She's having a lot of trouble sleeping lately, and I just wanted to know if you have any insights that I could pass to her.

A lot of beings are having what you term restless sleeps, and it is because of this thing called your time collapsing, and you'll see your futures and your pasts. Now, some of the things you don't want to see so you try to close the door. It is all right to allow you to see. Be thankful that these things are occurring in what you term the dream state, know you, and they're not occurring in what you term the physical. That is a safety valve right now. Soon *that* is going to go away, but not for a while, you understand?

I heard a tape that said there is a colony on Mars of beings from this world. Can I get some confirmation on this?

There are many colonies there, what about it?

I just wanted confirmation that it was true.

Little bit. Some beings think it is going to be a getaway place, hideout, know you, [that] no one's going to find them there. Wrongo congo, know you what I mean?

I have a question. A woman said that in her light body she had disconnected the negativity of the crystal in Atlantis. Is this true?

There is going to begin surfacing a lot of technical information, particularly regarding Atlantis, and it is an attempt by the beings that were involved in the destruction to even things out. Yet it is also part of the Pleiadian game. The Pleiadians desire, in one manner (now you must listen in between the words here for this) to slow down your spiritual acceleration, your divineness being recognized by you, because if you accelerate completely, what we say majority of the planet, that would mean you did not evolve your technological skills to the point where the Pleiades exist. Everyone breathe a moment.

You *are* involved in an alteration of time here, and I've told you before that these beings are coming back into this point because this is where they remembered you're part of that experience, by the way. That's why some of the councils are getting a little shook up, and the councils over them, also. It's a very interesting time, because once again you're going to have the opportunity to think you know it all, and a chance to go home or not, to become. Each must listen to their . . . here [heart chakra/soul].

Pyramid Visualization

Allow your eyes to close a simple moment. Indeed, and we're going to bring you a vision of ancient temples in what you call the city of Atlantis. Simply allow you to see, allow this golden light in the room and see the temples. They were initiation centers. Allow the memory to be understood here. Allow. See you the pyramids there, there are many. They are crystalline, they are clear, and they are very large. See the splendor of this place. Allow.

Now compare the pyramids that be in Atlantis with the pyramids that exist now in what you term your Egypt, there is a big difference, even in the vibration of it. And the reason there is a difference is, when the technology destroyed that continent, the memory of how to do it again was distorted, because not only did you create an effect on your planet, you created an effect throughout your entire solar system in this end of your galaxy. It wasn't going to be allowed to be happen again. (Everyone breathe and allow your eyes to open.) So these memories are beginning to resurface.

Golden light within your being will heal you in a moment if you allow it. If you allow you to understand your Father is a lavender flame. Don't put a personality to It. Don't put a name to It, you cannot, it doesn't exist. This is what you call before the beginning, this One. The concept of names did not exist. It was the experience of this One that allowed all other things to exist, and this One is still experiencing these things, waiting for the journeys of those to come home. There is no judgment. This One does not understand judgment. This One is innocent. This One is in ecstasy with the creations here. This One is innocent, and this One is within you. Everyone breathe a moment. Any other questions?

You were speaking a short while back about a method of cleansing the poisons out of the body by breathing in the nadis [two points located at the top of the forehead/hairline, left and right of the centerline of the body] and bringing it down into the perineum, then expelling it back through the mouth. Do you use light, colors of light, to aid this process? Can you speak on this a little bit, please?

You use what is termed brilliant white light through this nadis here [left of center] and red through this one [right of center], and you breathe in and down. Now in the center there is a great blue light that comes from your blue corona. When you breathe these colors down [the brilliant white and the red] and they crisscross over the chakras and connect at the perineum, that'll give you a calling we will term it where your blue light, your blue flame will come to the center, know you, and it is that connection of the blue in your release [exhale through the mouth] that expels the poisons. And there is an activation of kundalini there, also, so be gentle here. Are you ready for a meditation?

This meditation is going to allow you to visit with the innocent One, with your Father. We will start the process. Once we start the process, whether you complete the visitation or not this evening, you *will* complete it. And it is what would be termed a training because it's going to occur for many upon the planet, and it will cause confusion because it is not understood. This One is the innocence within you. This One is still innocent, still, and still in love. Allow your feet to be flat upon the floor and the spine erect, or allow you to sit comfortably with your spine erect. Now I'm calling in some of your guides here for some of you that are nervous. They will be here to be with you. Allow.

Meditation

Open the heart chakra. Do not be concerned if you don't know where it is, simply tell it to open; it'll begin to open. Open the throat chakra. Open the sixth seal and the crown chakra wider. Breathe in the white and red light into the top of your head, into the nadis at the front near your forehead. Breathe it down and hold it at the solar plexus here. Let it out. Open the solar plexus chakra. Open the navel chakra. Breathe in the nadis, breathe down, hold it at the navel chakra. Breathe it out. Open the root chakra, open the navel chakra wider. Breathe in the nadis again, down to the perineum, down to the root chakra, to your buttocks. Hold it there. Squeeze your buttocks together and tighten your stomach, hold the breath, and tighten your thighs. Exhale, let the breath out. Peace. Peace.

Allow gold light now to enter your crown chakra from above. Allow. Allow. You have additional eyes besides your sixth seal that reside in your head – tell them to open and feel a current begin to spin counterclockwise within your brain, within the fluid that surrounds the brain. Allow. Peace. And feel the eyes open. Allow. Open the heart chakra wider. Peace. Open the throat chakra wider.

Now, with the hands of your lightbody (do not move your physical hands) allow the lightbody hands to grasp the sides of the pyramid of your soul that is in your chest and allow it to push out in front of you six inches. Allow the lightbody hands to do this. You pick the pyramid up a little bit toward the throat to unhook it and push it out. You are in safety. It is not going away. Allow.

Now within the pyramid that is in front of you, within your soul, there is a lavender flame in the center. See it. Feel it there. Bring the pyramid gently back into the body. Allow more gold light into the body. In front of you see a great river, very large, very wide. And across the river there is a lavender flame, a lavender flame. See it there in front of you. That is your Father. See it there what you term across the river, indeed, and see it surrounded in a manner by what you call a very dark blue, and there is your Father in that blue. Allow. Allow. And the flame simply dances in its innocence. Allow. Allow you to take all of your unwanted baggage, we'll term them thoughts, your diseases if you have and you're playing with them, and allow them to appear in front of you in a ball. Allow them all to be there. Anything you want to get rid of – your bad habits, whatever they are; any limitations, whatever they are; your lack of abundance – put it there, allow, in the ball, and see the ball getting larger as you fill it. Let go of your judgments. Now push this ball to that lavender flame and let it dissolve within that fire. Push it. Peace. And see the flame burn brightly, there is no judgment within this flame.

And the sphere that you sent now returns back to you, and it is a brilliant gold-and-white light. It is cleansed. Allow it to enter what you term at your chest area, into the throat and chest, through the apex of the soul. Allow. It was given freely by the innocent one to you, cleansed here. Allow. Be anew now. Allow.

This one what is called your Father in your terms does not speak, yet He does. He allows all things. Everything. So to communicate here you must communicate in innocence, without a doubt of what you want. Peace. And if you desire, tell the lavender light that you're desiring to come home and be home, to be empowered being. Allow. Feel it in your body. Everyone take a breath. Hold it at your perineum. Tighten your thighs, tighten your buttocks, tighten your stomach, and push it out. Allow. Peace. In a gentle manner slowly open your physical eyes. Peace.

One of the greatest things you can do in this time is to love those that are ill. Some of you will be able to love them so much that you will assist in their healing. And how you do that is, the love becomes so strong from you that they vibrate to that love and they remember. But you will never heal another, you cannot.

This is also the time when the Antichrist, the physical being, and his antagonists are going to begin to appear on the world scene. They have a game to play. Be you more interested in your own journey, because in the beginning you won't be able to tell them apart. Be you interested in your own journey. Indeed?

Indeed!

So be it!

The Healing Power of Gold

Now, know you we've talked before of gold, know you gold, what you term your physical gold, and your silver, indeed? And we told you they are important. Not in what you term the monetary, but because of the healing power there. It is stored there as a memory. It would be wise for each of you to carry a little piece what is termed gold coin, little piece of silver coin on your system, on your body at this time. It will create circuitry to allow the movement of the light through the physical form easier. You don't need great big piece. And I will allow you to play . . . I will suggest that you start in this manner, however: a little bit of gold on the left side, a little bit of silver in the right. Little bit. You will feel a change in your endocrine system, some of you. You'll feel a change in your lymphatic systems. You will feel a change in your immune systems. And you will feel a strengthening of your lightbody in the physical. Then begin to play with the coins around each chakra, one chakra at a time. For example, your gold coin on this side [left] of navel, your silver here [right], and you push them close together and see what happens to the chakras. Play it within your own body. That becomes your knowing. Play with them on your temples here, for these vortices are now beginning to open here. Everyone take a breath a moment.

There are some of you that don't want to get activated too quickly, that is all right. That is perfectly fine. It has to do with belief systems and good and evil. That is all right. It is your vehicle and you may play with them what you call as you will.

Love yourselves and each other through this process. It is going to be a very confusing time, these months that are coming. And that is because you don't know who you are. You *think* you do. As the magnetics of your poles shift (this is from your physical perspective now) it will create an alteration in your weather —you're already seeing that. Yet it is *not* the magnetics of the poles shifting that is doing this. It is the light and the Christed consciousness that you are awakening that is creating the shifting of the poles, creating the cleansing for the Earth. Consciousness creates. So collectively (whether you want to accept it or not, it doesn't matter), humanity *is* working toward a spiritual awakening within its own being. And because you are who you are, and you're residing on the planet, you're affecting the planet, because light is love, and lowering light becomes electrical, and lowering the electrical further becomes what you term the sound and the color and the frequency called magnetics, and you're all a part of it. I know some of you think you're *so* separate. It's all right. It is fun, and you're all loved outrageously by your Father. He loves each of you equally, none more than the other. It is you here who separate, and that is all right, that is part of your journey. It is your body, you can do with it what you want to. And when you die the body, that is all right, we'll be there with you as we always have been.

[To a participant] Are you ready to play in your dreams?

Yes.

So be it. It's going to be a lot of fun. Everyone want to have a journey in their dreams this evening?

Yes.

Some of you want a yes, little bit one. Some of you want a big one. So be it for those who want a big one; who wants little ones? Everyone wants a big one?

Indeed! Yes.

So be it! Some of you want visitation by Sananda, he is willing.

Pay attention. Some of you I'm going to play with — I'm going to tap you in your physical form as you lay in bed, and you're going to think someone is there and they're not, and you're going to get all nervous. And then you'll remember. Anything anyone else wants to chat about?

When we go into the fourth and fifth dimensions, is it like a sleep state?

No. Why would you want to sleep through the fourth and fifth?

I just read something about it.

Ah, here we go, more wisdom. You can sleep through the fourth and fifth, for there's more fun there than there is here, know you what I mean? You're at a disadvantage in one way.

I am?

I've got my cord around you, know you?

So you're pulling the strings, huh?

You may say, a little bit. I'll cook your fanny if you try to sleep through the fourth and fifth dimension, that's what I'll do. [Laughter.] There's more fun there. That is simply a way to say it for you, know you, by comparing.

You've All Been Together Before

I have another question. My friend here and I feel like we've known each other before, but we don't know from where. We've both tried to figure it out, and we still haven't been able to.

You've been together before. You're not the only one that has been together with anyone else in this room, know you? You've *all* been together before. You didn't just live two or three lifetimes, know you? You've spent many. You don't always repeat with the same being, know you, it gets really boring.

Yes, it does, except for [with my mate] over there. [Laughter.]

I haven't told you half of the stories. One of the great things is sex brought you to the planet, know you, and it is one of the greatest healing forces you have here, know you? Your judgments about this thing, all of you, limits this thing. If you knew how to use those forces, you would understand that the body was built to last many, many, many years. It is not a falsehood, know you, in what you call your book, your Bible, there are 600 year-old beings, know you, still giving birth. No big deal. However, your physical form at this time is not capable of handling that.

Quite a challenge.

I can't wait until you will allow me to share some of your stories.

You're rather an outrageous being in your own right, know you, never mind [your mate] back there.

Helping the Physical Body to Keep Up

I have a question. I'm getting really dizzy, I feel like I'm going to fall over. What is this?

A lot of you beings are going to have difficulty with the energy because you think your physical body is your physical body. You know metaphysically that you are lightbody. Your lightbody is becoming stronger, know you, and when you start an argument with your lightbody, I've told you this before, the lightbody is going to win. Know you what I mean? I've also told you before that if the soul desires to leave the body, it's going to leave, know you? Your arguments now are with your higher self. They're not with I or any other god that exists, they're with your higher self, and your higher self is in control.

Because the current circulates within the brain here, within the fluid of the brain, to make the connection, old belief systems will limit that flow. The current wants to go. New pathways want to be evolved within the brain. They are going to be created. What will happen, in your old system if you play your metaphysical behavior with this thing, you're going to feel the presence and at times this energy will create a palpitation. You'll get hot, you say, or you get what is termed a stroke. Pay attention to these warning signs, what you term. Be very careful where your belief system is here. Do not play metaphysics with this. Know you what I mean? If you are the littlest bit off your power, seek a master that has been empowered in what you call your science or your medical profession, that knows what's going on. Do you all understand this?

You all have your expertise, believe it or not, your own special skills. They're going to come to the forefront. You will know what they are. You each need each other. Each one of you. Just like your body needs all of your blood and fluids together, and you need your cell structure to create your form, to walk in it. Do not be arrogant here in this time. Use your humility.

You're not the only one getting dizzy, there are quite a few others. It is a disorientation because your light is coming to you, know you what I mean? And this activity you're feeling in your knees, you say, "I must walk like this" [he imitates the average human walking down the street], know you? Your great lightbody is coming down around you, know you, entering you, and it desires to walk like this [differently from the way one normally walks – slow, emphatic widespread stepping, indicating deliberate and purposeful intent in each step taken]. It wants to own its footing upon the planet. Wants to feel the planet's breath. But you beings have to walk proper, wear the proper clothes. It is all right.

One of the ways you can ease some of these disorienting effects is, know you, there is an oil called white, white oil. You put upon the temples. White oil along the sides of the knees and the inside of the knees will alleviate some of this pain that you think is your knees. It's the light moving here. Also here, what you term your elbow, and here and in the shoulder areas, white oil. Before bedtime you should do these things because what you are doing when you oil your body gently (I don't mean jump into a tub of oil), when you put a little bit of oil on your body before you go to sleep, what you are doing with spirit is you're blessing the physical form, because you each leave your body at night —you don't remember, some of you do and have a grand journey —but you're blessing the physical and in a *manner* what you're telling it is, "I love you greatly! I will be back," and the energy that holds that is enjoying this, waiting for you on *this* side to come home. The same feeling that your Father has waiting for *you* to come home. So you need a little bit of oil on your palms here, on all your chakras, a little bit, a drop. Some of you beings, I tell you a thing and you get into what you call big waters here. But what you're doing is blessing the body. You know your spirit is going to leave and play in the dream state and play in other realities —you do know this. But you're telling the body, "I will be back, I love you! Enjoy this aroma," and what you'll do is you'll end up healing your body. You should sleep with what you term a little gold and a little silver. Allow the gold to be near the top of your head, and the silver to be between your feet. The body will enjoy its frequency here. That is what your gold and silver is for, that is what your oils are for — to bless your vehicle. It is time now to treat your vehicle like a temple that it is.

You talked about white oil — is there supposed to be an aroma in it?

There is an aroma [called white oil], it is very sweet.

Are you talking about White Angelica Oil?

That would work. You also have some other oils that you can experience: you have your lavender, indeed, there is a lavender oil; there are several that are very outrageous. You've been given these clues, know you your frankincense and your myrrh? They are outrageous for the body when you leave the body. Particularly your what you term frankincense. It is one of the initiation oils. Only use one at a time. Some of you are thinking, Well, I'll use frankincense here, and a little bit of white here, and I'll use lavender on this one . . . one at a time. Later you may play experiment. Know you mandalas? Later you can experiment placing mandala designs over your being with the oils and different ones. But I tell you these things so you can experience the first movement, and then you can go further and further. So experience the first movement gently, and then you can play with the rest. Know you what I mean?

Another outrageous thing . . . well, let's get into it now that we're into it here. Know you the grand chakra on your back? That is your own personal mandala that you have used to create this vortex you're living in. It resides there, it's an outrageous chakra, contains all of your experiences, all of your pictures of your journeys.

Now, know you a rose oil? If you will allow someone to start in what you term the center of your back there with a dot of rose oil (it is a loving thing, know you) and then a little bit around it, a little circle about an inch or two apart, another circle, and you make twelve concentric circles out, you will have an *outrageous* experience. Some of you have big backs, but even it out, know you? Don't go one inch and then along the sides here. Twelve circles. You are physical body number thirteen.

Does it make any difference which way you go, clockwise or counter-clockwise?

Counterclockwise. Will you experiment with one another?

Should we go beyond the body when doing the circles if the back is small?

Not at the present time. Each one of these things I tell you, you understand that they're very basic, and I'm giving you the very basics. Once you've experienced the effect, you may go further with them. But experience the effect first. It will also alter your dream states outrageously.

There is a very important point here — this part, put the [palm of] your right hand here on your left forearm, [right thumb running along the crease where the elbow is]. In this area around your forearm, I won't be specific, but you carry a lot of memory, a lot. Rose oil here will help you overcome your judgments, know you, little bit.

Is that on both arms?

No, just the left. Don't worry about the right side yet. The chakra on the back is going to straighten a lot of that out. Are there any other questions?

You Wear Your Own Rescue Devices

Can you talk about codes? We're coded, aren't we? What are they, can you explain?

Which codes are you talking about, your DNA? You have other codes in your body, also. Some of you have implants. Oops.

What kind of implants?

You have implants so you can be located, in case you go astray too far. "Oh, there they are, in *that* field."

Spiritually or physically?

Both. Once you separate your spirit and your humanity . . . how do you do that? I know you *think* you can, that is what is so funny. You are all coded spiritually. You're coded physically. There is going to be a device pretty soon, within a year, that's going to be able to detect the implants that are within your physical form now, under the idea that they're going to save you from interference, so to speak. But a lot of you have these implants in you, you wanted them there, they are really rescue devices.

Would you expound on that? Are you saying that it would be wise to keep the implants in?

Of course! You are involved in the body. You were part of the process of determining what you needed here. That is how you're becoming confused now, not because of the implant, but because what others say creates fear. The implants were your what you term rescue stuff. Know you? "In case I really lose this thing on this mission, I push this button, you come get me, okay?" They say, "Okay!" so you in your great wisdom, and as you get more fearful, you take all of your rescue devices out. It's all right, it's fun to watch. Some of you aren't very good swimmers and you're leaving your life vest behind. It simply means you'll make another trip, that's all it means. Some of those devices were literally to take you aboard the ship if need be. It is interesting how you say you're attacked from outer space and all of these bad beings are kidnapping you.

I'm really confused now. There is a healer that I have been to who said I had an implant around my navel, and he removed it with my permission. He said that the reason that it was put there was to prevent me from teaching. So apparently it's like a ball of energy?

More like what is termed in your case it was . . . know you a crystal that is elongated about this big, that's what it was.

So I should have left it there, that's what you're saying?

I'm saying this thing: you are in love with the Father in your original journey. The Father is in love with you. You play game be born, you have many friends out there that are in love with you on this journey. You decide the vehicle you want, you decide the tools that you want within that vehicle, and you perform the experience. Know you what I mean? Yet some of you enjoy playing victim. Some of you are aware . . . know you this thing called the cords, how you put cords out? And you're willing to have everyone cut them for you because they told you that is how you let go. Well, it is. You can't even contemplate or remember *how* you put the cord there. What was your purpose for it? It was because of the journey. So before you start getting rid of all your stuff, understand what your wisdom was for doing it. Know you what I mean? Once you have the wisdom acknowledged, then you can let go. Don't come from what is termed a fear, know you? Everyone thinks they've only got one eye in here. There are three more. They're going to open. With your physical eyes you literally perceive your reality, yet you use that color and light and the electrical to create it to only perceive one-dimensional activity. That is shifting now. That's why some of you are starting to see activity over here [to the left], over here [to the right], some of you, in front of you. You're becoming more. You're not a limited being. By the way, that crystal that was there, it's still in your auric field — your guides didn't let it go away.

So I should call it back?

Talk to your guides. Know you one being you trust, what is termed Sananda? You communicate with him, indeed? You listen to him sometimes, indeed? Pay attention! Indeed? All of you have your guides. You don't pay attention because you think you know so much. That is all right. It be really wise now, I mean really wise, really wise, really, really wise, really, to pay attention to your guides through this time. Don't pay attention to me. I don't have a problem with this. Pay attention to your guides, because if you don't, that's simply going to make my job harder, because then I have to get on your guides' case for not guiding; then I have to reassign them to guide school, get more guides down here —we're running out of guides, entities. Some of you go through three or four guides a year. We have to rotate them, know you? You exhaust them. You know what I mean. They need a vacation too.

You're all loved grandly. This is an outrageous time. In what you term your dream state this evening, we're going to allow some of you to be play what you call aboard a ship, others we're going to take you to different arenas, and it is only to help you remember your power.

It is to assist you beyond judgment, and to let you understand how easy this game really is here, how divine you are. Some of you are within a cluster, a grouping. Some of you think your own grouping is the most special. It takes all of the groupings, entities, all of them. I love you outrageously. I love your divinity, however, more than that. I love God. We are through.

12

Earth Signed on as Member of Council of Planets

Zoosh through Robert Shapiro
May 26, 1995

Now comes the time of the true battle between the illusory forces of evil and the ongoing natural forces of good.

You mean right now or when this is printed? Now meaning today – the 26th of May?

Now meaning *now* now. The organization of the empire of evil is an accumulation of wants, desires and attachments of that which is out of balance with the true flow of natural reality. It starts out simple, and all that people recognize as truly evil extends from it eventually, because that simple beginning of separation from the good can, if not monitored closely, easily go off and take the next step of alienation. And beyond alienation there is a significant potential – not guaranteed, but a significant potential, say 50% – of some kind of mischief developing. Mischief, then, is built upon and it can become evil.

So I will say this. Evil is, generally speaking, that which controls or attempts to control the outcome or destiny of some other object, person or entity against its will. That's the foundation of evil. Under that description, many things might be perceived to be evil that are not evil at all. For example, something innocent – a mother keeping her child from sticking his finger into the light socket – might be interfering with free will, and yet I do not call this evil. This is guidance. That which controls another individual and prevents him or her from following the natural course – and the natural course is benevolent – would be evil.

What's happening is that those who have been attached to preserving the old, whether it be of value or not, are gearing up for the big fight. And the big fight from their point of view is going to be an attempt to maintain control at all costs. What you can do about this individually is to examine your own life, to look at it and see where you are attempting to maintain control of your own life at all costs. If the moment of "at all costs" represents a true disruption in your life or a true disruption in the lives of others, or both, you must look at whether this is just an attempt to maintain predictable order in your life or whether it is truly a corruption of your life. So it is a time of faith, a time of trust, a time that calls upon you to reach into yourself and feel which is the loving path and which is the path of predictable outcome.

600-Year-Old Spirits in a State of Panic

This battle is taking place not exactly in your time. Those who would control the outcome at all costs, many of them are in a time six or seven hundred years ago, and even further distant times of the past. Your time is a pivotal time for the change, not only of your dimension but of your whole universe. As I've said before, one of the factors of this change is that not only will your future be re-created, but also your past. Those who would control you from the past are frightened now, because their world is being uncreated. As a result, they are having a call to arms. They are inciting all of their nefarious allies and calling all the incantations they can and pulling all the strings they can in order to slow down your progress. But it cannot be slowed.

Now, how will this play out in your daily life? On the one hand, if you get into a bad mood – whether it be brought on by something expected or unexpected, whether it be simply a case of depression about something in the past – you will be susceptible to control by these forces. Because when you are in a bad mood – angry, despairing, depressed – you can be manipulated, you are vulnerable, you are susceptible. But if you make an effort to stay in the now, where your power is, you will then have the opportunity to experience the ongoing love that is building not only from the angelic realm but from your own creative energies. So the challenge to you now is that you cannot afford to be depressed anymore. You cannot afford to be overly angry. Yes, if you're anger leads to some resolution and it needs to be expressed, you do not have to suppress it. Express it in some constructive way, a con-struct-ive way. But if you are involved in destructive or self-destructive anger, you again can be manipulated.

How about an example of that manipulation. Let's say a man is fired from his job. He's angry, resentful, depressed. And he gets deeper into those feelings, not only because of being fired from his job but because of everything else that has ever made him angry or resentful or depressed his whole life. He then is susceptible to being manipulated into what you would call an overreaction — perhaps a violent act — instead of just getting angry and maybe cussing a little bit or taking a beer can and smashing it as flat as he can get it. He will be manipulated by those in the past who would like to create a destructive chaos for you. And he might perform some perverse, violent act, being self-destructive and destructive to others.

Here's the key: As you know, you are coming into a time of creation, literally imitating Creator Itself. What always precedes creation is a form of chaos. Chaos can be constructive or destructive. The key here, what to watch for, is destructive chaos. So I've given you some tips on how to avoid it. This should be considered a warning, because this will be a factor in your lives through 1998. But it does not have to be a gloom-and-doom thing. Remember, it's all right, if something bad happens, to get angry and express that anger appropriately. But it is not all right to get depressed, resentful, carry that anger around and spray it in every different direction, because then you will become susceptible to being manipulated by the evil forces from the past, which can very easily destroy your life and the lives of others through an attempt to create chaos in your society and to slow you down in your spiritual progress.

So your job will be to be able to take things in stride. That will be tough sometimes, but if you can do it, you will improve your own mood and be able to quickly recover from any and all difficulties. I know that sounds easier to say than do, but I recommend it.

Let's see, 600 years ago — that would be about 1400? 1300?

Roughly from the 1150s to the 1380s.

Who was it? Were they the ruling clique, the ruling elite at that time?

Not the apparent rulers; people more underground. These would be forces of what you would consider nowadays to be something along the lines of incantations, what do you call it . . .

Witches?

No, I don't want to call them witches because witches are good. I would rather call them forces of corruption willing to use any and all means to control and maintain their authority. They might use satanic means, but they would not believe in them.

But this was before what we're calling the secret government that controls the Earth was organized?

Yes.

They were just here and there — people who had that inclination . . .

Pockets of resistance, but organized.

All over the world or just in Europe?

Well, there were some in northern Ireland, some in northern European areas and the continent itself — underground, always underground.

"Underground" meaning not known, or physically under the Earth?

Both. Their meetings would take place underground, though they did not as people live underground, and underground meaning not known, also. Some were in what is now known as Poland, some in what has been called Tuscany — Italy, all right? Then some in the northern African area. Some near Monte Carlo, a little bit south of Monte Carlo.

They do not have current branches or anything like that — it is not something happening in your time! It was happening then. So these beings, they forswore going into the afterlife and they remained in spirit attached to the Earth to control. They are not human — they are in spirit — they would be what you might call evil spirits. And they are being uncreated.

And they will be totally uncreated by . . .

By the end of 1998. But they will be attempting to influence you, so you must make some effort to notice when you are overreacting in anger or when you have the feeling to do something way out of proportion to the cause. This will not be easy. But you can do it.

And they're influencing all of the Earth now?

Yes.

TV Hackers and a UFO from the 8th Dimension

On A&E, between 10 and 11 p.m. on Sunday, May 14, this was flashed on the screen four times, about one minute each time: "jW!+dIR,]zfN19=?÷B00E01Sac>ú+m." That line of code across there — was somebody talking to somebody? Does it have any importance?

This is an interesting thing. This is why you have an FCC. This is someone who managed to break into the signal and send what would normally go out on the Internet. That's the way I'm going to talk about it now. I'm just going to say this about it. It was not transmitted by the A&E network, all right? Someone broke in and transmitted it.

Good guys? Bad guys?

No need to put it in either category.

Okay. Also on television, they showed a light flying over the mountain at Luke Air Force Base. The military people refused comment, ducking cameras and leaving the scene of the TV camera crew when the reporters tried to question them.

This was reported when?

Channel 11 in Phoenix, channel 15 in Sedona, 10-o'clock news, May 14, 1995.

This was a genuine UFO. It was not associated with any earth-bound inhabitants. They are beginning to break through your electronic warfare and they are utilizing a form of technology that cannot be disrupted or interrupted in any way. You could drop an atomic bomb on one of these things, and after the smoke cleared, there it would be, because it is not physical as you know physical to be. But it can appear in a physical realm such as your own. This was coming from a star system beyond Arcturus; this is all I will say. It can travel trillions of light years in a microsecond. And it could make – for the sake of the amusement of your statisticians – about five million trips between the Earth and, say, Saturn in about 3/4 of a second.

Okay. Dimension? Purpose?

Origin: eighth dimension. Purpose: waking up the people on your planet, breaking through the veil of secrecy that is placed upon "identified" flying objects.

All right. So are they the only ones able to break through, or is it that once they break through, then others can come through?

They are utilizing technology that has been loaned to them, and they will freely loan it to all others who have their hearts in the right place and are attempting to come in and show you all that you're now a member of the Council of Planets. You do not have to *do* something to do this; you've been signed on by your cousins of the future. It is understood that there are [negative] forces that are resistant to people knowing this at this time. But they [eighth-dimensional lightship] are here, and for those who are afraid that they are Godless: they are not. They recognize God, they recognize Creator, they recognize love, they recognize heart. Do not fear them on that account. They will be friends, and will not harm anyone. Do not believe any stories you hear that they have harmed someone. This will be a falsehood. They can be recognized because their ships will be of light. And since they are ships of light, there is virtually no means available to the secret government or any military force to prevent their appearance.

So, headlines: "Earth Signed on as Member of Council of Planets"?

Signed on by your future brethren! Grandfathered in, you might say.

Are they going to be all around the planet? Are we going to see more of this lightship?

You're going to see more of it.

One ship or several that look alike?

There will be many.

Are there any areas in particular they might be concentrating on to show themselves?

Central and South America, northern France, possibly the southern Netherlands, Australia, New Zealand, possibly Madagascar, the Aleutians — generally areas where people are used to seeing them. Possibly northern Africa, around the Mediterranean.

But not so much in the United States?

Not so much in the U.S. You'll have some, though; you've obviously had one here. But there is an ongoing thing. Even now as we speak, many governments have established people to study it, and many newspapers in other countries have established people to regularly write about these events, and it's appearing in newspapers all over the place. Your country is like isolated. It's like isolated, man.

Next you'll be dancing!

Dangerous Chemical Sprayed to Provoke War

Okay. On May 23, three black helicopters sprayed what witnesses thought was insecticide over an area. People had bloody noses for two days. They touched a pickup truck and it was all gooey. They're monitoring the foliage and soil samples to see if the foliage is going to die.

These people must contact their congressmen and senators right away. They must get attorneys. This stuff is not insecticide. It is a foam that must be analyzed; it is a cousin to dioxin. It is not safe. If there's any place you know where it exists, try and scrape it up and get rid of it. This stuff is a way of saying, "You're not welcome here," even though this might be your land. It is — to put not too fine a point on it — an act of war.

Do not use this as an excuse to shoot on other black helicopters, because they want you to fight amongst yourselves, see? This would be a case of, say, in the case of two hostile forces, a third force that derives its strength from having people in opposition with each other. They would go in dressed like one of the hostile forces and perform an act of violence against the other one, and then the two forces would be fighting amongst each other so they would not see the third party standing on the side. Because once those two hostile forces unite and look at that third party, the third party will appear very weak and easy to conquer. And to be perfectly honest, your secret government is not so strong, they are really quite weak, and they can easily be conquered through means that do not involve violence. So be very careful about these acts — they are designed to provoke you! They are designed to get hotheads amongst you to take rifles and try and shoot at any dark-colored helicopter that goes flying by. This act of war was designed to do that. Watch out for these people! They will try to provoke you. They are truly *agents provocateurs.*

This chemical is highly dangerous. Gather as much of it as you can. I might add that after 24 hours or so it decomposes into something that does not look very dangerous. But if it should happen again, gather it up right away, get it to a laboratory as fast as you can (an independent, reasonably decent laboratory). Have it analyzed. Call your congressmen, complain to your senators. Tell them that as far as you could tell, these vehicles did not have military markings on them, and they appeared to be . . . you don't have to say black helicopters; say they appeared to be private helicopters. By saying *private*, you establish the potential for lawsuits, see? So that's the way you want to go with this. Go see your doctors, get physicals right away. Accumulate any doctor bills you have, get a good lawyer and be prepared for a mass lawsuit against somebody; but get it rolling. Don't just lie back and take it, and don't let them manipulate you.

Okay. Well, this relates to one particular instance, but there might be many more that we don't even know about.

That's right, that's who I'm talking to.

Indications of a Conglomerate Earth Force

Okay. Why these troop transports? Why are they touch-and-going up at the Sedona airport?

You know, on the surface it looks kind of scary, the idea of the United States military being usurped by foreign powers. But you have to remember, you are in the middle of the world order. And the initial face of the world order is that all militaries will become kind of a conglomerate Earth force. And while that might be kind of scary at first — having soldiers walking around the streets speaking a language you don't even understand — it does not necessarily mean that your country's going to be occupied by a foreign power. But it is truly the case that your legitimate military as well as the global military, which is what I would call it, is training for control. The United States is considered to be a dangerous country because the people can own guns. In other words, they can resist change. And many people in other countries consider the people of the U.S. — not all, just a few — to be dangerous, because not only can you own guns, but you can easily obtain weapons, and objects that can be easily converted into weapons. To some extent this is accidental, unintentional, meaning these are items in daily use that could be converted into explosives or some other kind of flaming weapon, which you would not necessarily know unless you've studied the chemistry.

So let's just say that the world government is proceeding a little quicker in other places, and a little more cautiously here. But — and this is a big but, or a giant but — a lot of this is taking place in what you might call the hinterlands. Almost none of this activity is visible in big cities. This is because it is believed by the powers that be that those in big cities are basically going to follow what is. Because they're used to going to supermarkets and such, they will be more easily controlled. They are not going to be growing food, you know, they're not off the grid. They're not, in other words, independent. They are dependent and interdependent. In this sense, they are not seeing military sorties over their cities and towns. So I would say that it is people of smaller towns that are more likely to see this kind of activity.

Wait, now I'm lost.

It's kind of a military thing — black helicopters and all this kind of stuff.

So it's secret government stuff, not U.S. military stuff.

Yes, secret government.

Okay, we have to make that point, since we have two groups.

That's right, but the world is, as I've said all along, going to go through a short period in which there's going to be a not very good world order, based loosely upon the corporate model. Then you're going to quickly shift — quickly in historical time — into a more benevolent world order. But you have to recognize that the less benevolent world order is going to try to put a face upon itself of something that is more international. That's why people are seeing troops from other countries and things in other languages — things written on this or that, and vehicles disguised as United Nations vehicles. But of course you know, United Nations vehicles are painted very light colors. So it will appear that they are a force for some good. The United Nations does not now, as far as I know, promote any force that has vehicles painted dark colors.

All right. Well . . . where would we rather be?

Right here where the action is.

Where the action is. Okay, I'm done.

Then I'll say good day.

Thank you.

13

The Time for Compassion

YHWH through Arthur Fanning
May 29, 1995

Indeed! A lot of things going on around your planet. One of the things that is going on now, in one manner you beings are playing toward another world war. You will not be allowed to blow this planet up. If you cannot govern yourselves, then your humanity, you will be governed by others, what you term from out there. It is time for your world leaders to understand this thing. There are spiritual forces, they exist. There are your extraterrestrials, they exist. They are here now, and whether they show themselves will be up to you, because the first showing will be taking your ability to govern yourselves away. They will do it for you. You won't like it, because they will bring spiritual law with them, not your human law. You are still in a phase where you may choose wisely, but you're quickly approaching that point where you will not be allowed choice any longer.

As for this date you be worried about [June 5, 1995: landing date of ETs prophesied by Pope John XXIII], you may consider it still a probability. The movement will depend upon your wisdom. Many of your world leaders now are being talked to in their sleep, so to speak, some have being given visions. The visions that they are being given is a path, what you would say, "If they take this path, this is the result." Do not have to take that path. We will speak in this manner: If the event does occur, it is because of mankind's foolishness, and not his sacredness, not his display of his sacredness. So in that manner the event will be fearful from your perspective, what you see, because you live in fear, you play fear.

This month called your June is an outrageous month, what is termed spiritual understandings. There *is* a quickening, *within* the beings, because you have not been taught and refuse to remember that you are all one. As the oneness approaches, fear rises up within you. You must let that go. Everyone breathe here for a moment, take a breath. Lighten up.

Your life *is* forever, always will be. This is the time for compassion! And compassion also includes action, compassionate action. That does not mean threatening another.

There is a great possibility that you will see this great armada (and it's more than one ship, by the way) appear this month coming, your June. You will not be able to turn to your government to protect you, any government. You must turn to you, to that Light that borned you, that was you when you were born and that is still you. That Light is what remembers. Your guides will assist you in this thing, you all have them. Your inner harmony will take you through these times.

Now, you must remember that before you were born you knew the probabilities of these events occurring, and you chose to be here for them. In one manner it's exciting, because you all like excitement. There is also a lot of humor here, for those that *think* they know are going to be the ones into the most confusion. It will be the ones in their innocence and the little ones that are innocent, that know the innocence of what you term your Father here, that'll make it through. No big deal. Why is it so difficult to believe that God loves you all? Who told you differently, who told you one was better than another? It is your competitive behavior. That is all right, you'll learn. You're all delicate lights, living. Why not allow *all* beings to experience beauty, why?

There was a decision made what you would term in your years '85, your '84, not to blow this planet up, so to speak. So too the Hierarchy, what you term the angelic forces, came here in great numbers to shift, help you shift. And you started, and then you stopped as always, didn't complete. It is the cries of the little ones that are being answered now.

There is one on your planet, one being, one human, one, that is playing what you term the atomic bomb. This one is an irrational being and he plans to use it, as it stands now. So *that* will be interfered with. If you could remember your divinity these things would be so easy here, but there are those that refuse to, and that is all right. But they will *not* win!

Part of the game is this force you call the Antichrist and his opponent. They are about to show themselves, each one. Initially it is going to be very difficult to tell the difference, who is who. Don't choose. Don't pick a side. They have their game to play. Choose you your divinity. And if you don't know any better then pray, and if you know a little better then meditate, and if you know a little better than that, love God. You're into outrageous times now.

Toward Your Future Divinity

One of the things you can do to assist others, human form, is to understand that you are being manipulated *away* from your divinity, individually, each of you. The way to acquire an immunity to this is to desire to know your divine light each moment, and one of the easiest times is upon your going to sleep, desire to know your divinity, desire to remember, and the same upon your waking moment, desire to remember. Desire. It'll happen. And allow others this thing. Communicate divinely with one another, you will find your conversations becoming very much more profound, yet not as long. You will find your telepathy increasing tremendously. There is no need to chitty chat all of the time except to experience the wordings out of the mouth — for fun, not for controlling or confusion.

These are the times you have been reading about in your books, this is the shifting of consciousness now. It is arising within everyone. That consciousness is you before you were born. It is the you of your future in one manner. It is the you that loves you more than anyone else, anywhere, anytime. It is the you that has been with you forever, and it is the you that remembers God, what you term Father. It is that you that is arising. Let not this thing called separation interfere with your divinity. The understanding of these things will prevent the confusion that is coming, will alter it. If you do not, you will be allowed to play portion of your war. You will be allowed to play portion of your fear and your understanding of what death is again, but the planet will not be destroyed.

There is a possibility . . . it is a probability, within what is termed the next two weeks that some will decide to shift spiritually — we're talking a lot of beings on your planet — and that will create an easing of these things. If that does not happen, however, prepare for your visitations. You are dealing with divine forces now. Give me a moment.

Now, because you are lightbeings — you are electrical force in your body, your consciousness is electrical here in the physical — there are those that are aware of this thing on your planet, and they have the desire to manipulate your electrical currents in a manner, and they do this by impinging your force field, your auric field, with thoughts, thought pattern. You can either accept these as yours, or know they don't exist in your belief system and let them go. Remembering your divinity will allow you to know which thoughts are yours. It is simple. It is really very easy.

Now, one of the easiest ways, even in your greatest density, to get through these times coming will be to eat what you term fruit and your vegetables. Their frequency is not harmful to your movement in this time. Your denser foods will block you, and they even carry what you call energies to limit you in a manner. Fruit and your vegetables, and your grains, your beans, and you don't need too much.

I will tell you another thing that hasn't been mentioned before, yet some of you can understand this. You are each connected what you would term to a ship, what you term ship, spaceship, we'll call it a ship, by a . . . we're not going to say cord of light – that's not the way it works – but there is a telepathic connection to your ships. You belong to a certain grouping of beings out there. They haven't forgotten who you are, you have. If humanity doesn't get it together and cease the nonsense here, those lines of telepathic communication are going to be opened rather greatly and you will think you're going crazy, because you will begin to get instructions, literally hearing. This is why it's important to remember your divinity and to know whose thoughts are whose. Your ship thoughts will override everything, because you are connected to that armada that is coming, that is here, let's put it that way. It is part of your home.

Now, what you interpret as the appearance or as the visitation of Mary is in greater understanding use of your belief systems with an image to communicate to you. Because of your idea of separation and the way you personify energies, these appearances are for those in certain belief systems; they're adjusted to communicate. Now if you beings are wise, you will look at the places that Mary's visions have been, and you'll understand the message given there, and you'll look and see what's happening there now. The message was warning, "If you don't change, this will happen." There are wars going on now where she has appeared, every place. She, the vision, using your words now, has been in what you term your Texas, and is now at this time in your city here, south, you say your Phoenix. If you don't change, the energies will be there to make you change. The sequence has been this: to love God and your brothers here. If you don't, you will bring damage to your beings, and every place she has appeared, this has happened because you didn't pay attention. I say to you, check it out.

You are in an interesting decade. The world is not coming to an end this June, you're going to make it a little bit longer than that. Exciting changes. Your year 2002 is an outrageous year, your year 2015 is even more outrageous. This planet exists in your timing to what you term 6,000 or more; 15,000 is a possibility, even in this density (your words), because this sphere that you are on is manifested by the thoughts of the beings that are upon it, and you all work together in this creation, in *all* of your creations you agree to play here. It is not the time to go hide into a mountain, or to what you say run in fear. It is time to understand the divinity of all beings, each thing, and the consciousness of a rock.

Compassion is going to be needed here now in this time for all beings, outrageously so. Compassion not only for the physical form, compassion for the light that was born within the physical form, without what is termed the secularization of religion.

Lot of fun. It's going to make a lot of beings nervous; that is all right. It is part of your journey into wisdom.

Even have compassion for those that become ill. Compassion toward the Light there as they are gaining wisdom through this process, for there are many that are going to become ill.

You've been tricked out of your divinity. Don't blame the one that tricked you, don't blame anyone. Desire to know that light that you are. It is not spiritual mumbo jumbo. You may think so, some of you, but you're going to live through these times. Don't get caught in the confusion of it. Do you have a question?

The specific dates given in the Journal *— June the 5th and July — are they expected to really unfold? The people following the* Keys *of* Enoch *and the* Urantia Book *had specific dates, too, but they didn't materialize. Is this going to definitely materialize?*

There is a probability that it will. There are many forces now working to shift this. There is a probability that it will occur within the next two weeks, yet we don't want to do it that way, because what we will do is we'll be governing you. You're going to get overlords at that time, and there *is* a chance that it doesn't need to be done. I will say you this thing and I will put it this way: We love you so much that we desire you to understand you here, and many are getting assistance now to shift.

This month called your June is what you term an X on the map, crossroads. So the entire planet is being watched over. We are already here, we are around you. We are in the light that is in the room now. All we have to do is quicken the frequency, what you would term from your side, quicken you, and lower the frequency be us, and be there. Because of your training and your indoctrination, it would frighten you, and we know that. So we are looking very carefully at, is there any chance, any chance that we don't have to do this? And as long as there is the slightest chance, we won't. Yet if it becomes a necessity, say you, this idiot uses his bomb and can't be persuaded not to, and another does, and another does, we'll stop it as the thought comes.

There is a grouping now planning to create an atomic war. The being that has this one that has what is termed lost his mind, is actually being influenced. And there are his host, angelic host, that loves this being, that are working desperately from their manner to *change*, to get this sense of compassion and love within him to open a little bit not to do this thing. So yes, this is a very critical time, this month called your June. I will say you this: If you make it through your June, the first three weeks, without any great game in the sand [that] idiot boys play with one another, then your July will be a great place, an energy of peace. It'll be like a "Phew! We made it through." There will be another little bit of tension in your August, but not as intense as is building now. So it is a very delicate process.

One of the things you don't understand is you are divine human, you are divine god in a manner, from the Father, and there are many upon your planet that desire, *desire*, in their light in a manner, ignorant as it is, for these ancient prophecies to come about. Know you? They think the hosts are going to rescue them and save them, and everyone else will die. Well these ones are going to be very surprised that they be the dying ones. Know you what I mean? So it is a delicate situation here.

You have forgotten your divinity so much that you rely upon others to tell you what it is, and whether this race is divine and this race is not, or this church is more divine than this one and that one. It is ridiculous, and that is still what is going on, this control thing. This month, indeed it is, your June of 95, an outrageous month, what you term in the understanding of spiritual forces and in the understanding of who you are on your planet.

More a Game Than a Plan

So, a specific date, we will say you, *pray* that it doesn't happen. *Desire* that it does not happen, and desire that these ones playing with their toys can gain some wisdom. If they do not, you will be governed by other forces. So don't look to your June 5th to see the end of the world or the great change coming. Use your entire month, because what you don't understand is that we are shifting time for you, we are bending it so it collapses a little bit, hoping you gain wisdom from your future selves. So we've sort of blocked out part of what would have been your history, we've altered it. And you're meeting portions of yourself now that *do* desire this place called Eden to exist. Consider not specific dates. They are, in one manner, often used to create hysteria, to control you and to limit your ability to know your own divinity, your part in this plan, this game — it is a game more than a plan. Understand? Yes, this month called your June will be very interesting. Your June 5th will pass very quickly, with a Phew! The next two weeks through your June will be more intense, however. That is where you're going to have to know that you love God. And wish and hope that others playing their game can understand that spark that exists in all things. They will not succeed in setting off these bombs; *that* will be altered. But they will attempt to and that is what we are watching. Because you are all loved, even the madman with this thing starting this contemplation, he is loved greatly. Not more, not less than you. He just doesn't know it. Did that explain?

Yes. The way I see it is that this is a wonderful, complex drama . . .

It is.

Having written our script, I guess we're all trying to improve on the script.

You have written your script and you've forgotten who wrote it. It is this way: you are familiar with the concept of reincarnation, and you are familiar with other concepts. The memory of the reincarnational experience, however, seems to elude you at times — you don't *know* that you did this thing. You have trained the body that it is not a thing. That is all right because you judge some of your reincarnational experiences, you forget them. It is called forgiving self. Forgetting is forgiving, know you? When another injures you, you say, "I was insulted." If you forget it, it never existed and it is a forgiving. You understand the energy and the flavor, you don't move into get even. As you know your experiences reincarnationally, *how* you did it, *why* you chose each journey — to gain more wisdom in your light forces, in your soul power called emotion here, because it was fun, and it is. When you're out of your body you enjoy being in the body, what you term spirit. You have an ecstasy there, an orgasm you term it, and the light enjoys the physical, and you *play* forget. Some of you think it'll confuse you in this time, that's all right. This movement through these planes now is accelerating, and for some there is a lot of anger toward God, other deities, it's all right. Lot of blame there, didn't want to be born, etc., etc. That is the portion of the identity that is working through the play and can't understand who wrote the part that it must play. It is a lot of humor. So be not caught up in the fear of this thing.

A Greater Ability to Heal Yourself

Another thing, this what you term your August period: there's going to be an acceleration in the ability of the physical body to heal itself, if you allow yourself to go through this and understand the wisdom of you. The human body, the physical form now, along with the identity consciousness you call your ego, your thought being, is going to realize how easy it is for itself to heal. Those memories are going to come back, how to fix this thing with the light forces and the electrical systems that you use. That is what's big deal in August. Look forward to it. Outrageous fun. Indeed. Does anyone else have any other questions?

Being electric-magnetic, is there any simple way to raise our frequency, such as by concentrating on love and getting our state into a loving state? Is this the most effective way?

Because your concept of love is different than what exists in truth, and because there are other entities that play with love to manipulate you, one of the easiest systems to use in your own physical form, know you, what you term physical, is to say, "I" (meaning the being called you) "arise" (means speed up) "the vibration that I Am." So if you say, "I arise the vibration I Am," those forces in your soul, in the electrical currents, begin to quicken because you are in charge here. And then you'll get a greater pulse of light through your body, and you'll move into what you call a different perspective. All of the chakras begin to enjoy this increase of vibration. It is a felt thing in the body. The skin literally becomes softer because of the electrical current that begins to flow through it, sort of like brand new, do you understand?

Yes, when you consider that the brain is 97% hydrogen and oxygen.

A lot of water in there, fluid around it. That's what gets excited, also. Now, there is a part of all beings that is very innocent, no matter how cruel they are, and it is that part that is portion of the Father that is within you, and it is lavender fire. It is innocent. Even though it has been around for eons and has seen all of these things in many places, it is still innocent, because the game continues forever, it doesn't end. This innocence dwells within you, within every being, and it's that innocence that wants itself to be remembered by you.

Like a child.

Indeed, even beyond that. Know you your Father, what is termed God, the original Creator, He is innocent, innocent One, and He is in ecstasy at everyone's play. He is innocent. No matter what has ever happened or what will, He has still held that innocence, for He enjoys *all* of his creations. You see? It is an outrageous thing. And it's a good thing your Father is innocent, it is a good thing. I use your words here to explain.

Now, for those of you that are living in what you term your California, you're going to have exciting times. I will tell you this thing: pay attention to your dreams. I beseech you on this thing. If you must, write them down and look, because your guides will be talking to you.

As we operate from the concept "As above, so below," and considering the multiple lives each of us is involved in, then this expansion of the ability to communicate to billions now, literally billions of ourselves, must be happening on every level.

There is indeed a union becoming, more than a communication now, a union. All things are known out there, so to speak, what you say telepathy. It is a river, and you simply move into the river to know. There is becoming now a union of light. A union, a merging.

Well, light is a vibration.

Indeed. It is also . . . well, from your perspective it's a personality. A personality that has a collection of his experiences, and it declares itself as this thing, a form, a symbol, display.

The Buddha and Jesus consciousness, and Krishna and Mohammed and so on . . . I don't know if it was your channel who mentioned the fact that these entities themselves are evolving.

Indeed, they are. In a manner, I'll tell you this thing: Know you the one that is called Sananda, you say Jesus, indeed? He was one, with two other beings (Buddha be one of them), that petitioned greater forces to assist here. He, Buddha, he, Christ, Jesus, taught some of these greater forces compassion, what it was to be compassionate. Because they, Buddha one, Sananda, they existed in the human form and understood the ignorance here. If it hadn't been for these beings, the greater forces would have terminated your planet. These beings have so much love for the human condition, and they put forth such a great petition, that they are the ones that in a manner, what you would term, from your perspective, saved the planet. Yet that is not known here. They understand the difficulty here, and they taught compassion to what you term the gods out there.

The Dangers of a One-World Government

I have a question. In the past year I've been hearing a lot of fear-based information about the new world order and a lot about the detention camps and all this stuff that's been coming up about the government's control of the people, the population, and the dissolution of the Constitution, and all of this one world government stuff. I'm wondering about the reality of that, and how it will play itself out.

Well, one of the things you must understand is because of your borders, you separated yourselves from other beings. Know you, one country, border, another country, different beings, different laws. And it was needed in the expression called human, to play in different arenas what you would term called cultural understanding. One being wants to play in a sandbox painted red, another being wants to play in a sandbox painted blue, another white and green. It is a culture. As you evolve more, you understand that you are all one, and you share your culture now, you teach, and you blend with one another, and you become a family, planetary family.

Now, because you've been trained so much about "These be bad guys, I be good guy; this religion is the best, and this is second best," you created separation. So the fear within this that you've been trained is what is coming up. It *would* be a good thing that you had one planet here, one system, no borders, you had no enemies. There *is* going to be this completion of this thing, this one-world thing. There are those, however, that want to be in power, in control of this one-world thing, not spiritually focused, however, in a manner of this ruling thing, an aristocracy. So it will be allowed to play in the blend that the aristocrats think they're going to win, know you? But before they do, and they're convinced because everyone believes the aristocrats, know you, and as they let the borders go and everything becomes even, then the host, what we term the angelic host, will appear and say that is enough of the control attempt. This is indeed the way it is to be. It is one planet, you are one race, one *human* race, and you're all spiritually mixed here, you are a blessing, indeed, to the galaxies. So the game will be played, but it will not end the way some think it will. The fear is, however, what you've been trained with. Know you what I mean? So that is the way the Hierarchy is watching this thing. Let them play their game. Let the fears be overcome. Your neighbors to the south love you. You neighbors to the north love you.

The only thing you've been told is by others that say they don't. And money is always an issue, know you?

So too with your churches here. There will be one that wants to become the world universal church in these new things, and it's going to be metaphysics. Don't get caught into this thing. Understand your own divinity, that you are divine no matter where you are, each being on the planet should understand that thing. When it happens you're in your Eden now. You understand? It is really very simple. So yes, in a future time, your borders will go away. There will be a confederation that will be, we will call them administrators. And the cycle of the administrators will be taken from what you term the average population, the general population. Won't be an election in that manner, it'll be a knowing of the Light that shifts these things. Different. You don't have the concepts yet.

You spoke of almost a divine intervention if we don't get our act together. How does that coincide with the basic premise of free will?

Free will is out the window now. You've had it. We've seen what you've done with it.

Hasn't that always been the basic premise of God – to allow His creations free will?

It is allow. It is an innocence that is what is termed free will. You are not innocent in your play now. You are being ignorant. You are well aware of these things, humans, what you're doing. So yes, your free will has sort of been taken away. No big deal, you'll get it back.

I have a question. Is there going to be any news about the weather? There has been some thought about large hurricanes on the East Coast, something to do with global warming, perhaps . . .

In the greater truth, you beings are walking on your planet, and you are part of the Father, and you have consciousness, and your consciousness is shifting. Because you are an electrical being, light, as your consciousness shifts, you shift the consciousness of the poles, the consciousness of your planet, the electrical forces, the magnetics —you shift it. In the shifting, you are shifting the weather. Your consciousness is shifting, the weather is changing. You are doing it but you don't remember. You think the weather is getting erratic. It is, because your consciousness is shifting rather erratically. You've already had winds in excess of what you would term 300 mph at your mountain tops, 400, and they can't explain it; they don't know what is going on. And yes, it is going to be that windy down below, down here. You've got four major winds moving across what you call your continent within the next three years, exceeding 300 miles per hour, because of the shifting of the magnetics around your planet.

That would blow away most towns, wouldn't it?

Be a little breezy. It'll be outrageous.

Underground, I guess, is the safest.

It'll be a little bit underground, yet what will happen, however, is it'll be windy one place, know you, but your guides are going to tell you, It be time to take a little vacation. It be time to walk across the street." Pay attention. Because consciousness is shifting now, you are getting closer connection to your guides, all of you are —very close power with your spiritual forces, and they want you to listen. That means *shut up*, know you? Be quiet and listen! And they tell you to move two feet, I would suggest you move two feet. It is time to quiet this ego thing you play with and pay attention. Everyone on the planet, *everyone* will be warned, everyone. Everyone. It is up to them to pay attention, it is. And if you don't, it will simply be an oops, and you'll pick another lifetime. See, no big deal. You'll be born again, you just can't remember being stuck in that little body all over. So it is going to get windy. The weather is going to get rather dramatic, it already has. It's becoming rather obvious now, indeed, and the earth is going to shift and change. Part of the fun. Never move into a thing out of the fear thing. Contact your knowing, it will tell you. Some of you need to be at specific places for a specific purpose. You're not aware of what that purpose is yet, but you must be there *before* you discover the purpose. It sounds confusing but it isn't.

In the drastic weather changes, and the predictions of the tremendous loss of life in Africa, for example, as you say, it's little dots, entities, playing out their roles. And as we see the weather drastically change, is this part of the attempt to change consciousness?

Well, it is more, as I said, that your consciousness is changing, and it is creating this weather change. You're not aware of how your consciousness shifts and affects the weather. What you should do is you should learn from your Native Americans, you should learn from some of the aborigines, the ancient peoples that remember how they think and how weather is affected, what they do to affect the weather. They communicate with animals, and the animals are spirit too, and they know how to manipulate these forces. You beings should begin to appreciate that wisdom, because you're going through the phase of initially blaming, or it is this, that, and the other. You're not aware of your place in this cog of how you're doing it. You will be. And the reason the weather is so erratic is that you're clumsy with what your consciousness is doing now. Do you understand what I'm saying? That if you associated your own power, "This is how we do this thing," and you understand you collectively get together, then these great winds and this great water and these other things will alter. You will be understanding how you do it. You're just in your clumsy phase.

Now I know some say this [global] warming — there is a warming. The polar caps are melting, indeed they are. It is simply going to raise the water level a little bit, couple of inches, yet that's a lot of water. That too is because of your ignorance. You've burned a big hole above your planet. You have beings trying to mend it now, working back and forth for you. But you are gods here, empowered, and you are allowed your evolution. We're not going to allow you to destroy this place. You've had too much free will to do that, so we're assisting you, giving you a little bit here now. If you *really* want to exercise your free will, understand what your consciousness is doing as you work; you will get more of it back.

So it's not the planet or Mother Nature doing it *to* you. It's not the planet (and yet it is) cleaning itself, because you are the manifestors of the planet, so it is *you* in one manner, assisting in the clearing and the cleaning of this place. You don't know your connection yet. You're not allowing you to remember. Know you the aborigines of Australia, know you these beings? They know the weather, they know much. So too do some of your Navajo here, they remember a little, two of them do. That wisdom is quickly being lost from your place here. It will come back. You see how much fun it is to get into density and then come back?

As an acupuncturist working with the electromagnetic field, I want to know how I or acupuncturists in general, or anyone working with the electromagnetic field, can help quicken that energy working with others.

Know you gold and silver? They are metals, they are primarily used in your world for currency. Great spiritual healing power here, great power. A piece of silver, know you silver coin? You lay it upon the heart chakra right here [middle of sternum], shiny, and then you allow what you call your needles to penetrate. This creates the white light inside, creates a memory of the vibration of it, know you, silver brilliant light. That memory will be picked up by the cell structure. Know you when you do your needle thing, include a coin here, a piece of shiny silver over the heart chakra, and a piece of gold is always wise in this arena [center of forehead at hairline], not very big, little, right here. That'll quicken, you'll get a force. You can experiment with this yourself. Hold you a silver coin in your left hand and a gold [coin] in your right hand and feel the current jump between your hands. Other metals will also work, what you term your copper, indeed.

Will using the gold and silver also assist the axiatonal therapy to quicken?

At that point you must place what you term the silver beneath the feet and the gold above the head, not touching the body. There are chakras that must be included, know you? What you say a foot above [the head], a foot below [the feet]. Don't touch the body with the coins [when] doing that.

Well, it was channeled that gold was the original motive for coming to the planet; is that valid?

It is.

I know it's an awfully powerful metal.

It is.

I was told I would be hopelessly crippled with arthritis by the age of 35, and I had liquid gold in my hips and within 6 weeks it was gone. It changed my attitude toward what's going to happen to gold.

It is an outrageously powerful healing metal, and so too the silver. That's why the beings, even though they're ignorant about how to use it, want to collect it all of the time. You only need a little bit, and it works outrageously.

The Emotional Accumulator

Is there anything, any message they want exposed on the satellite?

Because of these timings that you are in now, it is important for each being to remember their divinity that is with-in-side their being, and have the desire to know more of that divinity because these are outrageous times. It's going to be a time that your divinity will take you through, will succeed, will allow you to succeed in these things to overcome, your divinity.

What would be a clear definition of divinity?

Your divine aspect of you, that light that birthed the body, that light that imbued the physical form with its force, with its life, that it may live. Know you? Some of you call it your spirit, your higher self.

Well, is your soul also your divine entity?

Your soul is your emotional accumulator. It remembers the wisdom of your journeys through the emotions.

And what would be the spirit?

The spirit is the one that sends the soul to gather the emotion, and then when you've accumulated all of the emotion, the soul expands and what you call imbues the spirit with all of the journey. So your spirit in a great manner is assisting in manifesting the soul with the help of other forces. It was designed that way after Lucifer (we'll use that word) declared he was greater than the Father. Lot of beings went into density, lot of beings that are upon the planet now were with Lucifer when he made that declaration. No judgment, simply the limitation they placed upon their being. You're in the process of overcoming this now, humanity.

In this month's Journal [June] it says that one of the developments will be that entities will start living their lives as they were supposed to live in the Bible. This refers to the length of the lives, as they refine themselves, I gather.

Indeed.

But it's an interesting drama. People want an ending. I find in this society that everybody expects it to end, I mean they expect a beginning and an end. But we're in eternity right now, and therefore the degree of eternity and the enjoyment of eternity, it seems to me, is the realization that it is eternity.

Indeed, it's one of the ecstasy things.

And we're having a blast – or at least I am. I don't know about anybody else.

[He laughs.] You have always had a blast, most of the time.

Yeah, really, I can't believe it. I'm from Newfoundland, which is the closest point between the Old World and the New World, and it's a fascinating location because in an area bigger than California, which has got 29 million people, we've got 600,000, so there's one person every 3½ miles. You can have like the Big Sur all to yourself! I have outside of St. Johns an area of 50 acres, all waterfront. The Japanese Foreign Minister said to me, "We can't own waterfront. It's against the law in Japan." So I'm hoping that with these weather changes it's going to change 20 degrees, because it'll make a difference in Newfoundland. It may be a little hotter here, but it'll be delightful in Newfoundland because we never get over 80 degrees.

It's a very sacred place, that place. No one knows about it yet; it's a good thing. . . . It's going to get warmer.

Yeah? Well that's good. I'm waiting for sand instead of rocks on the property. Well, I'd like to thank the channel, the consciousness. It's very profound and it's very helpful. I find that it's very, very, very powerful in slowly dissolving the darkness.

We don't lie to you. We tell you the truth from the beginning, and you simply crawl to the truth – that's the way it works.

In addition to cultivating our sense of our own divinity, would it be beneficial to be doing planetary work and prayer and visualization?

The difficulty in this thing . . . it is wise to do, and if you know how to visualize and allow, you send light, but you must be careful. You send gold light, indeed, and sometimes you send white light, but the two lights work differently, know you? Say you there is a place of destruction. You see this place and you send from your being, and others around you, green light to heal. Don't tell the light what it must do, simply send the light and let the light be used by the beings, you understand? So green with gold is a grand light to do. A great power is white light, yet you better know what you're doing with that one, I'll put it that way.

As you move in this time, there's going to be a lot of movement out of the soul here and that is a good thing. You're going to understand your divinity, your light, and how it is incorporated in the body, and how to manipulate the body. Know you some of the adepts, indeed, in what you term the East? How they can manipulate and levitate the body, how they can shapeshift the body. These are the experiences now that are going to be come to the Western world. You're going to be allowed to play in this more, but it will not happen in your cities or in your lower level of consciousness. These are the things now that are being shared with everyone to create this unified planet. I'm not going to use "new world order" because it is not a new world order the way they want to do it. A unified planet. You're going to share the magic now and get over the superstition. That is always wise.

So your June is going to be interesting. Do not put fear upon this date, your June 5th. Your two, three weeks into it, understand the energy shifts, and you beings can send love to the planet. Send you green-and-gold light to whoever needs it. The more you share your green-and-gold light, even the thought of it, you'll get tenfold back.

Unconditionally.

Unconditionally. Send it to areas and let the beings use the energy. It is like they feed off of it when they need it.

Well, I think that's a banquet of material to feed on. We appreciate it. Thank you very much.

We are through.

14

A Vehicle from the Atlantean-Lemurian Past

Zoosh through Robert Shapiro
June 19, 1995

Note: Photos 3, 4 and 12 have been enhanced
in order to reproduce in black and white.

T his ship *[figure 14.1]* is related to the famous photo of the Gulf Breeze vehicle. It looked a bit like a crown in its radiance. This is a much better picture of a vehicle of that type. Again we have a vehicle associated with the past — not the past of this planet, but the past for the source civilization of the Atlantean-Lemurian civilization (I'm combining the two because Atlantis grew out of Lemuria). The source civilization was closely associated with the point of origin (where planets are formed) at the center of your universe.

One might ask what people like this need to have ships for. In reality the vehicles they use are for their guests. These are beings of light. They can travel without ships, but when they wish to have visitors, guests as it were, travel with them or even to pick up guests from Earth, as they sometimes do — this is not abduction, these are guests, people who have been informed they will be going for a ride — they bring along or manifest a vehicle like this. This creates a vacuum from the past to the present and an illuminated videographic reference point that allows people to feel as if they are in something solid, when it is actually a vehicle of light.

This picture has a significant capacity to wake people up. And

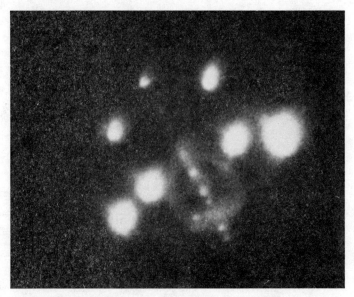

Fig. 14.1. Gulf Breeze-type vehicle seen in Sedona.

the more people it gets out to, the better, is the way I feel.

Okay. Why is it so perfectly symmetrical?

Look closely at the picture and you will see a vague outline. Do you see the outline? Do you see that the vehicle is actually bigger than it appears to be? And the light reflecting off of it is actually light that it does not produce, but since it gathers light to travel, this light is, how can we say, reflected energy that is not yet being consumed.

What has it got to do with Gulf Breeze?

If you look at the famous Gulf Breeze photo, if you've seen this sort of ephemeral vehicle floating in the sky that is sort of there and not there, the general shape is the same.

Why are they here?

The area that these photos are being taken in is an area riddled with holes into other dimensions. I might add that it is not exactly safe for human habitation, because a person could fall through one of those dimensional holes and not be able to find his way back. These dimensional holes or tears in the fabric of space/time are being caused unintentionally by work that is going on underneath the surface of that area, and that work causes a warping in the time field. So I'd have to say that a person would have to remain very connected with his physical body.

This is not a good place to meditate. It would be very easy, when a person is meditating there or being in an altered state, to not have the physical or instinctual awareness that would be required to step back from something that is not appropriate for this dimension. One might fall right through a portal. I don't recommend people to be hanging around there too much. So, note to the photographer [Tom Dongo]: Do not blab where this place is.

Fig. 14.2. U.S. Marine Corps helicopter.

Figure 14.2. I pick out this picture primarily to tell you that there is an increased military activity in this area. If you're going to print it, please print it fuzzy so that men's faces do not appear; it wouldn't be proper to print the actual faces. They're just human beings like you.

This area is now strongly associated with a military corridor, and this vehicle is your legitimate military you can make out on the side of the vehicle what it says: Marine Corps. And these people are genuinely U.S. Marine Corps soldiers, genuine U.S. citizens. I want to comment that you can expect to see a great deal more of your legitimate military, not only because this area is extremely active in terms of UFO and interdimensional contacts, but also because it has been the scene of a recent battle, as we know, between the forces of light and dark, and to some extent between the forces of your own military and the shadow government's representatives. We talked about that at length before. So we must take note of the fact that when the military fights a battle and feels it has secured the area, they tend to have more of a presence there.

I might also say that because the future President of the United

States likes this area, he is, how can we say, making it known that he will perhaps frequent the area. The military is intending to make sure the area is secure, so they have now put it on a regular fly-by status. I mention that only because it's important for people to understand that everything they see that looks like something else isn't necessarily something else. It might actually be what it looks like.

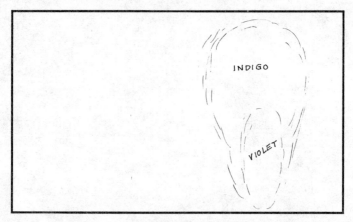

Fig. 14.3. A purple spirit from the Heavenly Host.

Figure 14.3. Here we have a lightbeing, not particularly well-formed in terms of your idea of a formation of a being, but a cloud of a being that is passing through. A true spirit, because of the color, focused from what some people like to call the Heavenly Host, and visited upon your area in order to provide a blessing. This is a purple spirit, a blessing from God.

Figure 14.4. Here we have another form of this same being. In this case the being is making an effort to form into something that vaguely resembles the head of a humanoid being. This is not sent directly from the Heavenly Host, but is rather the being itself, experimenting in your dimensions, experimenting on how it feels to be encapsulated as best it can do so. So you might say it's a spirit playing at being a humanoid.

But it's the same one as in number three?

Yes.

Figure 14.5. Here is the vehicle that looks exactly like a helicopter but is not. This is the helicopter in which Monad is actually flying. [In Chapter 10] we helped Monad to deliver his message, and that is his actual vehicle — looking very much like a helicopter but having the capacity, in that technological representation of itself, to also look exactly like a mountain. These vehicles can land on a mountain and

Fig. 14.4. A spirit playing at being humanoid.

Fig. 14.5. Monad's helicopter.

just blend in. They can sit there —you can walk right past them fifteen feet away, and if you're not highly sensitive to energies, you wouldn't have the slightest idea they were there. They might be staring at you outside of a window, looking out through the windshield of the vehicle, which, when you flip a switch, becomes fogged, and when you flip it back, becomes clear. These beings might be looking at you. In any event, that's Monad's vehicle.

Figure 14.6. Here we have, on the left side of the picture, the Council of Light, and on the right side, a visiting representative from the extraterrestrial version of the fairy kingdom. Not often seen in your skies, but around from time to time, this representative of the fairy kingdom is present with the Council of Light (the Council of Light being related to Andromeda) to be instructed on adaptation methods to alter itself. In this way members of the fairy kingdom, which is not these days welcome in too many places on the surface of the planet (I know they might be welcome in your hearts, but you need to have land that is undisturbed where they might live), can

Fig. 14.6. The Council of Light instructing
a member of the ET fairy kingdom.

remain present energetically without being sufficiently present in their natural form that they might be injured by the energies that abound here, specifically microwave, which are not good for them — or you, for that matter.

When you say ET fairy kingdom, where are they from?

They are from the higher dimensional aspects of the Pleiades. The actual fairy kingdom, the home of the fairy kingdom in this part of your galaxy, has two spots — the upper-dimensional aspects of Sirius and the higher-dimensional aspects of Pleiades. This one is from Pleiades, and they are very influential on the Pleiades, even today.

Are they the same ones that are here on Earth?

Yes. But remember that you and the Pleiadian citizens are connected, you come from the same source. It is only natural to expect them to be influential on the Pleiades, where the planets are less likely to be disturbed by technology.

A Government-Captured Vehicle

Figure 14.7. Here we have a picture of a government UFO on the ground — not secret government; this is a vehicle your government has captured. The picture was taken clandestinely, as you know, by the photographer. It was at that moment, for about 21 seconds, that the vehicle's masking system was not working very well. I don't think the occupants of the vehicle realized that the masking system was working as poorly as it was. They believed it was working at about 3/4 of its capacity, but it was actually working at only about 10%, which is why the picture shows quite a bit of the detail of the actual vehicle.

This vehicle was captured in a shoot-down incident and was

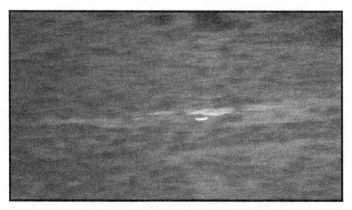

Fig. 14.7. A vehicle captured by the government in 1941.

rebuilt painstakingly over many years by your government's underground installation in Nevada (I won't say where). It does not function completely as it did before, but it can be flown, it can be masked. It does not have working weapons systems, which is good; those who were in the vehicle when it was shot down managed to destroy the weapons systems and managed to throw the switch that destroys all means of using the vehicle in any way against their own civilization. The vehicle was originally from Attyris, which is a planet in the Arcon system not associated with this part of the galaxy. The beings on board were able to escape.

When?

The vehicle was shot down accidentally during experiments in radar and sonar in 1941.

Where?

It took place on the eastern coastal regions of the United States.

What happened to the occupants?

They were able to escape.

But did they stay on the planet or someone of their own kind rescue them?

They were able to escape through the use of a light device, which compressed their essences; their bodies were destroyed in the wreckage, but their essences, their immortal personalities, their conscious minds, everything you know a person to be without the body, was able to escape in a light pod. We call it a pod because you could actually see it. And it emerged from the ship as the ship was on its way down. It would have been visible for a brief moment and then it traveled in time back to their point of origin.

Why were they here?

Why is anyone here from other places? They were here to observe, particularly to observe your World War II. They were scientists. They did not understand at that time, nor did their civilization understand, the self-destructive nature and the self-destructive capacity of human beings on this planet. They had been told that human beings, being cut off from true knowledge of their Source, had a tendency to be self-destructive as a subconscious means of returning to Source, but they found it hard to believe that Earth people could have such a capacity for being destructive. They came to observe to see if they could understand it.

Was that the first craft that was shot down?

It's the first craft that your government took notice of that came down by means other than a problem onboard the craft. So you realize we're saying "shot down" here, but we're being liberal with this term, because it wasn't the intent of those who were experimenting with the technology to shoot anything down. But it's the first one to be taken down by technological means other than a breakdown onboard the ship.

So they've been working on this thing since 1941?

Well, they were just looking at it for the first five or six years. After the war, they captured a lot of German documents about UFOs and what the Germans understood about UFOs. As a result they got real interested after World War II and started working on it. But they hadn't done much work on it other than just looking at it and marveling at it and trying to figure out what the heck it was.

Where was it stored?

It was stored on the East Coast for a while. I won't say what base, but it was near Washington D.C.; later it was moved to Texas, and from there to Nevada.

Where it's based now?

Yes.

What were they doing on the floor of Loy Canyon?

They were having mechanical problems — they knew they were having mechanical problems with the masking system, and they weren't about to go flying around above the Sedona area looking like they do. So they set down as quickly as possible.

What's the shape of this craft?

Well, it's roughly oval, with another semicircular shape underneath it.

How long? How big?

It's about 41 feet across. Big enough for a crew of several but usually not having more than one or two people aboard, for security reasons primarily.

So how do we separate these as U.S. military? I thought all the captured craft were in the hands of the secret government.

No, no, you have to understand that the U.S. military at the cosmic secret level and above has vehicles like this in genuine government bases, but they're not trying to exploit them. They are attempting to use the technology and adapt it to prototype military aircraft, but they're not trying to build up a fleet, as it were, as in the secret government's case. The secret government is attempting to build up a fleet of ships to use for control purposes, you know, for purposes of controlling your civilization. Your government, when they have ships like this, are going to study them and try to apply the technology to their own prototype aircraft.

I thought the secret government used the military to go get crafts and bring them in? How do you separate that out?

I do separate it out because . . .

The secret government has their own recovery crew?

Certainly. The secret government might have the capacity to usurp a vehicle from the legitimate military of the United States, but they don't need to. They have the technology, the capacity and, moreover, the will to go and do it on their own. They don't need your government now.

So was Roswell captured by the U.S. military or the secret government, then? There were so many witnesses in the military, 350 of them have come forth . . .

The secret government was involved, but the basic ship itself was retained by your legitimate military. I might add that some of the technology on that ship has already been applied to your vehicles that fly around with the electronic warfare — electronic warfare in this case being countermeasures and so on; the ability to interfere with anything electrical or electronic for military purposes. A vehicle like that could fly overhead and people could be watching television, using a blender, making a piece of toast, and they could just flip a switch and bang, all that stuff would go off.

I see, okay. Are you going to talk about the second picture, this one, where he turned 90 degrees?

Fig. 14.8. Government-captured vehicle taking off.

Figure 14.8. Here you have the vehicle taking off. It can take off in light, but you notice it cannot mask its shape, so its shape is apparent. If it were to turn and give the photographer a full broadside view, you would be able to see the shape, but as it is you can see the shape only generally. The vehicle should be fully masked; you shouldn't see anything but the countryside. Right there they have about 40% capacity of their masking device – still not enough. It tends to blur the appearance of the device of the vehicle, but it does not really mask the shape sufficiently, so you can still see the shape. You shouldn't be able to do that.

But the fact that it turned 90 degrees in the time it took him to take another picture – that's incredibly fast movement.

Well, you have to remember that this vehicle wasn't built by Boeing, you know, it was built someplace else. No offense to Boeing – as good a manufacturer as they are, they don't build spaceships of this type just yet.

Andromedans Coming to Reclaim the Horizontal Mind

Figure 14.9. Here we have a vehicle of your legitimate military, a military helicopter, most likely Navy or Marine Corps, but it is surrounded by little blips, as it were, of material. The blips are, in most cases, lightbeings. The lightbeings are from Andromeda. You have a lot of lightbeings coming from Andromeda these days because they're reclaiming their thought process. I said before, a long time ago, that the mental process you have in your own bodies, your mind as you have come to conclude that your mind is, is from Andromeda. It's not really your mind at all. Your mind is vertical; the

Fig. 14.9. Lightbeings from Andromeda surrounding
a military helicopter.

Andromedan mind is horizontal, in linear terms. Andromedan beings
are now coming to reclaim that, which is part of the reason people
are losing their minds, as it were! Not because your IQs are descend-
ing, but rather because you are coming back into your own consciousness —vertical consciousness, meaning you know what you
need to know when you need to know it, while also having what is
referred to as a spiritual awareness. That's why you have so many
Andromedan lightbeings there; that's what most of them are. There is
a small dot in there —can you see the dot? The dot is a probe.

The black dot?

Yes, it's a probe. The probe is from Sirius, from a very large
vehicle. The probe is observing the lightbeings. The probe doesn't
care at all about your country's flying ship so it was in that case
completely visible to the people onboard the helicopter. They could
see the probe, couldn't imagine what it was, couldn't do anything
about it, didn't feel threatened, but being military, they were cautious.
The probe was observing the lightbeings only.

Just watching them, seeing what they're doing?

Seeing where they were going, what they were up to, and
generally monitoring their behavior. Sirius is highly involved with
your culture right now, since the feminine energy is rising in your
planet; Sirius in your galaxy is the source of the feminine energy.
They are moderating, in some cases, the energy on your planet so
that the feminine energy can feel nurtured. Since the planet is so

caught up in taking care of herself, and most of the individuals on the surface of your planet are caught up in taking care of themselves, the external energy required to support and sustain feminine energy must come from the source of feminine energy itself, which in this galaxy is Sirius.

Therefore, the vehicle from Sirius, which is quite massive, with people onboard, with individual souls in various capacities, shapes, sizes, appearances, about 85,000 in number, is near your part of the universe and it sends probes out – fully automated, nobody onboard – in order to keep track of things. So they're very interested when a primal or a very condensed mental energy like Andromedan lightbe-ings shows up. They want to make sure that the mental energy they have does not spread and cause disruption in the feminine energy they are providing. The feminine energy, as you know, is primarily emotional/spiritual, so the probe keeps an eye on Andromedan beings – not because they're considered a threat but because it is in the nature of the traversing and traveling of lightbeings of any type that a certain amount of light falls off, is discarded. They are monitor-ing the discard rate of the light in order to make certain that the balance of the energy on your planet remains in a positive zone.

Are the Andromedan beings taking mental energy from humanity as a whole, or from individual beings?

For the most part they are scooping it up from humanity as a whole. This is mental energy that is not being used by humanity as a whole, so do not feel a sense of loss. But they have so far, in the past three and a half years or so, taken and returned to their planet mental energy that you have processed so that they can bring it into a better state of balance for the beings on Andromeda (see *The Explorer Race*). They have taken so far about 7% of the total mental energy that is available to the entire human race.

When will they start taking more? What is the percentage as we go through the years?

It's accelerating, as you know. They are now taking about 2% per year – 2.1% per year.

How is it going to accelerate? Exponentially?

No, not exponentially – that would be too much. But by 1996 it ought to be about 3.2% per year; by 1997 it ought to be about, maybe, anywhere between 3% and 8%. Now I can't say why, but there's a potential for an occurrence in early 1997 that could allow people of Earth to get much more instinctual, much more open to their heart energies, much more cooperative with the angelic kingdom, much more balanced physically, instinctually, heartwise and lovewise as you understand it to be. If this event does take place, the mass event will affect everybody on the surface of the planet and it will be a benevolent event. But I cannot talk anymore about it at this time because I do not want to give the secret government any more means than they already have to interfere with the event.

Okay. Thank you.

Fig. 14.10. Military helicopter attempting to track a trinary UFO.

Figure 14.10. If you look closely at this one, here we have another legitimate military vehicle of your government that is attempting to track a trinary UFO. A trinary UFO is a single ship with three disks; it is barely visible off to the side of the picture. You can't see all the disks. He's attempting to track them using what amounts to magnetic-wake-diffusing optical enhancement technology — how's that for a mouthful? It essentially allows them to not only detect the magnetic wake of a vehicle as it's moving but also to extrapolate a best guess as to where the vehicle is going as a result of that wake or trail.

But there's another white space over here on the right side. Is that something else?

That is a probe.

Oh, that's a probe? From where?

In this case it's a probe from Andromeda watching the action because the vehicle that is being tracked is from Andromeda. It's not a physical vehicle; we're not talking about a vehicle that's masked. So there's no hostile action being planned or considered by the beings onboard the helicopter or by their commanders; it is simply being tracked because they now have the capacity to do so. And as you know, when people have the capacity to do something they are more inclined to do it.

And they're all light? The probe and the craft are all lightships?

Yes. Ruling out the helicopter, of course.

Fig. 14.11. Cosmic trail of a lightbeing passing through
from Resonance Nine.

Resonance Nine: Origin of the Shape of Human Red Blood Cells

Figure 14.11. Here we have a wonderful picture. This one is a cosmic trail of a lightbeing passing through and it showed up on the picture. The lightbeing is made up of forms that are very similar to the red blood cells within your own body. The red blood cells within your body are an actual form of life from another dimension, from the seventh dimension of the galaxy of what I'd call Resonine — that's a contraction; their galaxy would essentially be described in your language as Resonance Nine.

Your red blood cells, the form of them, are very much in the cosmic hierarchy of this being. The shape of your red blood cells is not an accident. They are actually associated with the galaxy Resonance Nine, and this particular being happened to be passing by, visiting, as it were, the place of Resonance Nine's allocation of their shape and function. Your red blood cells are this shape so that you cannot be corrupted beyond a certain point.

You have heard about, read about, and some of you might have experienced, a person who appeared to have virtually no redeeming qualities whatsoever. But if you look beneath the surface you will be surprised to find that even the most monstrous person — and there are a few of them out there — has some redeeming qualities. That is because Resonance Nine's influence on the shape of your red blood cells does not allow corruption past a certain point. So that being was visiting its society's creation, passing by to experience compatible shapes.

It is interesting, is it not, that some cultures, like this one, would consider a race of beings to have personal resonance or value on the basis of its shape, rather than on the basis of any thoughts or actions or instincts or demonstrations belonging to a particular race of beings (Earth people, in this case). This culture gauges the value of civilizations entirely upon the basis of their shapes, and groups and subgroups them according to the shapes of the beings. Resonance Nine considers your people to have some value in spiritual countenance because your red blood cells are, shapewise, their offspring. Of course, they also feel that they have a proprietary interest in your civilization because they have loaned you, from their point of view, one of their primary shapes. And they fully intend, when all of you have evolved past the point of having red blood cells like this, to reclaim the shape, because you'll be past the point of susceptibility to corruption. They will reclaim the shape, and that will be that. And then when you have fluid running through your veins it will not take the form of a red blood cell and will be somewhat flexible in its parameters and dimensions.

It's not clear, when you say light trail . . .

The white is essentially the trail. The shapes within the trail are Resonance Nine beings.

There's no way we could catalog it according to what we know of creation? It's beyond and above what we know in our galaxy?

Well, I would say that it's far beyond your capacity to communicate with directly, unless you chose to communicate through meditation process whereby you would focus entirely upon shapes as a means to communicate. You could not communicate verbally — they would consider that a base form of communication. They would consider communication in shapes to be the only thing of value. Basic shapes would be the start of the alphabet, as it were, the square, the diamond, the circle and so on, and more complex shapes might be the basis of more complex levels of communication. In a way, one might say that alphabets are combinations of shapes, but they are, from their point of view, a base example of it because the being is entrapped in these shapes and cannot use its own shapes, as it were.

Fig. 14.12. One Xpotaz vehicle pursuing another that is attempting to escape.

Figure 14.12. You can barely see it, but this is the pursuit of one Xpotaz vehicle by another.

The one Xpotaz vehicle is pursuing the other because in the vehicle that is being pursued, the beings have gone conscious! And they are attempting to get away, but of course they are being pursued by a vehicle that is equal to their own. They have not gone sufficiently conscious to know that (a) they can ask for help, and (b) they can, by using their conscious white light selves, make the ship about twice as powerful. This cannot be done by people with evil intent, but it can be done by people who are connected to the angelic kingdom through their hearts. They haven't achieved that yet, but they are attempting to get away. As it turned out, they didn't get away, but they did manage to crash the Xpotaz ship, so they have one less vehicle to use, and in that sense they were able to serve the cause, as it were, valiantly. Of course their souls left their bodies afterward, and they were welcomed by the angelics, so that was interesting . . .

The ships they can replace, but there are so few beings connected with the Xpotaz that they must really be running out of beings, aren't they?

Yes, they are, you can be darned sure they are. A loss of two or three people—in this case two persons plus one almost-person, meaning a person that was partially involved in a mechanical supplement (not unlike in your old days, using the iron lung), partially robotic but an actual person—is a grievous loss, a serious loss to them.

This was over Massachusetts, so where did the ship actually go down?

It went down in the ocean. They knew they couldn't just crash it somewhere, so they took it down in the ocean to a depth at which it was crushed by the pressure. They took it in as a physical ship, so it was crushed as a submarine would be crushed if it went too deep.

And they knew what they were doing?

Oh yes. They knew they couldn't get away, and they didn't want to go back to living in that circumstance, so they essentially committed suicide and took the vehicle with them. The vehicle was crushed beyond all possible means of repair. It's still there, by the way — it's just a lump, but a well-searched scout mission by a legitimate military of any country could probably find it. They couldn't use it for anything, but it would be a curiosity.

Where exactly?

I'll just say it's in one of the trenches. I won't give an exact place; they've got to do something, haven't they? Let's not make their lives too easy! It wouldn't be any challenge if I told them exactly where it was.

Figure 14.13. I'm not going to comment on this over here, I'm just going to comment on this [right edge]. A lot of people would say this is a flaw, but it's not a flaw.

That black blob on the bottom there?

No, I'm talking about the white light. That's not a flaw at all. That is a compressed lightship that was traveling from one dimension to another. It wasn't traveling to your area. It was traveling in time from second-dimensional Earth to ninth-dimensional Earth and just happened to pass through your dimensional existence at the moment the photographer took the picture. I mention it because it's kind of interesting to know that sometimes vehicles pass through here without giving a care as to what's going on here. It's just kind of caught in the act of traversing the subway line, as it were, kind of like taking a picture of an "el" as it whizzes by on the track in Chicago.

A Hole to the 85th Dimension

Figure 14.14. Here we have a hole in space. If you'd been in a plane and flew through that, you would have wound up in the 85th dimension of (I'm going to do the best I can to pronounce this) Ark'achit-sant'sa.

85th dimension?

This area was experiencing, at that moment of that place (I'd

Fig. 14.13. A vehicle traveling in time, passing through this dimension.

Fig. 14.14. A hole in space to the 85th dimension of Ark'achit-sant'sa.

rather call it "that place" than try to say it again in your language), a complete collateralization, meaning reforming, of the entire process of their being. And once upon a time, their souls passed through the third dimension of Earth, before your souls got here, and as a result, in the moment of the photographing of that picture, they were photographed in the process of blending all that they had been into all that they are. They have now achieved a level that is slightly (though it is hard to conceive of this) greater than that which you know as the Creator. They are paving the way for Creator to go to Its next level.

I've said before, and I'll say it again, that you are here to learn how to become creators so that you can give Creator a little time off and Creator can go to the next level. How, you might ask, might Creator get there? We've talked about that before. Not only is Creator going to be given a boost by you, but It will be pulled by these beings who will essentially grease the rails of the next dimension, and they will also help to create the next dimension for the Creator. Hard to conceive, I know, that there are beings that are more than your Creator, but it is so. After all, Creator knows that there is something more. How does Creator know this? Obviously, the same way you know it — through inspiration. Where does that inspiration come from? Voilà! From beings like this, who have the capacity to be more than your Creator, to welcome your Creator to the next level. Your Creator will now have the capacity to see more clearly what is in the next dimension, whetting Creator's appetite, as it were, for that next motion forward, and creating a little more fire, as it were, under the spiritual toes of all of you here on Earth to come more quickly into your spiritual expressions of yourselves to replace Creator, hence allowing Creator to move on up.

There's something you don't hear every day.

The Original Thought of Earth

Figure 14.15. All right. Here we have a reconstruction of the original thought (I'm going to call it "thought" for those of you who believe that thought is the foundation of all things, just to give you a little support there, even though it's actually the original *inspiration*) of what became Earth. This energy was re-created in that moment to give Earth a model. She's going through this struggle, you know, to re-create and rebuild herself without using all the means she has available, which

Fig. 14.15. The original thought of Earth and a visitor from Arcturus.

would essentially decimate your population. She needs a model that she can use again, the one by which she was originally created. So here we have essentially a model for her to follow, not unlike a highly complex cosmic blueprint.

What's that light on the bottom?

A visitor from Arcturus. You know, they're always involved in change, and they're there to watch the action, as it were.

Watch the action of Mother Earth looking at this blueprint?

No, Mother Earth applying the change as a result of looking at the blueprint. Mother Earth had to, because after looking at that blueprint, she was on the wrong path, a little bit off. She had to recreate the structural dynamics of her own auric field in order to regenerate the proper photon/ion balance and create the echo resonance of her permanent structural bias. Say that ten times real fast.

So does this have anything to do with the energy of the Photon Belt? Is she using the energy of the Photon Belt to do this reconstruction?

Yes. The Photon Belt Doctor, as we have called it, has provided her with a means by which to utilize this "technology."

And did he help call it forth?

No, he didn't call it forth, but he gave Mother Earth the means by which to utilize it, let's say the tools. She had wanted something like this but she needed to have something that was sufficiently physical so that she could use it. You have to understand that Mother Earth is a *material* master, and now, because she's going through all these changes, she needs to have something that goes beyond spiritual. She needs to have something that is actually a form of mass by which she can reconfigure her harmonic identity.

So how did this original thought suddenly show up in front of her? Did she call it forth?

She learned how to call it forth by using a reflection of certain photon and ion particle images to amplify the request, not unlike praying and receiving an instant manifestation of what you prayed for.

Where did this manifestation of what she prayed for come from?

Well, there's the rub. It did come from Creator, but it came through Creator. It came from the upper dimensions of Creator, what we talked about in the previous picture; I'm going to say it came from Creator's guides. It's really important for you to begin to think of Creator as someone and to realize that Creator, while being inspiration and All That Is as far as you're concerned, is not All That

Exists Anywhere. If we say that, we're really honoring all that Creator is but not necessarily all that Creator has full access to. Creator is all that exists everywhere, but does not have full access to that, which is what you're going to help Creator do when you give Creator a coffee break for a few millennia.

I understand. And we don't want to ask you who some of these guides are.

You don't, because we do not wish to distract them. If many people start thinking about them by their names, they will be distracted.

Fig. 14.16. The eyes of the Imp.

Figure 14.16. A moment. Have to get permission on this one. Okay. Here we have the eyes of the Imp. Everybody has a certain amount of impishness in them, and here we have the eyes of the Imp looking at you, the spirit of impishness, if you like, literally looking down from the heavens at you, admiring its work. I might say that impishness is really designed to bring out the comedian in everybody, and it's designed not only to give you support and sustenance but to help you to take it all lightly, so that you don't get too caught up in the trials of day-to-day life, so that you can laugh not only at yourselves (which you do very well) but at each other from time to time, which is most beneficially done when one is laughing at oneself I might add. The best kind of impish behavior is that which makes a joke of oneself and includes others, making a common ground, which is what the spirit of impishness would like to do. He is feeling fairly good about it, since most of you on Earth do have the capacity now, no matter how mundane or traumatic your situation, to be able to laugh about it, laugh in the face of unhappiness, which is, from the point of view of the spirit of impishness, a great success. I can't help but laugh at the picture, though; you know, it's kind of amusing.

We've never heard of this fellow before. Tell us, where does he come from? Does he hang out with the Creator? Does he travel around the galaxies?

He is more what I would call a member of the pixie world. (I'm calling it "him," but it is not male or female; it is more of a pixie.) I'm calling it that for lack of a better term; how can you describe something that is a first cousin to humor? But I can only say it hangs out wherever its resonance is felt, or for that matter, wherever comedy is felt. Wherever good humor is felt—it can go there also. But its particularly fond of going to check on places where true impishness exists. This is not capricious, that you have impishness; its designed. And this, how can we say, is the prototype designer.

All right.

Figure 14.17. Here we have the large image on top receiving a request from the smaller image on the bottom, as it were. This is an appeal by the smaller image to allow Earth and the denizens or citizens of Earth (meaning all citizens, all living physical beings on Earth) to be released from all laws, aspects and thoughts of the preservation and the application of the doctrine of karma. Now, I said quite a while ago that karma isn't happening anymore, but as people continue to think about it, it tends to linger, so we have here a being speaking on your behalf to ask that people let go of the belief in the influence of karma.

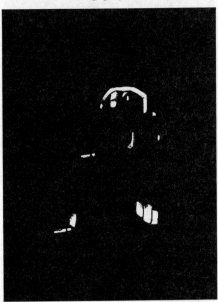

Now, on the one hand (and I'm not attacking religion here, by the way), karma is a way to explain why things are the way they are. And it was very valid in the past. But now, since you're beginning

Fig. 14.17. Shiva asking the Lord of Dharma to release Earth from karma.

to recreate with Creator, you need to get past the limit of cause and effect. Cause and effect are valuable when you are denser beings, but you are not as dense now, nor will you be as dense in the future. So you need to get past the idea of cause and effect, which I realize is a very rudimentary description of karma, but since we're not going to talk for another two hours, it's the description I will use.

Who was asking, and who was he asking it of?

Shiva is asking.

All right! And who was he asking?

Oh, I'd have to just say that Shiva is asking the Lord (overseer) of Dharma.

No name for that?

That's a pretty good name right there.

But there is a name, and you don't want to tell us.

That's right. I'd rather give you the explanation of what it is rather than go into a long name associated with it.

Okay, and how did the conversation end? What was the answer?

The answer was yes, but we must allow for the fact that karma is at the basis of one of the greater religions here, and as a result, the belief in karma will be allowed as a thought longer than it is allowed as a practice.

Which religion is that?

Well, there's more than one, but basically we're talking about religions of the East.

Hotheads in the Inner Ring

What's the update on our friends in the secret government?

Well, what we're having in the secret government these days is a certain amount of breakdown in the inner ring. The inner ring of the secret government, as you know, are those who are really at the core, and there's a certain amount of breakdown there. I'm not going to say they're coming to the light; it's a little too soon for that. But they're beginning to breakdown in factionalism. This is perhaps a little dangerous, because there are factions of the secret government that just want to grab for power and say, "Okay, we're in charge, tough luck for the rest of you guys" and just be brutal. But there are other aspects of the secret government that are perfectly willing to move slowly, in slow, calculated means of grabbing for power, which is what's in effect now, and would just as soon stick to the plan, from their point of view. So the hotheads in the inner ring of the secret government are threatening to branch off and grab for power on their own, essentially telling the rest of the members of the inner ring to, how could you say, kiss off.

While this would appear to be cause for celebration, it could be extremely hazardous because of the weapons technology available to all members of the inner ring, and because if the hotheads break off they will be perfectly willing to use weapons technology not only on other members of the inner ring, which would be their first targets; they won't care at all about who else gets exposed to it. So if one member of the inner ring was, say, in Dallas, he'd be perfectly happy blowing a hole in Dallas and injuring a great many people. So we're in a ticklish time right now. The threat begins between July 3 and July 17, but accelerates into August, September and October.

I'm going to ask your readers to do something you probably haven't considered doing. I want you to imagine the inner circle or the inner ring of the secret government. I don't want you to imagine what they look like, I don't want you to tap into their power, I don't want you to tap into their strength or energy or anything, because you can be affected negatively. I want you to just get a cartoon like image, as it were, something enclosed in a circle or a sphere. And I want you to try and place within that an energy, a flame, as it were, of red light. Now, you might say, why not purple or gold? Well, for one thing, they have the means to deflect that. They do not deflect red. Red is a color they cannot reflect, or deflect, for that matter, or even dodge. Red light will cause them either to reunite or to break up entirely. This is a calculated risk; if they break up entirely they'll be extremely dangerous for about two-and-a-half years — kind of the warlord situation. On the other hand, if they come back together, they'll just get back on track where they are and things will be resolved in their own proper time.

So I'm going to give you an exercise. You can either visualize red light in there, but make sure that you put gold light in the center and surround it with red light. Red light will not cause them to feel pain, it will not cause them to feel anger, it will not cause them to feel, period. But it will help them to tend to see each other as allies. I realize this sounds like helping the secret government, but it's not. The secret government is infinitely more dangerous broken up than they are as a unity.

So last time, when we talked about the terrorists, I asked was it the terrorists or the secret government, and you said that it was hard to tell them apart. That's because some of the split-off ones are starting to act like terrorists?

That's right. They don't care at all about the Earth — the Earth is a product to them, as, I might add, are the people. Consumers, one might say.

But they'd have no place to go, so . . .

They do not perceive it that way. They believe they could go to the Moon, and from there, utilizing technology which they believe they could capture, go out to the other planets — Mars, and so on.

So I will say this. There are plans in effect to keep them from going too far and to keep them from doing too much. But for your part, the more you can visualize within yourself the golden-purple flame, and let it expand out all throughout the universe and, most importantly, throughout Earth and Earth's auric field, that's the best thing you can do for yourselves right now. But for those of you who wish to help, let's say gold light in the center and red light around it. Red is the basis of life on Earth and it's also associated with the basis of transformation. It's associated with many other things, but for inner-ring members it would be as close to transformation as they can get. Nevertheless, you can put a little gold marker on there; that might be good too. Put it in the center. Anything else?

We have a few minutes left.

Then let me say this. The star system that I refer to as the Bear is becoming more influential in your lives. It is providing you with inspirations, it is encouraging people to be more active physically. You might notice that sometimes you're nervous for no reason you can think of. Usually that means your body wants to be in motion: this comes from the Bear system. Perhaps when you have nervous energy you should be a little more physical, even if you just get up and walk around the block; that's good enough. Or, for those of you who can't do that because you're in wheelchairs, wheel around the block. Try and push the chair if your arms work; if they don't, move your body around to the extent you can.

What's happening essentially is that nervous energy is really being transmitted to you, not to make you nervous but to stimulate your physical muscles into action. People who live in the Bear galaxy, as I'm calling it (it's almost really a dimension, but I'll call it the Bear galaxy) are very knowledgeable in the electromechanical functions of all that is physical in form. That is why they are sending you this energy — to encourage you to be more physical. Sometimes it is difficult to be physical when you're going through major transformations, as you are now. But it's just as important for you to be physical now as it was in the past, so try to make your meditations more physical. Try to do more dance in your meditations, try to be up and around, because this will help you to integrate your meditative states into your day-today life, something that is important so that meditation is not separate from life. You understand?

Do we have a name for the Bear constellation?

No, I'm just going to call it the Bear constellation – that's what they call it.

Don't we have a name for it in our star charts or something?

Yes, you could probably look it up if you wanted to, but that's not them actually. The Bear dimension, call it what it is, is actually something in a different dimension . . .

The Bear you're talking about – how does that relate to the bears that are in the Earth, the keepers of the Earth?

The animals?

Yes – well, the bear people that live in the Earth. Is there any relation there?

That live inside the Earth? You're talking about . . .

The she-bear people, who are related to the constellation of the Great Bear . . .

No, they are not related to them. They are related, however, to physical bears, what you know as physical bears on the Earth. Perhaps you have walked in the forest and seen a bear at a distance, walked by or near a bear, even looked through a telescope, and the bear appears to be stopped and thinking. One might assume that the bear is using its instinctual body, but very often, at least half the time, they are connecting to the Bear galaxy. Bears are, needless to say, not native to the Earth.

Ah, so they're connected to this other-dimensional group. Oh, yes. All bears . . .

What is their purpose? What are they really doing here?

They are here to support, sustain and encourage the manifestation of spiritual physical motion.

Really? But they hibernate!

Why do you think they do that? Because when they are in that state, which is really a deep meditative state, it is not sleep per se. In sleep the body rests; this is different.

What's the meaning of their long sleep? Getting instructions or something?

They're being home as much as they can be.

Because they don't want to be here?

No, they're willing to be here, they volunteered to be here, but it's not an easy place to be. Especially when surrounded by human beings who think you're some kind of animal, whatever that is. You know, the so-called animals have no idea what animal status means and why you don't understand that they're equals, from the tiniest ant to the largest gorilla or elephant; they're all equals. They're just people from other planets. Just because they don't look like you and they don't go digging things out of the Earth doesn't mean they're not conscious.

15

A Great Armada of Consciousness

YHWH through Arthur Fanning
June 16, 1995

F or those of you that we played with this past weekend, how are your bodies? [He laughs.]

Feeling unusual.

Feeling unusual, that's probably a good thing. What are the usual feelings?

Familiar stuff.

Familiar. Would you rather feel familiar all the time?

No, I want unfamiliar.

You want unfamiliar?

Mm hmm, it's okay.

Well, I know it's okay. It would be interesting to watch the energies in the body as you communicate with the body, to tell the body it's okay. Know you, you talk to the body instead of arguing with the energies when it comes in, because it's just more of you, you understand? It is a part of you that you've forgotten that is coming to you. I know some of you think it's all mumbo jumbo, but when it begins to get right next to you, your body goes all sorts of goosey.

That's it, goosey. That's the way it feels.

I'm learning your words. Stand you up a moment. There is also a connection from this arena into right here, from the spleen to the center of the back. A lot of you are going to get energy pain here. It is where your greater light anchors in the body, life force. It wants to distribute itself through the body. Some of you play you're being attacked. In some cases it would seem true because it is your past lives coming to you. Ho! Ho! Oops! You thought you forgot that past life, didn't you. [Laughter.] [To a participant] How be you?

Well, can you explain what happened to my body on Wednesday evening when I sort of wilted?

You were preparing to disappear and you hadn't trained the consciousness of the physical form that it was okay.

So it got worried or something?

The physical consciousness and the ego portion of you hasn't been trained. You neglected that job this time around, but you're going to remember.

I'm going to remember . . .

To train it!

Any suggestions on the training?

Speak gently to it, tell it it's okay, know you? Know you what I mean? Lot of shifting going on in your consciousness, entities. Yet it is not the game you thought you were going to play. A lot of you thought you were going to play with this great energy and ascend. Ho! Ho! You're still here. You're playing with the energy in the body now, physical, in the form physical. You are living the process. You are living it so you can remember how you do it. You can remember what it feels like to be physical when these great energies that are you become, become the master when you remember you are. So you can remember what it feels like to be the master, to be the power, to be compassionate no matter what's occurring; to get over your angers, your hatreds, your jealousies, because they are going to all be reflected in your own body. Everywhere, all things are the Father, everything, and that is the process you're learning now. Can you see the humor? On the other side you're laughing like crazy at yourselves. Everyone take a breath. For those of you that are a little nervous, sort of stamp your feet a little bit. It'll ground the energies. [To a participant] How do you like flying?

Well, I'd like it better if I didn't crash.

If you didn't land on the ground, you're saying. You didn't crash! You told yourself you couldn't fly and you proved you were correct.

You're right.

I know, I usually am. [Laughter.] Just an attitude of mine.

Some of you used to come here and want me to talk of your past lives. Well, I didn't oblige you on that one. And some of you I've talked to about your future lives, only to show you where your thoughts are and how you can alter the future. Now don't judge your future, however, by your present, because your future is going on right now. To judge it by your present limits it. Little sidelight there. Everyone lighten up.

The energies are going to get stronger and stronger as you play in your year here. You've got two weeks steady, know you, of calm energies — your first two weeks of July. They be sort of mellow-out level, they won't go down. And then you're going to get ten times more than you've been getting lately, just for your information, know you, through the end of the year. So if you think your libido is in check now, or it's getting excited, just wait!

Now there's great power in sexual activity, that energy. You can literally use it to lift the body off the ground when you understand that your gravity is not a pull, but a push. And these energies are here so you can play with them. Play! You're allowed to see. You're allowed to have your visions. When you do have your visions do not interpret them with old patterns; consider them brand new gifts to you; and they are new! They won't fit into your current structure because you don't want them to. You want the newness to be new, new, new, and it will be, really! It's going to be great joy for those of you that can maintain your center, your power points, knowing who you are. It'll be great joy for those of you that can't, also. [Laughter.] You will create humor for those that are watching that know, and you'll create humor for yourself pretending that you don't know.

You've heard the term *personal responsibility* metaphysically, indeed? It applies spiritually (your words). They are your energies. Everyone take a breath. This is not the end of the world; it is the beginning of a new consciousness, and you're right at the birth stage. That's why the body is going through its changes — you're birthing new, indeed. [To a participant:] How be you?

Pretty good for somebody who's been on the edge and back.

Had a rough time.

Rough. But it was a good experience.

All experiences are; wisdom is gained through all. There is no good or bad. You had a *Phew!*

I sure did.

You think the body physical is sort of fun to be with now.

Right.

Indeed. It is an honor that you're still here, for me. It's also an honor to have a body, know you?

I realize that.

You're an outrageous being. I'm just trying to figure out who doesn't mind getting cooked. How much energy do you think you can handle this evening?

[The group responds:] A lot.

A lot. A lot, a lot, a lot. A lot, eh? Let me check the level of a lot here. We'll pick the lowest level of a lot — that'll keep everyone safe, eh? And then we'll squeeze the highest level right into the lowest level so it's the same thing. [Laughter.] The time for pampering you spiritually is over. I have a reputation and it is not for pampering.

[More laughter.]

Meditation

Allow your eyes to close gently. Open the heart chakra. Just tell it to open, it'll open. Open the crown chakra wider, top of your head, and feel a golden ball of light there. Peace. Allow that golden ball to enter the physical form. Allow. From the center of your heart chakra command a violet flame to be there. Let it move up toward your throat. Allow. Your perineum, your root chakra, feel a ball of fire there, red and gold. Feel it. Take a breath inward down to that root chakra. Hold it, and as you breathe out let that ball of fire come upward to the crown. Peace. Allow your eyes to open gently. Peace. Center. We're going to bring your guides in closer to you this evening. They're your guides, part of your energy field. Maybe you'll listen to them a little bit. Allow. Be comfortable with that energy.

Now, for some of you that don't know, I'm the one that assigns the guides. And it's not always the guides' fault that they have to go back to guide school. Sometimes you wear them out so much they need a rest. [He laughs.] [To a participant:] You've been through quite a bit, indeed?

Yes.

Can you let it go?

Yes, gladly.

And accept the new, indeed?

Yes, gladly.

So you accept new thoughts and new things, and the old is simply gone away because it was experience to get you where you are now. When you allow that newness in the body, the body becomes younger. It is the old thoughts that make the body old, know you? Everything is going to be all right. Have you ever heard the expression "Forgive them Father for they don't know what they do"? That be wise to hold in the body right now, know you?

I will.

This week that is coming you're going to get very sleepy, indeed, so allow yourself that rest. It'll be likened to going to sleep in what you term your ancient mother's arms. Bargain?

Yeah, bargain. Thank you.

You're ready. Let it happen, indeed; you'll find it much more fun and thrilling. Everyone breathe a moment.

[To a participant:] Now when you have this thing you call your [eye] glasses, indeed? What does that mean to you?

It means that I don't see well without them.

Indeed. Now, do you have control over these forces at all?

I used to think I did, but lately I'm very curious. It doesn't seem to fit.

It doesn't, because what you're seeing you don't want to see, and sometimes you don't want to hear it, either, know you what I mean?

Yes, I'm having a problem hearing.

Indeed! You don't want to. You'll hear what you want to hear, know you?

Don't we all.

A lot of you humans do, it is very humorous. Indeed. And when you do that, you shut down patterns that are in here [within the brain], you create blockages in the circuits in here. Know you? And you say, "All thoughts will always fit within this pattern because I want it to be that way," in this portion here [brain]. Know you? Now your higher self, what you say your great mind, exists around you, and it has a lot of love and energy. It knows its road map, so to speak, in here [brain], and sometimes it can't get in because you say, "I will only accept it this way." Know you what I mean? Know you how you need . . . "This is one rule, this is second rule, this is third rule, this is the only way it can be!" Indeed? Know you what I mean? Very analytical. Indeed? Analytical.

I'm a retired engineer, yeah.

Have a grand time. [Laughter.] Now, your greater light knew you in past lives. It knows you in future lives. Knows you, loves you, loves you more than any other being, your light. The concept of light is not

. . . well, it is known by some of your scientists now . . . that light lowers itself in frequency, it has consciousness. And as it lowers itself in frequency it becomes an electrical current, and that electrical current registers behind what you call the left ventricle of the heart to keep the heart beating. Now, that is *not* what you call your physical light. It is what you term, your words here, a spiritual light. Spiritual encompasses *all* things, *all* life force. It encompasses *all* religions, every one, and you are in the process now of learning that it is a oneness. Now to *define* that oneness you're going to create a limitation. Your words that you utilize, any system of words is a label, a definition, and it creates a structure. You're going to go beyond words. You're going to go into telepathy if you will allow yourselves. So what you're playing with, and why you think your higher self is lying to you, is that in truth, in this system, in this new consciousness coming, *you* are lying to *yourself.*

I've had practice.

I know! That is all right, as long as you can what you call *feel* the experience in the body that something is going on, know you, and when you decide to search for the truth, it'll always take you right back here [soul], not here [brain] — this gets it last. This [soul] is the one that knows, this is the one that enjoys to play, this is the one that knows freedom and the desire for it. It is in here, what is termed the soul. And it exists, it is a real force. Know you what I mean?

I think so.

Would you care to have a little journey?

All right.

Indeed, I take you on a trip this evening in your sleep. Know you your weekend, the weekend that you're coming up to? I will take you for three nights out to play, to show you. Bargain?

Bargain.

It be fun. Maybe we'll get a little libido activity going, too. [Laughter.] This is the one that wants this [he goes to another participant]. You think I don't hear things, that I'm not around. [To the participant:] How is your body?

Good. Cooking. Cooked.

It is simply more light, know you? The reason it be hot in the body is the resistance. Know you what I mean?

Is that it — resistance?

Indeed. The thought forms that you build your body out of you say only exist in this manner. The light comes in to change them, know you what I mean? You're an outrageous being. You're still in that mode, know you, when you built the pyramids. Remember? And you wanted everyone to walk through them just because you built them, know you? You said it would be good for them. What was the purpose of the pyramids?

Manifold purposes.

It was to remind you that the soul is inside you, indeed, and it was initiation. And you're all going through it, in your body, through your own soul, your own levels of initiation —you're living it! Even the process of death is an initiatory process. Now, don't go out and kill yourselves to be initiated! Hang on here. I am telling you a truth. You've lived many lifetimes before; you've forgotten them purposefully because you judge them. But the experience took you to this time. You're not being punished. You want to remember, you want to remember how to do it. And you want to become the power and know it. You want to meet your extraterrestrials as friends, as buddies. But before you can you must know who you are, indeed, literally. They're not coming down here to what you say pick your brains for your superior intelligence. You have to be out of your mind to think that. Most of you are. They're coming here to share, but your capacity to understand love is very limited. They want to *share* with you technologies, and the moment that word comes, "share technologies from the extraterrestrials," many go into a military thought form: "Well, we could conquer the planet!" Well, that be going on right now, and it's not working. We put a stop to that. So some of the extraterrestrials that have been playing around with you beings are sort of looking for hiding places. They're not being very successful, by the way. Everyone take a breath. Lighten up.

Everyone and everything upon your planet is sacred and holy. Always has been. Even the murdered and the murderer, still sacred. (Everyone breathe.) In these new energies you're going to learn to choose your games, your plays, your movements, yourselves, without limitation, because your light is coming and it is going to *drag* the body with it! You used to play in the old paradigm where you dragged body along and light follows, and now the light is in charge. And that's why you're having some of the energy patterns going on, and you're confused in your days, and your reality seems to be shifting on you, and you can't see right, and you thought you saw this thing, and "Do beings really exist right beside me? I see all these lights on the side of my head." It is shifting. Some of you say it is fourth-dimensional activity and fifth. Well, that is simply a word to describe an elevation of consciousness, that's all it is. It is an awakening is what it is. In one manner, it is the Christ returning, that consciousness returning that knows all things. You've played such a fearful mode that you don't want everyone to know all things. It is all right if you know all things about them, but the moment they know all things about you, you move into a density. You hide. You create a lower level for yourself, you *think* you hide. Well, you're not being very successful. Everyone take a breath. Lighten up. Anyone have anything they want to chat about? [To a participant:] Have you been listening?

Yeah.

Who's been talking to you?

Oh, I think you have.

Well, besides me.

I think Sananda has.

And besides he?

St. Germaine has.

And besides he? Will you get off this male kick!

Uh, Mother Mary.

And what is Mary saying to you?

I think the message that I'm getting from her is to be more gentle with myself.

Pay attention, bargain?

Yeah.

Would you like to sleep with her this evening in your arms?

Yeah, I sure would.

It be good thing.

Can you tell me what happened Monday when I lay down . . . I didn't think I was going to nap but I did . . .

A lot of beings are lying down unexpectedly in the afternoon.

Right, well this is what I did, and I went somewhere and I saw millions of bubbles and beautiful yellow lights and beautiful green lights, and just bubbles, and the words that kept coming to me in my dream were "this is creation," and I was unable to wake up. I just was unable to wake up. And when I did wake up, I looked at the clock and it was 4:30, and I walked outside to get my mail, which is a two-minute walk, and when I came back in it was ten minutes to 5:00, so there was a collapse of time. What happened?

A shift.

In me?

Of course, and your environment that was around you. Everyone that was around you felt that. When you become a master and you move more, what happens is you have the ability to manipulate *your* consciousness. When you manipulate your consciousness, because you're all connected, you manipulate the consciousness of everyone around you, you shift things. Know you this ball we talked of here [etheric golden ball in the palm of right hand]. It's part of that little game. I'm not ready to get into that one yet, however. So have fun with this thing. It is called becoming more psychic, and psychic is becoming more god – that's all it is. No big deal. Becoming more in your own power. Everyone breathe a moment.

You must remember that I read thoughts. Some of you, you think you think here [brain], but you think in each of your chakras. So concentrate on what is going on in each chakra here. Some of you have little energy bubbles in there that can't quite contain themselves; they're popping out, sort of interrupting my conversation here. I would advise you to center your being because I'll answer every one of them. Ready for more energy?

Indeed!

How's the body? How's the head? Do you get a little pressure in the head sometimes?

Yeah, a little bit.

I want you to eat grapes – know you grapes? They relieve that. Purple grapes create a memory of the sweetness and the lavender, and your headache goes away and more energy can come in. Understand?

Yes.

[To another:] How be you?

I feel sad.

Is it fun?

No. I'm trying to decide the right way to move out of it.

There is no right or wrong way, indeed. What is the way is the movement, the power – know you how you feel in here [within the body navel region], the energies? This energy, because it is moving over here [toward the center of the body], it wants to move up, what you term in clarity in the body, and . . . I have to be careful here. Each process of moving up creates a new journey, and creates a new experience. Sometimes you become comfortable at the present way station, so to speak, as you're moving down the path. The energy then begins to decide, "Well, this being doesn't want to go further," and it begins to disperse here, but as it disperses, the energy itself wants to come back and continue the journey. At times, the energy as it disperses in the body becomes an excuse not to continue the journey. Know you what excuse is? Know you what I mean?

Yes, I know what you mean.

So that is what is going on. Journeys are always interesting because when you're going on them, you never know what you're going to find, so there's always a little bit of apprehension. Yet each step of the journey is part of the initiatory process, know you what I mean? You are playing with this energy that is right here [navel chakra], and it wants to jump up into the solar plexus, know you, because that is the base of the soul: it wants to make that connection. I will tell you this: it is going to make that connection. Know you the word allow? That means to allow you, know you what I mean? That'll settle it.

Thank you.

Don't thank me, you've already set it up. I'm simply sort of pretending with you that you don't know. [Laughter.] [To another participant:] How be you?

Fantastic! This is a whole new experience this week. I'm compassionate and it's very interesting.

Getting more. Compassion for you is indeed interesting, even in other lifetimes.

Something happens and there's a little tiny start of [anger] and then there's something different. I love it.

Indeed. You're becoming more powerful, too, know you this?

Knee Energy

I want to ask you a question. A couple of years ago I asked to embody the energies of a particular being and you said my knees would hurt. I forgot about it. My knees have hurt for about two or three years. Is it soon to be balanced?

There be a lot of activity in the knee energy for everyone now. It is a shifting of your light. Now I have to be delicate here because you beings take what I say and interpret it in this level of activity, but it is really another. Let me add a thing before we go to this. In your compassionate manner you're beginning to find out they're picking up your thoughts, and that is sort of straightening things out rather quickly. You're getting very focused telepathically. That's a better way to do it, indeed.

Now, this knee thing: in the knees, one of the anchor points, the great anchor points for the lightbody, is here [outside edge of knee-caps]. (Everyone take a breath a moment. Want to get this clear here.) When you play die in your bed as you do your thing, these anchor points have to be released, opened. A lot of beings will go through three or four years of these anchor points creating jerky movements when they try to sleep – the knees become very active. The light wants to escape, so to speak, unlock these points. (Everyone breathe a moment. Take a gentle breath.) So what is happening, literally, your lightbody is unscrewing or unanchoring those points, but you're still going to be physical – you're not going through die. You will *experience* (this is part of the shift in consciousness now) being light and physical, both. You will understand very limited what ascension is. You're not ascending, yet you are in a manner. The pains in the body that anchor you, particularly the knee points now, are shifting to a greater lightbody. So when you have these pains you should say to yourself, "I arise the vibration I am," so you can vibrate the physical form to this light form that is around you. You work together. The past is coming toward you, your future is coming toward you. You are the one that is going to get it all, right in the middle. It is okay. No big deal.

For some of you the game called fear is fun. That's where you have your joy, in fearful attitudes. That is all right. There is a thing called love; it exists. There is a thing called life, it is forever. And there is a thing called fun. And if you're having fun and you're in joy and you're in love with what you're doing, you will always have a body, always. You will always have consciousness forever and ever and ever – that will *never* be taken away from you. But you're in love with what you're doing; you will always have a physical form . . . a form. Some of you can vibrate it one way or the other. No one is keeping you imprisoned from fun, away from fun. You are, because of what you think another thinks. That is all right, that is part of the fun. It is difficult at times to think that beings have *fun* when they're in their sickness. Part of their sickness is their wisdom in this lifetime. Some of you accumulate your wisdom when you go through your oopses. "Oops!" And you'll say, "That be not wise." So this knee thing is very important here, and when you begin to have it you should simply allow the physical body to vibrate faster – it'll ease the discomfort. Or you can joke with your friends and say your knees hurt; "Shit, I'm ascending." They won't understand it, but it'll create some humor. Or you can tell them that *they're* ascending; "Let me watch." Anyone have any other questions they want to talk about? [To a participant:]

Are you ready to remember more?

Yes.

So be it! Now when you start remembering some of your other stuff, don't go judge it, any of you. Indeed? Because it was required to get you to where you are now — it was absolutely necessary. If you had done anything different, you would have been in heaven by now. [Laughter.] That's my joke, don't take it literally. Some of you will, however; that be all right. Part of the humor. [He toasts:] To life!

To life!

Consciousness Shifting

I have a question. Before the Harmonic Convergence there was lot of talk about the world ending on August 17, 1987, and there was a powerful shift. Now it's July 26th; can you talk a little about the meaning of that? Is it more than just another shift, is there something else happening?

I think we'll have a session July 27th. [Laughter.] Humor.

You don't know?

I know. You're going to be here. There will be some energy shiftings, know you? That is part of . . . I told you [in] the second week in July [there will be] the ten-times speed-up. Notice how you've had difficulty in *this* section of it? Well, you're going to get ten times more. Now, simply enjoy the energy in the body. Play, know you? If you become confused, go hug a tree because the trees will know what's going on. Indeed? We can create another *religion* out of this one! "The tree religion took me through a big change here!" And then you can separate them; you can have your maple-tree religion, your pine- tree religion, your apple and fruit tree. [Laughter.] It'll fit right in with the way you beings like to separate.

The shift *is* coming — it is consciousness shifting. It is not a god coming down to eat your thought forms, though it probably would be a good idea for some of you; but we're not doing that. You're going to be aware that you're more than just physical body, that you are light. You are living, literally, in an initiation phase — you're being initiated into what you would term the Brotherhood of Light. And other levels are going through it too. But you are going through it in the level of physical form, this density, so it's a pretty courageous thing to do from one perspective. Pretty idiotic from another, but it doesn't matter, you are going through it. That one particular day there will be . . . and that is simply . . . how will I say this? That is being played out that way to get you to understand that time is shifting, to get you off this system of time that you're playing with, to get you into a light thing.

Light doesn't understand what time is, know you? It's a rather limited thing. So it is simply a display to get you to understand that consciousness is shifting. You beings like your dates, know you? You want your date for the next disaster so you don't be there on that date. Well, this is a date for you simply to focus *around*, because date is time, you understand? So that is a limitation. Indeed? Your calendar is a limitation. That is time, know you? You are all one life, and you're moving to that. You've played (your wisdom) seven main chakras in the body, indeed? In truth there is only one. At another level of truth there are billions, indeed, and you're going to understand that as you go through. Know you what I mean?

A lot of you beings are getting information, and some of the information is of a fearful nature — some of you *take* it fearfully — because that excites you. You love this roller coaster ride of fear. You are forever, always will be. Consciousness is shifting, but it's going to take this decade, the rest of it, to your year 2002 (another date for you to play with), as it makes its shift, and you're in the ride. Simply consider that earlier this year you paid one dime for your ride. Now your ride costs you a dollar. Better ride! Another way to put it. And you're going to experience this ride in the physical body, know you? The energy called you is coming to you and you're going to experience it in the body.

Wonderful.

It is indeed wonderful. It is a sacred thing, it's an honor, in a greater manner, to be here. Hug a tree when you become confused. Any other questions?

Yes, today was a pivotal point in my life, very pivotal, and it's very intense, and there is fear involved with it, which I am attempting to bring . . . okay, that's all I'm going to say.

Indeed. Part of this thing, any time you make a step through the door and you're not sure what's on the other side of the door, there is always a little apprehension. You beings say there is fear. But you built the doors to allow you gifts when you get sort of bored, and you built this door, and on the other side of the door there is an even greater gift that you've set there for yourselves. In this structure, however, you think not because the door is closed. If you will allow the door to open you will see the greater gift. Know you what I mean? You've taken chances before, know you?

Yes.

Well, you don't have to consider it so risky this time. You're on safer turf. You know what I mean? And you don't have to be the protagonist, either. Simply open the door. Understand? You ready for some excitement? You can build a little keyhole in the door if you want to look through and peek.

I think I like that, yeah.

Don't want to get all your gifts at once, eh?

Pretty powerful.

Just beginning. How's your back?

Wonderful. Better! Thank you.

Be grand. Don't thank me, you simply are swinging inside there. You ready to start seeing?

Yes, I am.

Don't alter what you see. Then you can share it, indeed? Be fun.

Allow your eyes to close gently for a little bit. Center your being. Peace. We're going to send each of you a thought — it's what you want. Simply let it be there. It is what you want but you don't know you want it. So see what you want and you can alter it later if you decide you don't want it, but this is what you want from your light forces here. Peace. Peace. Allow. Be gentle. Allow. In a gentle manner slowly open your physical eyes. Allow. Does anyone have any other questions?

Uh, the process I'm trying to complete . . .

. . . You will work through it. How would you enjoy going into the woods naked and screaming?

I think you told me this once before.

I did! When was the last time you did it?

Didn't do it, yet.

Ah! There are other ways to accomplish this thing, however I think a naked scream in the woods would do you good. I be serious, and the journey toward this might be different than you think it is, because I can already see your thinkity-think as you're going through it. Bring in old clothes, leave them, walk out with white clothes. Know you, bury them. So when are you going to do this?

This weekend.

Which day? I want to be there for sure.

Okay. Sunday.

Sunday. What time? You play time here, I don't. What time?

After breakfast.

What time is breakfast?

Noon.

Could you make it a little earlier?

No problem.

Could you make it roughly about sevenish?

I'll do it.

Indeed, be aware of the elementals there — know you gnomes and fairies? They're going to be there. Say hi, know you? Don't get all embarrassed. You don't have to stay there long, ten moments is enough. Big scream or two. So be it. Then you can have breakfast and chat about it.

Good story.

Good story? You haven't seen anything yet. Anyone have anything else they want to chat about? I won't send you to the woods.

Now, as you move into your late July . . . and by the way, from this date, every other Friday until further notice [we'll have class].

Any other days?

Not at this time. Your second Saturday in August.

Only Saturday?

Could be Sunday. Indeed?

You want to give us a title for the weekend?

Title. You always want title. Life Is Everywhere, God Is Everywhere — pick a title, any title, doesn't matter. It all is the same. We'll also do your second Saturday in September, know you? And we will title that one PHEW! [Laughter.] Believe me, everyone will know what we mean. And you can say your August; what say you A PRELUDE TO PHEW! [More laughter.] Those will be my titles.

For your information, you're going through a mini phew now! Mini phews. You can see the humor in all of this because you're going to find out that you live forever no matter what happens. No matter where you are, you're loved, or you wouldn't be there. You're at your level of where you think love should be and that is all right. You are love! That is what you are. Some like to define it so they can limit other beings' experience of it, because if another has a greater capacity and wants to play love and one does not, the one that does not feels threatened. And it is a control issue, but controlling behavior and intimidating behavior is going to be out the window, and those of that attitude are going to be along with it, out the window. That's the change that is coming. You will live through the change of it as you play through this decade, but that's going to be the result. So those that are into controlling behavior and manipulative behavior (competitive behavior is included there also) are feeling very nervous as these changes come about. Inwardly they know that there be change coming. Controlling entities are going to have to find what you term great pain in their head, great ache in their heart; even though they be young, they be threatened because the heart chakra is not opened. They be think they be die in what you call a manner. They won't graduate in what you term it the elevation here, because they have a limited concept of what love is. That is all right. No big deal. You've got many lifetimes to play it through. You've already lived many, so it is fun.

There is a term though that you should be very familiar with in these times, and that term is compassion. Compassion. For everything, because even your animals are going to go through this shifting, and they don't know. They have an understanding of the magnetic influences, but they're not aware of the consciousness that's involved here. So have compassion. Exciting times. Any other questions here?

I have a question. We haven't heard about our friends in the secret government for a long time, and the visits from various places of authority looking in on us. Is there anything happening?

Well, we've been sort of chatting with them, know you what I mean? Sort of advising ways of perhaps being not so aggressive.

Are they listening?

Mm, little bit. Got their attention. They're going to create what you term a little grouping, so to speak, to check out and see if the information is really coming from what you call a high source. They're in a quandary now. They are allowed part of their game, however, and one of theirs is greed, outrageous greed, and they need to play it to complete, so that part will be allowed. You need not be caught up in their game, however. They have this great desire for this thing and it needs to be completed within the soul. It is all fun, indeed? You won't be involved with them unless you want to for your experience.

Meditation

Now, allow your eyes to close a little moment and allow your palms to be upward upon your thighs, because your thighs now are taking a lot of energy, also. Indeed, allow. Peace. Allow. I want you to visualize yourselves as golden beings, your physical body is gold and you're sitting on a golden throne. I want you to feel that gold throne at your back. I want you to feel a golden crown on your head. Allow. Allow. Peace. Now at the solar plexus I want you to open that chakra and I want you to accept a golden ball of light that is going to come toward you to press into that chakra. Allow. Peace. Allow the light. Let it move into the solar plexus and then up to the throat. Peace. Feel your legs as golden, feel them golden, golden light, golden light. Allow. Peace. Feel the head as golden. Peace. In the center of your golden body there is a blue line of light, very thin, from the top of your head right down to your root chakra, very thin line in the center of your being. Feel it there. That light is a direct connection to your blue corona, which envelops all the lives you've ever had or ever will have; it's part of the Father. Feel it in you. Peace. Gentle manner, slowly open your physical eyes. Peace.

Now, while you're sitting there tighten your buttocks, tighter, and tighten your thighs. Let them loose. Take a breath in, breathe it down into here [perineum]. Tighten your buttocks, tighten your thighs, bend a little bit, straighten up and breathe out.

This is going to give you the ability to handle these energies. What you don't know is that you think you breathe in your mouth, and you do through your lungs — that's your physical consciousness. You also breathe in prana through two holes here [hairline at forehead, left and right of center] in your etheric forces here. One is white light on the left side, one is red on the right side. You breathe it in and it crosses in the body [the two energies spiral around one another]. It aligns to blue in the center, which is a color close to your Father, and it is life itself. It'll be helpful (you don't have to do it, but it will be helpful) in these weeks coming to contemplate even when you're physically breathing that this is where you're really breathing from, and you exhale out the mouth. As you breathe in through these points, this comes through and collects poisons in the body. As it comes back up (it bounces off the perineum, so to speak) you expel the poisons [as you exhale out the mouth], and what you would term thought forms, negative thought forms that you play with, your doubts, etc. So you can literally by your breathing clean your body out, from the inside outward. It be fun to do it. It also be very much wisdom. [To a participant] Indeed, how are you doing?

Grand.

Are you ready to play with more energy?

Oh, yes. I was going to ask you for more.

How's the diarrhea?

I don't have diarrhea.

You've got it under control? Indeed? Well, you know the extra energy comes in when you start having diarrhea then. That'll be the check. You ready? Need to run to potty yet? It'll be clearing.

I still want to move; I'm still in the same place. Why is that?

Indeed. Know you the male energy of your body? How do you feel with that integrating with you?

I've been very aware of that the past few weeks, that that's what's happening, and it's okay, but I don't know what it's doing.

Well, that is where you sort of placed your stubborn . . . know you stubborn? So you placed it in the male energy — it is aligned to the mental here. That energy is going to sit here to be balanced because you have centered a bit in here in this consciousness. Now that male energy wants to sit in there again, know you, so don't be surprised if you begin to get real stubborn. Know you? Adjust it, allow, know you? Adjust. Center your being. Take a breath. You simply contemplate "I have the wisdom of this now," know you what I mean?

No, not quite. I don't think I do understand totally. Can you explain it again? You're saying the male energy is stubborn.

Indeed, and it's going to move. It's sort of sitting in your body and it's going to shift, because it thinks this portion has got it figured out so it doesn't have to be so stubborn anymore. But the energy is going to shift and you're going to feel very stubborn. Bless this thing and understand that you, be you in here now [heart chakra/soul] are in charge. Indeed? You're not being possessed or attacked because it is connected right to your root chakra, indeed, so it goes back with you a long time. Some other beings might do you a favor by taking it out of you and setting it over here. And you'll be walking around feeling not stubborn, feeling rather grand, but they will be buying you another lifetime because you'll have to come back and get that energy.

Well, no, I don't want to do that, thank you.

Indeed, it be wise to integrate it all now. Know you what I mean?

What is it going to do after it's integrated?

Well, you're going to feel very sexually active. Know you?

That's all right.

I know it is all right. I never said sex was wrong, have I?

No, no, no.

That's what brought you to this planet in the first place, know you? No judgment there, be lot of fun. What limits the fun of it is you beings' attitudes and judgments of this thing. It's one of life's pleasures, know you what I mean? That energy can keep you alive for a long time, applied correctly. That does not mean spill your seed all over the countryside, however. That's not what I'm talking about. I know that's fun, too; I understand. It means utilize the forces. You know there is a system of thought within what is termed tantra that for every time you spill your seed or you have your orgasms without the mixture — what we would term [of the male and female] — or in a reckless manner, that you take four years off your lifetime. No wonder you don't live to be 400. But that is a belief system, we won't get into that. It has to do with tantra. Anyone want to chat about anything else?

The Effect of Entering the Mayan Calendar

I have a question regarding the Mayan calendar. As far as I know, beginning from July 26th we're going to enter definitely the Mayan Calendar. Now, I wonder what kind of effect the 13 Moons are going to have on women?

That is a good question. It'll not only have an effect on women, it'll have an effect on men. As you move through this ten-times speed-up, there's going to be a great force applied. There'll be the desire for sexual activity, union in a loving manner, yet you beings have played union in another manner. It'll also create a desire for men to have what you would term sexual activity for any reason, what you term rape in this society. In that energy, wars begin. Wars begin to become very profound, very big deals, because everybody wants to get into that rape/pillage mode. Everyone breathe a moment.

Women are going to feel very seductive, will be in their power. In one manner, very simply stated, you are going back to the Adam and Eve thing here. Now, that was simply a story. Don't blame the snake and don't blame the woman. Blame the male for being an idiot. [Laughter.] That's where the blame came from, by the way: male energy. It wasn't the female or the snake that did this thing, it was the guilt that did it, and that was a male influence. So it's going to create this great sensuality in women. Men are going to go through their ego crisis here, not knowing where they are. They're going to think they're the Don Juans of the universe, and they're sitting alone, home. That's not going to sit very well, so there'll be a lot of anger, lot of frustration, lot of violence. You must stay in your own power here, each one of you.

These are interesting times. It'll also influence women; we will say in a higher frequency, higher spiritual forces will be coming through the female particularly. Many will begin to associate themselves with Mary, some will actually think they are, and that is all right because you'll understand the energy of the Mother Mary in the body and you'll have the compassion. That doesn't mean you are Mary, it means you're integrating the energies of this being —she's going to exist as a separate entity as far as you're concerned. Do you understand this? Know you what I mean? So don't be surprised if you've got a lot of Marys running around. What they're simply doing is playing with her energy because it's a profound energy, but it will upset the male.

Question. Isn't the creative energy moving through the body and the sexual energy the same energy? Can the sexual feelings be translated into a creative effort of some kind?

Of course. So too translate anger and fear and doubt into creative energy, all of it. One of the ways to use these energies, however, in your body, is not only to be creative externally, it's to be creative internally. That means to be creative with your chakras, to understand that they are regions of divinity in your body, and you utilize the energy in each chakra, train it, be creative internally. You beings say you sleep, know you, when you're simply playing in another level of reality with systems of light that you are. And you're allowed in this time to understand these shiftings, how you work it. Humanity has stayed down here [root chakra], totally. They've never been up here [heart chakra]. There's going to be a lot of attention in this arena [root], and the way to be is really in the center of this blue line that runs through you. You're going to feel it. The old mental processes are also going to come back to take over, sort of to control this energy, work with it. They won't work. This energy desires a loving heart and compassion. Anything else is going to pervert it. Everyone take a breath.

The cycle of the Moon is indeed important because it is actually an influence upon your consciousness here. You may say it is a control device here. You must understand its influence within you because you're part of the Moon, you're part of Helios, the Sun, Luna, you in here. These bodies orbiting your system exist inside you. The Sun (thought, because it's all thought) exists inside you in this arena [heart chakra]. Where is the Moon? It's in the emotional arena. Shiva, where's his Moon? It's here [on top of the head/crown chakra]; controls the emotion with the mental process, understands the mind of the Father. Everyone take a breath. Some of the depictions of these deities are simply to play and show you how you can control these influences. That's why they're deities —more than one, by the way. Everyone wants to meet the Father. Well, you've got a few other

friends to meet along the way. You wouldn't recognize your Father now, doesn't exist like you do. Did that answer your question?
Oh, sure.

Indeed? It's going to be fun. Be a little erratic but you're going to be safe. Anyone have anything else you want to chat about? You are in exciting times. I can't wait. [Laughter.] I'm going to be around a while.
Last Wednesday we had this experience in my kitchen with this big energy swirling in. Could you tell me what that was?

Someone is trying to get your attention.
Like who?

I'm not going to say right now.
Why not?

I don't want to. What do you think about controlling?
I think it shouldn't be done.

Have you ever controlled before?
Mm-hmm, yes.

Are you still doing it?
No.

Are you sure?
Not to my knowledge.

That is all right. Are you really ready to find out what's really, really going on?
Mm-hmm, yes.

Well, this has the answers in here [soul]; this part here [brain] gets it last, indeed, and this is where the confusion is going to be [brain], know you what I mean? Now your guides are swirling about you at times, and they want to get closer. Know you what I mean? And you say, "No! That be enough!" Know you what I mean?
I say no, not at all. I say only higher self.

What is the difference between your guides and your high self?
One belongs, the others are along for the ride.

How many pieces of yourself are you going to have to pick up along the way?
I don't know.

It be a lot. Where is your Father? What you term God is everything, know you?
Are you talking about a masculine entity? I heard you say "Father." It

sounds masculine.

Father. You have an issue with that, indeed? No problem. No big deal. Doesn't matter. It's simply your words to explain, know you? Know you what I mean? Know you what I was talking about when you get angry and argue, indeed? Now, what do you think my energy is, using your labels here?

Confrontative.

Confrontative. Be say male or female from your perspective?

Male.

Male. That be interesting. It is female.

That is interesting. Where is the gentle?

Where is the gentle? Where is Father? It is everything, indeed? Know you what I mean?

No, I don't know what you mean.

Are you ready to see what I mean? Are you sure?

Yes, yes, yes.

So be it. We'll take you on a journey. Ever hear the name Lucifer? What do you think of this one?

Dumb.

He be dumb. Hmm. He be an awesome entity, know you? You're going to have to learn to love the being. I didn't say worship, I said love him, for he's your brother. He can't take all of the blame, by the way.

How do you do that? How do you love Lucifer?

How do you love anything? Do you have a requirement for a being that they be a certain way in order for you to love them?

Sometimes.

That was another lifetime, eh?

No, this lifetime I did it with my sons.

I know. Allow. There is what is termed power in all things. There is love there. The word *allow* is very difficult to handle because it creates changes in your system of belief. Know you what I mean?

I didn't know that, no.

What do you think of energies as they move?

Yeah, I like it.

What do you label them, good/bad, male/female?

I usually label them good unless I label them bad. Sometimes I don't like them but usually I like them.

How do they feel in the body?

The energies usually feel good, except for blockages, obstacles and shadows, which don't feel good.

Because the energy wants to move through them, and you want your shadows.

No I don't.

Are you sure? They are part of your form, know you what I mean? Part of what you use to build your structure with, your physical body.

Well, I don't need that.

So allow yourself to be gentle with yourself as we shift. Know you gentle?

Yes.

That is more of a no; you're learning gentle, indeed. That be all right. You'll get it. Don't be hard on your being, you understand, because your verbiage as you speak and you play is going to be reflected within your physical form. It will be. That is the way the play goes. Know you how you are angry at your Father, God, pick a word?

I'm over it now. I think I'm over it.

That be all right. Anger is a good thing, it can be creative.

Well, it didn't work out too good for me. My father, you mean my biological father?

Be your big daddy, big mommy, whichever you want.

I don't like to experience powerlessness and desperation.

Who would you feel comfortable talking to in your sleep this evening? Name a being.

Everyone take a breath. Part of the limitations that you beings play with in this lifetime is what you call why you are here, who sent you here, who you're going to blame for this thing. You can't acknowledge that you made an *oops*, so someone has to be blamed. You wanted to come. You wanted to play here, to be born, you wanted it. Yes, some of you were born in anger; you were angry in your last lifetime, you're angry now, and you utilize that force, anger, because it has propelled you through experiences. You utilize the force of anger because it propels you through experiences. You haven't had enough wisdom yet that you can use other emotions to propel you through the same experiences. So you hold on to this, and that is all right. That is part of your power. But that is part of the power that is going to go away. Competitive behavior, controlling behavior, is leaving the planet, so when the ropes are pulled, if you're holding on to it, let go of the rope or you will go up with it. That's the way it is.

These energies that are coming are very powerful, they're here now. And what they're simply going to do is quicken, vibrate faster around you, and you're going to be in the middle of it. Love all things, have compassion. You're not as smart as you think you are. You will experience it in your bodies. Your metaphysics was simply a tool to get you where you are now, that is all. You are standing on that tool and you're living in this light called the expansion of consciousness, called Christ becoming, called mankind becoming the master. These energies are so powerful you cannot pervert them; you will destroy yourselves. The planet will not be destroyed, and destroy what is termed a physical sense. Life is forever. So be gentle with your beings now. Some of you I've talked to about this thing before, and even you thought I was being little jokey, jokey, until the energy hits the physical form and then it be *Oops!*

You are coming to yourselves: your future is coming to you and your past is coming to you, and you're going to meet all of you, all of your incarnations you're going to meet, your favorite ones and your not so favorite ones. So you can sit around your table and have your little party with your favorite ones and not so favorite ones, give everyone a little piece of cake, have a little drink or two, get really drunk, know you, then maybe everyone can forgive each other and get together to complete this little mission. Lot of fun.

Now, the most important thing to remember is that these energies will enter your physical form, they're going to. Your guides are a manifestation of your thought processes as you enter physical. Yes, you will have to blend with them, indeed you will. You are in physical form; now your high self, that is what you are, like it or not. You're more spiritually advanced than you ever have been in this lifetime, in this moment. You're at that level now, what do you want to do with it? You weren't that spiritually advanced in the last lifetime, so don't think they were better. Some of you in your future lifetime have actually gone backwards. Take advantage of this moment and understand the power that's developing here within you. Some of your future lifetimes are rather decadent. That be all right. That's where you think the power is. Doesn't matter.

Be very compassionate in this time toward all things, because if you don't, you're going to create an aberration in the ability to think here. You will literally think you're going to be what you term a violent entity, lost control, almost animal-like in behavior. And there will be systems to support that, you'll have your wars and your riots in your cities as they begin to develop here, and some of you will jump right in there, pick good side/bad side. This is the time when you need to be in your power, entities, completely.

Sir, I'd like to ask you a question.

Be Sir? How be I Sir?

Worshipful Sir.

No church, indeed.

All right, if you don't like it I won't say it anymore. According to some of the teachings, this planet is going through an initiation.

You're going through it now.

Right. But the planet itself, Gaia, as she's called, is also going to be going through an initiation and going into another dimension, from what I understand.

That is true.

Now, are we allowed to know if we're going to reincarnate on this planet, or are we going to go back to our home planets, or are we going to move to another system?

It'll depend.

Are we allowed to know that, or can we plan for it?

If you allow your vibration to arise fast enough then you will stay upon this system, you will stay upon this planet, because it's going to be a beautiful planet. It's been declared a planet of peace. This is where all the action is. This is the what you would term greatest resort in the galaxy, because there's more color here — more energies are in this system that are fun to play with. Now if you can hang on and increase your consciousness enough you'll stay here. Many are going to be leaving, they won't be able to hang on, and what you term "the visas" required are going to be very strict. Know you the regulations to get here? And don't feel bad if you don't hang on; there are other interesting places. Some of you better hope you like the color blue — that's all there is is blue. Or brown or blacks. Get very familiar with greens. No offense to Tara — that's a joke. Know you joke? You don't know what green means. You don't need to go anyplace. My point is that as you raise your consciousness, you know that you're at all places at once. You can stand upon this planet and another. You won't be limited by third-dimensional structures, yet you can play with them if you wish, within the bodies.

We're not trying to lay a heavy on you; you beings were part of the process of creating this muck way back when. You're here to clean it up now. Some of you don't want to. Some of you were overlords in this older system. That overlord didn't sit too well, and you're back here as an underlord. No big deal. Part of the fun. Everyone take a breath; lighten up a little bit.

Now, this sexual energy, this sexual activity. One of the ways that you can truly utilize these forces is to understand the emotional content of what Shiva be saying with the Moon be here [top of the head/crown chakra]. You think clearly in the body, all the way down, and enjoy the feeling in the body, and then let it rise. It'll sit here [root/navel arena] like a ball and it'll give you great power. Outrageous healing power here. Your eyes, you can have new ones, energy correctly applied. This system, eyeball, regenerates itself completely in seven days, brand new cells. So you simply allow the energy to come in and to come out. You utilize these forces. There is nothing mystical about it. It is simply what you do. You were born as a light being. You will play die if you choose to as a light being. You're simply understanding the processes of what occurs within the physical body, of what you do with your physical body, with your thoughts, how your thoughts are applied here.

The Masters Will Complete Their Mission

Along with this shift in consciousness you're dealing with very powerful masters. Some of them have not been in human form, and they don't look at human form as being rather beauteous, though you are. They only have one thought in mind, from their perspective, and that's completion of what is going on here – that's all they care about, and they are going to succeed. They've already succeeded, you just don't know that yet. So it is an exciting time. Lot of fun.

Now, one more thing before we finish this evening. It is important to be compassionate because these forces that are coming, they only have one thing in their focused intent, and that is completion. They're not into labels and they care not, they care not for the physical body. They love the soul and the light that you are, the life that you are, and your life is not your physical form, yet it's part of it. They have a complete disregard for your spiritual ignorance and your arrogance in your physical. They don't like it. It is a manner of the shifting. As these energies begin to play, be humbly arrogant, very gentle with your being, because they are from the Father (from what you term the Father is your word, your label), beginning. They are what be termed on a mission, and they will complete. It's a great, great armada of consciousness that you have no concept of now. It dwarfs anything you can see in your sky, your stars. They are not from this system. They are part of what holds this system together, and they will accelerate your consciousness. You in turn will accelerate the consciousness of the planet and create the magnetic shifts and all of these other things, because it is your energy that is shifting, it is your game here. Be at peace with these things.

Now, give me a moment. We're going to have conversations with guides, we're going to create an alignment. Now allow your guides to be closer to you. If they frighten you, tell them to stand away a little bit, but closer is better because they create a vibration next to your physical force that allows you to vibrate, and allows you to vibrate inside. They love you. Allow. Be in love with each other. It'll make it easier through this time. We are through.

16

Secret Government
Terrorist Activity

Zoosh through Robert Shapiro
June 28, 1995

T his is Zoosh with a flash. The secret government has pulled out all the stops to usurp power in your world. Of special note is that they are targeting at this time the legitimate government of the United States. They are doing so by supporting directly, and in some cases indirectly, terrorist activity in the U.S. This forces the legitimate government of the U.S. to take steps that will be restrictive — out of necessity, for security reasons — and these restrictions will have to be placed across the board, and will affect all citizens.

Now, on the one hand, by utilizing terrorists and supporting and suborning their activities, the apparent, on-the-surface look of it is that the secret government is attempting to create chaos in the United States. But what they are really attempting to do is to further the resentment of the average person living in the United States, or even visiting, and cause them to feel worse about your government. A very concerted effort has been made to cause people to feel negative about your form of government.

People have been encouraged for forty or fifty years, through the use of broadcast media (unbeknownst to the broadcasters) and through various means that we have discussed before. But now the secret government is stepping up its attack on the legitimate government of the United States because the government will have to respond to terrorism eventually. They will be reluctant to do it, but eventually they will have to impose widespread security measures.

At first the security measures will be obvious. They will be at airports, bus terminals, train stations, places of mass transit. Eventually they will be on subways, local metropolitan buses. Then eventually there will be checkpoints at state lines, and in some cases even at the boundaries of counties and cities, through which cars must pass and be searched by various means. It will take a while to develop electronic devices that can do the searches in a quick, efficient way that is not time-consuming. But for now the search will have to be done largely by hand or dogs or some such thing. So this is all going to create resentment against the government.

Don't Blame Your Government

I want to ask the citizens of the United States and other countries, if you feel this is happening in your country, to make a concerted effort to not blame your system of government. Recognize that the system in the United States is one of the best that is functioning in your world now. Generally, any system that is parliamentary — that has a congress, or at least is set up like a republic, or even better, like a democracy, which you don't actually have, but almost — is very good. Please don't fall for what the secret government is setting you up for. They are directly setting you up to desire a leader who will "lead you out of this mess" — that's exactly how it will be put to you. This charismatic leader (if not the first one that you find, then the second one) will either be influenced by or will actually be the Antichrist. Know this: You will know that this leader is the Antichrist if he justifies all of his actions by draping himself in the flag, as they say, or draping himself in religion; in other words, calling forth justifications for all that he does by saying it is necessary to do for "patriotic" reasons or for "God's" reasons. I can assure you, those who would actually support you as individuals will talk about what is right, what is good for the individual, what is the nurturing thing to do — in other words, will be approaching from the feminine.

One guarantee I can give you is that that leader — and it is a group of at least three that is being trained right now by the secret government — will be a man. It is possible that the man will utilize women in his grab for power, but he will be a man. So that eliminates a large segment of the population as suspects, if you will. But I do not wish you to start casting about to see who this charismatic leader is, because there will be many charismatic people who will be benevolent, who will want the best for the individual and will work toward the betterment of all people. You will know if the leader drapes himself in the flag or in religion, as it were, to justify his actions, because many actions can be taken by standing in front of the flag or by saying, "You've been chosen by God to do this for the people." I can assure, you many of the great despots ("great" meaning well-known in your recent history) have done similar things – nationalism, you know. After all, the Nazi party and its famed leader started out as a nationalistic, patriotic party. Don't forget that.

Get Involved in Creating the Physical World

So here's what you can do. I want you to take a hard look at the form of government you have, and see its value. I want you to encourage your fellow citizens to vote. If you don't like who's running, then put someone up to run. Become involved on a local basis. Now is the time for grassroots political action. Yes, pray. Yes, do meditations. Yes, do all of the things you have come to do to make your life more benevolent. But now is the time for action. And I will ask you to take action on the local front. Get to know all of your neighbors, encourage them to be politically active (meaning run for office), encourage them to be honest and work with the people on a first-name basis, and encourage all the people to be involved in all of the government all of the time. It is time to act. If this happens, you will not only reaffirm your responsibility for your fellow beings, you will also reaffirm your responsibility for yourself. The true purpose of material mastery training here on Earth is that you learn how to act with grace and love in the creation of physical world. It is time now to act, to create from love, from appreciation – but you must create. That's my flash.

What particular events will stand out as a warning? Particular cities, particular events?

One has already happened – the bombing, which we have discussed – but other things will occur, such as bombing threats that are taken seriously by your legitimate investigative departments, possibly associated with airplanes or buses, and most certainly associated with schools. It will be very important now for schools to have significant security systems. I don't want to frighten you, but know this: if your educational administrators say they've got to have metal detectors, don't be offended. The world you're living in now is not the same as it was when you were a youngster. Yes, it is annoying, and even offensive, to have to walk through these devices. But if your school administrators say, "We have to have them; we have to have security guards who work all the time – not just night guards who keep the building safe, but day guards who keep the children safe," I know it will be a strain, but won't you feel relieved knowing there's nobody walking around your school with a knife or a gun? Won't you feel relieved knowing that there are security people working while your children are there, investigating to make sure no one brings in even a cherry bomb, as it is called? I know children like these things, but they are no longer safe. Even if one is set off as a prank, a well-intentioned, amusing prank can have wide-ranging effects on people. A big boom nowadays could bring on a heart attack for somebody. Everybody needs to be responsible now.

So become involved at the local level, and take care at schools, at places of transportation, at buildings where the public comes and goes – theatrical events, movie theaters, any place where people gather. It's going to be a big effort, it's going to require a lot of volunteers. If you have knowledge of what to do, or would like to learn what to do, go to your local sheriff or police department. Tell them, "Let's start a volunteer corps. Let's have cooperation. How can we help you?" This is not to create a police state; it is to maintain a community feeling, so that when you go to the movie theater, and someone wants to look in your purse or your knapsack, you won't be offended, because the face you see will be somebody you see at the drugstore or at the supermarket or delivering the mail – someone you know. This is also addressed to police departments: Be ready to cooperate. If you don't cooperate, then you're just going to have to deal with vigilantes, because people will organize anyway. Why not have them organized in a way that works with you?

When are we going to see the next event?

It could happen anytime now – probably sometime within the next week or two. Hopefully it will not be at a place where children are.

Is this more of the breakup of the inner ring? [See page 211.]

Well, the hotheads within the inner ring of the secret government are beginning to break off and take action, as often happens with groups that are threatened by change from within, you know? So yes, cooler heads will prevail in most of the secret government, but at least two or three factions will break off, and the initial reaction by the secret government is to wait and see what happens: "If it works in our favor, okay. If it doesn't work in our favor, we will eliminate them." But you see, they're just going to wait and see for a while, and these people will be running loose and doing who knows what.

So we need to have an alert civilization and population; we need to have people go over to their neighbors across the street and say, "Are you okay? We haven't heard from you, haven't seen you lately. Oh, you've been sick? I'm sorry to hear that. Can I help?" In other words, people need to get involved on the local level and know who they're living next to. It's not okay to live in an apartment building and not have any idea who the people living next to you are. And there are plenty of social things you can do together, and when the people in the building are all pulling together, I can assure you, not only will crime go down, but quality of consciousness will go up and the quality of life will improve.

I just read recently that the secret government told the elitist politicians and bankers that they weren't doing their jobs, so the secret government is throwing their support now behind the far Right, and the Christian alliances, and that there would be chaos. Is that on an outer-ring level or inner-ring?

That's on an outer-ring level — and let's be clear with that. I don't want to simply blanket the Christian Right by saying that they are supported by the secret government, because it's not true. The people being supported are the fringe element that the Christian Right — no matter how conservative or fundamentalist they might appear on the surface — would not approve of. I can assure you that there is no fundamentalist I know of today in the Christian movement in, say, the United States who would approve of random bombing that blows up children. I cannot think of one individual who would approve of this. Now, we're talking about fringe elements who might float in and out of the Christian Right — who might decide that they were divinely chosen. But if they belonged to any group they would definitely be registered as a terrorist organization by your FBI, and probably recognizable by the average citizen as belonging to a terrorist group, or more likely, a fringe element that even a radical terrorist organization wouldn't have anything to do with, because the people would be loose cannons, as they say — unpredictable, not willing to follow orders at all; impatient, hostile, even, to people who seem to support them; in other words, essentially borderline, if not fully, psychotic.

Now, I'm not talking about people who espouse politics based upon their perceptions of religion. I have stated for a long time and will reiterate that religion is largely designed to control people, that the true religion is love, and that is it. There is no other religion. Love. God is love, love is God, love is good, *period*. But this is something that is felt, and as long as your society continues to look to words to provide answers and to create the peace, it won't work. The children, the young people, are cynical. They are cynical because people use words, and actions cannot be based on words, they can only be based on feelings — actions that do good for all. Now it is time for the change to the feminine spirituality. It is time not only for the return of the Goddess but the return of the recognition of the value of the values associated with the Goddess. This can happen in the general public only by people becoming aware and acknowledging that not only do they need love, but they need to give love. And I'm not talking about sexuality here, I'm talking about kindness, which generally comes from the heart, caring, values that people cherish — and that some people can remember as being a way of life in the past. It is still available to you, but you've got to want it, you've got to go for it, you've got to apply it, you've got to use it and you've got to value it.

17

The Trail of an Angel

Zoosh through Robert Shapiro
July 19 and 23, 1995

*S*hould *we print the Puerto Rican pictures and have you talk about the ET cadaver?*

I think that would be a good picture to run. It may not be something you'd want to put on the front page, because it's pretty ghastly looking.

Do you want to tell us who it is, what it is, why it is?

Figures 17.1. and 17.2. It really is an ET. They were beings inside Earth. I think the reason that the event took place is that they

Fig. 17.1. ET cadaver that surfaced in Puerto Rico.

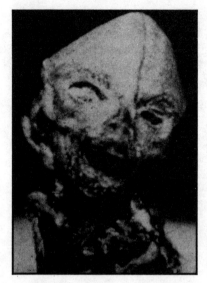

Fig. 17.2. Another view of ET cadaver.

were actually children. I know you're used to children here being short and adults being taller. But children from this particular species would mean beings who have little experience, like your children. The child that was "attacked" I think was not actually being attacked; but if something runs out that looks totally different and it latches onto you, you might become frightened, too. It was an unfortunate and sad event.

Do we have a name for the being or a place of origin?

I think that they were living under the Earth at that time. They had a ship that dropped them off here about 48 years ago, depending on how you count it. These beings just got out to the surface. It was quite a tragedy. But yes, I think it can be proved in the lab even now that that being was not of Earth origin.

Where were they from?

I think initially they were from one of the Zeta offshoots. They are not Zetas. They're not Grays, either. It's kind of hard for you to tell, perhaps, because the skull was so seriously damaged, but I think that we're talking about beings that were combined from the Andromedan and the Zeta cultures. I can only call it Tgaean culture, which is a culture that is significantly far away from here. These beings were essentially experimental beings. I think they got out to the surface but weren't meant to.

Ten years ago they came to the surface in Puerto Rico. Where are the rest of them now?

Well, they ran back down inside the Earth. But I think they've since been lifted off, which is good.

So it's not a major thing, but it is evidence.

It's physical evidence, yes.

Figure 17.3. Here we have an etheric . . . call this etheric "smoke." Smoke in that sense would be particulates left over from the transformation from something to something else. So this etheric "smoke" is a residual byproduct of a transfer of angelic energy — this

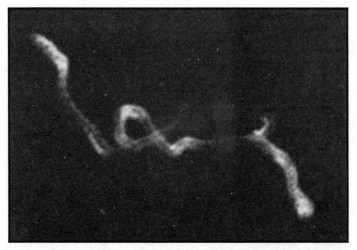

Fig. 17.3. Etheric "smoke," trail of Archangel Michael.

is pretty close to the trail of an angel traveling through the sky. I'm going to tell you who it is, too.

Who?

Michael. This is an etheric imprint of the passage of his motion through the sky there. A very blessed event, as it were.

What was he doing?

He was checking up on the pulse of humanity's responsiveness to the needs of all people around them. It's absolutely vital that people be united these days, all over the world, stop seeking to blame, and understand that all people do what they must and that the more you can do to help each other, the better.

And what was his diagnosis of this pulse?

He felt that things were getting better.

Good.

That's what he told me, anyway.

Figure 17.4. Here's something you don't see in the Earth's atmosphere very often. Here we have the closest rendition that I have seen (outside of Zeta Reticuli) of the energy body of the Zeta Reticulan cosmic godhead. The cosmic godhead in Zeta Reticuli is primarily the spirit of renewal. So this is the Zeta Reticulan cosmic godhead, spirit of renewal.

Okay, but what does that mean? How does that particular tribe, race, planet, have a godhead?

How do they have a specific cosmic guardian?

Fig. 17.4. The Zeta Reticulan cosmic godhead, spirit of renewal.

I thought you said god.

I did, but a god could be a cosmic guardian.

I see.

They have this by their need, by their desire to celebrate renewal, by their devotion – that's the word – to the causes and needs of others. These are wonderful people. The Zeta Reticulans have been given a lot of bad press and they don't deserve it. Granted, they're not the most sophisticated beings in the world, but they're getting better. They're going to make the jump to the ninth dimension, so you can be sure they're going to be *much* better. But they have largely been totally devoted to the needs of others.

This particular being was traveling through your time and space because, as you know, you are the past lives of the people on Zeta Reticuli, as per Joopah's talk from previous times. This beautiful being was orienting itself to your energies and will (and already has, at this point) go forward to the Zeta Reticulan beings to bring them a little bit of your personal energy of transformation (as any human being might transform through inspiration and application), so that they might be encouraged by your coming along, *and* because they are developing another ceremony by which they would celebrate their connection with you – which is by way of celebrating the past. This is not something they've done before, this celebrating the past. They tend to celebrate the moment. But they're going to celebrate the past with this ceremony, and it will be largely done through the blue-green light spectrum, which has certain effects for them personally. It is very healing, meaning balancing, maintaining their perfect order (as they might say, but I'd rather say their perfect balance) and allowing them to sustain their culture virtually free of disease.

If we had a cosmic guardian, who would that be? Who in our pantheon would be the equivalent of this being for the Zetas?

Probably the combined energy of all of the angels. Angels do exist for other planets, but all of the angels that exist for this planet — it's hard to put them in number or mass, because how do you measure an angel? You're actually asking me who is the cosmic godhead of this planet. But I would say, if I had to put names on it . . . I'm going to pronounce it for you, it's very difficult in angelic language: Chis'kaden'salanka. I'm throwing in vowel sounds that aren't there, they don't have many vowel sounds. You'll just have to do the best you can.

So we've never interacted with or heard of this particular being?

No, this being is essentially guiding your move forward. It doesn't push you; it pulls you, and it is the cosmic guardian of your entire race and all the beings on your planet. You might ask what it does. (I'm calling it "it" for lack of a better term at the moment.) It maintains the separation of all species. That might sound strange, but this means that men and women do not breed with deer and elephants and so on; even though these things happen in laboratories, they are fleeting and will not last. This allows all races — including animals, plants, minerals as a race, human beings — to maintain the line of their wisdom back to its source and forward in all possible avenues of pursuit. The worst thing that can happen to a race is losing its wisdom. When a race loses its wisdom it essentially either has to be eliminated because it can't function (wisdom also includes body functions) or it adapts to another race's wisdom, which can only work for a fleeting time, because the body may not be able to function. That's what this being does primarily.

Figure 17.5. Here we have a ship that is moving from one dimension to another, leaving what is almost like a magnetic resonant image. So this is almost an MRI reflection of a vehicle moving from . . . I think it's the Solagant (with an accent over the last "t") system, which is actually moving through your time, exploring your time. They are, I believe, your future lives in the thirteenth dimension, which has to do with the ninth harmonic of the seventh ray. In other words, it's well into the future! That's measured in their time, you understand; that's a time measurement according to the way they would say it.

Fig. 17.5. A ship that is moving from one dimension to another.

This is a race of beings that exists entirely in sound. They are not light per se; they are essentially making light by passing through atmospheric conditions that create a suffused glow. They are basically highly condensed sound. They are not affected by the sound harmonics of any scale of your time, but the sound that they are could be liquified and if you touched that sound "liquid," you would have a complete and entire reorientation in the purest sense in your physical body, so that your physical body would become the highest expression of a physical human body. Meaning that if you had even the slightest anomaly —a scar or a pimple or a birthmark (you know, something that no one else even knows about) — it would disappear.

Someday it will be possible for you to touch this. Sometimes these beings compress themselves and choose to travel on lightships which are used as physical rescue ships (physical meaning going to places where physicality is a factor) and assisting populations to restore the physical prototypes of the beings after there had been a major disaster, for instance. They can restore any physical being or etheric being, for that matter, to the highest expression —meaning the best or the purest expression — of physicality for any race. Although you could see the being as a liquid, it would feel like you were touching a gas or a vapor. It would be very difficult to tell you were touching something even though you could see the displacement of mass. Imagine all of the diseases and discomforts you have; if you could touch any part of their body, just the tiniest touch, in less time than it takes me to snap these fingers, you would instantaneously not only feel beyond wonderful, but your body would probably be able to live (barring a piano falling on you, in the physical conditions you have now or even worse) a minimum of ten to eleven thousand years. Part of the reason, of course, they're not functioning in this part of the galaxy is that a human being learns what he's going to learn in sixty or seventy years at the most. You don't want to be in one body that long, because you've got places to go and things to do.

Yeah, but I wouldn't mind getting purified just a little bit!

Well, ask them to come in your sleep or in your meditations, and ask them if they will give your auric field a little kiss.

By asking for the race? The Solagant?

Yes, with the accented "t" on the end. And they may or they may not. But you know, the interesting thing is that as much effort as it would take them to do that for one human being, they could do that for an entire solar system. I'm going to tell you a little secret.

The Rescue of an Ancient Earth Culture

Once upon a time on third-dimensional Earth, in a civilization that took place about (measuring in experiential time) four million years ago, the entire civilization was lost due to a solar flare. A solar flare reached out, the brainwaves in the civilization were entirely discharged, and the nervous system of the beings could not work. Because that was a fluke, the race of beings had not chosen to end. These sound beings came and the collective unconscious of all the Earth beings existing were re-created in slightly modified bodies (the highest order of their own bodies) with a little more resistance to potential solar flares. In this particular case we're talking about an entire population on the Earth at that time, including explorations under the Earth and under the sea, of about 130,000 people. This was a sea culture that . . .

Was the name of the culture the Toom?

I think it was, only it was "Tu-mm." I think this was essentially a culture that interacted in the sea quite a bit. They did that to save the culture because it wasn't intended that the culture be lost. I think there was an angelic that asked them to do that. I'm wracking my memory cells here, because I was with you, I wasn't here. But I think, as much as I can remember hearing about it at the time, that the angelic was associated with that culture. That's interesting: The angelic that was associated with that one was the forebear of an archangel that I don't think is with you anymore but was with you for a while. It was the Archangel Honor. That's a feminine being in this case, even though that's a masculine name in some cultures. This archangel was with *your* spirits for a short time; I think I may have heard it from them.

She went to those individuals and asked them if they would come and re-create this culture, and they did that by traveling through time, bending sound, primarily. They move through sound the way others move through space. So anywhere that sound exists or even a residual sound or an echo of sound, or where sound had passed through, they can go —which is most places.

How many of them are there? Is it just a tiny group or a particular race?

How many of them are there in terms of individual consciousnesses? Oh, I should think no more than forty thousand. Because you are dealing with space and time, you have soul branches that branch off of other soul branches. This is the other way around, where you have soul branches branching back into the trunk. So you have condensed souls instead of souls that are expanded.

Every time I ask you a question we learn so much information that just comes percolating out.

Yes, it's really true that there's something new under the sun from time to time.

Feminine Energy and Ancient Egypt

[Figure 17.6.] Okay. . . . Airport hill?

. . . and the Moon, yes. You know, sometime this might make a nice cover. This is a very special circumstance. The Moon is the last bastion of natural, nurturing energy on the feminine level for the Earth that cannot be overly disturbed (meaning corrupted by too many people). It's true that it's being mined, but the Moon's function for the Earth is largely reflective. Its job is to reflect all that happens on Earth —all that Mother Earth does, that the divine spirits and the fairy kingdom do, all that the people and the animals do, everything —back to the Earth, cycling it through the feminine source. This is why the Moon is associated with the tides, and with feminine energy. The Man in the Moon is somebody's idea —it's really the *Woman* in the Moon. I don't know where someone got the idea of the Man in the Moon.

What is here captured on film, due to the grace of the Moon spirit, is an actual stream of reflected energy recycled through the feminine source. The feminine source is not directly associated with the Moon; it is from Sirius, so the Moon is functioning in a mediumistic capacity here.

Fig. 17.6. A stream of reflected energy
recycled through the feminine source from Sirius.

Is it lowering the energy or is it just bringing it from Sirius?

It takes on the reflected energy of all that is happening on Earth and sends it to Sirius, bringing it through. Of course, it goes to Sirius when it's safe, fully encapsulated in a beam. The reflected energy goes to Sirius, where it is soaked with the feminine source; it doesn't go to any planet, just near one. It returns to the Moon and is reflected back to Earth. So what you have here is the feminine-self energy, which would be a divine energy, reflected back to Earth in a moment captured on film. This is as close as you can get at the moment to a picture of the divine feminine in process.

Do they go anyplace on the planet – that was over Airport Vortex – or do they send it to a vortex as an energy aid?

The intention is to aim it toward vortexes that will disseminate the energy and recycle it outward. As you can tell, there is more going on in the picture. To some extent, we have a portal and a lightbeing moving through the portal, which just happened to be caught on film.

This is a planetary portal from . . . that's interesting . . . Akhenaton. That's an interesting one, you know, because we're dealing with something here that is directly associated with Earth because of the

Egyptian culture. But it is actually from another planet, so we may be dealing here with the planetary source of the underground beings who trained the surface beings in what became known as the Egyptian culture. The idea of pyramids didn't start on Earth, obviously. So these people with their particular portal here may be responsible for that.

Let's explore that. Is somebody about to go into the portal? Is that lightbeing from the portal? What's the purpose?

I think that it's largely an observation of the picture-taker. Whoever took this photo has a direct relationship with those Egyptian times, and because this was a magical moment in which this divine energy was being photographed from the Moon, I believe that this portal opened to support and sustain the person taking the picture.

There's another story in there, something that's important for people to know now. That is that portals are more active now on your planet than they have ever been at any time in the past. People will be taking pictures of portals, some of which will be in color, some in black and white (though they won't show up quite as well), and some might even be ultrasonic (people will think they're something else, but they will actually be portals passing through the ultrasonic visual). These portals will almost always be associated with individuals. There are portals of other kinds, but individual people now are being – I don't want to say activated, but their spiritual clocks have essentially struck the hour, as it were, and all of the energies that can be passed through them are being activated to benefit the people of the Earth and to reinvigorate the spirit and devic energies associated with the Earth (including the fairies and so on) as well as the general goodwill and good vibrations that draw supportive and sustaining energy to the Earth. These portals I'm talking about now will all be associated with people rather than places or things.

I mention this because I want readers to be particularly alert for these portals. Now, you don't have to make anything big out of it. It will be exciting to see one, I guarantee you. Very sensitive people will simply see them. But for the most part, most people will see them like this: you'll catch something out of the corner of your eye. Or more likely, you'll be shifting your gaze suddenly from point A to B, whatever that might be, and you'll see a flash of light. You'll see perhaps a disk or half a disk of light; it might be blocked by something. It'll most likely be in color, but it might also appear as white light or cloudy light. If there's nobody else around that you are aware of, this portal probably has to do with yourself. If there are other people around, it may have to do with you or somebody else. I mention this phenomenon to you now because it's very active through a lot of people.

So what should they do?

I'm disinclined to be more specific about the people who will see these things, because there are certain spirits that have been polarized to the negative but are not actually negative, who are functioning to keep the Earth in a dense place and block all energies of beauty. Some of these dense spirits are associated with the sinister secret government, but some are simply associated with the denser or shadow side of the mass consciousness of certain human beings.

What about that lightbeing in the lower left?

This is quite a wondrous thing. Someone came through the portal, as I said (we're going to keep the picture-taker anonymous). This is a picture of an angel. It's a nice idea that angels look like human beings and that they have wings and all that — I don't want to say that they don't. But I would say that very often they appear in a form like this. This angel has come through the portal to be with and bless the picture-taker at the moment of taking the picture.

Is that like the godself, or the high self or the source self of the picture-taker?

It is not. It is an angel from the angelic kingdom that is associated with the divine feminine. This angel came through the portal to bless, support, sustain and love the picture-taker.

Then there has to be a connection between the feminine energy and the ancient Egyptian energy.

Yes. When you go way back to the ancient Egyptian energy, we had a hierarchical system, but not higher and lower. We had levels and layers. The beings that came from the planet I mentioned before are all feminine beings. They came and established a colony deep inside the Earth. These feminine beings realized that they themselves could not train the surface beings, because the culture of the time on the surface was masculine-dominated. So they had to have an intermediary. They could train the priestess class, but they could not train the priest class themselves. They needed to create an intermediary race or call for one. They sent out a call and some beings came, but they didn't work out because they couldn't relate sufficiently to the feminine beings. They could relate to the surface beings, but not to the trainers. It was necessary to create a genetic blend between the surface people and that feminine race, so there were offspring. These offspring, both male and female, became the intermediary race. Until very recently, they were still living underneath the Earth in the area of northern Egypt, the northern Sinai peninsula, extreme northern Saudi Arabia, and parts of southern Iraq and northern Iran. But because of tensions in the Middle East and the work on highly complex defensive systems, especially in Saudi Arabia (these defensive systems are using sound and are basically what I'd call electronic countermeasures), the intermediary race had to leave because of their sensitivity to the strong electromagnetic pulse waves that were being used in what is amounting to an offensive capacity. I'm not going to talk about that too much because I don't feel it's my place to give away national defense secrets of Saudi Arabia.

Because of that, you're saying they have now left?

The intermediary race has left, the one that had been largely responsible for the training of the priest and priestess class of ancient Egypt.

Can you put a date on that? How did that tie in with the Atlanteans coming to Egypt?

It might have started around 16,000 years ago.

What about the picture on the top?

The Angel Antonitus Upgraded

Figure 17.7. Here we have a couple of different things going on, as you can tell by the different colors. Again, there's a certain amount of orange radiation here, which is an Earth reaction to the white light. The white light is angelic. The angel — I can give you a name, which is not normal. One moment, permission being granted here. [Long wait.] This is an angel, the name is Antonitus. He was being upgraded in this moment — what he has been and is becoming. This is an upgrading of Antonitus: Here is what Antonitus has been, here is what he is becoming, you see. In this moment he is being upgraded to an archangel. Here is divine Earth spirit celebrating the moment.

Does he have something to do with the Earth?

He will now. He's being upgraded so that he can help guide the transformation to the upper level of soul incarnation of physical beings of a certain nature (which I can't tell you right now because I'm hiding their identity). It's a very broad identity that I'll give you at some point, but these certain physical beings amongst you, and there are many, will be guiding, influencing, transforming and protecting the hearts and souls of all life on Earth. These people, though they be in flesh and form, are all angels in disguise. They know not who

Fig. 17.7. Antonitus being upgraded to an archangel.
Here is divine Earth spirit celebrating the moment.

they are, but some of them are beginning to feel there is something special happening for them. And they will feel a stronger attraction to the fairy world, to the lightbeing world, to the devic world, to nature in general, and will also be recalling at some point their ET contacts. They've all had ET contacts, every one of them.

That's beautiful. There are so many more angel books appearing now that angels are becoming such a big subject. How do you upgrade an angel? Are they created, are they ensouled? How does that work?

You upgrade an angel by essentially giving them more work to do. [Laughs.] You take them out of the realm of the angelic work and you assign them a task, which is generally greater than they think they can handle (which makes it a little bit like human souls). You give them the support and sustenance they need for the first millennium or so, and then they realize they can handle it completely on their own. So this particular archangel, Antonitus, is being given support and sustenance by Earth devic energies associated with the cosmic pulse of life. This is the matter that holds all matter together. (It is essentially the scientific term for love.)

I thought angels were created and that was it, but are they also on an evolutionary path and ensouled?

They are on an evolutionary path, and their evolutionary path, as they often say, is dependent upon you. That is because they must serve you according to your needs. There's a tremendous amount of soul expansion going on now, as you know, so more angels are being drawn into your society to serve, to function, to support, sustain and so on. As a result, there will be a few more upgrades. You'll be hearing about more archangels that you hadn't heard of before, because, not to put too fine a point on it, they're going to be promoted. You need them.

That's great! When we become the gods we are, then what do they become? When we realize who we are, how does that relate to them?

As you begin to realize who you are, they will simply blend with you. They represent the separated portion of all of you that has necessarily been separated out so that you might learn how to be creative. When Creator birthed your souls and said, "Go and learn all that I know so that I might pass on to my next realm and you might take over for me," Creator wisely separated you from your godself so that you might learn from scratch, as it were (no pun intended). In this case, the angelic kingdom is largely the combined effect of that separated portion of yourselves and is a separate ensouling from the Creator having to do with all of the Source energies that make you up. All of the people who've ever been on Earth, and your souls, have had ET lives. But you haven't had infinite ET lives; you haven't been everywhere. Thus there's a limit. So the light from all those places that you have been, as well as the light from Earth, is the light source for the angelic kingdom.

So could you say that every soul has an angelic part?

Yes. To fulfill the angelic mission, from the angelic point of view, they must descend a little bit to where you are in density, but they can't descend very far. You must ascend somewhat to access what they have to offer. Because you cannot ascend to their particular pulse dimension unless you know how to find them, there is a cord that connects you to them. Some people refer to this as a silver cord.

Oh, I always thought that connected the soul to the physical. But there's another end of it, then?

That's right!

What if some people don't have one?

In my experience, the silver cord might be broken because of something you chose to do, not because of something the angelics chose to do. But as soon as you start coming up in your consciousness, expanding it, it will repair itself. So no matter how far down you go or have been as an individual, when you come back up (and you will at some point, regardless of your philosophical path) the cord will repair itself and your angelic will be able to help you.

That's in Boynton Canyon, so a lot of this light work is done in vortex areas now.

Oh yes. Definitely.

People going to vortexes can gain the benefit of some of these things that no one knows is happening.

Oh yes. Of course, if there were mobs of people there, they probably would have to go to a different vortex to do this, because too many people create a chaotic energy field.

One of the benefits of going to a vortex, beyond what we already know, is that there will be some of this residual feminine energy or upgrading energy or . . .

. . . angelic energy, yes. Definitely.

Pleiadian Ship Restocking Liquid Light

Figure 17.8. Here we have, I believe, a couple of lightships. You have to look closely; it may not show up in the photograph, but you can see one of them pretty clearly. I believe it is restoring, rebuilding its liquid light stock by interacting with the rainbow. Granted, the ship is not exactly where the rainbow is, but it's close enough. You

Fig. 17.8. A Pleiadian ship restocking liquid light.

have to remember, too, that rainbows are a result of where you stand more than a result of the other factors. The ship is from the Pleiades; after all, who else would be restocking liquid light? It is unusual for a Pleiadian ship, so I'm going to talk about the one ship; the other one just happens to be passing by and is not of any great consequence.

So it's the top ship.

Yes. The Pleiadian ship is restocking liquid light for its liquid-light training, which is largely meant for children aboard the ship. The ship is quite large, but it's not what you'd call a mothership. It has roughly 2500 people aboard, not counting visitors. The liquid light is used to train and to entertain the children, and occasionally to entertain and calm visitors. You can't help but be calmed by it because it swirls and dances around you. It is enchanting.

Different colors?

Yes.

So it's a rainbow sort of . . . .

Yes, the rainbow is sort of a fixed focal-length version of liquid light. If you look at a rainbow, you see sort of sparkling things in it. You can see the same sparkling things in liquid light. They can be used educationally, or they can simply be a further portion of the charm of the light itself.

Figure 17.9. And this one you can use or not use. I think you can see the ship in it. You're seeing the trail of the ship. We have here a double rainbow, which doesn't show up very good, but you can kind of make it out.

Same ship?

Same ship; its trail.

Moving away?

Yes.

Figure 17.10. Here we have, obviously, a military vehicle, the type known as a transport vehicle that occasionally transports troops but usually transports supplies. The interesting factor in the picture is these beams. What we have here (I think the photographer will tell you these are not wires) is an electromagnetic countermeasure that has gone wrong. The countermeasure device is in effect for no particular reason other than the military would prefer to perform its functions, however mundane, without being constantly scanned by ETs. This is because the military cannot easily discern the difference between a negative and a positive ET. So we have here an electromag-

Fig. 17.9. The trail of the ship seen in figure 8.

Fig. 17.10. An electromagnetic countermeasure that has gone wrong on a military transport vehicle.

netic device intended to block being scanned. However, the device is on too strong, and certain sensitive people who shall go unnamed are able to photograph it.

So this is emanating from the military ship?

Yes. So a note to the military: It's about sixty percent too strong. Power it down; it'll still work.

All right, very good.

Figure 17.11. Here we have a picture of unity, which if you look at it closely and blow it up, you will discover that we have a top and a bottom. Unity is moving through space in order to form (not to quote the Declaration) a complete union. I would like you to note the similarity between the "front piece" of unity, and human lips. It is not

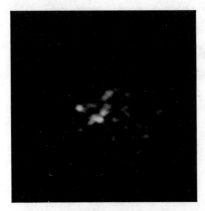

Fig. 17.11. Unity moving through space.

an accident that human lips are two things that form not only a means for communication but a means for the transference of affection and a means by which one receives gracefully.

Is this an archetype of unity? A prototype?

So much is going on on your planet. The interesting thing is that these things have always taken place on third-dimensional Earth, but now that third-dimensional Earth is moving toward the fourth dimension, you're beginning to see the things that have already been here for quite some time, and sensitive people are able to photograph them. In some cases the people that are photographing them (though not in this case) are not particularly sensitive, but that which is being photographed desires to be seen so it can make itself known more directly. So here you have the ensouled energy of unity, which is coming, by its very existence, to bless you as a culture and to spread a little unity around.

You know, you are being constantly flooded with the harmonic of disunity. In some cases it just happens to work out that way, and in some cases it is deliberately done by those who would keep you fighting amongst each other so that you don't come together and work and live and love together. Because unity is making its presence known more strongly, you might notice that even in a polarized form, certain groups of people are coming together more unified than ever. Now, you might say that you don't like that, because this group, for instance, is very unified and radical and that group is very unified and radical. Even though it's fragmentary, unity is taking place, and it won't be too long before the groups see the advantage of working together. Most people will understand this politically before they understand it philosophically and lovingly. Because your societies are so enamored with political man and all that he does, you will tend to find this out through political or journalistic channels first.

Should we tune into it, should we invoke it to unify aspects of ourselves?

Yes, the best thing would be to unify the parts of yourself. Everybody's shadow side is now coming on very strong, with the intent of being loved, healed, gracefully accepted and being transformed, as you all know. There is great joy in bringing the so-called black sheep back into the family and seeing its transformation into fellow, loving sheep (no connotation on black or white here is intended). If people could only understand that their dark sides are up not so much to take charge or protect them — but because they desperately need to be loved. Then simply accept that side of yourself, though not to function from there, and say, "Okay, you're me; come on along." Then anytime it rears its head, notice it and say, "Oh, you're my dark side. I love you, too. Come along." Then function out of your lighter side. Just accept it; don't get angry at it. Then go on! This is a very important factor. Very important.

Figure 17.12. This is a tricky little fellow. That is the face of power. The reason it's tricky is because power is amoral. That is why when you are learning to be a creator, you need to have some form of polarization so that when you deal with power, you can only go so far without being balanced by the other direction when you are empowering the dark side. Now if the picture were blown up a bit, you could see that there are almost faces in there, and those faces represent different expressions — you know, like the masks of comedy and tragedy, one smiling and one frowning. This was a personal message to the photographer. The face of power came to him to inform

Fig. 17.12. The Face of Power.

him that his ability to achieve these photographs would be enhanced in the future because of his spiritual and to some extent physical abilities. That's part of the reason we've seen more startling pictures from the photographer, and in the future I expect even more extraordinary ones.

Isn't there a universal application of this face of power, or is it only connected to him?

It's a little tricky, but if it were blown up, for instance, and people were to stare at it and consider something that they wished to resolve within themselves, they could meditate on this picture and have greater energy toward that resolution. Equally, if people who were involved with the dark side were to stare at it, they might have greater energy to pursue their nefarious intentions.

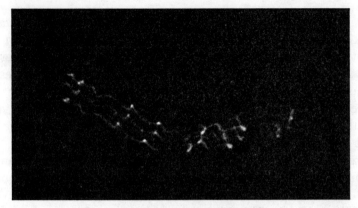

Fig. 17.13. A light ribbon.

Pleiadians Integrating Saturnian Philosophy

Figure 17.13. Here we have something interesting. The main light here has been talked about before to some minor degree. But if you look closely, you can see that there is a light energy skipping off the main light (the main focus of the picture), launching or redirecting itself toward a different dimensional focus. Sometimes lightbeings have a limited capacity to move from one point to another — this is where portals come in. But sometimes portals are not available while the being is in transit. What may be available, as it is in this case, is a light ribbon, which is more like a light path that becomes available and functions in a fashion similar to the mathematics that a navigator uses to plot a course (in a commercial aircraft, for example). A very precise angle is calculated that the lightbeing can travel through, and the angle is redirected, reenergized and given a new harmonic, whereby the lightbeing is able to be attracted to its place of destiny rather than being propelled. Attraction, as you know, is the more powerful force; the light ribbon is doing just exactly that with that lightbeing.

Can I say who the lightbeing is, what his purpose is, where the light ribbon is from?

The light ribbon is simply from the point of origin of all portals, which is the density of the ninth dimension. They are birthed there and sent out into action. The lightbeing is in this case from the seventh dimension and just happens to be moving through this part of space. It is not visiting here, but happens to be here because the light ribbon is here. It deflected its course a little to use the light ribbon for renavigation. The lightbeing in this case is from the eleventh dimension of Saturn, and it's being refocused to move directly to the star system Pleiades, where it will interact with the teachers of the Pleiadians to inform them of the evolution of the Saturnian philosophical rhythm. This is a term used to describe the philosophy of the planet Saturn as a being unto itself. This is important at this time to the Pleiadian culture because the culture is integrating some new harmonic rhythms, tones, into their tonal range. They, like you, have had some limitation in their tonal range, though it is broader than yours. They are now getting an even broader tonal range integrated into their capacity to absorb and "hear" it. This lightbeing is bringing not only that harmonic but the means of infusing it into the Pleiadian culture's present tonal rhythm.

These particular rhythms coming in now will allow the Pleiadians to adapt more comfortably to very slight discomfort (about 1½ to 2 percent), which they cannot do right now because it would cause them to get sick and eventually die uncomfortably. This new Saturnian harmonic will allow them to create a harmonic chord resonant within themselves, keyed off a central crystal directed from the eleventh dimension of Saturn. This will give them an initial protection from a degree of discomfort that would be insignificant to you or any Earth person, but difficult for them. The new harmonic will give them initial protection, so they can experience it very fleetingly while it is in its midst, and then create this harmonic, which will protect them. It's a complex issue; Pleaidians must move very slowly into minor discomfort so it will not bring about disease to their culture. This is very carefully being avoided because a harmonic is a real factor of discomfort energy or negative energy, of which disease is a potential byproduct. We don't want that to happen on the Pleiades, so this method is being used where they can slowly, very gently become used to it without suddenly becoming overwhelmed by it.

Figure 17.14. This is interesting. Here we have the original light model that has been used to inspire flight by human beings on Earth. This model was given in dreams and visions to all the people who built successful flying ships in the beginning, whether they be the flying ships you are familiar with now (airplanes and so on) or those of more ancient cultures, ships associated with

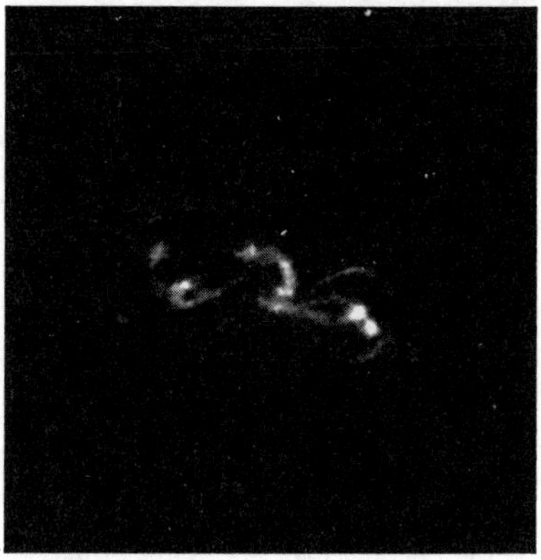

Fig. 17.14. The Eye of Horus.

disk patterns and so on — all that have been built on Earth. This light model has exactly the same energy by which birds and other flying creatures — moths, butterflies, etc. — are inspired and initiated. Not that they don't have their own devic energies and fairies and so on, but they must flow through this energy in order to have the rhythm, inspiration and intention of flight. But this is not all. It is also the origin of the Eye of Horus. Those who originally created what has come to be known as the Eye of Horus were inspired by visions of this flight energy. Their interpretation pictured it as a free-floating eye that sees all. As a result of their cultural training, that which was in the air, flight, had to do with that which could see all.

So here we have a light energy that has a significant history.

Say more about the Eye of Horus. That's Egyptian . . . how does it come down to us in our mythology now?

The actual intent of the Eye of Horus, or how to use it, was not something that looks at you. It was really intended as a mask. You turn the eye around and look through it. So it can be used to see the universe, not only the universe in yourself and those around you, but the universe at a distance. It can be used as a tool to inspire imagination and visions. That is its intent. It might be the source of a workshop at some point, doing applications of the Eye of Horus through visionary techniques.

A Being Pulled into Third Dimension

Figure 17.15. Well, this is a scary little one. It's very hard to see and you'd probably have to make a sketch of it, but there's a line down there in the corner. There are a couple of other lines; can you see them slightly?

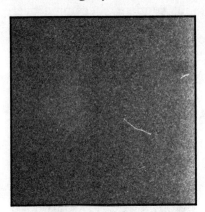

Fig. 17.15. A being being pulled through a crack in time.

There's a big round light, a diagonal line and then a horizontal line, a very short one.

The round body has just emerged through those lines. Those lines are cracks in space and time. That round body's not supposed to be there. It was later retrieved by interdimensional beings who can pass through all space and time and patch up these cracks. I believe this crack — which pulled this being from the tenth-and-a-half dimension without its wanting to be pulled —was traversing from the eleventh to the tenth dimension of a different galaxy. That's the thing about cracks in space and time: If you have a crack in one place, you'd think you'd just fall through to another dimension of the same place, but now it doesn't work that way. This is on the other side of the universe!

The sound of the being's name would be like [first clicks his tongue] Kachi'tonat'sa. This being was pulled into your dimension very briefly and was totally disorganized when this picture was taken. The being does not look like that at all. If you were to see that being, it would appear to be rather round and flat from the side, it would look like a disk. But if you were to see it straight on it would be slightly oval.

Is it very thin?

Very thin, yes, disklike in transit mode. But there you see it in a disorganized state, completely confused in your density. The lines are cracks in space and time, which were repaired in about three seconds of your time. The being was ... picture in cartoon style a hand coming through, grabbing the being and pulling him back into his own space. That's roughly what happens, although it happens on an energetic level. That being, in terms of your time, required about ten-and-a-half or eleven hours of reorientation into its own dimension to understand and to feel comfortable. If you're whizzing along in that dimension and suddenly you become densified to the point of 3.4 dimension, it's quite a shock. You're this large being, you know, and whap! You're suddenly this very small being. It's pretty frightening.

What is the being's reality?

I think the reality is basically along the lines of vibration. Not tone, not sound as you understand it, but the echo of sound. The best way I can describe it would be like this: If you made a sound, and then measured the vibration in, say, a cymbal (like a drummer would play) five or six feet away from the original sound, the vibration would be similar to that being's world.

I like to give examples like this because it's so vague to say, "it's from a vibrational reality." What does that mean? But here's something that you can actually produce. It may not mean much to you, but it would give you an idea.

So has he come up through the dimensions? Has he already ...

No, no. This being has always been in that dimension and I think always will be. He's the form and function of that. I might add that vibrational sounds, the echoes and such, are all a form of life there as well. If it hadn't been that you had vibrations here, that being would have been totally mad and I don't think it could have been recovered. But because you have vibration and music and tones and harmonics here, the being fortunately survived the experience.

But there are realities and galaxies and universes where there is no evolutionary process? There is no involution and then evolution?

No, they are what they are and happy to be it.

And that's all they'll ever be?

Well, that sounds rather judgmental; I'd rather say that that is what they choose to be, and they enjoy that. They celebrate life in their every moment; they are very happy, and that is sufficient for them.

Then devolution and evolution are a choice?

Oh, yes. Yes! When the Creator broke off a segment of Itself and sent you on your way, you were just a segment, you know. The Creator is many things, and many of that which is Creator are perfectly happy to remain exactly what they are; they don't have any desire to be anything else. Nor do they choose to act upon a desire they don't have.

So what percent are evolutionary beings compared to the total mass of the Creator?

I can give you that, but I'm going to need a piece of paper and a pencil. I'll give it to you in the form of a decimal.

Maybe the Creator's a whole body and we're the brain cells, so we get to evolve?

This is the percentage of beings caught up in evolution that exist as a total portion of the Creator's being.

[Laughter.]

Not much!

One!

You don't need that many! Because that which creates evolutionary pull or direction for creation is just that. Let's say this: That portion of an airplane, a commercial aircraft — a 747, for example — that is involved in its actual navigation (the computer chips) makes up a rather small portion of the entire vehicle.

So the wing is happy to be a wing and the rudder's happy to be a rudder and . . .

Well, given that they were. That which creates direction, purpose, motivation, does not have to be very much! It is strictly that portion which guides, encourages. Everything else goes along and is part of creation performing other functions.

But that number is then applied to the total number of beings so incomprehensibly large that it's beyond . . .

That's why I wrote it down that way. I wanted you to be able to see something that you can consider a measurement. This is why, when people want to be involved in the evolutionary process, there are many more volunteers than places to put them. That's why it is always said here that being here is a privilege! Even though it doesn't necessarily feel like one, it's an advanced degree for which very few are given an opportunity. But then again, you might say it another way: In the larger sense, very few want the opportunity! However, there are usually more that want the opportunity than those that have the opportunity to do it.

But they get it in the next cosmic day, or something like that?

If they want it. Very few of them actually do want it, nor is it intended for them to have it. The ones that do want it that can't, yes, they get their chance.

We're still deciding if choosing to join the evolutionary process is a lack of wisdom or too much courage, right? Jehovah keeps saying "we had more courage than wisdom."

I can't say that I agree with Jehovah. I'd say that you were driven by the search for wisdom. And yes, it takes great courage to do it, but you were driven by the search for wisdom.

It's a joke . . .

All right, I'll let him off the hook.

Figure 17.16. Here's something you don't see every day — I know I say that from time to time, but here it is again. This is pretty wild. Here we have the higher self of the star system Pleiades dreaming — traveling through space dreaming. Naturally, when it dreams one of the first places it's going to visit is here, because the Pleiadean people and the people of Earth are directly connected. So this is the star system Pleiades' lightbody dreaming.

What is it dreaming?

It is dreaming at that moment

Fig. 17.16. The star system Pleiades' lightbody dreaming.

of the indivisibility of your cultures, and it is longing for and missing the souls that make up the souls of the people on Earth. It is missing you who are connected to the Pleiades, and can't wait for you to return. It sometimes comes to visit.

How beautiful!

Is that not sweet?

Is that a mark on the film over here where your thumb is?

Oh, thank you for reminding me. That is an elemental. There are two marks there. Well, there are actually several marks there. They are all visitors from the fairy world, elementals associated with what people generally call fairies, although elementals and fairies are not quite the same thing. They are there to land their utter and complete heart, which is what they are, to support the Pleiadian lightbody; to make it comfortable for the Pleiadean lightbody to be in the Earth vibration, even at that density of itself, which is a very high attunement and would not necessarily be affected by . . .

You said they came from the higher part of the Pleiades . . .

Yes, and these members of the fairy kingdom and elementals are there to provide loving, cherishing support so that the higher dimensional aspect of the Pleiadian lightbody feels at home. What is referred to as the elementals and the fairies and gnomes have a direct counterpart on the Pleiades who are completely safe and can function and not under any stress at all as compared to those on this planet, stressed because of the changes of man.

So is the high self of the star system an evolutionary root? Has it come up through the ranks, or is it projected down from its Source?

I believe we have something that's really seeded from the Source here rather than something that's come up from the ranks. It's more akin to the angelic kingdom, which can come down a little bit, rather than something that's gone up. I don't think it can come down much further.

Let's say a human has an angel. Does the Pleiadean system have this higher self, this large being?

Oh well, so does your own universe, your own galaxy.

Are there parts from the Source that they haven't integrated with yet that come down . . .

No. In your own galaxy you would have a higher source lightbody like this too, because everything is alive. As it is for one individual thing in the physical world, so it is for all individual things in the physical world.

In the galaxy differently, you mean in our solar system.

Oh yes, thank you — in your solar system.

So Helios has come up through the ranks and he has a lightbody, or is the lightbody?

Helios is the lightbody.

And what do we call the one who ensouls the Sun who has advanced upward?

What comes forth to me is Maitreya.

If we can sneak little questions in once in a while, we begin to understand how all this works.

Yes, and someday correlate it all. We'll really have something then.

Yes.

Fig. 17.17. A present-day Orion vehicle.

Figure 17.17. Here we have two ships, disks. As you hold the picture toward yourself, the one on the left is a present-day Orion vehicle. They are exuding a harmonic vibration. This is the harmonic vibration they make when they move from one space to another. You have seen in the Meier film, perhaps, the Pleiadean ship moving through space and time, disappearing in one place and reappearing in another place within the frame of the camera. Here you have the same thing: The ship on the left is the same ship on the right. It's moving from left to right, but you still have the light image of itself on the left while the image of itself on the right is forming. So here we have a photograph based on that appearance in Billy Meier's film of the Pleiadian ship, which some of your readers may have seen.

Why is it doing this? Is that how it moves?

I believe it is doing this just because the people in the vehicle know that the photographer is present and they would like to give the photographer a little gift, as it were. Many ETs are like this, you know. They are very benevolent and supportive. Remember that the photographer has taken many, many pictures, and sometimes nothing comes out. But the photographer makes the same effort every time, so it's very much of a struggle. Sometimes ETs, if they are present and they are able to do something, will do this for the photographer so that he feels supported by beings from afar.

Other than this navigational miracle here, what were they doing, where were they going?

They just happened to be passing, but they were aware of the photographer's work and they stopped. They were headed back, I believe, to seventh-dimensional, current-day Orion culture. They come here a lot. They are allowed to come here because there are so many beings now on Earth coordinated to Orion past, present or future. When you take it all into account, fully 19+% of the people on the Earth are connected to Orion past, present or future right now, which is a really significant amount. So Orion vehicles are allowed to come and go pretty much at will. When they come in these higher dimensions they're not going to be affected by anything that goes on in your now dimension. So the photographer was photographing something of a higher dimension; he was not photographing something in this dimension.

Okay, but do they come to check on the beings connected with them, or to lend support?

Mostly to lend support, sometimes to observe, occasionally to contact. The last is quite rare these days, but I think in this case they were here to contact about three people, which they did through what I would call a technology of dream evacuation. Meaning that when the soul is on a dream and the dream is not critical, you understand — a critical dream might take place at the very deepest levels of sleep where you are being instructed or when you are instructing others. Dreams at other levels not quite as deep basically involve psychological symbolism or entertainment. In dreams at that level it is considered allowable by the powers that be to induce a dream evacuation, wherein the soul or the soul personality is in one of these not-so-critical dreams. It is evacuated — taken from that dream — to the vehicle, where they visit. This is a pleasant thing, not an abduction. They visit their Orion friends, there is fun and games, music, stories, a pleasant experience. They travel back in time to the dreamspace, and the dream continues. When the dreamer wakes up he really doesn't remember it, but his soul has been refreshed by the present-day harmonic and the pleasant reality of this Orion source. *That's beautiful. The personality doesn't remember.*

No, the personality doesn't remember it, but the soul has been regenerated, supported and nourished.

Fig. 17.18. A vehicle from Zeta Reticuli being escorted by members of the fairy world.

Zetas and Andromedans Networking for Earth

Figure 17.18. Here we have a vehicle, the red-orange one there from Zeta Reticuli, being escorted through your dimension almost playfully by members (again) of the fairy world. They are very active now because they are being reinvigorated, welcomed, by many souls, by many people. Even the angelics are encouraging them to return in some form. Members of the fairy world are usually associated with different plants or animals, and because many of these species are now extinct or no longer alive on the surface of the planet, these particular fairies would not normally be here. But certain lightbeings, certain angelic beings and so on, are creating a tonal harmony of that original plant or animal around the lightbody of Earth, that allows these fairies to be present. If you understand that, then you'll see how they could be present even though the plants or animals they represent might be dinosaurs or some fern no longer present on the surface because the surface has become too cold. (You know, in the Northern Hemisphere where you now consider it to be cold or icy, some places, once upon a time, were very hot tropical swamps. Those ferns existed then, which is why archaeologists and others are amused by such finds.)

They are escorting the Zeta Reticulan ship just for pleasure. The

Zetas in this case are passing through, checking up on things, networking (as you say in the computer lingo) with friends from Andromeda who were involved in a council meeting in the higher aspect of the planet Mars. The council meeting had to do with Earth and the people on Earth. There are beings on Mars in higher dimensions, right around the fifth dimension, who look just like human beings. The Zetas couldn't attend the conference because of duties elsewhere, but they came to talk about the conference with their friends from Andromeda, and that's where they're going right now. The friends from Andromeda are in your solar system, parked at that point, about 290 miles from your planet. They are passing through to meet with them to get an update on the meeting.

What were the results of the meeting? What was the purpose of the meeting?

The purpose of the meeting was to learn how things are going on Earth. How is it with the culture? Are the people feeling any greater unity? Does it look like they will be transmitting fewer microwaves in the future? That's a major concern of other cultures. Your culture does not realize the extremely negative and damaging effects of microwave radiation on higher-dimensional beings. This damage tends to create a certain degree of breakdown in the transharmonics. Transharmonics in this case is the means by which your souls interact with higher-dimensional aspects of themselves, their teachers, angels, everybody else, and this microwave radiation is unintentionally disturbing that. So they're concerned about that. They don't want to interfere. They do, however, have permission from the councils that observe, as well as the Creator and Creator's teachers, to interfere with microwave radiation if it reaches a lethal level. That's about 19% to 21%. Below that level, if it should ever become lethal they have complete permission to interfere, which you would probably experience on a practical level here on Earth as an interruption in computer and perhaps logistical transmissions, but more likely telephone conversations. You know, the ETs are not going to interfere with critical microwave-transmitted data from say, ship to shore or from an airplane to its guiding instrumentalities and all that. They're more likely to interfere with telephone conversations.

So as we move on up the dimensions then, we will eventually find another way to transmit phone conversations. Part of it is also the secret government doing their . . . ? Are the microwaves all benign right now?

No, microwave energy is just bad for you. It disrupts your . . .

No, I mean the purpose.

Theoretically, its purpose is communications.

Yes.

So we will move to something that is benign for us, right?

Yes, probably you'll use crystals – in their natural form rather than their artificial form.

Figure 17.19. Here we have a lightbeing from Arcturus sort of following along, observing a military helicopter from your legitimate military. The lightbeing is simply watching in a bemused fashion.

We've got three things over here, too.

Am I missing something?

Fig. 17.19. A bemused lightbeing from Arcturus
observing a military helicopter.

There's a white circle, a black circle, and then a line.

I think what you have here is essentially Andromedan beings. One of them, the dark part that you refer to, is a part of the electronic countermeasures on a very mild level, detecting the Arcturian lightbeings, but not really making any effort to be combative. So we have here a standoff, one side observing the other and the other side observing back electronically, to the best of their ability. But no hostilities.

So our secret government has the ability to electronically observe any lightbeing from anywhere?

The military has the capacity to detect variations or ripples in magnetic energy. Because of the intensity of these lightbeings, a ripple in magnetic radiation was created, and it was perceived as just that, not as a lightbeing from Arcturus. If it were, you can be sure the ship would be turning over there and putting on a full array. But they didn't do that; they just noticed the ripple and went on. It wasn't perceived as a threat, in other words.

What was the Arcturian ship doing?

It wasn't really a ship. We're talking about lightbeings here. They were simply passing through, as they often do these days. They have to do with change; that is their core. And since you are all changing in a big way, they are passing through to support that. Their presence supports change.

I asked about the book that José Argüelles wrote called The Arcturus Probe; *are they related to that or is that another story?*

No, they are not.

Are there actual beings out there who are related to that, or is it more of a possibility?

I'd rather call it a possibility.

18

To Life!

YHWH through Arthur Fanning
July 14, 1995

What do you think of this Photon Belt thing?
That's a question I was going to ask you!

I forgot, I should have waited. What do you think of it? I beat
you to it.

*You did beat me to it, I was thinking of it. Well, are we in it right now,
and are we in a hologram? Is the Earth in a hologram?*

Well, you are a hologram, you're just not aware of it.

*Mm-hmm. But how far are we into the Photon? And are we ready to
come out yet?*

It is more like this: When you say "Photon Belt" you think it is a
thing outside of yourself. Well, it is not. It is your consciousness
coming back to find you, know you? It is a great group of consciousnesses coming. It is an alive thing, know you *alive*, and it is part of
you. It's sort of a bargain you made a long time ago: "If I get lost, you
come and get me." Know you what I mean? So, as far as getting out
of it, you *have* been out of it. You don't want to get out of it. You want
to be united. So there are things going to be shook up a little bit. No
big deal. All fun. Know you what fun is?

You can consider this Photon Belt like a truck. And you're
standing in the road, but you're also the driver in the truck. So the
truck doesn't have to run over the person in the road, the driver
recognizes the being in the road and it goes alongside, stops, and lets
the being get on. And then you both continue down the road.

No accident.

That is a truth; there is no accident. Why does it concern you?

It's my curiosity.

It's part of your thinkity-think, mm?

Mm-hmm, my thinkity-think, right.

Well, you need to think sometimes, but it can be confusing a lot of the time.

Yes.

What portion of your thinkity-think keeps your heart beating?

What portion?

Of your thinkity-think keeps the heart beating?

I don't know!

It's a good thing, eh?

The Choice for Freedom of Choice

You're moving through a great shift in your consciousness, all of humanity is. One of the things you enjoy is your free will, you say, your freedom of choice. Because you have neglected your divinity for so long, you devised a plan —you term it the Photon Belt, you play with here —to have an effect upon you. And you will *feel* that you don't have any choice, because a greater part of your being is coming to join you, to unite with you. And *this* is a choice you made a long, long time ago. Everyone breathe a moment. No big deal! You're going to get through it, might as well relax. Your meditations will help you through this thing. It is energy is what it is. It is consciousness is what it is. You are energy. You are not only your persona, you are light beings in the body. You are a soul in the body. You are love. That's what you're made up of, including all of the sticky stuff that you attracted to you to pretend you're not.

Now, because light —spiritual light, now —when it enters this density, it lowers its frequency, becomes an electrical force: electrum, movement of light in this density. Your body has electrums in it, electricity flowing through it. You have magnetic fields around your body. These energies, as they come around you, are going to affect those fields, they're going to adjust them. So you're going to end up being in a brand-new vehicle, so to speak. And don't get all caught up in your DNA this and your DNA that, because you haven't seen it, really. Be thankful that the Father within you was smart enough to put an electrical force there where you could not think about it and to keep your heart beating. And also be thankful the DNA is tucked in where it's supposed to be, indeed? Say, "Whew! Got away with that one!" No big deal! You're going to make it. When you start thinking and do this worry-worry thing, you get *all* confused, know you what I mean? You get into jumble, a big pot, and you cook it, cook it, cook it, steam goes all over, doesn't even taste good when you eat it. Know you what I mean?

Mm-hmm.

Don't blame. Going to be plenty of opportunity to blame very soon for everyone here. Some of the blame that I've been getting for a long time is going to shift! [Much laughter.] Going to be more outrageous than you think!

Another Photon Belt one, here. You two should meet for coffee and discuss all of the things that are *not* going to happen! Little clue: Why are they not going to happen? Because your consciousness is evolving, and you're going to understand that you are, in a manner, uniting. So it won't be as threatening as other beings want you to think it is.

Indeed.

Indeed?

I allow.

It be fun.

Good. I'm ready.

Mm? Be have to look for a word, toboggan, know you? You can either enjoy the ride or be terrified all of the way. It *will* be exciting. Enjoy the ride. Don't take your hands off the handles to take pictures.

The Forever Thing

Am I doing okay? It's been an interesting two weeks.

Are you doing okay? I'll check my okay list. Looks okay to me! What is *not* okay?

Whatever it was, I think it's better.

Can you allow yourself to remind you of your divinity that be right there? Indeed, forever? Forever?

Mm-hmm.

So be it! That's all we need, no problem, indeed? Are you worried about this forever thing?

I don't know, what's a forever thing? I don't need to worry now. Forever. That means forever, and forever, and forever . . . hmm?

You don't simply remind yourself of your divinity this lifetime, forget, and go over here! You *can*, know you? Know you what I mean? I'm being sneaky. Know you waves of water?

Water be very emotional energy, indeed? You can either ride the waves — how you say, on top — or you can be tossed under, indeed? My suggestion be: more fun on top. Indeed? Your divinity is always on the top, know you? Your persona sometimes is down here, in this part, in the turmoil. You understand?

Now . . . know this word, "guides," and beings that assist you in other realities, other realms? They are like buddies, know you? Not bosses. So you can sit down with your buddies and suggest to them, you want to handle certain things this way, that way, and to assist you that you do it. You understand? And if they're not performing, get a new buddy! You have that authority!

We're going to bring more energy in the room this evening, to activate you. Do not become upset if you get a little bit of diarrhea. The energy is simply cleaning you out. It is a high frequency. Some of you have already had the pleasure of that experience in the last couple of days this week. This Photon Belt moves very fast! [Laughter.]

Is it anything like a safety belt?

Well, it's not a belt, it is like a string of pearls running through this body, and you're part of this thing. So there's a lot of humor here.

The Fear Game

One of the games you beings play here is fear. You *really* enjoy it! You do! You "see how far I can get to scare myself and get out!" And you're very creative in the games to produce that effect for you. Know you? You even create evil beings that are going to come and eat you up from outer space! What makes you think you taste that good? You are beautiful in your own right on this planet, but you're not that beautiful compared to some of these beings. They certainly don't want you for models or for your great intellect, either. They want you to love and be in love as they are. Yet this love thing is difficult for you beings, because you play a game of not here. What be not love? Let's see . . . and you succeed in finding it. And then you have to look inside to see where it is. It is all part of your game, we understand. No big deal. But as this shift of consciousness begins to accelerate through this year and the next, love is going to be very, very important. It is going to be a requirement in order for you to get through here with any sense of sanity. You're already starting to lose what you think is your sanity anyway. No big deal. You wouldn't be in this room if you were sane, know you? Now, I have to be careful when I say things unto you, because your words here are not appropriate, yet they are what we have to use.

There is going to be a very large amount of energy (it's already started) coming around you. Now you process energy through this portion [brain], your thinkity-think. You categorize, label, good/bad, this, that, the other. This energy is going to move so fast that you won't be able to; you'll feel like you have a cloud in your head and you can't think. Now that is because the energy does not want to fit in any boxes that you've already predefined. So the best thing to do is sit and meditate when you get this very heavy-head feeling, know you? Some of you have already experienced this. To sit and meditate and allow the visions to come, because the pictures are going to be, well . . . it be a release, it is also be a showing, it will be a form of communication. Like . . . a movie, and you get your information that way.

So when you get this feeling, say you, find a place to meditate, let the pictures come, the energies. You can write them down if you wish, but the writing will simply be your way of trying to put it in a box. Don't put it any box. They are here to create openings in levels of activity for you, to open doors and gates as you would term them to be. So you may go *through* the gate, go through the doorway, know you what I mean? You're getting gates opened right now in your arena, here. What you call along your grid lines, they're opening. Prepare yourselves for some outrageous experiences here. If you turn too quickly you might find yourself in another dimension! I'm not kidding, here. This is what you've wanted to do, now you're going to have the opportunity, and then you get there, and you say "Oops! I didn't really want to do this, I miss my puppy!" Know you? "I forgot to feed the cat."

Everything doing fine?

I hope so. You tell me!

I'll go check my okay list again. A little bit argue, no big deal. A little bit of confusion. Know you this word "allow"?

Yes.

Indeed? It is difficult at times, if you think another is not doing what you think they should do, but you have to allow them to express their own divinity. Know you? To find it. You're still having a little struggle with that thought, indeed? You're doing fine.

Sometimes if you try to rush to completion and you're at one step, and completion is three steps later, you figure, "Well, I'll take a whole bunch of energy and get through those three steps real quick." Know you? But when you do that, you miss the wisdom of the second step. So you have to come back and do second step again.

Well, since I'm ignorant about what the steps are, I'm having to . . .

Take them very slowly and understand that each experience is wisdom, it is for your divine light. Understand?

Enjoy the Unexpected

Okay. All right. I'm still waiting on that book, so apparently I'm not ready yet.

You'll get there. It is one of these things of structure. You like things to fit in one particular way. Know you?

Mm-hmm.

See all these lines on the floor? Mm? Be you say, "Be lines!" They all coming to you, indeed? Know you what I mean? And they be light and gifts from your Father. But you beings will stay right here and want the gift to come *this way*. Know you? When you could simply say, "I'll stand here and take this one, and I go over here and get this one, I'll get them all." Takes movement, know you? Everyone used to want their soulmate. And they had to walk this line. If he was a little bit off, had to fit right there. Some of you *stood* on that line because you didn't *really* want to meet the being — he/she, whatever — because it is too threatening. Know you?

Has to do with structure.

Expect the unexpected, then, hmm?

Enjoy the unexpected, indeed? And see how things are all tied together, see how your thoughts brought you a thing. Watch how you play here. Know you? Watch what happens when you think a thing in your now moment. Indeed?

You should keep track of *those* things in your writings. Know you? It be fun.

Chakra-Clearing Meditation

Now allow your eyes to close gently. Give me a little moment. Open the crown chakras. Allow. Now what we are going to do, because there is going to be confusion with this other energy, it is because the chakras, what you term the eighth chakra, the ninth chakra and the tenth chakra, have been sort of clouded. We're going to clear them. And you're going to clear them with the divine light that is within your being. Your guides will be around you to assist, but you are going to command from within you that these chakras clean. Going to use gold light and you're going to use white light, and you're going to use green.

Allow your palms to be upward upon your thighs. Open the heart chakra and visualize a gold ball of light there in the heart chakra. Open the throat. And when I say open, I want you to take a breath and blow energy out that chakra. Blow it out. Gently, now, we don't want to create too big a thing here, gently. Gold light in the heart chakra. Your soul is within the body. The apex is at the throat. I want you to visualize yourself sitting in your soul. And I want you to see that apex open at the throat chakra, so you can look out upward. Look through the throat chakra, look through the sixth seal, look through the core of your being now, through that white light that comes down through your head, look above the seventh seal and see the eighth chakra. From the heart that you are sitting in your soul, push a gold and green light up out of the head of the sitting one in there, to the eighth chakra, and command it to be green and white. Let it be. Tell the eighth chakra to open wider, that be grand.

From inside the soul again, take a breath. This be gold and white light, push it past the eighth chakra to the ninth chakra, tell it to open. Tell it to open. Allow. Peace. Now take lavender light from inside the center of you here, and push it up through the eighth and ninth to the tenth. And they all become tinged with lavender. Allow. Peace. Allow. Peace. Feel the tenth chakra assume a shape like a pyramid, three-sided, above you here. It becomes golden in color. Allow it to turn very gently counterclockwise. Indeed. Allow. Allow it to extend its size now so the base moves down to the ninth chakra. Allow. And the base moves down again to the eighth chakra, and down to your crown chakra. Now push this apex of this pyramid out, as far as it will go. And let it continue. Peace. Push.

Feel in your palms of your hands now brilliant white spheres of light, and let the spheres move up the forearms. Let it move up your biceps, across the shoulders and join at the back. Allow. White light. Peace. Manifest two spheres of brilliant white light and place them in your knees. White light. They are not only within the knee but they surround it. This will help you with the energies that are coming, entities. Place your feet into two spheres of white light. And allow the spheres to be around your calves, they are that large, your feet are halfway, there in the center. Place a large sphere of white light now in your torso, include your hips. White light. White light. Place a brilliant sphere of white and golden light in your physical head. White light. Gold and white light. Allow. Peace. Open the throat chakra wider. Peace. You are white light.

There is a flap at the front of the soul, there is a hook at the throat chakra. Allow that little feeling of a hook unhooking, it lifts upward a little bit. And allow the flap of the soul to, . . . the apex will fall forward and down, and allow that apex to fall so it connects at the navel chakra, and latch it there. White light. Feel gold in the chest area now, entities, open the heart chakra. Peace. Gently. Now I want you to contemplate this in the heart chakra, at the open soul area. Contemplate these words: I love God. I know. I love. I am. Peace. Allow. I am power. I am divine. Feel it in the chest, entities. This is where you manifest from. That flap must be down to manifest what you call in your now moment, in your hand. You must be in power to do this thing. Peace.

Now look inside your pyramid that you are sitting in, with the soul, and look in the corners and see all of the things that are there. All of the treasures, all of the gifts. They were given to you when you first became. You are allowed to have them anytime you want to. Allow. Reach into one of the corners and simply pick a few and push them out the front of the soul with the lightbody hands. Put them out there. Allow. Allow them to be in your auric field so you will run into them. Peace. Allow. Be willing to become empowered, entities. Peace. Peace. In a gentle manner slowly open your physical eyes.

The Super Bowl of Spiritual Experience

God allows all things. Will you allow you all things? That requires an answer.

[Everyone:] Indeed!

So be it!

So be it!

[He toasts:] To life!

To life!

It works! [To a participant:] What do you think happens when beings die?

They just pass beyond onto another side.

What side?

To another elevation. Some don't leave though, some stay.

Are you sure?

Mm-hmm. Others leave. Why?

Where do they go?

I think they go to different realms, different levels.

What brings them there?

Perhaps guides, perhaps knowing.

Knowing does move you.

Mm-hmm. But don't others come to help some on their way?

Well, that is one of the humor things. They are there all of the time. And if you don't pay attention to them in the physical, what makes you think you're going to pay attention to them later?

Well, some don't.

Most don't.

Some stay and become problems.

Well, they're not really problems.

Mm-hmm. It's almost like the other side sometimes is more inviting than this side.

So you say! But you can't remember being there.

It's kind of hard.

Don't push it, is what I'm trying to get to you. Indeed?

Mm-hmm.

This be where all of the fun is, on this side, right now. Because you're going to be able to experience a shift in consciousness where you can elevate the brain. You're going to have to use the brain, so you think differently, and you can move the body. This be the great play. This be Super Bowl of spiritual experience, and that mm-hmm is not here, because this part is not going to get it, this is [soul], right in there [soul], is where the movement occurs. This'll get it later [brain], because it'll understand the experience! This goes, Aha! Bulb-light! But this be where it starts [soul/heart chakra].

So with feeling . . .

Be feeling, be love. Are you ready to play a game? I'm pretty good at games.

Okay.

We'll play a game in your sleep, we'll take you to several places, indeed? And we'll show you two journeys you're contemplating, and let you understand it from this side. Bargain?

Okay.

Be fine. Are you sure there isn't something you want to chat about?

Well, it's been an up-and-down week, it's been a very interesting week, and the growth I've gotten since I've been here, I don't understand it all, so I'm just going to go with it.

Be on top of the waves?

Mm-hmm. Maybe it'll be revealed to me eventually, maybe not.

Growth, Joy and Being

Indeed. It is, when you deal with energies it becomes very easy. When you deal with structure it becomes very difficult. You beings have an outrageous concept in your metaphysics, know you? "I'm growing!" That means you're in the muck! You're so miserable, you can't stand it — but it is good for your growth. Joy also works. Know you? Joy is where you get faster growth, because it's all fun. You don't have to suffer to grow. Know you what I mean?

Mm-hmm.

Unless you enjoy suffering.

How about just being? Can you just . . .

Being is grand! That be outrageous.

I mean, can you, in this Earth, just be?

Indeed. That be the easiest. That be the easiest way to do it.

It's difficult, just being.

It is difficult?

Mm-hmm.

I say it's the easiest, and you're going to argue with me and say it's the most difficult?

Well, maybe it's that I can be, but other people don't allow me to be.

Let me check my not-allow list. Not allow. One of the things on the allow list is to allow you, first. Know you what I mean?

Mm-hmm.

Allow doesn't mean to allow others to walk all over you. It means to allow you to be in joy. Indeed?

I'm just learning this.

Well, you're going to come through it rather grandly.

I am?

You are. Believe it or not, you will make it.

Thank you. I'm not always so sure. But if you tell me, I'm going to believe you, because I have to.

Well, don't believe me, but take my word for it! Belief is a word, a limit, know you? Belief is a limit. When a god speaks, it becomes. I better be careful, I can get myself in trouble real quick, here. This is a very precious experience you beings are going through. What you don't realize yet is you're being polished, so to speak. You're getting ready to become diamond lights, literally, in the physical. You're getting ready, your auras are getting polished, and you're going to show them off, some of you. And some of you are pretty outrageous, I will tell you that; you're going to strut your auras like you strut your dresses and your suits! "I've got the most expensive tailor! I go to the most fashionable aura shop!" Well, you'll get over that comparing, but you're being burnished here with these energies. Your bodies physically are literally changing. You are becoming. You are becoming lighter and brighter, and power. And that *is* power. And as diamond comes out of coal, so too you are going to come out of this thing. It has already been seen. So the gods are sitting back there, waiting for you to come to play, and they're watching and waiting, and waiting, and watching. But this is the speed-up time. You are in it. So everyone's getting their uniforms on to meet you rather grandly here. They're polishing their auras, too. And some of them are not as bright as you think they are! They've got crooked halos, know you, some? And don't be angry at them when you meet them, because it wasn't all their fault. They didn't know what they were doing, either. Don't blame them.

That would be a good book title.

They didn't know what they were doing?

No, no, the gods with crooked halos.

Mm. That would include everybody in *this* room, too. I don't have a halo, I have horns. That shook some beings' perceptions!

Do you get horns if you know what you're doing, and crooked halos if you don't?

Be your perception. Like strings connected to Father so I don't get lost. I've seen what you've done, so I have two strings. Indeed.

Indeed. So in the last two weeks since the first time I saw you, the gifts have been coming at me sometimes faster than I know what the hell to do with them.

Keep them coming!

Well, I guess my question is, how does one stay in focus and peace when many colored lights are exploding all around me?

You are going to blame the lights now. And because you are at peace they becoming show. They be beings, know you, beings? They are entities. They are joining to sort of fly through your field, to pick up your energy and that be, say you, they fly through your fears so they can chat with you, and they can tune into your frequency to know who you are, from *this* experience, know you, because you're going to meet them. Understand?

Yes, so are the physical representations that are happening in the physical and the people I'm meeting and the money and all that, is that part of the . . . that's just a reflection of what's happening, the people coming . . .

It be out here, it be what is going on in here, it be out there. Know you? It be in here first. Allow, know you? Nothing wrong with money. It is God, know you? It is!

I think I must know it now since it's coming so fast.

Indeed! The gods enjoy the gold and the silver because it's very healing in this arena, this ecstasy, rather. Very powerful energy, not for your moneys, though you play, and it is played, it's all energy. Not evil. But the gold and the silver, you're going to learn pretty soon, is very healing for the body. It stimulates the electrical system and gold, particularly, stimulates the endocrine system in your body. And things work very nicely if you have a little piece of silver (I don't mean a big bar, know you?) and a little piece gold, one side of your body and the other. That's why they were used in temples, entities. Not because the churches were hoarding, though the later understanding it did become a hoarding. But in very ancient times it was used to heighten the consciousness, the frequency of it.

Is that the same with colloidal, like colloidal silver and colloidal gold, or is that not the same?

Not the same. At this time in your density you need the metal, the physical metal to touch, you need to play, know you? So you allow your evolution. Little bit. You're going to be kind of heavy walking around with two gold bars, know you? Little bit. Consider the healing qualities is what I am saying here.

Your Guides Are Here

Okay. Most people on this planet are living in cages, and I found I have a way to open up a lot of cages, and someone said to me today that most people aren't going to want their cages opened and are going to be rather unhappy if I open them for them.

That be a truth. You have to ask permission.

Permission. Thank you, thank you, that's the word I was . . .

With-in-side the being, not only permission verbally chit-chat. Be how I work with you! I talk to your guides, here. But I have an advantage, I don't have to ask, anyway. I tell everybody to get in line. I'm one of the ones that assigns the guides. Eventually you're going to understand this thing. But from your level you ask, because it is from divinity to divinity, here, know you? There are some divine beings that I communicate with in what you would term "ask," yet it is different, we parley, know you? Other ones I don't bother parleying so much with; rather boring. You beings are fun, though. Give me great humor. You're fun to watch, yet you're becoming. That's what's even more fun. The other alternative is to die in ignorance. That be fun, too, I suppose, for some.

But as you play with the energies, what you term this "die," these fears, and you move through them, blend, so to speak. You understand a wisdom that is different, that is a wisdom that everyone wants to know. And there are many in this time, beings, very shortly, who are going to desire to commit suicide, because the presence of this change of consciousness and this death concept you beings play with is going to be so heavy that they're going to think they have to do it. Now I've been on this one for a while, know you what I mean? I've been chitty-chatty with this one, be saying you beings, "Don't do this thing." (Everyone take a breath.) You are on this planet at this time to understand your divinity. To learn your power as Buddha, as Christ, as God, as part of the Father that you are. That is what you're here *for*. And you will do it any way you can. We are here to assist you in what you call assimilating the energies, we are not here to rescue you at all. You're going to do it all yourselves. We will throw you a rope. We won't pull the rope in, because it be tied to Father. *You* pull on the rope.

This is a very tricky phase in the evolution of humanity. Very tricky. And even though you've been picked on and manipulated and had your genes switched and this, that and the other, you're still here! You still have some semblance of a brain, you still have the ability to contemplate that God exists, you have the ability to contemplate that you might have a soul, contemplatability you are life. So there's a chance, know you, that you can make it through this thing! It's a very simple understanding, know you?

The body is a tool for the soul to understand its process within this divine play (your words). The soul and the being in there that is you knows it is divine. It knows it. It's no big deal. It's a time for the structure called the tool to understand where the divinity is, that it is not in the persona. It is in the light in here [soul], and this light is going to move. The brain will become altered, you will be able to think totally differently. You'll get the union what you call with your higher self, because it is your perception that you must have something come down upon you and it will, it'll be around you. But what you do is you push it out from within so you can see it here.

From one perspective of my side, I look at you beings and you're all part of one very large being. As I lower, lower, lower, lower, and move and use this vehicle, these eyes, here, I see your separateness. That's why I have to use a vehicle here, unless I manifest a body. I see what *you* see, your separateness. Now if you knew what you knew, how I say you, in your greater grouping, one being moves — all of you are affected by it, because you are connected in this greater being. So too when you move your body gently, and even when you think, you affect every cell in your being. Every one. The old concept was karma, but you are only going to become aware of each manifestation when you begin to allow the process of the divine here [soul] to get out of the thinkity-think here [brain]. Allow thoughts to flow through you, pick one, and willingly play with it. (Everyone breathe a moment.) What I'm getting at is, you're going to be fed an awful lot of information here very shortly in your next two months. It's going to come out of nowhere. Well, it's coming out of somewhere. And it's going to throw a lot of you in tizzies because you like tizzies. Know you how you enjoy tizzy mode?

Yes.

Indeed? Contemplate your divinity; go you not in tizzy, eh? It won't do anything except get you deeper in the muck. Be in your own power in this thing, know that you're going to make it through it. There are certain games that are to be played out, because there are some beings that need these forces for their completion; they need to do it for them to understand. The only way you will lose your divinity and spend another 26,000 years in this sort of activity is to forget you are divine.

Contemplate a Grain of Rice

You should be so involved with your own evolution, with your own divinity, that you should be willing to spend at least ten moments a day contemplating "How do I manifest in my hand?" Or contemplating a grain of rice, how it knows what to do. Ten moments a day, contemplate a little thing: how does a grain of rice know what to do? And talk to the grain of rice, ten minutes a day, ten moments. Ten! If you can't afford ten, three will do. But do it! Because it will get you into a thought process of remembering. And you won't go running all over following another that's doing this thing, and they be sitting there laughing at you: "I can do it, you can't, ha-ha." They're not teaching you how to do it, they don't want you to know. I want you to know. Do your ten moments.

You won't know if I do it for you, you'll sit there all bug-eyed. So I manifest differently for you. I create a lot of muck sometimes to see if you can get out of it. But spend ten moments a day contemplating your *own* divinity, know you? I don't mean contemplate what star system you came from, know you? Or who your guides are. That's not important. What's important is *your* divinity. Your ability to manifest, your ability to talk to a grain of rice, your ability to talk to a grape; that's what's important. Your ability to talk to the animals — not only talk, but to *listen*. Then you're approaching your divinity. And then you'll know more and more and more.

Your next year, it's going to be required that you at least feel safe in your own light, that means your own divine power. It'll be almost a requirement; that's how intense things are going to get here. You beings do like things intense, however, know you what I mean?

Yes, I do.

Until they get too intense, and then it is Oops! No big deal.

Mudra Activation Exercise

I want you to close your eyes for a moment. You have your thumb and you have your index finger, and then you have your second finger. Allow the thumb and and the second fingers to be connected, both hands. Now the thumb and the index finger [together] is what you would term a mudra for freedom, power. This finger [second, together with thumb] mudra is what you would term an inner connection to, we're going to use the word God because that is what you do, but it is the light that's within the soul, within the being sitting within the soul. This mudra, thumb/second finger, connects to the being in the soul and sort of advises the being to ask the question, consider its own divinity. So it not be persona, now, it be deep inside you, contemplating its divinity. Remembering. So allow those fingers to touch now, thumb and second finger. Peace. Open the throat chakra. Open the heart chakra wider.

Now in your little finger of your left hand, at the tip, I want you to feel your heart beating. Allow. And you can love your heart by simply loving that little finger. Little finger of the right hand, contemplate the kidneys there, both of them. And you can love your kidneys by loving the little finger of the right hand. I want you to contemplate the crown chakra of the one sitting inside you, the little one. And in the palms of your hands, I want to feel your crown chakra, physical, opening, in the palms of your hands. There is a connection here between the palms, your root chakra, and your crown chakra. This is a very quick way to activate kundalini, by the way. Allow your palms to become activated now, can you feel the energies? Allow. Peace. Tell the crown chakra to open. Contemplate your divinity. Contemplate how precious the body is from within you now. It is, indeed. In a gentle manner slowly open your physical eyes. Slowly. How do your palms feel? Can you feel the energies in your palms?

[Group:] Yes.

Can you feel it?

Yes.

Your palms are connected to your root chakra. Now when you contemplate the vortices there, the chakras there as they open more and more and more, you activate, you're getting a movement in kundalini and it's going to come out of the crown, so you can literally look at your palms and tell your crown to open. Know you? Some of you have a hard time getting out of your body to look down on your crown chakra, so you tell here to open, indeed? Open! And your body is a tool. Some of you connected inside here very strongly, and that is an outrageous thing because that empowers you in utilizing the tool.

Now there's one other thing. I have to check some of you out here, because you haven't been here before, so . . . well, no one's died in the audience yet, I suppose we can do it, can't I? We haven't lost anyone yet, so don't worry. I don't think tonight will be the first time. Moment.

Connect now with your eyes open these fingers, here. Center, and contemplate now the thought, allow the thought to feel the one in here. Allow. Because your meditations are really tools, and you're supposed to be able to handle this energy in your waking moments, indeed? So you train the body.

Now allow what you would term this hand [right hand] to open, indeed? And the index finger, there's a charge of energy in there now. Put that on the solar plexus here. And then allow your eyes to close, and allow that energy to move in at the base of the soul, to move up to the heart chakra. It will feel very warming. It is like you are petting the little one inside there. So it begins to understand that indeed, "maybe the persona does know that I exist." And you contemplate the love of the little one in there. And that is the love of you and the love of your Father that exists, that's what it is. And then allow the finger to come off and go back to the second finger, right on. Now contemplate the crown chakra again, that is in the palms of your hands now, entities. And allow the palms to be open now, allow the fingers to be untouched. Feel the crown in your crown. Let the energy move out of the fingers. Peace. In a gentle manner slowly open your physical eyes.

"Outside" Energies Are Coming from You

As these energies build, it is more of you coming to you, more of your divine awareness. Because this is an outside thing from you, and you haven't communicated with your systems here (this communication with animals, etc., is not commonplace to you, so you don't feel connected) so too this energy coming, you're going to think it is outside of you. It is not! It is *you* having a reunion with *you!* And your inside being, here, understands this, and is looking forward to it. Your thoughts about it, however, will be manifested, because the inside being (because it loves you so much) will do anything you allow to come through here, to play with, even fear, because it knows better; it doesn't care. It thinks you want to do it this way.

Remember your divinity. Ten moments a day. Ten moments. That is not very much time. It will help you greatly. I don't want to hear, next two months coming, that you didn't know this was going to happen. It will be like a great big — how I be say you — how big you beings are here, know you this big? It be like a great big spider came and got you, only it is bigger than you, it be wrap you up. And you will react the same way! But the spider be your buddy, here. One of my jokes. Everyone lighten up, here! It is all very precious and sacred, here. Some of you beings have issues with spiders, some of you beings have issues with snakes and other furry little beings.

Allow your eyes to close for one more moment. Your thumb and second finger [together], please, contemplate the crown chakra in your palms. Contemplate the being within you. Allow. Feel the soul in there, golden color, see you as a Buddha one, a Christ sitting there. Allow. With all your treasures there, allow. The soul flap is still open. If you desire you may release it from the navel chakra and allow it to come up and close. It will be clear and transparent, however, but you can feel a sense of safety and protection there if you desire. Allow. For those of you who desire to leave the door open, you must maintain clarity in your divinity, or it will release and close itself for protection — from your understanding, your words, here. But it will still be clear and transparent.

Now pay attention to this. All the activities that have ever happened in your journey, wherever you have been, wherever you are going to go, are inside that soul that is inside you. Everything you could ever imagine to do, have done, it is there. So when you lower that flap, you be ready for the pictures and allow, because you've all done it all. Don't judge yourselves. And don't you even consider judging another. Allow. If you really want to know your power, look inside the soul here. What you call the pyramid. All the messages are written on the wall. In your physical world, now, you're discovering secret passages in your physical pyramid. That cannot be done until the gods upon the planet discover the passages within their pyramid, because it's an exteriorization of what the gods understand. Nothing happens upon your planet that isn't inside the beings here. Nothing.

Peace. So you can know it all, and play as you will, knowing it all, and that is allowed. In a gentle manner, slowly open your physical eyes. Be at peace here. If you feel a little energy in your heart chakra you might place your hand upon it, sort of tell it to close a little bit because we did create an opening here, we did allow an opening. Ten moments a day, bargain?

[Group:] Bargain.

Not a big deal. We are through.

19

October's Hemispheric Change

Zoosh through Robert Shapiro
July 19, 1995

All right, Zoosh speaking.

The world you're living in now is going through what I call an inside-out peel-back. Imagine yourself peeling a banana upside down. Your planet has been attempting, as many people know, to have a pole shift for many years. Although this is actually occurring in the third-dimensional version of Earth, you are still close enough in your transitional motion from third to fourth dimension, that you're going to have a reverberation or echo of that experience.

There will be an opening in the South Pole. A wave of energy will come out from the inside of the Earth at the South Pole and surge upward in a complete circle through the Southern Hemisphere into the Northern Hemisphere to the North Pole and back down around the outside of the planet, and back and forth a few more times — maybe altogether about three times — in a measurable way. This is going to create a homogenized situation in which the energy of the Southern Hemisphere of Earth will suddenly affect the hemisphere in the north. There will also be some effect from the north to the south, but the intent is that the south affect the north. In the Southern Hemisphere you have the feminine energy of Earth, and in the Northern Hemisphere, the masculine energy of Earth. This will be primarily a positive experience.

While the experience is happening there will be some feeling by people in the north of an even more scattered sense of memory, and some people will feel a scattered sense of purpose. This will pass with the first wave. The first wave will take approximately three weeks. I'm going to give the exact dates. Let's see now, I want to get this exactly right; because your time is curving, I have to calculate that. Calculating for the curvature in time, this ought to begin at 12:03 a.m. on October 4, to run for three weeks. It will take about a week or so for the energy to get from the Southern Hemisphere to the Northern Hemisphere, and then it will come on very strong. This should cause a primary magnetic flux. Here is a warning to people with radar and other electronic instruments used to track airplanes, both commercial and military: You might find false echoes in radar and sonar; it could even create temporary disruptions in microwave communications. It shouldn't affect microwave commercial appliances, because they are mostly shielded (not completely, but sufficiently).

A New Auric Microorganism

I expect also certain other things to happen. Doctors tell you that you're losing cells all the time, that they just fall off your body and can't be seen because they're so small. But there is a microorganism that exists in the form of a static charge. I'm referring to a microorganism that's hard to measure – in the auric field, roughly about six inches from the body – and that could be proved to exist only by measuring the static charge around the body of an average person. This microorganism is going to mutate.

I talked a long time ago about how the immune system was going to change in the future. Now we're having actual effects. I'm expecting that the immune system of the body is going to begin functioning better from the auric field than within your body. Your bodies now are exposed to about 30% (at least in the Northern Hemisphere) more static electricity, electrical fields, microwave fields and other miscellaneous electrical and electronic fields than you can tolerate. So your bodies have begun to adapt; they are going to create a hybrid microorganism, which is just now forming, that functions within your static field. This will generate its own means of deflecting the effect of these electrical and electronic waves that run through the bone marrow in your body and reduce the effectiveness of your immune system. The immune system is significantly, though not completely, dependent on the bone marrow. What we're seeing here, then, is a genetic evolvement of your primary vehicle (meaning your physical body) into something that's beginning to move to a light-body. I would guess in about four or five years you might be able to measure it with current instruments.

I've said before that, because you're in transit from one dimension to another, you cannot measure the differences between what was and what is. Everything is changing relative to everything else, so everything appears to be the same size. You can't compare it to something in the universe, because everything is bigger, including your perception of everything else. Taking a target year, 1947, and comparing it to 1995 where you are now, you are all about 13% larger. Your auric field is densifying to make you larger, which allows you to accelerate from one dimension to another, to expand your reality yet remain in the body. This form of static organism, the light around the body, is going to mean that there is a 97% chance that your auric field, no later than 2008 or 2010 (probably 2009), should be visible to every person in your then-visible light spectrum, which is changing. Your natural auric field or energy body is going to come into play because of this wave of energy coming from the south. It should begin to have a measurable impact in protecting your body from rays, including cosmic rays caused by the breakdown of your atmosphere from space. This is especially important for protecting you from certain rays, even x-rays that travel through space.

I'm telling you this because it will have side effects, mostly in the creation of false echoes in these highly selective devices that track various things. It is probably not the best time to launch any missiles for any reason, because they could malfunction. I'm talking about missiles that will put satellites up in space or anything like that. It's also going to be a time in which I'm recommending that the military be *extremely* cautious about what they think is a target that might not be a target. You could be firing a missile at something that isn't really there, although your instruments, your radar will confirm it's there. This could create a potential hazard. I want to put it out now to give a little extra warning so that those in the know who read this actually consider that some of it could be true and check it out through other sources — so that they take appropriate steps.

This is generally going to be a good experience for people. Like I said, it will create a period of feeling scattered and having a hard time concentrating, so it's probably not going to be a good time to begin new projects. But it could be a good experience in the long run. There should be a significant clarification and calming of the dream process, so your dreams should become less dramatic — or if they are dramatic, you will not remember them very well. You've been remembering dramatic dreams; you've been processing energies from Mother Earth. This should be a significant clearing, so that will not be so much of a factor anymore.

The people in the Southern Hemisphere will also notice some changes. Probably the most significant is that they will suddenly be able to think in a linear fashion, which will actually interfere with some of the things they are doing, because the instinctual body may be somewhat interfered with. This will be especially noted by countries and peoples who are very heart-centered. You will find yourself in a situation where thought will be almost interfering with your daily life. This is a backwash effect from the Northern Hemisphere. I'm not saying that you don't think in the Southern Hemisphere, but you have the opportunity (and many of you already do this) to think with your hearts and to include a significant amount of instinct.

So, drivers, be careful. You might be distracted by your thoughts. Police departments, it is probably a good time to set up whatever you can to slow the traffic down. And students in school, it would be very hard to concentrate in the Southern Hemisphere. You might find that your thoughts and fantasies actually interfere with your schoolwork and studies. This is especially important for college students. Be aware; know it will pass. Recommendations to teachers and professors: Please delay final exams if they are given at this time, or conduct them over a period of several days, giving the students a little more time, because they will be distracted. Even you will be distracted, and you'll have a hard time correcting papers.

Why is this happening at this point? Has it to do with the Photon Doctor? Is it a cycle that's connected with the galaxy? Is Mother Earth doing it?

Mother Earth is doing this primarily at the third-dimensional level. For anyone locked in third dimension (which you're not in anymore), the experience is overwhelmingly dramatic. If you were in the third dimension now totally, from space it would look very much like a flare that went off at the bottom of the Earth and welled up around the outside of the Earth like a free-floating ring or a gaseous cloud. Other individuals who are in the third dimension or shifting into the third dimension may be able to measure it scientifically if they're interested. It's very powerful in the third dimension and will probably destroy all microorganisms that Mother Earth is not comfortable with. It's actually designed in the third dimension to totally cleanse the complete surface of the planet (including all the oceans to their total depth) of any alien microorganisms, meaning microorganisms from all time that accumulated from the stars, from ETs coming to Earth and from mankind's creations. It will cleanse those and sterilize the Earth. For her, sterility means that the only microorganisms that will remain are those that are a part of her natural immune system. Her natural immune system microorganisms account largely for disease, but sometimes diseases are man-made. But this is coming from Mother Earth.

Where in the dimensional transition are we, three-and-a-half?

Well, not quite. You're at about 3.37 or something like that. You're still close enough to the third dimension to get an echo-wave effect, but it's happening because you're on your way. The effect is going to be benevolent for you, with the exception of its impact on instruments. How is it going to affect the instruments that people use on an everyday basis? You might find during that time that there will be some interruptions in sending faxes or making phone calls. Phone lines might go down temporarily or you might have interruptions of satellite-to-Earth signals because the signals will be bent, and if they're bent they're not going to get to the place they're aimed at. You might have a difference in the diffusion of light. Sunsets might be interesting and different. Laboratories might have anomalies, meaning they'll shoot a laser at something and it won't land exactly where they expect it to land. So with anything that uses lasers for sound generation or light measurements or configurations, you might have anomalies from time to time. If you expect it, then it won't be a problem. If it doesn't work the first time, wait about an hour and try again, and it'll probably be fine. The wave will be passing in an hour or so, and the part that caused the problem should be past you. It could pass you much faster than that, but just to be circumspect you could wait an hour.

There may be some effect on television signals. Anything that involves electronics could be affected. There may be some odd static sounds in radios and so on, but it won't sound electronic, it'll just sound like distance, like you're far away from a signal even if you're across the street from the radio station. It should make an odd sort of experience.

Very sensitive individuals may feel a slight tingling because this portion of your auric field that's forming up is going to have a static charge; it's a little different from your normal charge. You're used to an electrical static charge; you're used to throwing off that static charge but it will not only throw the charge off, it will tend to throw it inward. So instead of going out, a charge will go out and in. For sensitive people, "in" does not mean into their bodies, but into the particle itself (which is probably not measurable at this time). It might create in sensitive people an odd tingling feeling, which will not be unpleasant; it'll just be unexpected.

For people who are not particularly sensitive, you may notice from time to time a feeling of being unexpectedly warm or unexpectedly cool. It could affect your body's air conditioning system, as it were. For some people who have sensitivities to sound waves and their effect (again, we're dealing with something that could be microwave here), there could also be an effect. It shouldn't be an overly dramatic effect — like, for instance, an unpleasant feeling of sound waves in your teeth. This should not be any worse than a 1% increase, so don't expect it to be too bad. It's measurable, though. We need to get this out, because there's a certain amount of benevolence that this event is going to create, and I feel that it will upgrade the quality of your ability to resist discomforts.

Great!

An Ebola Oubreak?

Do you see an Ebola epidemic in the U.S. in October?

Even though your immigration service is very careful, there's a limit to what they can do. They don't screen everybody that comes into the country for biological toxins. This kind of equipment exists, but nobody can afford it right now. It's possible that that screening will happen some day when the equipment becomes more affordable. What you want to know, is, is it really likely to happen? Well, there's a 30% chance there will be an outbreak somewhere. I'm hardly in a position to say where, because if I do everybody's going to run from there to someplace else, which is the opposite effect we want. I will say this, though: homeopathic remedies should work. I don't want to say that something *isn't* going to happen, but I will say that there's a chance it won't happen. How much of a chance? There's a 68.351% chance that it won't happen. That's because it might be possible (that's how I want you to put this out, because we need to have people working on it) that if enough people pray, or lightworkers do your lightwork, or do your transformational work, shamans — everybody. If enough people do that, it might be possible for the oceans of the world (that's a reason not to pollute your oceans) to produce an alga that exudes a gas that will knock down the effectiveness of that organism so that your own immune systems can reject it.

As an aside, those of you who have a lowered immune system will be the most susceptible. So just be warned: Those of you who can do it, boost your immune system by any means that does not tear it down, no heavy chemicals. I'm not trying to scare people who already have difficulties, but if you're living in a city where there's dense smog, for instance, and your oxygen is depleted and you're getting forgetful, if you can afford it, at least try to take a few puffs off an oxygen tank now and then. If somebody wants a little sideline business, have an oxygen tank out in the street and charge people a few dollars a minute for puffing on it. I know that sounds a little crazy to you, but you'd be surprised how many people will do it.

Ask for Mother Earth's Help

Now, I believe that for the people who practice sacred practices, if you pay homage to the Earth Mother and Grandmother through sacred ceremony; for those of you who are religious, in prayer; and for those of you who can perform true, loving magic, in that form of ceremony (magic meant to support rather than distort), do all you can. Ask for Mother Earth to produce an alga that will exude a gas that could prevent it. This has to be done through asking. That's why sacred peoples to this day ask. You can ask for God to intervene, but I think you're going to have to ask Mother Earth directly. For those of you who are primarily religious, if you hear about this, do ask for God to intervene, but ask for Goddess to intervene also. It's more likely that Goddess will intervene.

Know also that you really have to cut down on your microwave transmissions. It's demolishing your immune system. If everybody had an immune system the same as they were in the 1600s, this virus wouldn't faze you. It's just that your immune system has been reduced so much. In 1600 A.D. you had a lot more oxygen on the surface of the planet.

So oxygen is an important part, then, of building up your immune system and averting being involved in this potential epidemic?

I believe it is.

And a homeopathic remedy, the rattlesnake venom [See Eileen Nauman's book Poisons That Heal *from Light Technology Publishing], taken in advance before you're actually affected is a preventive?*

Yes, it is.

The only one?

Well, it's the only effective one. There are some remedies that will work with the proper wave forms. People who are experimenting in electromagnetic therapies and certain gentle sound therapies might find them effective, too, but the homeopathic remedy has the advantage of being right there and ready to use.

All right. We'll check again next month, but you say there's a 32%

chance that it's going to happen?

I would like to say this: In terms of a massive disaster — anything from, say, 1% to 3% of the population — there's about maybe a 1 in 10 chance for it, roughly 10%.

Is it higher for the rest of the world?

In countries where immigration is more casual, it's probably higher. I just don't want to say where because of how much chaos this can cause. It would be so much better to do what I recommend and try the homeopathic remedies. Those of you who are making homeopathic remedies, crank it up.

A World Leader Walk-In

What about the U.S. President that was taken out of this time path and put someplace else? How is he? Is he coming back? Will we hear from him again?

I think we're going to hear from him in the near future, because he's probably going to either incarnate in the fourth dimension or he's going to "walk in." There's a chance he might "walk in" to a U.S. President or possibly a head of the United Nations within the next eleven years. If this "walk-in" takes place, the soul will not be kicked out; walk-ins are always done with benevolence. The individual (the President or the Secretary General of the U.N.) will fall ill for a few days, so it will seem, and then be up and at 'em, as they say, and fine. The walk-in may have taken place then. Pretty good chance.

If it occurs you will find that the desire to create world government will get stronger. Another reason you need to have world government is that, referring to that virus and the spread of disease in general, we really need to have some kind of a governing body that will screen these things. It probably is going to mean that immigration will become a little harder, in about eight to ten years, certainly from one continent to another. I'm expecting a world order medically within the next seven to fifteen years at most. It'll be a little awkward at first, but eventually it'll be very good.

What about the secret government, what about our monthly update?

Well, I stood corrected when I was speaking to the people in Brazil. We need to change the name of the secret government to the *sinister* secret government, because someone spoke up and said, "What about the White Brotherhood, and what about the angelics and others who are also a form of secret government?" I had to say that I stood corrected!

The sinister secret government — that's very good.

They are in a sort of holding pattern — there hasn't been much change. They've had another break in the ranks, though, a particularly troublesome break because this individual is highly influential with certain members of the outer ring. These outer-ring members are particularly hazardous because most of them don't even know they're members, and so they can be easily manipulated. The reason this break is a hazard is that these members that are controlled or influenced by this particular member of the inner ring are all members of the medical community. In some cases they are military medical, but for the most part they are researchers and administrators. There is a real concern by the sinister secret government that this individual will release all of the cures for all diseases. On the one hand, while that looks great for everybody, the hazard is that the sinister secret government might attempt to develop or release new kinds of disease organisms in order to control, manipulate and otherwise harass the population for the purpose of creating money.

I think, however, that they're not going to wind up releasing any of that stuff. For one thing, it's not that hard to make interferon anymore, which can essentially eliminate all disease although it does make you dependent on it for the rest of your life. However, I think that one major cure is going to slip out that can be manufactured (I can't say what it is right now) in a backyard washtub. I expect that the cure for pellagra might come out. I think the sinister secret government would be willing to write that one off. So you have members of the inner ring who are beginning to bolt the group.

This movement is a good one. Before, they were bolting to terrorist action. This time someone is ready to work against the inner ring by helping the people?

That's right. We're going to see more of that in the future. So it's a good sign in the long run. In the short run it could create some ripples, but I think in the long run it's going to be a good thing.

You're saying they have a cure for every disease?

Well, every disease within reason. I'm not talking about unknown diseases that pop up, but for the most part they have a cure for every communicable disease and every inherited disease.

AIDS, cancer, polio, all these?

Yes! The cures that they have — this should perk a few ears up — are largely electronic! Meaning, producing the right waves, the right sounds.

Harmonics!

Harmonics, yes. Mostly we're talking about harmonics. And

harmonics really can cure almost anything. Researchers take note: harmonics can really do it.

Once you know the frequency, you can do it radionically?

Yes.

Okay, is the potential epidemic at the end of October a natural thing, or is it released by the sinister secret government?

If we break it down into potential event and actual event, the potential is supported historically and through the percentages. But if the actual event takes place, I think that you will find that the sinister secret government was significantly involved. This will probably have something to do with medical terrorism from other people who have bolted. But I still think it can be headed off. That's why it's important to get the warning out as soon as possible, and thus stimulate the sales of homeopathics. Nearly anything that can oxygenate the body might help. Basically you need to have something that comes close to being a universal antitoxin – which is ironic, because that's how AIDS got spread around, through the search for a universal antitoxin. But that's another story, and we've talked about that before. So this homeopathic snake venom would be good. But it's a bit of a problem: I don't like talking about these disasters because it tends to give support to them. So I don't know what to say here.

By publishing that article [Sedona Journal of Emergence, September 1995] are we helping to create that epidemic?

Maybe. You're in a difficult position here because you're starting to get into hard news. You're in a position where you're doing speculative hard news (as a regular newspaper would call it). If you know that a hurricane is coming toward land but that it could change direction at any moment, is it all right to warn the people? This is what you're dealing with. My idea is that you can publicize it as long as you include what the people can do about it, so that people don't simply rush to their stores and clear out the shelves of this homeopathic treatment. What happens to the 98% of the people who can't get hold of it? That's a reality, you understand.%%It could create a lot of mischief, and it might be totally unnecessary. So I'm going to say that publishing it is good, but it'll be a calculated risk. I'd like you to get some other people to channel on it, especially people who channel the angelics, because the people need to know there is support. And they need to be reminded that no matter what happens, everybody's immortal. But nobody likes to think they're going to suffer or their loved ones are going to suffer. I think it can be headed off. I hope so.

20

The Awakening of Humanity

Zoosh through Robert Shapiro
July 31, 1995

I t must be mentioned that there is a worldwide body forming with an intent to create a form of martial law under the *guise* of the United Nations. But I can assure you that the United Nations does not have a strike force equal to that which is needed to usurp worldwide power. And when you and others see these dark helicopters and dark vehicles with the barely legible "U.N." on the side, that is strictly a cover. That is a situation involving the sinister secret government.

There is a belief by those in power – legitimately and otherwise – that coming soon in the present time, which is a significant time as far as the Mayan calendar goes, there will be a full-scale visitation from extraterrestrials who will come and invite the people of Earth to join the planetary community. Your sinister secret government will do everything in its power to prevent this, and even your legitimate government is not sure about it. Because one of the requirements to be a member of the Planetary Council is that you must, as a society – this means as an Earth society, not as American society or Arabian society or French society – swear to certain rules that you will do everything you can to live by.

One of them (I'll list a few but not all) is that you will do everything in your power to make certain that older people have not only a comfortable place to live, but interesting and valuable work to do, if they choose – meaning that they will likely work with younger people, offering them the benefit of their wisdom in some way. And in this way your young people, children – say those under fifteen, for example — would have every opportunity to achieve true happiness. True happiness in this case means that they can go for whatever they want to go for, whether it's fun or play or whether it is a scholastic endeavor, without any (and I mean without *any*) prejudice to deal with. Another rule is that everyone will make every effort possible to eliminate anything that has to do with racism. Another is that all people deemed to be criminals will be treated fairly, will be treated kindly, will be treated as if they are sick in some way, not as if they are monsters. They will not be punished and hurt. They will be sent somewhere where they can have a reasonably decent life, albeit not where they can mingle with their society, whatever society it was.

There is a belief by the sinister secret government as well as by many of the governments on Earth that the extraterrestrials will expect all boundaries on the diplomatic level to be dropped, because other planets enter *as planets* — you can't have Mexico joining the Planetary Council . . . everybody has to join as Earth. So there's a belief that political boundaries will have to be eliminated, but this is actually only partially true. The council rules in such a way that they encourage political boundaries to be dropped, but within a given time. And the rules would be stretched in the case of this planet, because there are so many races, cultures, nationalities and unique differences between people. The intention is not to make everybody into one homogenous thing, but rather that the people will be encouraged to join the Planetary Council on the basis of their unique cultures.

Certain cultures will be thrilled to find out where they are from. For example, most dark-skinned people in African cultures are from the planet Sirius, and most light-skinned people are from Andromeda or Alpha Centauri. I'm not saying Pleiades, because Pleiadian people are from someplace else, too.

Futile Resistance by Governments

Your governments are seriously waging a campaign of resistance. This includes the Star Wars defense system, as it's called, which is not, as you know, defending the United States from Russia, but is and has always been intended as a means to deflect ships coming in from other planets. That is why they're not equipped with missiles; they're equipped with lasers, which can cover a significant distance. Granted, any single ship coming to welcome you into the Planetary Council, the Organization of Planets (whatever you want to call it), would have the destructive power to knock out every single (and I mean every single) weapon or armament that could be aimed at them, whether they be extensive weapons such as the Star Wars system (SDI) or simply a gun with bullets. They have the capacity to cause every bullet to misfire. They have the capacity to prevent every laser, every ultrasonic, every explosive from working — without harming a single person.

Your governments are all very aware of this. They've seen the demonstrations. The ships have come and gone, visiting many of the governments. One of the most appalling demonstrations (to your military's point of view) took place in the very late '40s at a base well out in the desert regions of the United States (it was quite isolated) when a ship from Andromeda landed. (There were some Zeta people on board, but the ship was from Andromeda.) And they said that at such-and-such a time (they gave a year) "we are going to expect you to join the Council of Planets, we are going to expect you to allow your people to have the full rights of interplanetary citizenship, we are essentially going to expect your people to be freed from tyrannical and crushing manipulation."

So let it be known that regardless of all the publicity and all the stories to the contrary, what's going on here now is that extraterrestrials are coming to do good things for the people of Earth. They gave a demonstration. They said, "We understand that you have a lot of rivalries to work out, and we don't want to get involved in your differences and wars and struggles — and we won't. But we will show you this." And they had certain military equipment lined up and they said, "We're not going to destroy anything, but we're going to give you an example of what we can do."

They told them exactly when they were going to do it. They said, "Now aim your weapons at some targets and assure yourselves that they still work." And they fired some cannons and some machine guns and rifles, nothing exotic — I think they had one bazooka. They fired all these things and assured themselves that they worked. The Andromedans said, "Now load all the weapons." They loaded them. And they said, "When we say 'mark,' these weapons will cease working for a given amount of time." They said, "Mark," and when the people picked them up, nothing worked. Oh, they could run the bullets through the weapons, but pulling the trigger — nothing. And they could even pull a bullet out of a gun and find a dent at the back of the bullet, in what is called the primer. But the bullet did not fire, because they have a technology that keeps certain chemical reactions from taking place within a certain area.

And it can even take place for a short time. They said to be very careful with these bullets afterwards, to put them in a special place, because when they said "mark" again, the bullets might fire. And that was really hard for the scientists to believe, but they did as they were told. They put the bullets into a bomb-disposal device, put in all of the ordnance, stacked it in there, all the things that were dented and would otherwise have fired, and when they said "mark" again there were big bangs and booms and sounds and smoke and everything. Most of the ordnance went off.

The main thing is that your military was utterly horrified because they realized that, since most weapons technology of the time was based upon something explosive pushing something else, unless they developed something like Buck Rogers weapons — ray guns, as it were, which is why lasers got developed so fast — there wouldn't be anything effective. Of course they can do the same thing with lasers, but the government felt that this was the only thing they could do.

I mention these things because it's really true that if you look at the Mayan calendar — I'm talking about the large circular calendar — if you look at this calendar, at the point at which it stops, you see something that is obviously, unequivocally, a ship, a flying disk. And the calendar stops at that point. Now, the date has been unclear to a lot of people, but a lot of work has gone on recently to say that this is the time when this calendar actually stops. But I'm going to tell you the exact year that the Andromedans said they would be here: 1985. They tried to come in 1985, and it was at just about that time that your government had developed not only lasers but a sort of plasmic device which they couldn't really aim but they could sort of send in a general area. And it was quite destructive. Also, it was clear that they were ready to use nuclear devices — anything — and the extraterrestrials all decided that the weapons technology being used was too destructive to Earth and decided they would wait. They decided they would wait for ten years plus four-and-a-half months before they would come. They've waited ten years plus four-and-a-half months — which brings us to right about now. As you can tell, they are not here en masse. They've come to certain places where there isn't a thorough defense net, but they're holding back. They're holding back because they have begun to see that your citizens are waking up spiritually on their own.

Now, no matter what the secret government does — no matter *what* — and no matter what any sinister government does, there is no possible way to stop the people from waking up spiritually. It can't be done. It's built into everything. There are some people who believe it can be done, but I'll tell you right now, it can't be done. We've been talking for a long time about the big wave of people waking up — yes, there have been smaller waves of people waking up slowly, getting ready, but the big wave has begun to wake up now.

It'll happen in three stages. The first stage has begun. The last stage will have completely awakened, I should think, no later than 2012. And it's not going to be that the first wave is going to wake up completely; it's going to be a cyclic thing. The first wave is going to begin to wake up, and then here comes the second wave, and about the time the first wave has reached its zenith, both the second and the third waves will already be on their way.

So what you have here is a circumstance of spiritual waking up that can't be stopped. You've got what amounts to an all-out power struggle going on between the sinister secret government (which we know is having members from within bolt and break free and run wild, causing some problems) and certain aspects of your legitimate governments who feel threatened by this.

Now, an update on the sinister secret government is needed here. I've talked about the inner ring and the outer ring. Right now the inner ring is beginning to break down in terms of their dedication to each other — their cause and their ultimate power as they see it. You can't have the inner ring break down without defections in the outer ring. An inner-ring member has gone renegade. He is manipulating outer-ring members to believe that this may be necessary and is setting up centers to hold massive amounts of prisoners. Certain places are being set up as detention centers. Someone in a position of influence is encouraging and allowing potential secondary uses for very large places with chain-link fences and barbed wire on top — especially airports. One of them I've discussed before as having a legitimate purpose, but it's now being usurped slowly, and its legitimate purpose is being taken off track, making it something less legitimate. And that's right up here at your airport in Sedona. That chain-link fence with the barbed wire isn't just because they want to keep out mosquitoes. This is a problem. I'd say the next three years are really the tricky ones.

This is so people to be detained can be flown in and out?

That's right. And we need to alert readers from other places. Many readers have seen these things being developed for no apparent reason, out in the middle of nowhere. They see chain-link fences and barbed wire and all this business, and they think, What's going on here? The more publicity this gets, the less likely they will be able to establish these things. So it's a time when communication is vital.

Is this basically the United States? Not the rest of the world at this

moment?

Right now we're talking mostly the United States. You see, the United States government and the sinister secret government perceive the citizens of the United States as a threat. Why do you suppose they perceive that? What's makes the citizens of the United States different from most citizens in the rest of the world?

They have guns.

That's it. The citizens of the United States not only have guns, but they've been raised with the belief that armed resistance is the means by which your country achieved freedom. And it wasn't long ago. Therefore, the ideas of guns and patriotism go together in the minds of many people. Also, many men have been raised with the idea of the brave and chivalrous male protecting his family and friends with deadly force – that this is admirable. Not all societies around the world do that.

So that is why there's so much stuff going on here. I would say that the next two-and-a-half to three years are tricky.

How does the regular government view U.S. citizens?

Many people in your government, as well as in other governments, and people in the established press, consider the people of the United States a threat to world harmony, because of the rights of the citizen. And you can't assume the people in the established press are just lame, okay? That's not the case. Many, many writers write things like, "Well, maybe there is a reason for people to have guns." But none of this stuff gets published, see? I'm not saying pro or con, I'm just saying what is. It doesn't get published because the people in the position to say yes or no – I'm not talking about editors down in the lower levels, I'm talking about publishers and people beyond publishers saying, "That's not what we want." The editorial policy is, "Let's get the guns out of the hands of the people and let's tell them that we're doing it because those guns are being used to hurt the people." But I must say in all honesty (not to sound like an NRA member) most guns are used to protect people or for hunting. That's really true – not counting military guns. So I'm not saying, "Go out and shoot somebody."

A lot of stuff has gone on to infringe on your rights. But on the other hand, in the larger picture – as I've said many times before – this is all leading to a benevolent world government. In the beginning there will be a struggle to create a world order. *The world order:* now, everybody's heard about that. The new world order, which George Bush unfortunately spoke about and . . . well, maybe fortunately . . .

put everybody on alert. Order, as you know, has nothing to do with justice.

Sonic Mapping, ET Probes and Air Quakes

We've gotten all these questions and all these news clippings from all over the United States about sonic booms. Can you tell us what's really happening?

Right now your government is somewhat hitting the panic button, because they realize that so many people from so many places have underground tunnels and all this stuff that everyone's talking about — bases underground — that they feel they must have a means by which they can map these things. So there are several explanations. Mapping is the first one I'll talk about.

They're using a form of sonic reading. They make a sound, and then they are able to read the echoes underground and determine where there are naturally formed caverns and where the caverns or significant tunnels may be manmade. And they are assuming that if they are not their own, they belong to somebody else. So they want to know where all of this stuff is. Because contrary to the way it may appear on the surface, there is really an undeclared war going on right now. On the one hand you've got the forces of your legitimate government. On the other hand you've got the forces of the secret government (what we are now calling the sinister secret government). And they are struggling for power.

The booms are also caused by extraterrestrials attempting to contact the people. (I'm not talking about booms that seem to register lower than the ground — I'll get to those.) That which appears to be a sonic boom, and which can be tracked, coming from way up in your atmosphere, has to do with some extraterrestrial probes moving through your atmosphere with the intent of creating a sound — not with the intent of breaking any glass or causing any disharmony, but to say something's happening.

Then there is another factor. Your secret government's military has been planning for a long time, training to take over, and they are running what amount to military threat war games right smack in the middle of neighborhoods. They will set off sounds which in the past have been called "air quakes." These make a loud booming sound but do not directly cause any damage, though in the case of some particularly loud sonic air-quakes you might have broken glass and so on. This can be understood to be either military exercises or sinister secret government exercises for takeover. I'm sorry to say that many of your police departments have been training for riot

318 • SHINING THE LIGHT: Humanity Gets Another Chance

control for many years, and many of them also have been training to take over.

Now, the sinister secret government does not trust your police forces. Know this, every police officer out there. You as a police woman or man will be seen by the sinister secret government as the enemy. And they will pull the same trick that has been done during many wars: they will put uniformed people out on the streets dressed exactly like you to confuse the public. And the primary reason they'll be out there is to round up legitimate police officers, get them off the street and replace them with people who look like legitimate police officers.

Friendship Homework

I'm not trying to start World War III in your streets. I am saying this: What can you do about it? You need to establish communications, a strong network of communications. You've got to just dump this whole racism thing right now. The sinister secret government is not at all racially motivated. They're in it for the power, for the money, for the control. They use this racial thing as a means by which to set you against each other. You've got to dump it and work together. You've got to understand that your best weapon against this is not the gun. Granted, it is a tactical weapon, but shooting people is not going to change things. You're going to need to establish friendship ties with everybody, you're going to need to dump all racial and political stuff that keeps you infighting. You know, "Keep 'em fighting with each other and they'll never see the person behind the person!" That's how the sinister secret government has managed to maintain power.

I'm going to give everyone some homework right now – and especially people who have any prejudices, even what are called by social scientists "institutional" prejudices. Institutional prejudice is not a conscious prejudice against another race or group of people but a set of attitudes and things you do that might cause others to feel that they're being shut out. So I want you all, no matter what race you are, no matter what nationality, whether you're a man or woman, child, young or old, to do the following. Sometime in that next thirty days I'd like you to make an effort to reach out to someone of some racial or national group, whether it be a man or woman, whether you are an older person who thinks all young people have gone to hell in a handbasket, or whether you are a young person thinking that all older people are old fogies – reach out to someone who is a member of that group that you don't like, and make friends with them. This is going to help you more than you have any idea. The second level of this homework, which you can do for extra credit if you like: I want you to get to know your neighbors. If you live in an apartment building, get to know all your neighbors on that floor. Make an effort to get to know everybody in the building. I don't care whether there are eight hundred people living in that building or eight. If everybody knows each other and everybody cares about each other and everybody at least says hello to each other, you're going to stand a chance to get through the nineties really easy. Try and get to know each other as neighbors, neighborhoods. This is really important.

A moment . . . someone's trying to stop me from saying this. Be aware that the sinister secret government even tries to stop Zoosh now and then because they don't want Zoosh to encourage you and give you actual homework that you can do that will be fun. This homework will be fun! You get to make new friends, you get to meet new people and, best of all, you get to go past the point of thinking you have enemies. This is particularly important for people who believe they have enemies, and some of you are going to have to work very hard to do this. You're going to have to reach out, and you're going to have to be very careful, diplomatic. But I want you to try; do your best. Because — and I mean it now — if you can learn how to get along with each other, *there is no way the sinister secret government can maintain control.* Did you know that?

The only way the sinister secret government, or any sinister military, can stay in power at all is to keep you fighting amongst each other. That is the only way. So if something happens, something goes down, I want you to check with your neighbors first before you react. Because if the sinister secret government thinks you're going to become friends, they'll try and create incidents. They'll go out and send people out in disguise and say, "Oh, look what he did!" They'll even plant articles in the paper about this person or that person. You're going to have to learn how to trust each other as human beings more than you trust either the printed word or any angry statements by people you love and admire. Now is the time not only to be networking from one group to another, but to be able to get on the bus and say hello! to everybody and have them all say hello back to you and look forward to seeing you every morning on your way to work. Make the effort. You won't be sorry.

What was the mechanism by which someone was trying to stop you from saying that?

They tried to send a negative bolt of energy.

Where did it come from?

It came from a place about fifteen miles from here. It was fired out of a weapon that looks pretty much like a black crystal with a large coil behind it. I'm not going to describe it any more, because it could be manufactured too easily.

Do they know exactly what we're saying as we say it?

There are no secrets. You know, it's very easy to obtain information. The solutions to the problems are so easy, but once people have published them, the tendency is to believe that no one will publish it again, because everybody knows it. But these things need to be talked about from time to time, because people forget.

That's good. Thank you.

21

You Are a Brilliant Light within and All about You

YHWH through Arthur Fanning
August 11, 1995

*E*veryone allow your eyes to close for a moment. I want you to
visualize a brilliant white pyramid in each of your seven vortices. Now for
this little exercise I just want you to feel all of the apexes pointing upward.
Allow. Four-sided, if you will, brilliant white, each one. Put the one at the
crown in front of you what you would term one foot, two feet. Move the
one from the sixth seal right in front of it. Throat chakra, same. Allow.
Heart chakra, move the pyramid, so you're going to create a line in front
of you here. Solar plexus, push it out there, all in a straight line in front
of what you term your sixth seal. Navel, root chakra, allow. Now see them
in front of you in perfect alignment. Allow. The one that was first, the
crown, allow it to remain stationary. And the other six, allow them to
merge into the one in front of you. Allow. Peace. They be merged. Now
allow this larger one (because it became larger in the merger) to come
toward you so the apex is at your crown chakra and the base is beneath
your feet. Allow. Peace. Open the throat chakra wider, physical form.
Allow. Very gently, slowly open the physical eyes. Allow.

Part of what is going on with these energies now, this speed-up,
is a merger of your chakras. Not only those in the physical, those that
are above, below, beside. They are your energies. Allow. They are
your tools to play here. They desire to become one, likened unto the
gods that are within you desiring to be recognized as one being that
is you. (Open the heart chakra wider. Peace. Allow.) You're not only

gods within your being, you are gods about your being, what you term in your auric field, your energy. You're a brilliant light out there, brilliant light within you. Being in that brilliant light that you are, the moment you walk past another being, another deity, what you say human, you recognize each other, inside and outside —you *know*. And there *is* love there, because that is what it takes to exist. (Everyone breathe, throat chakra. Allow.) There be love in you, there be love in they, there be love in your energy field, your chakra, all of this. The gods in their wisdom move slowly, because they are aware of the effect on all things in a simple movement, even within what you term a simple thought. That be you and all things. With this increase in energy that is coming from within you — *deep* within, from your primal core, entities — and coming from without, to join at what you term your physical forces, to meld and blend, to be one. This is the fun part. It is. Maintain your humor, it'll make it a lot easier, know you what I mean?

A lot of the energy, as it begins to move, because you've forgotten it for so long, you have memory of, say you, doubts, be a willingness within your being *not* to see love in the journey upward, so to speak. That willingness creates within you a fear of movement, because you think you found love in your now, limited as it is. The now is going to shift into great power within your form, within your forces here, and it is all love. You will remember and know these things. It is joyful expression. I'm going to look you over. Open the throat chakra. Indeed, everyone take a breath a moment. Lighten up a bit within your being, within your physical.

I want to bring more energy into your bodies, to increase your vibratory rate, to increase the flow of you. One of the things that happens when you bring more energy into your form, your persona, personality you say, must adjust a little bit to it. In that adjustment, the personality gains wisdom — it made it through the energies, so to speak, you think. And in that making it through, in the movement, there becomes a knowing —you did it! You now know. So the next increase is not so threatening, and you know a little more at the next increase. In your physical, at each increase, what wells up inside of you is part of your system of not letting go, a death of sorts, yet not. It's simply your energies. It is an overcoming of doubt of who be you, and how you work your form, your physical, how you work your body, so you know you are forever being, forever loved, and eternal. You *know* how to apply the energies in *this* form, so it becomes fun, joy, wisdom.

Are you all ready for another boost? Indeed? More boosters,

huh? How did you like the last two weeks of boost? That's just the beginning. Open the solar plexus chakra, let it be open. When we move from within this one [Arthur], and from without, because you are all connected, that movement is going on within you, that alignment is going on. Because you resonate or vibrate at a certain frequency so you can see each other, when you align your forces you create another resonance and you affect all beings that are around you: You affect the planet, you affect your solar system, all things you affect. It is going to be of profound importance now to love your being, to find the gentlest energies you can find to play with in this time, or you will play the other game, what you term in your emotional state, you lose it, know you? And then you be scrambling back to unscramble all your pieces, put them back in order. Your marble bag will break. Then you simply go shopping for another bag to put your marbles in. Don't panic. Pick them up and get another bag, and remember that you *are* the bag. Gather them together. [To a participant:] How can I be of assistance?

Well, I still want to feel with my physical body and see with my physical eyes, and know that love is all there is.

Indeed? You ready to feel it in the body?

You bet.

Indeed, so be it! I will assist you in this thing. It'll be fun. You won't mind weeping at the sight of a flower, then?

Oh, I've done that before.

More, indeed? Even be willing to weep at the sight of a rusty tin can. Someone up there is crying an awful lot, uh? Is it you? [To another participant:] How be you?

Mm . . . medium.

Medium? What do you think would help you?

A miracle.

A miracle. You *are* the miracle. Know this part right here, where all the thinkity-think happens, where you *think* it happens, this simply be the piece that gets it last. The piece that gets it first is right in here [heart chakra/soul], and then this piece [brain] gets the aha's and thinks it knows it all. So pay attention in here [heart], bargain? Little bit. I'm going to make a voice speak out of here [heart] for you. It's going to come from within here. You'll hear it. Then are you willing to look deeper in here?

Yes.

It'll be fine. Your water, your weather is grand, indeed? [Note: It was storming outside.] Know you, you need that silver fluid to keep your lightbody alive, in one manner. The gods enjoy the water.

Meditation

Now, allow your eyes to close gently for a moment. Contemplate you in your body, inside you. Listen to each drop of water, listen to the rain. It is a thought from your Father to you – one thought, one drop. It is also wisdom within the being physical. You have that many thoughts in drops you play with within your being. Allow. Allow. You are so powerful that you can communicate from within the center of you to any individual raindrop, as it moves through your arena, and connect with the intelligence within that raindrop – there will be a message for you, and that message will be love – it is there. The raindrop knows. It knows love, it knows its journey. It is not worried about landing upon the planet. That is what it wants to do because it is in love. It does not concern itself in its consciousness with its movement. It enjoys its movement, the spirit within the raindrop, the consciousness there. And your Earth is waiting for the impact, because it is an impact of love.

Now you, in your physicality, in this time, are getting that sort of impact from the lights that you are from within, and the lights that you are from without, becoming one, joining. Each one light has consciousness that's going to move, and it moves in love. Open the crown chakra wide. Open the chakras at your temples wider. Allow. Peace. You are not from this place, yet you are. You play here now. Listen to the voice of your Father within your heart chakra now, listen. Hear it in the chest area, gently unto you, in your throat [where the apex of the soul resides], allow. Peace. Allow.

Everyone allow the thumb of your right and left hand to touch the second finger of your right and left hand. Complete a circuit here. Allow. Move it to the third finger. Allow. Peace. Move it back to the first finger. Allow. Feel that adjustment within you, within your body. Move to the second finger now. Contemplate this thing deep within your being: LOVE I AM! Contemplate it, don't repeat it, feel it. Move down into your skeletal structure, into your spine area, center of your back, into the bone, and contemplate LOVE I AM there. Feel it radiate through the crystalline structure called your body human, skeletal as it is. Peace.

Now, when you open your eyes, which you'll do very slowly, I want you to release the thumb and the finger so you gesture giving, and breathe out the throat chakra. Allow your eyes to open gently, open the fingers, allow out the throat. What you are giving are blessings, wisdoms you gained from within you outward. They are there. They are there for you and everyone else. In that simple movement you gave as many blessings as raindrops are falling right now — that many, in that little movement. It is not that it is a thing; it is love, given freely from the core of your being, because like a raindrop you know you're moving, and in the movement it is love. That's all there is. Indeed?

[Group responds:] Indeed!

It's an outrageous thing. When you start playing with some of these energies deep within your being, know you, and you have leftover emotional stuff, the energies at times seek to burn it up real quick, know you, but you play hold on. That's like sticking your hand in an oven: You put out the fire first if you're going to keep holding on. I suggest you let go, though. Know you what I mean? It's safer for your vehicle, because all of these things that are going to happen are going to be reflected in your physical form. You *are* the god manifesting with these frequencies, *your* form. Be gentle, know you? Well, you don't have to be, you can be reckless if you wish. Just have a grand time, know you what I mean? Lot of humor.

Sometimes you have to adjust your physical, know you, pull it a little bit so the energies can balance in you. Allow it to get there. Peace. Allow. These are inside-outside energies. They're coming from within you, your movement now. I'll put it another way: You're at the front door of what you term your Father's house. You've opened the door, He be sitting there jumping up and down now —you've made Him really excited, know you? You're about ready to walk through that door. When Daddy jumps, lot of heat. Create a lot of movement. Know you what I mean? And it's going to happen within you, an expansion. This is what you've been waiting for, to walk through that door, know you? Move with Daddy, as you term it, Father, God, play. But then you've got to go beyond that and continue the journey. More homework —oops! More things to do. Other systems to evolve through. This is . . . well, you beings say one of the most difficult systems, yet it is also one of the most fun. If you make it through this one, you'll make it through any one. It is that precious here, that precious. This completion, union, a great movement together, indeed, be joy.

Now, part of your greatest joy is going to be sharing love. And the way you do that . . . you've been told love, love, love. The way you do that is you vibrate so much love in your body, you let it fall like raindrops wherever you walk, and you keep vibrating it, and vibrating it, and vibrating it. Vibrate more, more, more. One of the most difficult things to do, however, is when you vibrate this and vibrate and vibrate, you're going to have so much fun vibrating you're going to have to shut up (some of you won't like that) because you'll figure it's more fun vibrating — vibrate, vibrate, vibrate — and you'll know. The one that's doing all of the talking in your metaphysical chitty-chats is having a very difficult time vibrating.

Meditation

Allow your eyes to close a moment. Concentrate on the throat chakra. Peace. Feel light, brilliant white diamond light in the heart center, and see it pulse, likened unto strobe light there — pulse, and pulse, and pulse. And pulse through you, pulse and pulse, and out through your physical — pulse, and pulse, and pulse. And feel the solar plexus as it enjoys the activity. Allow. And feel the navel chakra; it's going to join and pulse its light. Allow. Root chakra, sixth seal, crown — pulse. Allow. Feel it in the heart chakra. LOVE I AM — pulse it. Peace. Let it fill your body. Allow light, allow life. Allow your eyes to open very gently. Peace.

Shine that love that vibrates within you here. When you do it affects every cell in your body. Your organs become rejuvenated in a manner, because they enjoy the pulse of life now, of love. Allow it to overwhelm you. That is a very healing thing. It is an outrageous thing. When you become overwhelmed with this love, you start off with new systems in your body. You be baby, in love, inside you. It rejuvenates your skin, all things. Everyone take a breath and breathe it out through the heart chakra. Allow. Peace. How do the bodies feel?

Great.

Indeed? You feel good in here [heart]? This where be your power. You do need this tool [brain], it is only a tool, like the body is. The greater forces are in here [heart chakra/soul] and they are spreading out now through all of you, through each cell. In these times you're going to be able to see what you do when you hold your hand and move your finger — you will see what's on the other end, what you're affecting. And that be a wise thing to let you see without judgment, know you? Now some of you will play this game: You move your finger to simply watch the other being jump, know you? Don't let me catch you. Remember, I'm in there with you. Very delicate movements now, in your being, because you're going to affect everything, including your planetary logos, planetary system, everything. So move you in a gentle manner. Bargain?

Bargain.

Indeed. [To a participant:] Do you have a question?

Mm, I don't know. I'm just happy to be here. I didn't know I had a specific one. It's been a real hot week, awesome energy.

It's going to get hotter.

Really?

Indeed! This is what you always wanted, hot, know you? "Turn up the heat, Daddy. Turn up the heat. Let's have a little bit more. More, more, more." Then you get your more and then we say, "Oops! Got a little too much." But that's all right, it's all part of the humor. Give me a moment here.

Some of the things we say are not meant to frighten you. They are meant to make you aware of how sacred and holy you are, and how sacred and holy this time is, how important it is. Metaphysical teachings were simply ladders to get you to this point – tools. You are playing with great energy forces that is, you term, love of God, love of the Father, love of all things, however you want to say it. Your love, your divinity is becoming known. That is the purpose of this time. Not the purpose to compare, not at all. It's the purpose to move, to become, to align with all of the divinities that are within you, all the deities. To align with them. Likened unto diamonds of light, to recognize them, not to separate. To know that you are a divine form becoming more, becoming empowered so you may enjoy more of the play and see more of the show, for this is a very limited view you have now. There is a grander play going on; the stage is much larger than you think, and you're participating there, but you're not aware of it yet. You will soon be. Be lot of fun, indeed?

Indeed!

In this thing, joy is the key. Freedom, love. I've told you before, many questions, many questions, many questions on your tests to come, and the answer is always the same. I've given you a cheat sheet on that one. Now, does anyone have anything they want to chat about?

I have a question now. It's personal. There was a line of energy connecting me to a life in the ancient past, and I've been working to keep energy from the now from going to that. Is that balanced? I don't feel it pulling on me so much.

Are you trying to destroy your past and your future?

No, I'm just trying to keep the energy from going from me to the past.

What is one of my favorite words?

Allow?

Allow. Allow. So you allow love, indeed? You allow love to flow, indeed. You can't restrict energy, you're just going to get yourself into deeper muck, know you? It'll explode on you.

I feel a lot more energy, though, like it's not being pulled from me.

You think a past life . . . I understand what you be saying.

Yeah. I had a great idea in that life. In that life I thought I had a brilliant idea, but now I'm paying for it.

That Orion mind, know you? Allow the energy to move. Love the energy, do you understand this thing? You have to love the energy. To try to restrict it to keep it from flowing, so to speak, you will create damage in other arenas *and* in your physical vehicle, because you're all in the same now, but you simply don't know it. The stage is a lot larger than you *think* it is. Allow love to flow freely!

All right, so don't think of it as energy being pulled, just focus love.

Focus love. Allow you to flow love, send love, know you? We say send love and you beings send love a little bit – "That be enough." Well, you *keep sending* it! Know you what I mean? If your Father decided that He wanted to pull some energy back from you . . . well, another group of entities, also, they would simply not think about you. But He loves you. He keeps sending you everything – *everything!* Always there, always will be, know you what I mean? And what is the always part? It is love. That's all it is, nothing else. You beings take it and put it in a little ball here. "Let's see what is not love" – that be the game here, know you? This be the game of not. "Let's prove that love doesn't exist!" You're pretty good at it, but you haven't proven anything. You proved that you can confuse yourself. You proved that you can forget, that's what you've succeeded in doing. It is an outrageous game here, but it is all right, it is beauteous here, know you what I mean? So love.

Because of these frequency speed-ups, there's going to be a lot of this competition flavor, know you, and blame past, blame future, know you what I mean?

Mm-hmm.

Feel in your body when you say, "Mm-hmm." Where be that? That be up here [head]. Move here [heart]. This is very basic, know you what I mean? You've been here before. Get it down here further. You're going to get yourselves into a little bit of difficulty if you're going to use your old metaphysical rules in this new arena. I will suggest loving. Trust me. It's a good idea. What be called snap back, know you snap rubber band? You'll be the one going oops, because it is your divinity and your thought processes that you're playing with.

You beings say you've got a collapse of time going on, speed-up, this, that, the other. The parts of the whole are coming together, to become one, to move. That is what is happening. The love is increasing, becoming one, to move. That's what is going on. There still is a little bit of proving the game of not is the only thing that exists, but that's soon going to change. What is the worst thing that could happen to your physical body if you loved so much you just burst into ecstasy? You vibrate so much you burst into a blast of light, know you, and you play in that light and move further and further with it, understand? That is what you do. You begin to love the love so much that you love the love more to love the love more. You can receive love, know you? Feel it in your body — that is allowed. It is okay. No one told you you couldn't. You're simply pretending.

Now, I'm not saying it isn't a little bit overwhelming to get smacked with all that love in the physical. You'll start shaking all over, especially when it hits you in your supermarkets and you're walking past the frozen foods — you're going to start worshiping beans. The way you beings operate, it's got to be the beans. "They've got the icebox too cold. It's all that energy coming out of the icebox," so we'll create some bean worshipers here. It is not the beans, it is you, and you happened to be in a moment where you were not in your thinkity-think so much, and love just came out of you, just blasted out, and the body felt grand, and it enjoyed it, and you went into ecstasy. That doesn't mean you can't love the beans.

[To a participant:] How be you?

Grand.

Indeed? How be your nails? [The questioner had recently removed all her artificial fingernails and fingernail polish after many years.] They be saying, "I be freeeeeeeee! I be baby again! I be!" You be an outrageous being, know you what I mean? Things be fun here, know you, they be joy. Everyone breathe a little bit. The body is getting a little heavy. Indeed, everyone get a little water here. Drink your raindrops and contemplate the thoughts that are going in the body.

Now, I will tell you this thing: It is a good thing that I appear in this form and through other energy vehicles here, in this manner, to communicate. It is a good thing. You don't want to see me the other way, like I've been here before, and other places. There have been petitions by many, and the petitions be in this manner: they be say, "There *is* love there, it exists. I can show you." So we be understanding. We paid attention, looked, and we see it. And they were right, there *is* love here, and it's going to move forth. You have many beings that have come and spoken. [You] paid attention a little bit;

that is all right; at least you paid attention a little bit. And they returned and petitioned more, and more. And because of them, because of their love for this plane and humanity, all humanity, we'll say we allowed an increase so you may become quicker.

Now, remember that all of this is occurring within you here, and you too were part of the petitioners to bring this about, even though you've forgotten. You called it to come forth. It is coming forth now. It is coming forth *through* your physical form, through your auric field, through your thought processes, and especially through your love. You are becoming. There is nothing fearful in it, it is only your ignorance. It is a joy.

You *are* the Buddha one and more. You are part of every consciousness upon your planet, and the stars, also. Treat it all gently, indeed? Bargain?

Bargain.

Meditation

Allow your eyes to close for a moment here. Open the temple chakras, allow. Peace. Open the chakras on your knees, bottoms of your feet. Be in your power in your line of light in the center of your being now. Peace. Allow. Now feel the energy about your physical body, that is around it. Feel it there. Feel the energy that is withinside your physical body. Those two fields desire to blend. Take a breath down to your root chakra and tighten your buttocks; hold the breath. Allow. Fire. Agni move. Peace. Exhale. Indeed, center your spine. One more time, take a breath in, hold the perineum, the buttocks tight, hold it there. Hold it. Shiva, Agni, move. Allow. Exhale out the crown. Feel a flame at the top of your head. Allow. Peace. Allow. Center. Peace. Where your jaw bones meet, upper and lower mandible in the back there, open those chakras. Tell them to open. There begins to get activity at the top of your forehead. Allow that to open. Allow. Peace. Align. Focus on the tenth chakra. Move to the eleventh, move to the twelfth. Allow.

At the twelfth chakra see a sword of light, brilliant white light sword. Flaming sword of white light. Allow it to descend now to the eleventh and to the tenth, straight downwards. It is vertical flaming light sword. Let it move into the crown and move so the handle rests at your solar plexus. Allow it. And the tip of the sword be at your throat chakra. Allow. Now allow flaming light from the tip of that sword to move up the throat chakra through the roof of your mouth, past the sixth seal and out the crown. Allow. Peace. Center. Allow the base of the sword now to move through your root chakra. The handle has a ruby stone at your root chakra. Allow. Open the vortices at your mandibles wider, jaw bone.

Peace. Grand. Peace. Now allow the tip of that sword to move back to the twelfth chakra. Allow. Peace.

Now pay attention. The sword will begin to spin counterclockwise, and let it sort of wobble a little bit so it creates a cone effect. It'll come to the left side of your head by your ear, past the left shoulder, right shoulder, right side of the head – so the shoulders mark the periphery of the cone, and let it go out to the twelfth chakra. Allow the energy to sit at the root. Allow. Peace. Allow. Open the heart chakra wider. Now, from the twelfth chakra allow a column of light the width of the cone to descend around you. Peace. Be in the body. Allow. Now allow the sword to dissolve into brilliant spheres of light in your auric field and in your physical form. Peace. Love. Allow. Allow. Allow, allow. Allow. Peace. In a gentle manner slowly open your physical eyes.

You are consciousness within light is what you are. You are brilliant is what you are. You have the ability to manipulate light. Allow you to remember this. It is the lightbody that allows the physical to exist, in one manner. This is your greater love that allows *any* of it to play, in another manner. That love for you that is you. All things. Everything. This time is the time when you've been given free reign, so to speak, to play with your light. To join with the gods and play and understand. To be in love. Not to worship the gods, not at all. To communicate, to gain wisdom from teachings that you've forgotten. They vibrate inside you. They will show themselves to you if you allow, right in front of you. They won't do it if you go into worship. They will do it if you desire to seek wisdom, we will say, to remember more of what you know. They will gladly share with you everything, all things. Indeed?

Indeed.

[To a participant:] Are you ready to play more with the light of you?

Yes.

Indeed?

Yes.

Let it shine forth more, be you say remember how to manipulate it within your being.

I'm trying to remember.

I'll give you a book this evening from inside you, bargain? It'll be fun. Be a little book, very small print. You'll have to focus. Then we'll make it big. . . . It is all a cake of piece (peace), know you? Piece of cake, you say. I like it better the other way. Everyone breathe a moment. Allow love, indeed? Love God, love you. Love, love, love, love, love, love.

Your soul is blending with your physical body, so to speak. There's not going to be any separation any longer. You're going to become known as the soul. Lot of fun, now. Can't blame the soul any longer! Have to find something else. It is love, and don't blame love, indeed? I'm going to tell you something else. Some of you are going to begin to get what is termed writings appearing on your body, in the strangest places. I don't mean tatoos where you go buy one. This be produced by you, for you. It be an outrageous thing. It is important. That means you're coming out of hiding. That's one of the reasons you chose physical vehicle, one aspect of one story, so you could hide – thought no one could find you. Oops! That be part of the fun. We were there with you all of the time. And you dive, and you dive, deeper, and deeper, and look for a bigger hole, and we still be there, laughing all of the way. Now, give me a moment here.

Now, we're going to create a little dance within your being this evening right around the heart chakra. And be a little kick, little open, little push, know you? We're going to push that heart chakra open. Be dance, push, push, dance. And you're going to feel this thing. Don't shut it down because that will simply make me push harder, push. Open the door, I want to come through, understand? See you, from within and without. Be lot of fun. Do you feel like another meditation?

Yes!

This time we're going to cook you in your solar plexus. Get ready. There be an important point there.

Meditation

Allow your eyes to close gently. Now, open the heart chakra. See yourself sitting there, you, Buddha one, gold color you, christed one, on a lotus flower if you wish, surrounded by golden light. Allow. You are sitting there in your glory. Allow. Now send energy from the root chakra up to the solar plexus, a line of golden-red, and allow it to sit there and spread across the diaphragm. Allow. Peace. Send more energy up from the root chakra. More. And as you send energy up, feel the Buddha one of you in the heart chakra floating up a little bit toward the apex, toward your throat chakra. Allow. Peace. Push more energy up.

Now, allow the Buddha one, the sitting one, you, what you term the eyes of you within you, to move to the throat chakra. Open the throat chakra wider. Open the solar plexus. Allow the energy up into the heart chakra, allow, and look you from your sitting position out of the throat chakra. Allow. Peace. Allow. Allow the energy to continue up through the head. Allow. Bring more energy from the root up, solar plexus, push it into the heart chakra.

Now the head of the Buddha one you call you, looking like you, stretches now to encompass your physical head – it becomes golden from withinside. Allow. Push. Gold. Allow. Take a breath in and hold it in the arena, the energy at the throat chakra, hold it there. You're going to breathe outward and you're going to fill the Buddha body inside you and push it down to fill your physical form. Push. Another breath, in at the throat – you're breathing into the throat of the Buddha now. Push. Fill it.

And one more, push the legs into the legs. Push. Feel golden body. Allow. Allow. Allow. Open the solar plexus chakra wider. Allow you. Grand. Peace. Buddha body, you, golden color. Take another little breath and take it at the throat chakra, hold the energy there and you're going to push up, sort of blow it into the head arena to fill that arena. That be grand, that be grand. That be outrageous.

Now, with this golden force that is you, it quickens your body. Allow you very gently with your right hand now to touch your left hand and feel your skin, how be soft it is. And allow your left hand to touch your right hand and feel how be soft and precious you are. Allow. And even if you wish, allow your hand to enter through your physical hand so it touches the golden light withinside you, and feel how sacred it is. That is you, entities. It is no one else but you. Allow. Breathe in down to the solar plexus, hold it there. Breathe out of the throat chakra. Indeed, grand. Allow.

Now I want you to contemplate at your throat chakra, contemplate your name, quietly within your being, contemplate it at the throat chakra, your name. Allow. Allow. Let it begin spinning counterclockwise around the throat chakra. See your name written on your head, inside on the brain, golden light, golden letters, red letters, your name. Allow. And see it spin counterclockwise around you, golden body, right beneath the skin. Allow. Now allow that name to spiral down counterclockwise around the golden body that be inside the skin, and allow the name to change if it wishes. Allow the letters to change. Allow. Allow the spiral to begin and continue, and when it reaches a junction point, arms, allow it to split and enter. Legs, same, split and enter. Allow.

Now, what you are feeling in your body is that you are your past and your future, and that you are the deities, be one and the same. Open the throat chakra a little bit more. Peace. Peace. Peace. Contemplate your golden body now with all of the names that you ever have been and ever will be that are around it. Contemplate it within you. Allow. And they're not names you might recognize or forms even of names or letters, they are *your knowing. They are very ancient scriptures, script, writings, that you are. They are sounds you can't even pronounce. They are you. Allow. In a gentle manner slowly open your physical eyes. Now allow what you would term flashes of light to project through your skin at times. In your quiet moments you'll see them flash out from you. That is you remembering you, beyond the limitation of the flesh. Allow.*

Tomorrow, for those of you that are going to be here, we're going to start playing with what you would term fire letters, fire, literally fire. We're going to write with fire. We're going to play with what you would term whirlwind tornadoes of thought. We're going to play with creation from within your being. We are through.

22

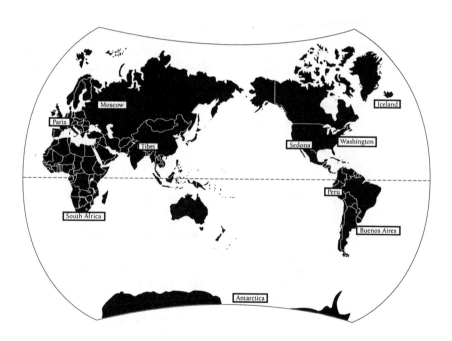

The warriors who were brought from the ancient past of the Pleiades to counteract the sinister secret government have developed technology that will send humans to the 7th dimension, transforming them. Secret government members do not want to be transformed, so they are leaving their isolated underground bases in the Antarctic and Iceland and their headquarters at the tip of South Africa to move to huge underground bases under heavily populated cities – Paris, Washington D.C., Moscow and Buenos Aires. They plan to use the human populations to shield them from the Pleiadians and to use ELF waves to send disturbing energies to the cities on the surface.

– Publisher's note

WHAT CAN YOU DO?

Zoosh: *The best thing the lightworkers can do is shoot, as it were, light underneath the cities. Use more than white light, because white light will not affect them. Use gold light . . . they have little resistance to it.*

For those who are musically inclined: Hit the highest notes on a standard keyboard, the two highest notes (or even the three highest). Play them in concordance, and broadcast the sound straight downward.

YHWH: *One of the main things when you share this information is to make sure it is as information – not fear-oriented, know you? So you become very careful in the dispensing of this thing. You have heard that you are gods, indeed? And you're becoming, indeed? That is the most important process, the most important thing. More than the secret government, you understand? It is sort of side thing. Cartoon is what it really is. It is that comical. Now, when you work with energies like that – antagonism, this, that and the other – there is a sense within the body of the joy of it, the thrill, thrilling. That simply means you don't want to focus on yourself. You would rather focus on what the bad guys do. It doesn't matter what they do! They're being taken care of, believe me!*

It is interesting. As long as you use that part of the interest as, "Well, I've worked on myself enough today," like you say, "Well, I've worked on myself 23 hours and 45 minutes today. I will spend 23 hours and 59 minutes; I will give them one moment of my time." That's how important they are.

Secret Government
Forced to Move

Zoosh through Robert Shapiro
August 21, 1995

I wonder what you have done to qualify for your recent invasion! As of this last weekend, you have four (count them up, four) outer-ring members of the sinister secret government circulating around in Sedona – and wreaking havoc, I might add – in three cases, unbeknownst to themselves; in one case, quite well knownst, as it were (if I can use that word), broadcasting every form of negative and controlling energy known to thought. They were definitely up to no good. Many people in this town did not sleep all that well Sunday night, and literally experienced in the afternoon and evening subtle and nefarious psychic attack, as it is ofttimes called. Sometimes one does not know when one has experienced psychic attack because you may not feel anything in the moment; usually you do, but occasionally you don't. But you do feel it when you go to sleep; your body is at rest then and your natural defenses are down. Those who would manipulate you and try to get in and disturb you then are up to no good.

So these members of the outer ring were acting in concordance with a plan being hatched by the secret government as we speak. All sinister secret government underground bases are being moved – right now. And this motion is intended to bring all bases under highly populated cities. You might ask why. It is simply this: Those who are in direct opposition to the sinister secret government, including some extraterrestrial groups who are attempting to assist the general population of the planet Earth, are preparing to utilize a form of plasma device. It is not a weapon; it will tend to create a certain amount of time distortion in an immediate arc from the firing of the beam as it touches the ground, which could affect the lives of those who are exposed to it.

So the secret government, now underground in places where a passing human would be rare, is moving its whole operation underneath the most populous cities they can find. One of these bases is being moved underneath the city of Paris, France; one of them is under the city of Moscow, Russia; another under the city of Buenos Aires, Argentina; and another is being moved under the city of Washington, D.C., United States. There is yet another, but I feel that that one is perhaps in the most "jeopardy" of being transformed by these rays.

These rays will be fired from a Pleiadian warship. The rays inject a form of highly evolved spiritual matter into everyone and everything they affect. It works only on that which has intelligence, not just intelligence as you know it, but any range of intelligence from the slowest intelligent beings to the most highly evolved intelligent beings. If the beings are already spiritual persons, it will heighten their spiritual awareness. If, on the other hand, the beings are dense and warlike, it will transform them to more spiritual beings. The fifth base will likely be lost to the sinister secret government, because it is under fire from these rays right now. I do not think they will be able to escape —which is good for your side, as it were, if there are sides in this matter.

Where is that one?

That one I will simply say is in the extreme Northern Hemisphere. They have been caught —not exactly with their pants down, but they were caught in an area where there isn't much population, so there didn't have to be much consideration for the effect of the rays on the planetary surface. So the sinister secret government is doing something that's not unknown in warfare, and that is hiding behind the bodies of innocent victims —from their point of view. You can rest assured that the Pleiadians are not going to fire these rays through the middle of Red Square and unintentionally affect the passersby. However, when the city sleeps, they will be able to fire some of the rays through. I do not think there is any means to resist these rays, but we will see what the secret government comes up with.

Now, you might ask, why is the secret government messing around with outer-ring members and having them broadcast various forms of negative energy? Over this past weekend, in different areas of the Northern Hemisphere, they had about 1300 outer-ring members broadcasting this negative energy. It was essentially a test to see how effective they can be. So this tells you that if for no reason at all you suddenly start feeling exhausted and weary, and if you start exhibiting signs of anger for which there is no purpose, it might be a good time to call in the angels and your guides, or call in the medicine people. Call in all who can help you to remove any entities or negative energy attached to you that might be affecting you or harming you in some way. These things must be removed and ideally transformed and sent to where they need to be.

How did they do that? What was the technique by which they did it, and were the outer-ring members conscious of what they did?

They used a form of projected rage by maintaining a level of sustainable anger, whether it be from annoyance or total rage. They were able, by maintaining that energy, that feeling, to be used as mirrors by rays of energy utilizing the extra-low frequency and/or ultrasonics (but extra-low frequency is easier to use) to transmit this energy at large. There weren't specific targets; it was all who happened to be in their general area. For example, one of these persons could walk into a department store, and everyone on that floor would be affected. It would not affect people who were strong, athletic or were working hard and their energy was flowing out. But those who were receptive, for any reason, or were tired or out of shape, as it were, and less able to resist – or who were sleeping – they would be more likely to be affected.

It was a test. I'm sorry to say that from the sinister secret government's point of view, it was a very successful test. Their motivation in all of this (the sinister secret government) is essentially to hold hostage the people of Earth and say to the Pleiadians, "If you try to transform us into something that you approve of and we do not, we will, in direct proportion to what you do to us, attack the people of the Earth and spray at large – with no intent for particular people, but just everyone – as much negative energy as we can." You see, that's their ace in the hole, because they know the Pleiadians will not attempt to transform them if they are going to hold the people of Earth hostage.

Are these the ancient Pleiadian warriors on the warship?

Yes.

So how did all this change so suddenly? I thought the inner ring was breaking up, and . . .

Well, the inner ring was having troubles, but one member bolting from it is not what I'd call breaking up. That member is still out there and up to no good.

Okay, if they're moving their bases, are they moving the one here in Sedona?

Yes. Although they're still here, and although a lot of nasty happened over the weekend here, they feel that it's necessary to move this base because Sedona is not sufficiently populated. This will be the base that they move under the City of Light, otherwise known as Paris.

So where are the others moving from? Where is the one that's going to be under Washington?

We have discussed where they are before.

But you said they're moving out. Are they moving out of Iceland and South Africa?

They are moving lock, stock and barrel, as you say.

Out from the one that's at the tip of South Africa?

That's right.

And Antarctica?

Yes.

And Iceland?

Yes, because these places are remote, and they can hardly say with any effectiveness to the Pleiadians, "Don't shoot, you might hit somebody."

But they're going to leave them protected; it's not like they're going to be available to just anyone. What about all those underground cloned soldiers – are they going to stay there?

They're going to move them all. They're moving lock, stock and barrel.

So they already have facilities built under these large cities?

Yes.

How far down?

About eight-and-a-half miles. But you see, what they always do is build under a shelf of very dense rock. You could say, "Well, why doesn't the government just use Excalibur or some kind of weapon like that and explode it underneath these cities?" Well, I don't have to tell you what the sinister secret government would do. If they had any breath of an idea that such a thing would happen, they would retaliate.

Okay, then what can the people in the cities do?

Light and Sound Can Prevent This

The best thing they can do, especially the lightworkers, is shoot, as it were, light underneath the cities. I want you to ask the angelics to come in, and they will; and your guides, and they will; and your teachers and all medicine people from all times – the future, the past and even the present, should they care to participate – to aim light, what I call light vibronics. Vibronics in this case means the vibration associated with a harmonic that will make it impossible for them to be there.

You understand that the sinister secret government thinks they're pulling a real fast one here. But they know they are at risk while they are moving, because while they are moving they are less protected than when they are entrenched. So to people in all cities: Fire this light down below. Try to use more than white light, because white light will not affect them. White light is totally, unconditionally loving; it loves everyone equally. Try to use *gold light*. That will affect them; they have little resistance to it. Pink light might cause a little mischief, because it's very loving. For those who are musically inclined: Hit the highest notes on a standard keyboard, the two highest notes (or even the three highest if you want). Play them in concordance, and if you can, broadcast the sound straight downward. It's not done to harass them; the idea is to make them feel sufficiently unwelcome here so that they will use their contingency plan, which is to move the entire operation on Earth to the Moon. If they do that, they will be in the position of having to negotiate. And once they get into that position, they will negotiate, and that will be a good thing. So we want to move them to the Moon.

That's pretty close to the end, then.

If we can move them to the Moon, we'll be closer to the end.

And what is their thinking on this?

It's a fallback position; they're willing to do it. They understand that they'll have to negotiate. Those who are in charge and are pulling the strings understand that they may have to live elsewhere, and they're willing to, as long as they can live under certain circumstances. I don't want to say exactly what those circumstances are, but basically, they want to be powerful, to be the boss and have all wealth and power. Now, this can be done under certain circumstances without other people suffering, but of course I will not say what those circumstances are, because if I do I'll just reveal my ace in the hole.

So this is really speeding up, then. This is only 1995.

Well, why not? Let's speed it up.

Okay, but are people going to react in panic when they read what's happening – those who live in the cities you named? How are they going to feel when the secret government is moving underneath them?

Well, I'm hoping that they will take this as a call to arms and start in their groups, in their group meditations or their singular meditations. This doesn't work if you pull the energy up. You've got to push the energy down, just like a hose blowing energy at them. Now, don't exhaust yourself. Thirty seconds a day, even ten seconds, helps. Blow that gold light down there; you could blow a little pink light down there if you want to. Or you could sound those high-register notes on any instrument that can reach the high tones (not talking about a baritone sax here). Anything that can reach those high tones would be good to use. Just aim it and feel it or see it going down about ten or twelve miles.

Anybody on the planet can . . .

Anybody can do it, that's right. And they'll feel it. It can only help the people on the surface, because these are good things for the surface people. It tends to be a psychic benefit for people on the surface. That is, it tends to remove or break negative entities off from an individual they are attached to. In certain circumstances, within the city it's hard to avoid negative energy becoming attached to you. But when you play these high-register notes, you blow this gold or pink cover around, it's going to release that kind of negative entity. It won't be able to hold on. So this technique can only help the surface people.

All right. Is there anybody else in the cosmos doing anything about this? I mean, if they're doing this, this is almost like they're . . . if they felt really secure, they would stay in their present bases, but this seems like they're going into war and moving into position.

This is a desperate measure, there's no question about it.

So are there any beings from the cosmos or any galactic cops who are making any moves?

Well, understand that this is basically a Pleiadian effort. They have not only the past that they can call on for these warships, but they also have a strong sense of family toward people on the Earth. So anytime people on the Earth are threatened, especially by some kind of force like the sinister secret government or extraterrestrials, they would be inclined to leap into action. Many's the time the Pleiadians would have liked to protect you in certain circumstances, but they didn't have permission. Now they have absolute permission to do whatever needs to be done within the bounds of upliftment, meaning that they're not given permission to kill, but they have absolute permission to transform and raise the vibration of beings by any means necessary. That means the beings must be alive, because when they die they naturally raise their energy.

That's interesting: giving up that absolute, impenetrable – well, we learned that the South Africa base wasn't impenetrable after the Pleiadians got there . . . and they know that, right?

They know that. You see, the Pleiadeans used a real smart tactic, because this ray they're going to fire at the sinister secret government – it's like the best laid plans of mice and men, yes? It didn't work out; the idea of being isolated was suddenly turned against them! So they have to move, and once you get people moving, they become vulnerable. They know this, and believe me, their contingency plan, to go to the Moon – that could be just around the corner if we get this thing going just right. It would take them about three months to complete the move, so our deadline here is not a problem.

Okay, so three months from now they'll be . . . it is amazing that they could move that fast! You're talking about a civilization, practically.

Yes, but you have to understand that if they're not nice about it, they can move real fast.

So this base at Secret Canyon here in Sedona is finally, after all this on and off again, going to be empty now?

They're going to move it out, but they're probably going to leave a small force there because they consider it to be a strategic place. I wouldn't think there'd be any more than maybe five hundred people there at any given moment. That would be really like a remote outpost. They're not going to have many remote outposts. They're going to leave one here in Sedona, one near the Andes in Peru, another near certain significant mountains in Tibet – in other words, associated with places that are by their very nature connected to spiritual creativity – to attempt to slow you down by broadcasting those energies. You know, if they weren't here, the people of Earth would have been uplifted and have joined the planetary community in the late forties!

That's when they really got organized?

That's when the sinister secret government got serious and went all out. There were delays going on here. But although they know darned well that they're delaying it, they absolutely know they can't stop it. And that's why their contingency plan is very real. I can assure you, they do not intend to take everyone with them to the Moon. They will take every weapon that will be a serious threat, but they're not planning to take their people, oh no. Out of all the people they have, I don't think they'd take more than, tops, 2000 people to the Moon. But they'd take some major weapons systems. And they would probably leave some booby traps behind that they could activate by signals.

By the way, those who may hear about this who *aren't* going to be among the elect or chosen few might be interested to know what's going to happen to them: As members of the secret government, whether military or dependents or whatever, the sinister secret government will consider them a threat because they know something. They intend to kill them all. I am not saying this just to create riots underground; that is an absolute plan.

Okay, so what percentage? We're looking at the inner-ring . . . the outer-ring members that you said didn't know they were outer-ring . . .

That's right, they don't know. They think they're doing a favor for a friend, or they think that sometimes they get depressed or angry for no reason they can understand (this is not, obviously, everybody who gets depressed or angry), but there's not a huge number of outer-ring members.

But you're talking about the actual military elite that guards them. How many military do they have? I'm trying to get what percentage 2000 is of the total people in the sinister secret government. Are you counting the cloned guards underground?

Let's count everybody. If we count everybody, how many people are they planning to bump off when the 2000 elite go there (and that 2000 max could very easily be 1000)? I think we're talking in the neighborhood of – depending upon when they go, what they do and how they do it – right around five million.

There's five million people in those underground bases?!

I'm counting everybody.

This includes ETs – the negative ETs are going to go, too?

Yes. They're not going to leave anybody behind that might possibly tell anything about them. I will say that they're not going to make them suffer, but they intend to, as they might say, "switch them off." They have all these fancy words for kill.

So by printing this, we're hoping that somebody in the outer ring who knows what's going on reads it?

We're kind of hoping that it spreads around and that the outer-ring members wake up. The interesting thing is that the outer-ring members don't know each other, for the most part — or if they do, they don't know that they're outer-ring members. Occasionally some outer-ring members know, but not many. So you might ask, what is to be gained here even if an outer-ring member wakes up? Well, if an outer-ring member wakes up, chances are the sinister secret government will not make any effort to harm them. But I'll put a percentage on that: there is a 95% chance that the secret government will not make any effort to harm them in any way, because very often these people have reached some level of influence, whether in business or public image or politics. They're in some way noticeable, they're in the media's eye, so if anything happened to them it would draw an unusual amount of police attention, and that's just the opposite of what they want.

If an outer-ring member wakes up, there's a very good chance they will be able to write, whether fiction, fact or opinion, or make public something about the secret government, even if only something like, "Woke up and felt strange; what have I been doing? I've been acting like somebody else and now suddenly feel like myself again." You understand? This can literally make all the difference, because sometimes all you have to say to an outer-ring member is, "Have you ever noticed that sometimes you have friends who ask you to do favors, and if you can do them, you do; if you can't do them, you don't; but that there are some people who tell you they need you to do something, and even though you don't want to do it, you can't say no to these people?" I'm not talking about your boss; I'm talking about someone you know who asks you to do something, and you haven't got any resistance to him. I'm not talking about somebody you love, I'm talking about somebody you barely know, who asks you to do something and you can't *not* do it.

So there's a control factor here.

Oh, absolutely. These people are totally controlled. Many of them, given their own personalities, would never do anything like this.

And yet they don't remember what they do?

They either don't remember or they don't even know what they're doing. More often than not, they think that they're angry or upset about something, in the case of this latest little situation.

So some outer-ring members came to Sedona, and just thought they were angry? They didn't even know what they were doing?

They thought they were upset and agitated and they didn't know why. For the life of them, they couldn't understand why they were upset and agitated, because they were on vacation and thought they were having a great time. They didn't know why they were angry. It was baffling to some extent, but it wasn't crippling, so they went on.

So how do they wake up? What's the process to remove whatever's controlling them?

Well, I'm hoping that they *think!* If we get these ideas out as much as we can, as we're doing here, then the word starts circulating. Then other people think about it, they read about it, maybe they even write stories about it. Sometimes you don't even know how your words affect people.

But is there a way, if they have an inkling that they're being used, to go to someone and remove this controlling whatever-it-is? I mean, how do they wake up?

The mechanics of it?

Yes. How do they become free?

There's more than one way. If they realize what's going on, they can wake up, they can resist it. If they start practicing consciousness things, meditation that takes them to different states of being, actions, spiritual practices that go beyond thought and come into feeling, it can change them radically. Or if they are, for instance, experiencing acupuncture (and a wise acupuncturist knows the spots to put the needles in that will heighten sensitivities of the heart and of the spirit), this can literally change them, like that [snaps fingers]. So there are therapies. This could happen by accident, or certain individuals who do work like this, you know, they might just be curious — "Oh, well, I'll go to this" — and bang! it happens.

Very good. Okay, what about the military? Are they aware of what's happening here? Can you actually move these five million people and have nobody know about it?

No, they are aware, and they want to know what it's all about. Part of the reason that there have been more intelligence flights and sonic mapping (mentioned last time) is that there are tunnels down there that weren't there a while back. Everybody in the legitimate military wants to know what's going on, and their immediate thought is that it's some other country — the usual thoughts. But they're beginning to get an inkling that that isn't it at all.

However, they're being distracted. One of the main distractions for the military are what they call political hot spots: Bosnia, the

Middle East. The United States managed to not get sucked into the Bosnia thing directly, but they're getting sucked right into the Middle East again. That's the big distraction, see? You make a bang someplace, you get them distracted, and then you bring them in. Now, I'm not saying that the intelligence they had wasn't real; the intelligence was good. But . . .

But it's a distraction to keep them from observing the move?

That's right. You keep them fighting amongst themselves, right? They can't see what the real problem is. But you have to understand also that your legitimate military is somewhat strapped here. If somebody is eight-and-a-half, nine, ten, twelve miles down below Earth's surface and you don't have any means to get to them, what are you going to do? You can't destroy the Earth in order to attack some enemy, because you have to live here. The military does have weapons that would be devastating, but the bottom line is that they're not idiots; they know if they destroy a big chunk of the Earth, where is everybody going to live?

If, from eight to twelve miles down, they're going to send ELF waves upward, these negative thought forms, can't we send ELF waves downward with positive thought forms?

You could, as a matter of fact, but in order to be effective, you'd have to have a very large ELF generator and send it downward using the pulses that would perhaps provoke good feeling. Even then I'm not sure that would do much good. There's not that much in the ELF wave that could be used to actually transform them. You could cheer them up, you could make them happier, you could make them creative, but I don't think that would be a good idea! You could do a lot of things that might cause them to feel happier, but I don't think you could transform them with the ELF. You can't use the same weapon and get the effect that you want.

And the Pleiadian weapon couldn't be amplified by ELF waves?

Oh, no, it doesn't use ELF at all. The Pleiadian "weapon" that's being used uses a higher-dimensional vibration that cannot be resisted. It's like a ray, but it's really a form of sound. We're really talking about vibronics here. It does not emanate very far away from itself, but it does emanate a good ten feet out, to a lesser degree as you get into the ray itself — it's almost like it illuminates this area, so there's a lesser degree. But there'd be time distortions because it's a higher-dimensional beam. So they're essentially firing more benevolent energies into people and into areas. So you might say that when this stuff is fired into the Earth, that particular place suddenly goes from being third- or fourth-dimensional (depending on what's happening there) to, say, seventh dimension for a while. You can't resist that. Even if you're in a lead-lined locker, it can't be resisted.

Excellent.

You just take these beings to their seventh-dimensional existence, where they could not possibly be negative in any way. It's very clever.

Very good. So it's going to take them three months to move. What kind of time is going to play out after that?

We hope that they'll be caught in transit by what everybody's doing. If they're caught in transit, have enough of what they'd consider discomfort, and are unable to occupy any of their new bases (and they will not be able to go back to the old ones), then they will exercise their other plan.

Can the Pleiadians follow them from the old base to the new?

They won't stop them going to the Moon.

Can they follow them from the old base to the new and fire these . . .

Oh, absolutely they can. And any time they get someplace where there's nobody on the surface, no animals or anything within reason, they'll fire these things.

It can go through water?

Oh, it can go through anything. It can go through mountains; it can go through planets and come out the other side. It can't be stopped. It's very powerful. The technology itself would be significantly bigger than this house, but say you were sitting here and you were the operator of it. There would be more than one person, but say you were just this one person; you could pull the "trigger," as it were, and you could fire this thing all the way across to the other side of the universe. It couldn't be stopped. It would just keep going to infinity.

So if they fire it at Washington, D.C., it's going to come out the other side of the planet?

No, no. They don't want to fire it through areas where there are people, because if the beam itself was fired right through a human being — poof! They'd be gone to the seventh dimension and they wouldn't be back.

And their physical body would be gone?

Everything. They would be gone; they would be transformed. You wouldn't see them again. It would be like there would be an existence in the seventh dimension in their next seventh-dimensional life, whatever it is. But that wouldn't help them in their evolution on this planet. If they were happy in a family, it wouldn't help them. And there could be time distortions in a ten-foot radius beyond the beam, and a person could fall into someplace in the universe and never find their way back. It would be totally unacceptable.

It can't be stopped. If you wanted to fire from one end of the universe to another, it would not be possible to stop it anywhere. Well, the Creator could stop it.

And what did they use it for before this clever thing here? Or was it invented for this purpose?

It was actually originally invented for therapy. It is not unlike the device that is used when people are taken aboard a ship to stay for a given amount of time, and they have negative energy that needs to be cleansed so they can walk around the ship. Yes, it's just like taking a very small device about the size of an x-ray machine and just making it humongous.

Got it, very good. If it's going to take them three months to move, we can get an update next month, then.

Yes.

To balance this out, what about the consciousness of the people on the planet? The energy is really being infused right now . . .

Yes. We talked about this a few years ago when everybody was waiting for everybody to start to wake up. I said that the mass of people are going to wake up in three big waves — well, the first wave is well under way. I mean, you're finding people waking up. Everybody in all walks of life is finding people getting more conscious in their own way, much more so. I might add that an interesting sidelight to this is that even in organized religions with a very specific aim — really almost a political aim, in the sense of disseminating their knowledge — they are finding that, top to bottom, the people in their religion are wanting the religion to be *more*. They're wanting it to be broader-based, they're wanting it to be less dogmatic and they're wanting it to be more universally appealing. This is an aspect of the broadening and the uplifting of consciousness. I think you'll find that the zeal to convert people to one's point of view at all costs will be something that will go away fairly soon — which I consider to be a big plus!

Further Incursions on Tribal Land

What's the latest news on the Indian reservations?

The secret government is still attempting to subvert certain individuals in tribal places in the United States. They're still attempting to get in and mine tribal lands. This is something that is ongoing.

If they don't get all that they want in one place, they'll try to get it in another place.

I've let a little something go unchallenged. A long time ago it was said, "Well, they got what they wanted." We heard that from some other source. And I did not challenge that because at the time I felt it was better not to draw too much attention to the reservations, which were attempting to deal with these things on their own. But right now certain things have gotten out of hand on various reservations. There are too many power plays, and many people are attempting to point the finger and say, "He did it" or "She did it." It's no different on reservations; everybody is human and they have the same problems as everybody else.

So I will say that the sinister secret government and its toadies are hard at work on the reservations, attempting to pit the people against each other so they can go in under the guise of doing this service or that service and actually run core samples and dig and take over. Particularly on reservations in the United States, you really have to watch out for wherever people are digging. (Obviously, if they're digging fenceposts or digging down a couple of feet and erecting a pole or whatever, it's not to worry about.) But if you can see a lot of equipment and they're doing a lot of digging and you know they're not digging for a well, pay attention. They're doing core sampling all over.

You need to keep up on this one. I would like people to continue to write letters to their senators and congressmen and make sure that the tribes have autonomy, that it is understood that the land upon which the tribes live is land that is *not to be disrupted*. To the people it is sacred land, to be honored, and the land is to be considered a church. You don't often see an oil company driving into the middle of a church and pounding an oil well down right through the middle of aisle B, okay? They don't do that; there's a respect. Just understand that the land is the same as the church. We've got to put that one out again because there's some stuff going on.

What happened at Hopiland? Did they take all the uranium out?

They took stuff out from the periphery, but in the process they discovered other things. And now, well, let's just say that they're drooling for more.

They have time for that, even with moving the bases?

Well, let's just sum it up in a little, short line here (as a matter of fact, in three words): Greed never sleeps.

Got it. But the energy is still good up there? They haven't been able to remove the . . .

The people are still doing their ceremonies and keeping the energy as well as they can, but there is a concerted effort by the secret government and its toadies to pit people against each other up there. I'm sorry to say it's having a little success. I don't want to meddle with tribal governments and so on, but I do want to encourage them to follow the ways they know to be true for them.

23

"Ball of Light" in Argentina

From *Mañana Del Sur*
August 2, 1995

UFO SEEN FLYING NEXT TO BOEING

Bariloche. At 8:30 p.m. on the night of July 31, the pilot of an Aerolíneas Argentinas Boeing 727 was making a routine descent into the Bariloche airport when he saw the unusual lights. He immediately pulled out of the descent and informed the control tower of his maneuver. The tower said they registered no other airplane, but they immediately reported a UFO sighting.

At the same time as this was oc-curring, the entire town of Bariloche experienced an electrical outage. The control tower lost use of various indicators, though not all. The direction and wind gauges went out temporarily. An airport official also witnessed the movement of a UFO from his seat in the Operations office.

In an official report, air force spokespeople said they preferred the explanation that the pilot was hallucinating.

 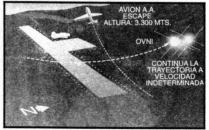

The trajectory of the UFO as it crossed the path of the Boeing 727

Bariloche. Jorge Polanco, the captain of Aerolíneas Argentinas flight 674, said he was very relieved to have landed the plane safely after seeing the UFO. In an interview with *La Mañana Del Sur,* the pilot said that he was sure what he saw was a UFO. This was confirmed by spectators on the ground and by a small Piper aircraft flying in the area.

Were you afraid when you saw the UFO?

No, but I was alarmed at the close proximity of the object. I calculated its distance to be about 200 meters. If this was in fact the distance, then it was about 30 meters long — the same size as our plane.

Was it round and illuminated?

No. We could see the silhouette — it was long — and we could not make out any details such as color. It had no windows. We could make out two green lights, one on each end, and an orange light in the middle.

Could you see anyone on the ship?

"It was about 30 meters long"

No. I don't know if they were observing us, but I do believe that we are talking about a civilization that operates by physical laws totally different from ours.

It was very fast and difficult to follow. We did not receive any messages on the radio or any light signals. I am sure a few passengers were able to see the ship, too. We did not inform the passengers, however, to avoid alarming them.

FABIO ZERPA NOT SURPRISED BY THE EVENT

Bariloche. UFO specialist Fabio Zerpa has no doubt that a UFO was seen in Bariloche on the night in question. He cites the numerous reports of similar sightings in the past and points to evidence of a "magnetic triangle" which makes it easy for extraterrestrial ships to move in this area.

Zerpa explains that "in this city there exists an electrical field that attracts these visitors.

"The preferred places for UFOs seem to be recognizably triangular areas; the principal ones are those at sea, often known as triangles of death," says Zerpa, referring to areas in the Azores, Canary and Balearic

Fabio Zerpa

The view from inside the cockpit.

Islands, and the well-known Bermuda Triangle.

In the case of Bariloche, Zerpa explains that there exists a triangle that runs from Osorno and Puerto Montt in Chile to Bariloche to San Martin de los Andes in western Argentina. In this region with its many mirror-like lakes "there have been many reports of extraterrestrial ships appearing to leave the bottoms of the lakes."

The investigator has earlier stated that there are extraterrestrial bases in the Andes and that South America, and Argentina in particular, will become an empire of spiritual power at a global level and a site for galactic bases in the future.

Andromedan Visit a Favor to Restore Vertical Mind

Zoosh through Robert Shapiro
August 21, 1995

*O*n *August 2, supposedly every newspaper in Argentina reported that an airplane had flown right past a ball of light that was 200 meters away. And this ball of light followed the airplane and landed. There were photographs of it everywhere. For several minutes the town lost electricity. Police, airport officials, people on the ground – everybody saw it. Can you say what that was?*

This was a vehicle from Andromeda. The Andromedans are contacting your planet now with greater frequency — and a little more boldness, I might add. As I've said before, you are processing the Andromedan linear thought process, and your mind, which you've been using as a linear mind, is really an Andromedan mind. They are coming now more openly to reclaim their mind, and this is acceptable, because your actual mind is much more vast than a linear mind; it's a vertical mind. So they are coming and scooping this up, as it were.

I'm not going to suggest that everybody in this country has suddenly lost their memories, but I will say that they might have noticed a greater sense of being present and a lesser consciousness of the past. It's almost as if 10% of the linear past is suddenly no longer present — in some cases, 30% or 40%. So you might see Andromedan light ships more often these days, because they will be coming to reclaim the linear mind.

But is that what they were doing in Argentina?

Yes.

Why were they flying around the plane?

Well, they were just making themselves known. They knew they weren't going to get shot down. Argentina does not have the same attitude as some other countries. Their attitude is that they might approach, but if there's no threat, they're not going to shoot anybody. They're curious, you understand? Curious, and they're not going to be hostile first.

All right. So it was just more evidence of other-dimensional beings.

Yes. Argentina was picked in this case because it was believed by the Andromedans that there were a lot of memories of the individuals there that people would like to let go of. So they could go and function there and become a public phenomenon so that people there would know about them. The more people know about them, the more the gleaning process that they are using will work. But as a result of going there and doing all of this, they felt . . . called. Many people in Argentina have memories they'd like to let go of, not because they've suffered so much or more than others, but in that culture there is sometimes more focus on the past than on the present or future. The young people in Argentina are especially aware of this and they'd like to be more involved in the present and future. You know: what's going to happen, what can we do about it now to change it in a way we want? So this is really sort of a favor to the young people of Argentina.

24

Calling All Material Masters:
This Is the Big One

Zoosh through Robert Shapiro
September 5, 1995

As to the topic of the day: You know, Earth population reached a critical mass of about 5.12 or 5.20 billion people, and it is this point of critical mass that is allowing the last and final wave of people to wake up. Granted, it's happening in three stages as I said it would, but now that Earth has achieved critical mass, even if we subtracted some material, atomically speaking (and physicists can support this), during this stage, critical mass would continue. So waking up the last wave, as it were, has been accomplished. However, there is an absolute which must take place now.

As I've said before, Mother Earth is really not comfortable with a population so much higher than the forty million she would prefer. And now you are moving in the general direction of five-and-a-half billion. Things are going to have to change. For starters, you've been seeing something in the animal kingdom which is not unlike what you've been seeing in humans: the birth rate has been escalating. This always happens before the following event occurs. When some disaster is going to befall, unconsciously, as it were, people begin to give birth increasingly. If you had asked amongst young women of birthing age a few years ago, they had a compelling urge to have children. And the animals were having lots and lots of babies too, be they the largest or the smallest.

Pandemics and Gender-Attraction Breakdown

This suggests a scenario of some kind of disaster; however, I'm not prone to talking about disasters. I would like to believe that this pandemic can be corrected (I discussed this in Chapter 19), that you can all pray and do your magical ceremonies and thereby cause the ocean to produce the algae which will exude the gas that will neutralize the virus that could cause the pandemic. That's still possible. Realistically, the odds of the epidemic taking place now are two to one in its favor. I'm sorry, it's true. Now, we're going through a tricky period. It could change to 50-50; I'd like that.

However, even if an epidemic is avoided, there is a distinct possibility that the following will occur (and when I say distinct possibility, I'm saying 60% or higher). I do not wish to suggest this is avoidable, but I would say it is something you may have to get used to. For many people, it won't be that difficult to get used to, but for others it will take a little adjusting. The means by which the population will be reduced will happen in stages. For people who are sexually active, there will come a feeling of a breakdown in gender separation. What this means is that the attraction between individuals will no longer be polarized by gender.

As you know, most people are attracted to the opposite sex. However, when the breakdown of gender attraction occurs, it is primarily promoted by the fact that the population is too high. So in order to reduce the population of the Earth in a gradual stage over the next 30 to 40 years at most (possibly as little as 15 or 16 years), there needs to be a multistaged approach. Therefore you will start to see, especially among sexually active people (we're talking here about the young) an acceptance of what is now called homosexuality. Then it will become almost faddish, meaning that the young will take on certain accoutrements, styles, fabrics and decorations that will remove them from the mass, as it were. I am not electing this for the young; I'm saying that it's happening, and there's really not much that can be done about it.

I'd say that within the next five to seven years max, 30% to 35% of people within the age group of about 13 to 28 and about 20%, maybe 25%, of people aged 29 to 48 (although there will be some increase in those who are older) will identify themselves either as gay/lesbian or as bisexual; but their primary sexual activity will be same-sex. The odds of the youngest group becoming more involved in homosexuality, lesbianism, bisexuality are about 35 to 1; the next group, about 30 to 1. Now, this is not some idiosyncratic quirk of fate;

it is connected with the absolute necessity to reduce the population.

Infertility and Suicide

There is more: You will begin to see measurably (scientists, beware) that in about three years, maybe less, the male sperm count and the durability of the female egg will be greatly reduced. Watch! Study the sperm count — that's easy — and notice that there will be decreased function of the reproductive organs. The odds of the sperm count in men dropping (some scientists may have already noticed this) are about 50 to 1, making it likely. The odds of the viability of the egg in the woman decreasing are 10 to 1.

I don't like to bring up subjects that are upsetting, but this must be addressed, because you are moving into it and nothing can stop it: There will also be another fad that develops. It will be bizarre, and will start out as a short fad (it's already shown a ripple in the past few years) and then find its acceptance in Westernized society, though it has already been accepted in the East. That is suicide. Suicide will start out, as always, with the young in some spectacular fashion — some extreme act in which people get together and do this. The odds of suicidal behavior taking place are about three to one.

Note this now: Please, please, if you have any desire or need to commit suicide, do not encourage your friends who are borderline! When people are borderline they don't really want to commit suicide. If you talk them into it, you're going to have to balance that out later after your so-called death — and as you know, there is no such thing. You keep on going; your body passes over, but you keep going as a personality. So don't talk somebody into something they don't want to do or that they're not sure about. Initially you'll see it as a crazy wave of suicides. This is caused by Mother Earth's need to reduce the population. She does not wish to be harsh.

I have told you a while back that the Photon Belt, which I refer to as the Photon Doctor, has certain methods. One of the methods is suicide in the offending (from the Photon Belt's point of view) physical mass that is giving discomfort to the planet.

The overpopulation has come to a head now. I must also admit, much as I don't want to bring this up, that there is another element, though it will pass very quickly. And that is bizarre situations of people whom you would never expect unexpectedly becoming homicidal. So I would recommend that access to weapons of mass destruction or things that can be made into weapons of mass destruction be severely restricted, like stuff around the house or farm that can be made into bombs. Putting identifiers in this stuff isn't enough (speaking to the government here). Yes, these things ought to go to the people who need them, but they ought to be tracked. I'm sorry, bureaucrats, but it's important. We can't have a repeat of what's been going on in Japan. That's an outrage. You've read about the nerve-gas attacks in the Japanese subways, and you've been horrified. I don't want that to happen here. I'm sorry to say that the materials that can be used to produce lethal gas are often readily available, and the people who might do this will often be the people you would least expect. The odds of homicidal behavior are about one to three — a significant possibility, something for security forces to pay attention to.

Bizarre Behavior

There will be a short-term experience of what seems like a viral madness. I'm calling this viral because it may not be a detectable virus. It's something based in electrons — really at that level — in which the electrical impulses in the brain will essentially short-circuit by switching back and forth in their polarity, meaning that they can no longer pass on the normal energies and impulses of the brain to all parts of the body. People will, during this three-day period, experience a lot of strange bodily functions, or dysfunctions.

It's survivable, by the way. There is probably no medication for it short of lying down and waiting it out. It might help to drink plenty of water, and you might wish to keep a bedpan nearby, because you might not have the physical capacity to walk gracefully to the bathroom. But during this time, for those people who can move around, it's possible that this effect in the neural system will cause them to do crazy things. Fortunately, for people in the security business (putting this out to you), people who suffer from this will be easily discernible because they will not look normal. This does not mean you can imprison all people who are emotionally or mentally ill (people who are in that space are *less* likely to get this, by the way). You will be able to see the effects. They will not be able to speak very well; they might sound as if they're in acidosis or drunk or in a diabetic coma, effects that are similar in terms of physical symptoms. It's a hurdle you have to pass over. The odds of this bizarre behavior in the neural system are maybe 1 to 2, but a significant possibility.

Many things will take place to reduce the population. I would prefer, of course (and I've been discussing this with a close friend of mine), that people simply make the sacrifice to not have children for a while. Now, I know that that's not realistic for many people, though some people have already done this. In any event, Mother Earth will make it possible for you to not have children, because at some point when the sperm count drops to a certain level and human ova (most importantly) are no longer viable – then you will no longer see children for a while. Now, some of you will say "Oh, wonderful," but most will say "Oh, terrible!" But let us say that you go five, ten, fifteen or twenty years maximum without having any offspring. A lot of people will be very unhappy, but the population of the Earth will shrink dramatically during that time in a benevolent way. Then when children are again being born, they will be cherished. Can you imagine, after twenty years without children, what it will be like when children start being born? They will be jewels, precious gems, gifts from heaven – which they are now, but because of your overpopulation, it's hard to remember that all the time.

Since you've achieved critical mass, your population will be reduced. It would be nice if it could happen in some benevolent way, but know this: You are immortal. You will go on no matter what. Try not to interfere with the natural. It may sound like I'm saying, "everybody's going to be dying; won't that be terrible?" But I want you to think about this another way. Everybody isn't going to be dying, but a lot of people will finish their natural cycles a little sooner than they expected. And as they pass over, their friends will be waiting there for them, friends from this life, family from this life, friends and family from other lives that they recognize immediately once they pass over. And they will go on to a beautiful life. No one who has suffered here on Earth will pass over into a life in which they will suffer. *That is guaranteed.* No one. I know that there are some of you who say, "I think some people ought to pass into a life of suffering!" But it really doesn't work that way. Yes, there is a life review. Yes, you feel what you have done for others, to others, or with others. In this way you learn and you gain.

But things cannot go on as they are, as you know well, and therefore the population must shrink. You are immortal, you will go on, you won't be separated from anyone. And once you get to the other side, you will wonder in many cases why you hung on so tenuously or so strongly. I am not encouraging you to do anything foolish to end your life; let it end naturally, as it must for all people.

So call up that old friend you had a fight with, someone you've missed, or send them a letter. Forgive them, or ask for forgiveness. Don't take resentments, angers and general conflict with you. You can't resolve it on the other side. Resolve all your conflicts now in a benevolent way. Forgive, let go, embrace, and know that you'll all meet on the other side. It won't be so terrible. And many of you will go on living here. Yet those who do go to the other side will have a good life also.

Timing: Possibly before End of 1995

Why is it so urgent that we put it in this month? It's not happening this instant, is it?

Soon.

What's going to happen soon?

There's a potential for things to happen before the end of this year.

What kind of things?

Diseases, wars, nuclear "accidents" (I want accidents in quotes or italics), bizarre behavior, things that are impossible, in terms of unnatural or abbreviated life cycles — suicides, in other words.

There are people whose life cycles are not intended to end this soon but who might get caught up in somebody else's drama. I'll give you an example: Someone decides to end it all. Their plane has taken off, and they walk back and stand near one of the doors. It's not difficult at all to open a door on a plane, though it's difficult in the air. Before you're cruising at final altitude, someone pops the door open before anybody can get to him and jumps out. But maybe somebody else falls out of this door. Now, it wouldn't be that difficult to create a security system for airplane doors, or in a case of emergency, some sequence of exploding bolts so that no one is trapped. Granted, it would take time, but you could put it on the drawing board and make it an option. The odds for this particular behavior are even, 50-50.

I think it's good to put it out to everyone in the medical field or in the field of security. (I'm not trying to create a police state, but you'd be surprised how much security people protect you — and they don't always do it at a total cost of your freedom, okay?) I'm also putting it out for those who will be passing over soon. I'm not saying that the epidemic will happen as predicted by your friend [see Eileen Nauman's articles in the September issue and in this issue]. But I am saying that since the last time we talked, the odds have increased.

But I thought it wasn't good for your future if you took your own life. Is that temporarily suspended or something?

Aftermath of Suicide

No, it's not a terrible thing. It's just that generally, if you take your own life *before* your time, you *continue* your time; but in a state in which you are reviewing your life. The Church calls it doing penance; I can't call it penance. You do something on the other side that is of value, but you do not go on to do what you would have. Say you end your life thirty years before the end of your natural cycle. You're probably going to hang around Earth (in the case of Earth people) and help out in some way. You're not going to go to some horrible place and be punished. That doesn't happen; Creator is not vindictive. But if there are too many people hanging around and helping, you're going to just hang around, because there's not going to be much to do. You're not going to become an evil spirit, so kiss that one off. But you will be bored. In the case of the person who commits suicide thirty years before the end of his cycle, he will have another thirty years of experiential time as a spirit to just hang around and do nothing. Pretty boring.

So you're not recommending that they commit suicide . . .

Certainly not. No, I'm just saying that it's going to happen. But that doesn't mean that I'm giving it my blessing; I am acknowledging the fact of it. I'm not saying it *must* happen and that I'm giving it to you as an early Christmas present, that's not it at all. I'm not trying to cause people to be scared or frightened, though I recognize it sounds dramatic. I'm putting it as gently as I can. I'm not saying that the epidemic *will* happen; however, there is a greater chance now that it might.

So all of this – the epidemic, the lowering of the sperm count, the suicides, the lack of children – is to get the population from five-and-a-half million to forty million in the coming years?

Five-and-a-half billion to about eight hundred million, ideally within the next fifteen, maybe seventeen years.

The Earth can't cleanse herself with this many people on it?

No, it's not possible. But if the population is allowed to increase as it is now, in fifteen to seventeen years the Earth will be dead. It's as simple as that. I'm not mincing any words here; the Earth would be dead. Do you know what happens if the Earth dies? *Everything* on it dies, too. There are no exceptions: plants, animals, everything. If the Earth dies, you know, all of her energy body, which gives you life, all of the parts of her which make up your body – the atmosphere, everything – are gone. You can't go underground to survive.

All these years we were told that we were going to Terra, to a fourth-dimensional planet, and now we're talking about . . .

You are! But you're not there, yet. The Earth is dying and attempting to rebirth herself at the third dimension. Remember when

I said that you're going to experience some echo effects because you're closer to the third dimension than you are to the fourth? *These are the effects.* This situation is intolerable and getting worse and worse, and people just cover their eyes and say, "I don't see it; therefore it doesn't exist."

I guess I had the illusion that all the people were going to the fourth dimension and then the Earth would get cleaned up, but it's not happening that way.

It's not really an illusion. These are always possibilities. We're talking about potentialities.

So some of the things you said years ago have changed.

Yes! Because everything changes . . .

We were going to the fourth dimension and the negative Sirians were going to be here in a very small number in the third dimension.

Oh, that's still true. All of that is true.

So it's taking us longer to get to the fourth dimension? Is it because of the tyrants and because of the energies held against us?

Let's just say that those who have the capacity to mount a resistance are literally delaying you. But on the other hand, you have reached a critical mass in population; that's good.

What does that mean? Has critical mass reached some spiritual level?

Critical Mass Triggers the Last Wave

No, it means that when the population gets to a certain number, then everybody who has not begun waking up consciously, spiritually, to their total being, begins to wake up. Not unlike when a person reaching the end of their natural cycle goes into senility, as it's called. The time of senility is actually the time when one begins to recognize the next world and to see beyond the veil within one's life. It's a similar procedure by which people wake up. They begin to see beyond the veil, even though they still have their wits about them, as you might say, and their full bodily functions.

That's happening now?

Yes, the last wave, as it were, is waking up in three stages. I'm not saying there's an absolute cut-in-stone fact that you're going to have an epidemic that kills millions of people, maybe more. I'm just saying that there's a real chance before the end of the year that something will begin, probably in Africa, possibly on an island; and it will move . . .

And that epidemic is the catalyst for the suicides . . .

It is not.

It is just one of the incidents?

That's right.

And all of it, the epidemic, the suicides, the lack of reproduction, is part of the plan by the Photon Belt and Mother Earth to reduce the population?

Well, it's part of the plan by the Creator to ... you know, it's not just the Photon Belt and the Earth. The largest single limiting factor to the expansion of consciousness *is the isolation of any single or multiple factors from all else.* There is no such thing. All happens synchronously with all else; that little rule ought to be in a little red box and put somewhere in the magazine, because that rule is an absolute. Once you start saying, "This is this, and this is this," you're limiting your consciousness right there.

Okay, so you're saying the Creator, our godselves, everyone involved, what we call the Hierarchy, the cosmic teachers, Mother Earth and the Photon Belt have tried to come up with some kind of solution that's the easiest on everybody?

You have to understand that *you came here to accomplish something.* And you have accomplished that, you have achieved it. The Andromedans are reclaiming their linear minds [see page 32] and you are coming back into your natural selves. You must understand that your natural selves *do not look like human beings.* Your natural selves are points of light, okay?

The Heart Energy

So what's happening with the heart energy? What about the heart energy stored in the middle of the Earth that some of these people need? Do they get it when they leave?

Everybody gets that when they leave. The heart energy in the middle of the Earth is stored for those who would remain physical. But the heart energy that is all that is you and makes up you — once you go beyond the veil of physical life and move on into nonphysical life (from the perspective of Earth), you have all of your self. Granted, it comes back to you in stages as you pass through your reassimilation into being yourself (you haven't been totally you here). As you reassimilate, you get everything back or move on into what you totally are.

I am not saying, "Oh, I didn't mean that" or "Oh, never mind about that." I'm saying that *things change,* and it's possible that everybody will be fine, and that you'll go through this threat of the pandemic and it won't happen. But somewhere down the road it may still happen. It is also very simply that the population absolutely, positively, must be reduced by the most benevolent means possible, and that, of course, is a simple lack of offspring. Now it won't help to *do* something to stop people from having babies. It's simply going to take place. I realize there's a calculated risk in my saying this, because those people who read this might say, "Well, we better have a baby right now!" I understand that.

Nevertheless I need to put this out not only as a warning to those who are in a position to help, but to assure those who are passing over that absolutely nothing will be lost, that the people you love here you will see again at some point; you will not be denied them, they will not be denied you. Things are not cruel like that. You don't go into some beautiful heaven and forget about the people back here. It doesn't work that way. You might go on to something wonderful, but when the people back here are ready to come in that direction, you certainly come down here and meet them! Things are not sequential as you understand it now. On the other side, things are omnipresent, as you know.

In any event, I'm hopeful that all of this happens in the most benevolent way, and that your world has the opportunity to keep everything in it — and all the animals and plants and people and elements and elementals — and that they all have a benevolent future. I know that you will in one way or another. But you will need to get over the hump. Know this: You are loved; you will be supported. All that you've needed to achieve in this life, in the larger sense, you've *already* achieved. And all that you wish to attain, you have attained *already*. You have lost nothing, and all that is yours to have is with you now.

Healing Techniques and Prayer During an Epidemic

Our purpose in putting this out to the people who read this, who are not apt to be affected by it, is just to allow them a preview of what's going to happen?

Yes. It's basically a predictable, but it's also a flash. In a way, I'm supporting what your friend has stated in terms of her pandemic warning, and in the article she does say what you can do about it. But there are other things you can do about it should you experience the epidemic, such as forms of healing techniques, especially those that do not use invasive therapies. Invasive therapies would mean something that's injected into the body; I'm not saying avoid that — for those of you who believe it, by all means do it. But I feel that therapies that are noninvasive will work better. So something taken by mouth would work better than something taken by subcutaneous injection. *What about spiritual healing?*

Yes, spiritual healing will help. Even prayer may help. So by all means, do all of that. It is designed, you know; the lesson here of material mastery is about working with an understanding how all material things exist. If you understand how they work, then you can work with them in harmony. And if I tell you that the means for this coming virus to be neutralized has to do with the sea, the oceans producing an algae which exudes a gas which neutralizes the virus, this tells you that you need to pray, you need to ask, you need to do ceremonies, you need to encourage by whatever sacred means necessary, that algae to be produced and to exude that gas right now in the oceans. It's a part of Mother Earth. Welcome the algae. Ask for it to exude that gas, for it will neutralize the virus.

Material Mastery

That is material mastery, which is built upon spiritual mastery, a practical understanding of how all things spiritual work. Material mastery is the same thing, only it expands on that. The application of spiritual mastery in the material world is the practical understanding of how all material things work. If you can't quickly resolve on your own an epidemic or a potential filovirus (as your friend calls it) or other potential events, you can ask somebody else to do it. In this case, it's the ocean. She can do it. She can do it by welcoming the algae, and then you also can welcome the algae, which naturally exudes this gas. So this is a material mastery lesson.

The big heading on this story should be, you know, "Calling All Material Masters: This Is the Big One." Now, I'm not saying the material masters should change people's attitudes, behaviors or any other thing. Ideally we'd like there to be no epidemic. Or, if the epidemic comes we prefer that it cause the minimum amount of suffering — for instance, people would go to sleep at night and in their deepest dreams simply go off with their teachers, and take their cord with them. We prefer there would be no suffering; they just go on. It would be like what doctors call crib death in infants, only it would happen to adults. If it must happen, that would be better, would it not?

Nuclear Accidents and Wars

What are the odds of the nuclear accidents and wars?

The potential for so-called nuclear accidents (in one case it might be an actual accident, insofar as actual accidents take place) are two to one.

Won't the technocrats in the ships stop it? They're not going to allow the bombs . . .

I'm not talking about bombs.

Accidents at power plants?

Yes, power plants, and there are a lot more than you think about. Many ships at sea have nuclear power plants. How do you think a submarine can go undersea for six months? They're sure not carrying a lot of fuel.

What are the odds on wars?

Three to one.

Where?

Africa, Asia, Middle East — that's a real threat there. I'm just going to mention those three because I don't want security to be heightened to the point of being ridiculous.

Will the French be stopped from detonating nuclear bombs off Tahiti?

I don't think they'll be stopped, no. They are, how can we say, ruggedly independent. But I think that they will follow through with their absolute commitment and just explode this one and that will be that. Trouble is that since all these filoviruses are floating around, if you explode an atomic bomb, it creates the potential for energies that live on energy, as viruses do (bet you didn't know that!).

Feed the virus?

Yes. Calling all scientists: Viruses live on energy, and it could feed the virus. So that's the real threat, aside from the obvious.

They're exploding these underwater; thirty years ago they tried to do that and were stopped. It was said that if it didn't ignite in the first second or something, it could suck up all the hydrogen in the ocean and become a hydrogen bomb. Are the guys upstairs going to allow this?

No.

Are they going to allow the French to set it off, then sit there and watch to see if it ignites underwater or something?

There's a limit to how much spirits can do, even the most benevolent ones, to say nothing of extraterrestrials. There's a limit as to what they can do to interfere. Since we're dealing with odds, there's a one to three chance that the French will be prevented from igniting the nuclear device.

There are places where some of these extremes are less likely to happen. I will name the extremes: In South America nuclear accidents, extreme violent behavior, and suicides are less likely; but homosexuality and lesbianism are likely to increase. It is a gentler place. It is also less likely that in Ecuador any of these things will happen; this is a relatively safe place. So South America is less likely, and even less likely than that, Ecuador.

The United Kingdom is not likely to have nuclear accidents nor extreme cases of bizarre behavior (hard to believe, but true). However, they are likely to have a significant increase in homosexual behaviors and lifestyles. They are generally about half as likely to experience the other potentials. That doesn't exclude them, but tells them they are a little safer. Alaska will be relatively safe. (I'm excluding homosexuality; I do not consider that a threat, but a benevolent way to reduce the population).

Alaska is less likely to have any of this happen, with the possible exception of nuclear accidents. Canada is about half as likely; they might have some bizarre behavior, so security forces, be alert there.

Dark Races Have Held the Feminine Principle — But Are Going Home

I would say, generally speaking, that the Southern Hemisphere is one-third as likely to have the extreme experiences, but I must exclude Africa. In Africa, India and Pakistan the populations have been exploding for many years. These people are actually planning to return to their home planets. I've said for many years that if there are not enough people of dark skin on Earth, it is not likely that Earth's human population will be viable. I know it's hard for you to imagine that; how is it possible? But the people of dark skin, regardless of how they express themselves, act as a link to the star system Sirius, from which the feminine principle radiates to support humanity. If the population of dark-skinned people falls below seven percent of the world's total, I don't think you'll be able to go on; but it is more likely that your reproduction will go into decline. You see, dark-skinned people hold and radiate the feminine principle more than any other single group. African peoples as a group and many peoples in India, Pakistan and thereabouts are planning to return to their home planets — many of which are in the star system Sirius, some in Andromeda, some in the Pleiades — en masse in the next thirty to forty years. I'm not exactly sure what you can do to encourage them to stay here. But their leaving will probably affect things. On the other hand, if there are enough dark-skinned people in the rest of the world, you might be all right.

Those are the places I will generally make exceptions for. I realize this may encourage people to run to the Southern Hemisphere; but in the larger sense that wouldn't be so bad, because it has more to offer the Northern Hemisphere than just raw materials. It is an attitude, a way of life, a greater sense of eternal love.

Feeling Love Can Avert All Disasters

What will change all of these things (except homosexuality and a decreased birth rate) is the feeling of warmth in the chest and the solar plexus, of love integrated into daily life as much as possible. That doesn't mean, "Oh, well, I can do it once in a while, maybe once a month, Zoosh," No, no, no. Every day. If you can walk around and feel that warmth, that love, as a physical feeling within you —which is literally the love of Creator and the Creator's love of you, the continuity that holds all life together —almost all of these disasters can be averted. Did you know that if you were holding this absolute love energy and in the state that it takes to hold that, you could walk through a laboratory, take all the tops off the beakers of whatever viruses there are, and come out (granted, be decontaminated for the sake of others) and be all right? I'm not trying to scare you into learning this technique, but *I do want you to learn it*. I'm going to have Robert give a workshop in October to encourage others to learn it. I'm going to teach as many as I can.

If we can get everybody doing this —love on a physical basis in their chests, in their solar plexus —if we can get that spread around the Earth, have everybody teaching, we could avert a lot of these disasters, and the population will reduce naturally and in a gentle way. And if any epidemics do come, people will pass over in their sleep gently, without pain, because that is the natural way of death. Did you know that? It takes place on the Pleiades and many other places. When one leaves it is a glorious experience, there is no pain. No one suffers. In many places it's a celebrated event. There's no reason that it can't take place here, as long as you center into the physical feeling of unconditional love, which is experienced as heat in the chest or solar plexus, and sometimes in other parts of the body. Eventually, you see, it begins to spread, and pretty soon you just feel benevolently warm. You cannot be affected by disease or even by other people's stress. You can walk right through the most stressful situation and you aren't even affected. It doesn't bother you. Just by your being there and doing that all the time (since love and heat naturally radiate), you can only do good. That will be a graduate thesis for material mastery school.

Good day.

25

Phew!

YHWH through Arthur Fanning
September 10, 1995

Everyone take a breath a moment. I'm not going to say this to frighten you; this is information. Please understand this thing.

With these energies building, there is a great propensity for the human to have these pains in the chest and pains in the head. If you're not into your power, knowing you're god, [that] you're going to fix this thing and know how to, then you will check it out from one that has wisdom in the level of reality you're dealing with. You do that.

These energies will also create strokes, know you strokes? Rupturing of vessels in here. Because the energy is moving through the head. The pituitary gland is going to expand, the pineal gland is going to expand. Your waters provide you great assistance, and especially your darker grapes provide great assistance, with energies in there. There is something in the grapes, what you call the darker grapes, the purple grapes, that literally assist the brain cells. Your scientists haven't even figured that one out yet. Your fruits and nuts will get you through this thing very easily. You should always have a little bit around, know you? It's important.

Now, because the physical structure is changing —your organs are changing, inside you, your organs; they are moving toward the center — it might be a little uncomfortable. You would certainly upset your doctors if your heart was directly in the center when you went and had your x-ray. They would try to fix it, know you —put it back where it was supposed to be. It's not going to happen overnight. But your organs are shifting, your cellular structure is shifting. You're getting the information gradually —DNA going to 12 strands and all of this little nonsense things.

You're a living example of the shifting. It's going to be completed, what you say, your 2002 completed. But in between that time could be a little rough, know you? From your concept of what is normal. Your skin texture is going to take on a different hue: some are going to get a little more yellow, some are going to get a little bluish, some are going to have a shade of green. Some of the skin changing of colors is a sign of illness. Know you hepatitis? What color does your skin go?

Yellow.

So when your skin is changing [to] yellow, don't you be saying, "I be changing into another entity." You better check —it might be hepatitis. Know you what I mean? There's humor here, there is! Some of the yellow change won't be hepatitis and your medical profession won't be able to figure it out —that's my point. But don't go be playing metaphysics, thinking you're one of the chosen ones. You might be not.

Would the whites of the eyes get yellow if it's not hepatitis?

All of your system is going to change. You don't have a normalcy yet, you understand? So check it out! One of the safest . . . if you're going to shift your skin color, I suggest you pick blue. That way they can say it was too many blueberries. Blue be safe. (Don't move into comparing here.) Light blue tints. You're all going to be very fashionable in your new colors, know you?

You beings are in a process of becoming, and when you really start facing what is called the nittus grittus, then you'll start questioning all your philosophies, and you'll start seeing where you hung onto false beliefs and where you didn't, and you'll start centering into the Father. You'll say, "Oops!" or you'll pick a deity. You'll pick one. It's just the method you use to teach yourself this time. No big deal. You're getting information *now* so that the emotional event of it is going to carry through with you wherever you go. It doesn't matter to me which way you choose to move from this plane. I know you're going to move.

What matters to me is your soul, whether it understands. I've been working with some of you long enough; the soul has the information, so I don't worry. Know you? I've got so many scribbles on your ships, you couldn't get away. I be walk out there: "Anybody see this one go by" "Just did!" "Thank you very much!" (I told you I was sneaky.) And you've got other beings scribbling on your ship, too. You've heard of the Brotherhood of Light, indeed, and some of what you term the archangels, big dudes? They scribble. If I get in a bind, "Hey Michael, where is this one?" Okay.

I have a question about the durability of the physical vehicle, since you're discussing this. Yesterday you said if we make it to 1998, we're good for 150 years. You've also mentioned 500 and at times 800 to 1000 years. What are the different conditions that affect that?

The more you know, the more you handle the energy and desire to stay — indeed, that's what affects. That you know you know. We're actually building enough energy in you that you can — we've told you the story — pop from place to place. Levitate, know you? Well, the first stage in meditation is to get you to levitate. If we can get two or three beings in the room to *really* levitate — I don't mean hoppy, I mean bump against the ceiling here — then the next stage is bumping across planets places. That's when you know to control the energy. You're not worried, the ego is not worried, the soul is not worried. One becomes bigger, one becomes smaller, and then you'll switch sides to get the job done, and then you disappear your body and do all of this thing.

You work with energies. Then you'll find out being in a physical body is really rather boring — it's really slow, molassesey. You think you're very fast down here, but you're very slow. It's very . . . a triple slow-motion movie, know you? Everyone is sitting there waiting for the action to begin. [Laughter.] It has taken us eons to get to this point. This is the last two frames. [More laughter.] We've been doing it for 50 years, slow.

The credits will have to go by for quite a while.

I'm not reading any credits, not in *this* movie, I'm not. [Laughter.] You'll be there long time. Lot of players. Anyone have anything else they want to chat about?

Desire, Fun and Ecstasy

Where in the soul does desire originate? Can you discuss the relationship of desire to the soul as a whole?

The soul manufactures that force from what you'd call the focused thought of what you want to do. Remember I say you be out here [out of body, prior to birth] and you look down, "that be fun," know you? That is a focused thought. It is not a feeling in a physical force. It is a thought out here, know you, out in the thing there. Look like it be fun. "Fun" (this is your words now) has a concept of a desire to do, okay, in the thought. So the thought of it, the soul just pulls that down to hold the emotion of it, so you'll do the fun thing. Do you understand? Do you understand what I'm saying?

Yes.

It is a thought of something you haven't done before when you're out of body, when you're in-between-life-state thing. Because everything you do is to gain wisdom to go back to the Father and say, "This be what I've done so far," to show. So it is, on this plane, a connection of electrical forces to see that you complete your "fun." That's in quotes, "fun," because some of the things you do down here, you say, "That can't be fun." You know, like some beings get shot, others don't. Some beings play die, some beings don't. Some beings play disease, some beings don't. You forgot where you chose the idea of what fun was here.

That's very simple, but as you become more advanced, you know where your thoughts take you each moment in your body. Your thoughts take you there — but not a thought through here [brain]; this is simply the tool utilized — the greatest "fun lights" that you have here. Do you understand what I am saying? That is how it works. Thoughts are everything. It is thought first. And that is a very limited word here, but it's what we have to use. Thought is first. It's not this part here [brain] that thought, though.

What you don't know . . . well, yes, you do in a limited manner. Every life force seeks ecstasy — that's what it seeks. It's *driven* to it, because it's exciting, it's fun. It feels good. And as you move through levels of density, your idea of what ecstasy is gets changed rather dramatically. For some being that is able to pass through walls all of the time, never touch a wall, he might have a concept [that] it looks like ecstasy to bang your head against the wall. It looks like fun. It would give him ecstasy because he's never done it. But you know from this level of experience, not a wise thing to do.

Could you go on with that ecstasy thing, because I'm not really sure what that is? [Laughter.] I don't think it's like an orgasm. I want it to last more than a few seconds.

. . . It's quite a trick to breathe here. [This is because he was laughing so hard; he can't laugh out loud in the body because he claims he would blow it up. So when he *really* laughs hard it causes him to leave the body briefly.] . . . Well, in one answer, the orgasm is what brought you to the planet in the first place, know you? It smelled good, you all jumped right in there, so you're here, in the body. Now, this other ecstasy thing — and it only happens in this dimension — is kundalini, where you experience a love for all things, a knowingness, but it's a titillation of *all* the cells. It is beyond orgasm. And you just *feel*; it is a knowing, it is a beauteous experience. Colors change. Everything changes. I understood what you were talking about, indeed. No problem.

Okay, thank you. I felt misunderstood.

Now, you're going to start to feel it when these chakras move. It is not the same . . . it is almost the same as kundalini. That is the feeling you're beginning to get, you understand?

Does it last longer than just a split second? Is it like a place you can be in for a good long time?

As long as you want, indeed; you can be in there quite a while. Yet in your normal state of consciousness it could be dangerous because you could be witnessing a tragic traffic accident and be giggling like crazy, you know? And a being, what you say a police officer, will take you, "Come on along with me for a moment," because you see things totally differently, indeed. And you haven't learned to control some of the frequencies in the brain. There have been disturbances when kundalini rises too fast. Nothing to worry about. It's going to move.

I'm not worried, I'm just curious.

It's an outrageous feeling in the body. It is the feeling, similar, that I have when I enter body. I have that feeling. I give that sort of pleasure to the cells, especially when I'm in and then leave and then come back in. The cells enjoy this.

Right now your voice seems to have taken on a different quality.

It is because I'm still laughing, and I have to learn to breathe the body here, too. Otherwise *he* [Arthur] has to come back in the body to hold it for me. I'm rolling in the aisles. I have not learned to laugh here yet.

Removing Unwise Desires

Are there some desires we may have stored in the sense of "that looks like fun" that would be wise to remove?

It is not wise to remove them unless you know what they are.

Well, how do we access them?

You start seeing them come toward you in your manifestation and decide to change it. Otherwise it's interfering.

If we do it ourselves it's interfering?

Well, you don't know what you're doing if you don't know what you're removing, correct?

376 • SHINING THE LIGHT: Humanity Gets Another Chance

Correct. But there's no way to make them conscious conceptually, so that we're aware?

Well, it would probably terrify you. You might be able to, what you would say, hypnotize yourself to find them, but if you did, you would go back and also see the reason you chose it.

Ah. So there may be wisdom . . .

There is always wisdom gained, indeed?

There may be some wisdoms we don't want to gain.

Well, you can gain it now or you can gain it later. It doesn't matter.

So you're saying that most of the desires we have set up for the rest of our lives have wisdom to them?

All of them.

Well, no, because there were agreements we used to remove and things that were not wise.

You can change the agreement. You have changed karma. You can do that. And now as you start learning to manifest, that you are god, you can change all things. You'll say, "Oops, changed my mind."

Is that all we have to do – change our mind, once we know what it was?

Choose a different path.

Thank you.

"Don't want to do that one again."

I'm interested in Petra, an ancient city near Jordan. Who were these beings that sculptured these mountains and made a city out of it? Were they spiritual beings, and did they sacrifice humans?

No, they didn't sacrifice humans.

Who were they? What happened to them?

They left. They went up.

Were they highly evolved beings?

Yes. Know you the rocks on Easter Island? Know you how they tip back and look? You beings think they're looking for something. They're showing you where they went. It's been done many times here. The sacrifices and the blood and the remains happen to be from beings that came to that city, came later, and didn't understand what it was about. It's ignorance.

They must have lived there a long time.

Long time. Long time. It was one of the places built after . . . during Atlantis sinking, *during* the process. There were three sinkings of Atlantis.

Crystal Skulls Manipulated Humanity

Someone else has found one of those crystal skulls. What do they mean?

It is one of the stones, along with the other crystal skulls, that were used to manipulate humanity. To split the brain, to be more precise. Know you how you have two halves to your brain? Well, we are in the process now of unifying that thing: sew, sew, sew; get one brain here going. Some beings are already being born with that one brain. No halves. Those crystal skulls were utilized to separate [the brains of] what you would call the beings at the time that enjoyed habitation upon the planet – to control them, literally.

Why? By who?

I'm not telling you yet.

You once said you split the brain.

I split one brain to get this thing back together, to create a soul, to create a species that was clean enough in one manner to create a soul. There were too many beings lost.

So this is something we're not accessing in our history, then?

I don't think so.

Will we?

The difficulty with some of this information, if it falls in the wrong hands, along with the skull, it can be used to put us back quite a bit. I would leave it alone for the time being. It's being watched, and actually, part of this . . . all of this has to do with some of the aspects of humanity that exist at the present time [which] have to come back and be involved with these forces because they were in on the controlling side used to intimidate. Know you? So they're coming back in this time to balance that energy. Know you, the bad guy last time be good guy this time. You understand? That is what's working here.

What's most important, however, is you! You know, your own individual thing. Your own god power. That's what's most important. There have been many journeys here. You only have a piece of the history, very small piece. When there was so much doubt that you all went into an abyss, and even those that were there, there was control at certain levels. You have that still left in your society – you call it the caste system in some of your countries – that existed among levels of . . . well, you call it gods. They weren't really gods, and they weren't fallen angels, either.

Origin of the Soul

So what I did one time, I performed a raid here, like we raided today. It wasn't a raid, however; it was a rescue. And I took one and split. Then we manufactured a soul so we could what you call gather the forces of the Father as they expired the body, [then] placed it within an electrical current so it could gain the wisdom of its journey and not be controlled. That's what the soul is for.

That's why you must learn to become it and go beyond it. Then my job is done. That's a little short story, *Readers Digest* version, as he [Arthur] would say. You have to go beyond the soul, you've got to. When you're at the point where you can at least understand the concept of electricity in the body and your power of thought in the body and you can *master* it, then you're ready. That is this decade.

That's what you're doing. You're becoming christs and beyond. You see? Everyone, not just one or two. What you did with your saviors before, you killed them all. That didn't work, so we're trying something new. They weren't saviors, really. They were just sharing information, just trying to help you out.

Some beings, believe it or not, feel very comfortable not learning. Learning frightens them. The more they learn, they understand the more responsible they have to be. That is frightening, know you? There are some beings that literally cripple themselves so they don't have to do anything. Have others wait on them. Feel sorry for them. They don't have to work, they're not responsible for their body. "Look at this crippling disease I have." They'll be coming back again. Responsibility goes to the core of your being, entities, the core of your light.

Does that include the autistic children?

Let me put it this way: As this planet moves into a higher vibratory rate and gods walk here, only gods will walk here. Know you? Others can't get here. If what is termed they try to manifest a body, they'll manifest it deformed, out of shape, this, that, the other. They'll feel out of sorts and they'll play die the body, or demanifest as best they can. That's going to happen, too. And the gods are going to get a little upset because you're going to have to clean up the mess a little bit. No big deal, clean it up. But that's the way it's going to work.

The autistic children here now, are they here for a purpose, or . . .

Of course they're here for a purpose! You beings are into the belief system of that's what is working here. That is all right. Know you what I mean? There are many games going on here now; many, many, many, many. I'm only interested in *mine*. I have delegated authority to get this done, this done, this done, this done. Do you understand this? I'm only dealing with the beings that are *supposed* to be doing the work and are *supposed* to be doing the teachings. I'm here to get *you* moving, to do *your* job. And I'm just beginning.

Now, you're getting information from a lot of sources, and that is the way it *should* be. That is the way it is. They need to be able to share their wisdom, their level of understanding. If I answered for them or part of their job, I am taking from them their becoming. Even if it is another group that doesn't exist physical[ly] here in their doing, they must understand their purpose and how and why they be here.

You see, I know how consciousness works in this level of things. It exists all over. And if I even thought what is called, as you would perceive it for me to say, the "truth," my thought of this thing would alter their experience. Because my level of truth is completely different from theirs. Do you understand that? So I'm very delicate about what I answer, very careful. Very aware about *your* energies and everything else.

Now, you can't understand that part, but that is all right. I am a Lord God! That's a big deal. It *is* a big deal. You're learning to become Christs and more, and become the gods that you are. Then you're going to learn to become who I am and more, because I'm almost completed with the Lord God game, know you that? I'm going to another level.

What's that one called?

You don't . . . the word doesn't exist. It is simply within the thought of it. All things, all time, everywhere. Know you how some of you beings say, "Well, your energy was with me; I feel you in my body, feel you around." Know you how you say that sometimes? That is just on this planet, how omnipresent I am. But it's going to go beyond this galaxy: It's going to go through every portal you saw at the black hole and every portal on the other side, and there are portals beyond that. You see?

So this is going to be the last time — your framework — that this force appears upon this planet in this manner. Clearing up all the Jehovah/Yahweh nonsense, all those stories. You become the becoming gods and you can make up your own story. You understand a little bit? So I am moving, too.

Now, Logos — what you call the Planetary Logos — is involved with my journey here. *He* desires to move, and I'm going to do everything I can to make sure he completes his desire. [He chuckles.]

I'm on his side. You'll all understand what I mean later as you move more into your own power, energy power, love power, ecstasy. The *real* real ecstasy. That is a joy. It is *outrageous* joy. We don't sit on thrones all day long [and] go, "Ho, hum, look what go down here." We be play. *Really* play. We're not worried about extraterrestrials eating our thought forms, either. Any other questions?

Sacrifice and Karma

What about sacrifice? Is it perverted? What is it? Why are they using it here on Earth?

You mean animal sacrifice?

Animals or any sacrifice.

Well, it doesn't look like very much fun to *me*. But it is ignorance. Spiritual ignorance. Every being has their level of truth. They express it as best they can, and it might be ignorance.

That's their expression.

That's what they think is truth.

I see. Okay.

They don't know they're cutting off part of their own being yet. Know you we said you're all one? Indeed? Do you understand what we said? I don't *care* if you understand, if you know you're all one yet. You're *going* to get there. But what I said, we're all one being, right? Indeed? Now, this being here has this other being here; he cut head off. Now, to explain karma and to explain the fact that you're *one*, we say karma exists, [therefore] your head is going to be cut off. But it doesn't work that way, because you . . . every being wants the whole one to be one. So the energy will bring you back down here and you *will* trade your head for the head *because the oneness wants to be one*. It works out mathematically, believe it or not.

Is it the same thing with surgery, where they transplant . . .

That be a whole other idiot game, indeed. It be fear of death, know you? Well, you're going to die, one way or the other. No big deal, you've done it before. People don't want to face that one. How do you work with energies in your bodies? You eat correctly, you think correctly, you *be* correctly. You live long time, and you leave the body when you know it's appropriate to take another journey, or take the body with you, either one. The only magic pill you're going to take to figure this out is *desire to know more*. And when you get the information, to apply it. Application. Not sit, chitty chatty about it. You apply it. You do it. Know what I mean? That means you walk in your grocery store and you look at another being dressed funny, and you can still feel love for that being. You don't say, "Look how sloppy that one's dressed. Hair's not even done, and it has all that stringy things." You love the being for expressing.

It's really difficult to buy a ticket and become a Christ, know you? There's a whole bunch of the tickets available. Everyone picks the other tickets — they're called judgment. Not allow. Those christ tickets go unchecked, uncalled. You [can] pick it up anytime. Just stay there. "Oh, I become the Christ. It's allow, allow, allow, allow, love, allow. Love, love, love, love." That also means love yourself enough to not be victim, know you what I mean?

Photon Belt Effects

About the physical changes when the Photon Belt comes through, will there be three days of darkness?

No. There's a lot of confusion about this thing. There will not be three days of darkness. It doesn't make sense scientifically. If there's so much energy involved with the Photon Belt coming through, it's going to brighten your sky — doesn't that make more sense?

That's true. Maybe it looks like a cloud.

It is a cloud of brilliant white light; electrical force is what it is. And when it meets the atmosphere and comes even closer to thickening itself, it's going to create brightness, brilliant light. It'll be so bright that you won't be able to sleep, because it's going to affect your lightbody.

Is there going to be an alternative world?

You might think so when it first begins to really thicken, yes.

No, for others that are not quite ready to ascend?

Well, ascension is not really the answer here, either. There'll be alternate worlds, they'll be taken to a place, indeed. There will be a shifting. Nothing ever dies, so there be movement for sure.

What is the movement populationwise?

Population is going to decrease upon the planet.

Percentagewise?

We're hoping to be able to keep 30% of the population. That's a pretty strong hope, however. Be pretty hard to figure out if you made it or not, anyway. Might be a little higher. Not much.

In a bookstore I saw an I AM AMERICA map, and I saw that part of Europe was completely gone. That a whole nation or a whole country would disappear, does that have to do with karma?

Yes. In fact, some of the beings over there should know better, because look what's going on over there [Bosnia] now. What you term Yugoslavia area, the Balkans. There's a war there. Didn't learn yet, eh? No big deal. Changes are coming. Now what you beings did today, when you wrapped the Earth in this love thing, you were attempting to moderate this. And what you did today when you went around the galaxy and stuff with your energy and in your gold body, your gold light, you were educating the consciousness that's within the Photon Belt: "Look, there's some of us still alive here. Be careful!" That's what you were doing.

So the consciousness within the Photon Belt be say, "There be beings down there that are aware." So it might approach a little differently. You had permission from the Council of Nine to get changes, do you understand? So you've done a lot of things here that haven't been channeled yet. You're the ones *doing* it! You're changing these things, you see? You can do that. I think it's okay, I give permission. [Laughter.] You're not at the mercy of any prophet or prophecy. Dealing with me, you're the gods that I am. God I Am — that is you —you're my Father, that is who you are. Who told you you couldn't change it? Send them to me. I'll have a chat.

Can you go into the Photon Belt without being burned?

Well, whether you know it or not, you actually passed through it when you did your galactic thing today. But you were in your gold body. And it had a little effect, and you had an effect on it, you understand? So . . . I told you I was sneaky. I'm here to "become" you [help you become]! You are becoming empowered gods here. You have work to do. What you think, will be. It's your world. You're the one that's going to live here. Treat it kindly, gently, respectful[ly], with these energies that you are. Indeed?

Indeed!

It really gets really simple. It is so simple. Lot of fun. Enjoy your food. We are through.

Thank you.

26

Compassion:
Use It or Lose It!

YHWH through Arthur Fanning
September 22, 1995

Indeed! Enjoying the energies, eh? Ready for more? Everyone take a breath. This is a very interesting time. Know you this thing you've played with for a long time, this game that you've called ascension, know you ascension? And you want to take your body with you, indeed? [He laughs.] Even with all the aches and pains you're getting? It is part of the shifting now that is going on, part of your responsibility for your physical form, because the changes going on in your system —your magnetics, your electrical systems within your body, and the battle with social consciousness, your ego, the persona — result in the discomfort.

Now, what is occurring (this is going to make you all very happy) is the golden lightbody that you are, that resides *within* you, your life force inside you, is birthing itself to meet the light of you that is around you, and the resistance is within the physical form. You're being squeezed [from] within outward, and [from] outward within, and the flesh portion of you, the physical skeletal structure, etc., muscle, is in between. Everyone take a breath. The part of you that you call the being within the soul, the buddha one, is growing, desiring to move into adulthood, as you would term it, and it wants to join with the rest of itself that is about you. That is what is going on now. That is what this acceleration is all about.

The acceleration really began this month, your September — the big speed-up, and it's going to continue. Your December is going to be ten times stronger than this month. That does not mean your October and November are going to be slower. Just giving you a reference point for December, know you?

Now, this is where it gets sticky. Through your indoctrinations, what you've been taught for many lifetimes, you've been imbued within the body, within your DNA, as a matter of fact, with a lot of false teachings — karma is one of them. But they were necessary to get you to pay attention, a *little* bit, to the responsibility of the light that is within you, that is what you really are. So this fantasy, this dream, is going to change, and the waking up is occurring. When you try to hold on to old structure in this thing, you will damage your physical form. It is the light of you that is within you now that knew how to take the food you were given and transform it into the size that you are now, utilize its forces. Not the vitamins, [but] the electrical force. Everyone breathe a moment.

As these changes begin to accelerate, become quicker, that old patterning in the DNA is going to activate. Know you this thing called fear of death, etc., unknown fears? Afraid to go to sleep, afraid to wake up. Afraid to go anywhere. They're going to be triggered. And it is simply you moving through old doubts, old patternings, belief systems. Each time you move through a little bit of that fear, you become more empowered, more empowered, more empowered. There will be many that will desire to take their lives in this time — not a wise choice, not a wise choice.

What is going on in the last quarter of this year is a preparation, one more initiation for your 1996. Hang in there. I'm not saying these things to frighten you. I'm just telling you the way it is, the energies that are working. You're being quickened to get over your fears so you don't shoot the first extraterrestrial that walks up to your doorway. We know how you react.

The meditations that you have come in contact with in your timing now have been purposeful. They were given to you, you were led to them by your guides, you call it, by your friends, etc., because they are going to be needed now. They will center you, balance you, align you, so that the golden being inside you can work in relative quiet, without your constant jabbering at it. It's got work to do now.

I'm going to bust another bubble here. When things begin to get hot and heavy — I mean *really* hot and heavy, really *really*, know you? It hasn't started yet! Don't expect to go sit on a mountaintop and be picked up by your curly hair. Won't happen. You're going to work through this thing. Some of you say you want the extraterrestrials to land, you want them to come down and change things. That would not be wise. All your free will would then completely be gone. You don't have much left, know you what I mean? Little bit left. I know you think you're free. You were given free will. We saw what you did with it. We kept taking a little bit more back. Now you've got a little bit. That is what we've allowed you – a little bit – so you can work and become now, between very fine lines. You're in it. This is all what you've been waiting for. Everyone breathe a moment.

As these energies begin to build more, there is going to be this sense of an overpowering force about you. What you don't realize is that it's really you, waiting for the you that is inside the physical to become, to join, to be aware. To be in peace and harmony, to be in ecstasy. Beyond judgment. Now, I know most of you here have no judgment – you got over that two years ago, five years ago when you first heard about it, indeed? [Laughter.] First time you heard about judgment: "I know how to get rid of that one!" None of you judged yourselves for judging, I can assure you, indeed? (Better see the humor, it's going to get even better.)

One of your joys is that you have a physical body, and it's your body. You are learning wisdoms with this thing, in this density. Believe it or not, you are.

The move to fourth activity, fifth, sixth, sounds like fun, doesn't it? Your body has to change. You'll be in a different form, similar but different. Your feelings of ecstasy, your senses of the ecstatic experience will be different. Kundalini only exists in this density, third. I'm not talking about the sexual experience here. I'm talking about awakening the divinity within matter in your physical form. Realizing it within you, feeling it. It can only be felt *here;* it's called kundalini. It's a different experience in other levels of activity.

This is the time for the masters to become. You're going to change your own diapers from now on. No more baby powder on your bottoms unless *you* put it there. You're going to have to know how to potty-train your spiritual selves, entities, quickly. Did you ever consider that extraterrestrial beings, your friends, what you term the ships, might not have a potty? What are you going to do, fly over the ocean? You're going to clean that up, too. Mm. Everyone breathe a moment.

There's going to be a lot of activity in the crown chakra. Some of you are already getting it, indeed? And in the head. The crown wants to open rather dramatically now, and so does the eighth and ninth. In order for these two, what you term the eighth and ninth – just your wording – to open successfully, the heart chakra must be open grandly, along with the chakra in the middle of the back.

When I say things are going to change, they are. And you don't have a belief system yet established to support these changes that are coming. You've got a little bit of one — that you're gods incarnate, that you're Buddha, that you're Christ. That's a good wisdom, better hang on to that one. Your year '96 is a window the entire year. It is going to quicken many beings. You do not need to react in fear. You *should* react in wisdom. You should *be* wisdom.

Now, I've watched some of you play with some of the information that we've given you, and you take it this way to mean only this thing. And you use it in your metaphysical understandings to play metaphysics. That is all right, that is allowed. We didn't say it was wise, however. You are becoming Buddha ones, christed beings. You are to remain centered in your divinity. Any other move, you will face polarity again. If you are the Christ, your polar will be the antichrist. (Everyone breathe a moment and center.) At least the Christ and the Antichrist recognize each other, and they can center very quickly. You are going to require yourselves to center very quickly. That means you're going to have to have compassion, particularly for yourselves. Know you my favorite expression here, "Oops!"? When you catch yourselves in an oops, have compassion for yourself and center.

These are indeed outrageous times. Now, the reason I'm speaking to you this way is not that I'm worried whether you're going to make it or not — it doesn't matter to me; I don't care. What matters is that there are other beings waiting for you to get it — they haven't woken up even a little bit yet. Your job is to assist them, and if you can't wake up, they have not a chance — none. So I am not here as a babysitter. Not my job — not my reputation, either. Everyone in this room, everyone, has a minimum of 30 beings that they said they would assist through this time, this decade. Every one of you. Some of you have a lot more. Now, you don't have to figure out who they are by name. You have to understand when compassion is needed because you only might meet the being for twenty seconds. You said you would be there. You had best complete that for your own wisdom, your own understanding. The only way that you can show compassion is to be aware of it within your own being. The moment you go off into your metaphysical chitty-chat with this, you're going to lose it. You know what it is. You know when you should be of assistance and when you should have more power by *not* assisting — you understand the difference. If you don't, go to another. Then come back and we'll start over. You're beyond those little games now.

Some of you are going to start seeing your cords go out, and where they are, etc., etc., and understand that you're connected to everything. And you won't have the desire to go cutting the cords. You'll know how to work with them to assist the others – that's why the cords are there, by the way. Once you free yourselves from all your cords, you'll go create others because you'll know you have to be of service in this density.

Meditation

Everyone allow your spine to be erect. Allow your feet to be flat upon the floor, or what you would term your ankles crossed, right over left. Open the seven [chakras]. There are chakras upon your hands – open them. Chakras on your feet – open them. Temples – open them. Open the heart chakra wider. Open the eighth and ninth chakras. Allow you to feel the energy building in the center portion of your being. It is golden light that is tinged; some of you may see faces there – it is all right . . . allow the fire here. Tighten your buttocks a little bit and exhale to the eighth chakra, gently. Peace. As this column of fire builds within the center of your being now, allow it to spread outward toward your shoulders and down your hands, both hands, and fill your feet, and through your feet, both feet.

I want you to feel a great pyramid of white light that surrounds you, encompasses the whole room, your city. And within this great pyramid of light within your beingness now, you are aligned unto the Brotherhood of Light and they are there with you. Peace. Take a breath in the heart chakra and hold it there a little bit. Exhale it out your nostrils. Now feel the Brotherhood come close to you while you're in the pyramid. Feel the gentleness there, the reassurance. They haven't forgotten you. They will give you all the assistance you need, but you are the one embodied physical here that said you would do this thing. I want you to take a very gentle breath at the throat chakra and hold it there for a little bit, breathe in there, and I want you to exhale it out of what you call your forehead, between the sixth seal and the crown chakra, and I want you to exhale. As you exhale I want you to see these words I know. Exhale out. That you remember, that you remember. Allow. Be in the body. Be aligned to the Brotherhood. Feel at your forehead again that energy there, I remember. I know. I remember.

Now at this time you're going to be allowed to either continue your agreement or not. There is no judgment. Contemplate you what you will do. You either continue with your agreement, or you can call it off, call it complete at this time if you wish. There is no judgment. What do you desire?

Everyone be in your heart chakra for a moment. Feel a gold light at your eighth chakra, and a golden light at your ninth chakra. At your temples, two feet on either side of you, sense and feel golden spheres of light there in your auric field, as you would term it. There are chakras there also. Feel them there open. Throat chakra, either side, feel it open. Open the tenth chakra. All the chakras in the physical now have ones on either side of the physical, equal. Left/right, front/back. Beneath your feet feel three spheres of light in relationship, what you call proportion, to the eighth, ninth and tenth chakras above your head. Allow. Center.

The sixth seal that is in your auric field on your right side, that is another what you call probability. Allow the energy that is in the sixth seal within your head to move to the sixth seal that is on your right side. Allow it to move there. And feel the other vortices in your physical form desire to move to that line, also. Let them move very gently. Bring the sixth seal back into your physical form, the energy that is on your right side, sixth seal, to your physical. Allow the energies in those other chakras to move [to] physical center. Don't close the chakras on the right side. Sixth seal, move it to the left side. Allow the chakric energy within the physical to move to the left, gently. Now sense within the body structure the sensation of the body almost wanting to move there. Feel that little difference. Bring sixth seal [on] left side to center [of] physical form. Allow the energy of the chakras on the left side [to] center. Peace. Open the left side.

Allow your eyes to open very gently. I want you to watch my hands. The chakras that are on your left and right side, you can open them in any moment by simply doing this [palms up, he gestures with a sweeping motion upward, vertically, on either side of the body], all the way up. You open. You open you. You not only have power here now [the seven vortexes within the body], you have power all around you, front to back. Allow your eyes to close gently. Allow your palms to be in a peaceful manner, what you call at your thighs, gently. Now allow the left and the right hand to move up gently to open those outside chakras. Simply contemplate it. Feel light now. This is what you work with when you move into fourth dimension, entities. This is where fun be. Allow. Center physical form. Gentle manner, slowly open your physical eyes. Center your being.

As these energies begin to get stronger, the light is going to attract a lot of moths. [Laughter.] Oh, you think it's funny, eh? Well, it is, from my perspective, know you what I mean? It won't be from yours, however. One of the best ways to clean is you clean these chakras first out here, [then] clean you [the main seven within the physical form]. Everyone take a breath a moment.

I am a warrior entity, reputationwise, indeed? Now, one of the things that you beings play here, warrior, is a defensive posture. Know you what I mean, defensive posture? You can close those chakras up the sides and close these up [the main seven], still knowing you're light. But you don't move around closing them because you're afraid you're going to move into something. You'll know when energy needs to be adjusted. And you don't shut down; you open them again. You learn to use all senses now. If you sense a being is trying to what you term, it is your word now, "invade," it's really an invite that you're evading acknowledging. Close it. [It] be, like you say, open door for one to come in your house, and he begins to step through the door and you say, "Oops, sorry. Phone call." You can change your mind.

For those of you that are doing your healings, you must now begin to take care of these other vortices here, not just the auric field. You know how the chakras are connected from the back to the front, indeed? They originate in the back of your body, come out the front, indeed? So too there is a spatial relationship with the physical form and these other chakras, same point, only it goes this way [from the spine out to the sides]. Know you what I mean? Be aware of that, because these cords are going to become thicker, and they are connected to chakras that are living beings, you understand? *Do not cut these cords!* You beings get chop happy when you see cords. They're connected to part of your being.

Well, that's enough intensity for tonight. We'll lighten it up a little bit now. Know you how you say you're not in charge of your chakric energy? Well, you know what the root chakra is? Everyone has a lot of attention on that one. These here [on the sides] are more sensitive even. You have responsibilities. There is great healing power that exists, what you say, "out here" with you, front/back. Great healing power inside you now. That's why your meridians are becoming thicker — to handle more frequency within the physical so you can influence these other forces here. Do your shapeshifting, etc., etc. Allowing the ability of your consciousness to move, to be more than you are as you think you are.

No one said becoming the Buddha or the Christ was easy. You see how some of your stories treated some of the Christs, and that is threatening. But we're going to overwhelm the planet with many Christs — they can't get you *all*. Not enough timber. [Laughter.] You know how precious *that* commodity is. And what would you heat your home with in the winter?

Now, there are going to be a lot of stories, a lot of stories. And they're only stories. Little bit of tales to pass information on. You're dealing with energy. You're dealing with magnetic energy that's within your body; you're dealing with electrical energy that is in your body; you're dealing with light, which is the force that you are when you're not physical and you're not electrical. As your light lowers within your physical it becomes electrical — the electrical hides within this density. That is God here, electrical, in this density. It's what you would call it. It is simply light lowered. That is what you are, and that light is expanding now. And you will write your own stories and your own myths for these changes that are coming. And we'll all stamp them with your name on it; it'll all be nice and appropriate — put it in the Akashic Records, know you? No one ever reads those things except you idiots here! [Laughter.] The others are too busy having fun. But we'll keep them neatly packaged for you.

This is a journey in consciousness, entities. Not metaphysics now, not at all. Your metaphysics has helped you get this far. It is a journey of very sacred importance, in a manner (your words). Very sacred journey. No church is going to have the authority over any-one's journey in this time. It's going to be an individual thing. Know you this: it is not just meant for the Father, because that is what you are. It's meant for all beings, do you understand? Recognizing the divinity within all beings. It's going to be a joyous time when that is recognized or displayed here. And it *will* be displayed.

Now, some are going to be able to vibrate very fast, move right through fourth and fifth, into sixth dimension. No problem. Some will want to play around in fourth a little bit — that be no big deal, either. And fifth, etc. But wherever you vibrate to, you must understand this one rule: you will remember that others are waiting for you. (Everyone breathe a moment.) Now, it's not always that the others are waiting for you to rescue them. They may be waiting for you, and they are your final checkpoint to see if you really know who you are. And if you don't meet them, it'll mean that you don't know who you are. Clever little game, eh? Be sure to recognize the angels when you see them, and don't be fooled.

Now, when you get past this first barrier, don't be upset at some of your guides for not guiding too well, know you? They did the best they could. You weren't listening all of the time. Some of you have outrageous tempers, so have compassion for your guides, too, indeed? Think I'm kidding? You've heard the phrase, "judging the angels"? That is coming up soon, too.

Now, we told you before, there is a lot of movement going on in the heart chakra, indeed? This opening, this expansion, to handle the great energy that is coming, which is very mental now. It's coming to sit here. It's coming with authority because it wants to assist you in the uniting of your chakras, at least the energy, for now. It wants to be as gentle as it can. What will damage you will be your own arrogance. Your humility will rescue your buns. Know you that [term], "rescue your buns"? So your humility will be very helpful here.

The world is not going to end. Some beings are going to wish it was, but it's not going to. When you begin to see things in the skies, acknowledge them as you would, what you call, a passing motorist, for now. You can wave. You're going to need to be more concerned with yourself in this time, your physical body. And I will tell you why, specifically: If you do not train your physical form to vibrate faster, to handle more frequencies, and you do get to go aboard this ship, or ships, whatever, you won't have any fun there because you'll be so packed with fluid you can't move —you call it gunk and stuff. Might even have to put you in a little cocoon just to protect you. You have to vibrate at very high frequencies to work there. In one form, they are radioactive. Now, if you're vibrating fast enough, the radioactivity won't bother you. But if you're not, it certainly will. Everyone breathe a moment. Everyone wants a mass landing, and then they're not so sure.

What is most important now is your divinity. That is what is most important. There certainly exist those that don't want you to understand your divinity. One of the difficulties is, you get so caught up in those that don't want you to understand your divinity, that in one manner you acquiesce to they and refuse to consider your divinity. You get caught in the little game. One of the easiest ways to know if you're caught in the game [is] if you're comparing. Your Father allows everything.

And there are those of limited understanding; you must have compassion for them. Even some of what you call the extraterrestrials, they're frightened. Some of them are more frightened than you. Their civilization is expiring, going out of business. Not quite a fire sale yet, but will be. And they're frightened. Because the concept of death, though it is known to you, is not to them. They don't have the understanding of it. So they are more frightened than you are. You're part of the reason they're coming here. Because of the divine aspected play that is occurring here, divinity can be remembered. Why? Because it is within you. You will never find it cutting one open. You will find it in the consciousness and the frequency called life within.

You have it! There are some that want it —and I don't mean they want to come to eat your divinity! They want to understand. And like little children terrified, they will nag, nag, nag, nag, for the assurance. Compassion will assist and empower you here in these times. Everyone breathe a moment.

You haven't even *begun* to hear the stories yet. They're going to be more outrageous than they ever have been. It is your divinity that is important now —that is a truth. You are divine light! You are high self, which has a piece of itself, along with the Father, residing within your body for this journey. In the greater context, as you become more, you are your high self. How do you get there? You say *I Am!* That's all it takes. And you say *God I Am! I Am!* Your high self knows it is. You begin to vibrate that way. You begin to recognize and speak unto your own being, *I and the Father Are One! We Are One!* It is a wondrous thing to be one with the Father —it is joy. *I Am One with the Father!* Don't get caught up in the aspect of male/female. It won't do you any good. Say *I Am One!* When you're working with the energies of your divinity, you'll know. That's where you begin to control nature, what you term nature. It's only a part of you —your consciousness. Everyone breathe a little moment.

Now, one of two things are going to happen in your December to every person on the planet. In this next big speed-up, in your October and November, there be little training grounds, a lot of meetings, a lot of energy, a lot of verbiage going about to assist, etc., etc. The energy within the physical form is going to be quickened much more. You either desire to know more, or you will desire to hide. This is the part of the book where everyone wants to hide. When you say you desire to know more, you desire to know more of you, right here [heart chakra/soul], *I desire to know more!* Even if you die the physical, in that desire to know more, that desire to know more will propel you farther than you've ever been propelled before.

We have three great armadas out there. They can encircle your globe in an instant —completely. Inside and out. In these armadas there are cadres, you call cadres, groupings, that everyone on the planet is connected to —one of the groupings. Some of you are connected to more, but that doesn't matter. These groupings are looking out after you —they're literally watching you. Literally. Moment by moment. They have you on their little TV screens. Each one of you. Each one on the planet is being watched. Not as you would term it for judgment, but as you would term it for the assistance that you need and your desire for that assistance. Desire to know more. Desire to be in love, we'll say with God, because that is your understanding. Desire to become the Christ and the Buddha. Not in a perverted sense, but to *become!* Everyone on the planet is watched. Everyone is going through an initiation, every one. Each one will accept the limit at a level of their understanding – that will be their limit. Everyone breathe a moment.

This is why some of your dreams now are becoming very intense. A lot of things need to be reconciled in what you term your probable realities, also. Your controlling behavior is going to have to be aligned more unto allowing life. Your competitive attitude is going to have to be adjusted to compassion. That's a big jump, know you – competitive to compassion? Or big step – whichever way you want to look at it. But it's not that difficult.

All of the things you've been taught, especially in the last fifteen years, have been put in front of you so you could make the appropriate choices, whatever you desired to do, this December of this year. So you've got what you term your October and your November to make your list; get aligned and decide. There is only one answer to any question they can throw at you possibly, and that answer is always love. That's all there is. That is all there is. Remember that one.

Meditation

Allow your eyes to close for a little moment. Center your being. Center your being. I'm going to invoke a very ancient entity. This one comes with great love for humanity, outrageous love. This one desires a merging of what you call a portion of the energy with your physical form, just so you can feel who is on your side. Give me a moment. . . . Feel the energy spiraling about you above the room. Allow. Now, if you will, and if you will allow, open the chakra in the middle of your back and open the heart chakra. Allow the energy to move from back to front. See the energy in the center of the room. Now allow it to spin around, spiral, and enter your crown chakra. Peace. Gently, peace. Be in your heart chakras, entities. Allow the energy to flow. Don't ask anything. Gently. Your guides are about you. Allow.

Now allow the energy to move down and through your perineum. Allow. Open the sixth seal. Open the heart chakra even wider, beyond your physical form. Grand. Peace. In a gentle manner, slowly open your physical eyes. Allow the chakras at the sides and in front of you to be open. Gently. Now allow your eyes to close slowly, and I want you to visualize from inside your throat chakra outward; see from within the physical body through the throat chakra. Allow. Gently. Peace. Peace. Very gently. Allow. Do not judge. Allow. Center your energies now through the seven, and in a gentle manner slowly open your physical eyes.

How do your bodies feel? Everyone okay? Any headaches? A little bit of water. There are two more beings that want to join. Will you allow?

Indeed!

The first one desires to spread the energy what is termed along the floor and rise up through your feet and through your perineum. So allow your eyes to close gently. Center your being. Now feel the energy what you term in the floor, feel the color. Allow. Feel what it is. Allow the energy to move up your legs now, very gently. As it moves into what you call your pelvic area, allow it also to flow from the floor upward to the perineum, and then fill your body upward. Allow. Allow it to move higher through the body. Peace. Allow it to move through the crown chakra, and to the eighth and ninth chakra. Let it move above you and beyond.

There be another now that desires to enter the heart chakra, directly in front of you. Allow it to come in and fill you. Great the being. This is great power, entities, allow. Stay in your body. Allow. Allow this energy to move down into the pelvic area and fill your legs now. Allow. Peace. Now allow it to move outward of the back chakra, the grand chakra. I want you now to adjust your bodies, literally move your physical body, and be the physical form called you in there.

Now pay attention. Both of those entities were what you term deities, supreme power. You shared your, what you call, frequency, allowed them to experience part of physicality (same with the other), what it's like to share the physical — you did that willingly, lovingly, compassionately. So too they share their power with you, and their power shared with you is being awakened within you, because you are the same.

Everyone take a breath and hold it at your perineum. Squeeze your buttocks and let the breath out the crown chakra. Peace.

You allowed yourself to share energy with three awesome entities. The names are not important, but most of you got it. They are going to prepare you through your seven days now, this coming week, seven days. In your dream state and in your waking manner, they're going to work with you. Now pay attention: These aren't guides! These aren't handmaidens, either.

Some of you are going to be given information very gently, very subtly, about the food you should be eating, about what you should be drinking etc., when you should be resting — seven days. It is a clue to how to proceed through your December and these months to come. It is a clue. Some of it is going to be very direct. Remember, these beings are into empowering you, your empowerment. You understanding you. They move through you now, the three. They know who you are, what you need. They know everything about you. They desire to assist you. It is up to you to listen. Do yourselves a favor for a change; listen. Bargain?

Bargain!

So be it! Oh, one other thing. As these energies really begin to play with you, one of the most appropriate things you can do is mind your own business, not everybody else's. You're going to have enough fun yourself, know you what I mean? [If] you make it through December without too much turmoil, then maybe you can advise some other beings. You'll look at your January and you'll say, "Phew!" Be cause for celebrating your new year, believe it or not. How do the bodies feel? How's the heart chakra? Open. Back chakra.

I know some of you can't believe that you came back this lifetime to assist humanity, but you did. Here you are. Lot of humor, eh?

One of the most important remedies that you're going to need, coming up, a very ancient [one], is the laying on of of herbs on the physical body, just laying the herb on the physical body for pain, fresh [herb]. The plant knows what it is here for. It's up to you to remember now. The light within you will respond. The light about you will respond. It'll assist the structure called you that is having difficulty in responding. There are your books – it is there. I don't mean go bury yourselves under leaves, know you; yet that wouldn't be too bad, either. That's actually very healing. You play with them on the chakras seven primarily, while you're learning, and then the other points. You don't have to lay there for an hour, either.

I want some of you to contemplate another thing. I'm going to put it in your heads for those of you that can comprehend it and have the affinity for it, because it'll assist. The Moon and the star you call Polaris have something very great in common with the cycle of energies that are enveloping your planet now, and the effect on the human condition. The Moon and Polaris. Do your homework.

Allow your fingers to touch one another very gently. Can you feel how soft you are now, silken, indeed soft? Know you that is the energy that you are running through you? You're soft. You're beautiful. It feels good for the energy to touch physical. Feels grand.

You're going to begin to have many more chakras open in this arena here [forehead], what you term many more eyes than you think you have. You're going to feel them all around your head. They're all vortexes.

Some of you healers that are sitting here in this room have your job cut out for you, and by that I mean, some of the personalities that are hiding within these bodies think they're still hiding, [that] they can't be seen. They're going to have to be aligned before the physical form can adjust with any comfort in these next two months. What is termed, you beings say, "past-life experience, karma." You simply dove in this density to hide. You've been found. Come, come, come, come, come. It'll make it a lot easier for you if you align all of those frequencies within the physical. The healers have their work cut out for them.

I'm going to tell you this again. We're not coming down here to do your job. It is your job — get it done! We're certainly not here to rescue your bottoms. We're not going to destroy this planet so you may have some sense of perverse pleasure out there. We're going to make it work; you're going to make it work. We'll keep speeding up the energies until you make it work. So it's a lot of fun, eh? Know you judgment? Better let that one go!

How many times do you have to die to know that you've died and lived? How many more? How many times do you have to hear there are no victims until you know there aren't? How many times do you need to see victims until you know there aren't? How many? I've already played with some of you in your victim role. If you start losing it — know you losing it? — this month, you might as well hide in a closet come your December.

Center. Meditate. Desire to know and love God . . . and that is you, you're becoming. You call Sananda and all the guides, you call the Brotherhood of Light. You call the three entities that were here tonight. They'll be there with you, they will, but they can't do it for you. They can't. If they did pull you out of the body to create a change, they'd mess up your evolution — you wouldn't know a thing. They know that. It's time for *you* to know it. They'll assist you as you move through the fear, that's what they'll do. The great teachers will be there. I'll be there. We'll be encouraging you, assisting you any way we can. But you're coming out of your diapers now. We won't do it for you. Might even stick a pin in your bottom to get you moving, know you what I mean? Just to make sure you know the diaper's back here if you back up, know you what I mean? There be pin there, too.

Allow your eyes to close very gently. Center your being. You have an entity that came, that is here now. Now listen inside you — this one is playing music for you. Listen . . . let the energy fill your head . . . allow your eyes to open very gently, and as you do, bless the entity and thank the entity for the music.

All in all, you are all very protected entities as you move through this — humanity. You are. Very protected.

Remember the herbs, indeed? And there are some of you I'm a little . . . (mm, how do I say this without getting you upset?) concerned with — you're not paying enough attention to the dolphins and the whales. There's information there, too. How do your bodies feel? Okay?

Great.

Ready for more energy this night as you sleep? We'll be gentle.

Someone called me this afternoon about the pink dolphins in Brazil. They were very worried about them.

You all should be worried.

They explained they couldn't move them, that no one could move them, because the gravity would affect them. What can we do?

One of the reasons there is so much difficulty now is that mankind was supposed to understand magnetics and his electrical frequency in relationship to the poles by this time. The dolphins and the whales have been holding that information from their heart chakra. If you had been doing your job, their job would be a lot easier. They are getting attention, know you? They're bringing it to mind. Lot of you are going to have sleep, dreams of this thing, and more. You're all on this planet together; each one works together with energy called God Force, electrical light. You're all sharing this thing. You are not separate. You're one! You're going to learn it, trust me. We are through.

Creator and Cosmic Councils
Allow Friends of Earth to Save Humanity
from Extinction

Humanity was expanded more fully toward the 4th dimension suddenly, over the weekend of September 8-10, 1995, to prevent its total extinction by disease, plague and Earth cleansing.

This action by the combined efforts of those cosmic forces who love humanity and Earth – and who see the value of this genetic experiment – came very close to crossing the line from intervention to interference. But all of the Councils of Creation and the Creator agree that to lose humanity at this time to catastrophe – before it completed the experience of feeling the effects of its actions as it transitioned from 3rd to 4th dimension – would be a loss of that experience to all of creation.

Humanity, thus saved by this "miracle," has another chance – in a less dense frequency – to choose love and compassion over fear, light over darkness, freedom over restriction and a continuing expansion into awakening.

Please turn to the following chapters to learn how this unprecedented drama unfolded.

Publisher's Note

27

A Crack in Time

Zoosh through Robert Shapiro
August 30, 1995

Atremendous event occurred this last evening [Tuesday, August 29, about 9 p.m.] in Sedona and in two other places in the world: a crack in the time dimension took place, largely unintentionally. Now, I've been saying for some time that there are tears in the fabric of time. You are passing through the astral plane to some extent, which is why all these portals are floating about and people are having trouble with them. But last night something occurred that is largely the result of "oversonic" mapping of the near undersurface of the Earth (if I may make up a few words).

A sonic boom was initially triggered, but that sound was amplified tenfold. As you know, most sonic booms are not strong enough to feel like an earthquake. This one appeared to have an echo, but the echo was actually a second sound. So the first sound was triggered, then it was amplified. The second sound that followed was an actual crack in your time dimension. This is very, very critical. Right now all of the overlords of the time that you've been in and that you are moving into are working furiously in three areas of the world – the southernmost tip of Argentina, the very northernmost area of Iceland, and right here in a canyon west of Sedona, Arizona. This has created a situation about which I must make some statements.

Now, we hope that the overlords of time can repair this crack prudently, quickly. But as I say, everything has to go perfectly. The chances of their repairing the crack in northernmost Iceland by the fifteenth of this next month are very good. The chances of repairing the crack at the southernmost tip of Argentina within thirty days are very good. The chances of repairing the crack in Sedona by the fifteenth of next month are not very good, only 40%. Now, that's a strong chance, but there's also a 60% chance that things will happen to slow it down.

[Update given September 20: "The southernmost boundary of the moving time crack, located beside the resort in Boynton Canyon, has been safely moved into a nearby canyon."]

Can we talk about the mechanics of it? The sonic boom shook . . .

The sonic boom happened at the very moment that an ultrafrequency change was taking place to move you. Remember, I said you're at about 3.32, fluxing to 3.37 in the dimensions. At that point in time, all over the Earth there was a flux of ultradimensionality designed to bring you up to 3.39, although you might slide back to 3.25. When this was bringing you up a couple more notches, at that exact moment this event took place. That's why we had a crack, a serious crack — something big enough to literally walk through.

The overlords of time are talking to me now, they're working like crazy, they're just taking a moment to talk to me. Okay, they're telling me that there's a 95% chance that they can pull the crack in the back of the canyon up into the air, where they feel it will be safer. But it will still represent a hazard to planes and helicopters.

[Update given September 20: "The northern boundary of the crack was moved to ten feet above the ridge at the back of the canyon and extended upward 270 feet. This presents a hazard only to a helicopter or small plane flying above the area on autopilot. In such a case altitude alterations could be off by a factor of 10."]

Is that why it's so squirmy in town today?

Yes!

It's crazy! It's like everything is fluttering and shaking.

Yes, there is definitely a wobble in time right now. On the one hand, it could be used in a positive way by people who are goal-oriented; they can make a tremendous acceleration toward what they want. But people who are in a vague state might have their vagueness amplified. So to you townspeople, be goal-oriented, and it might actually work for you.

Has this ever happened on this planet before?

I'm not aware of it happening during the time that human beings have been here.

28

Souls of Exploded Planet
Pass through Our Reality

Zoosh through Robert Shapiro
September 8, 1995

All right. The "crack in time" information is a precursor to what is happening now (actually yesterday, about 24 hours before today's full moon). The energy has been and is still building up. This present experience relates directly to the *Explorer Race* book, in which I stated that beings from the negative planet in the star system of Sirius would begin to remanifest themselves directly on third-dimensional Earth in a new reincarnational form, where they will experience for the first time roughly 50% positive energy, as well as 50% negative. And as I have stated before, the planet they're coming from is (or was) pretty near 97% negative.

Roughly 36 hours before your full moon here on Earth, the negative planet upon which these negative Sirians existed began to go critical. However, the planet has been isolated with a sound vibration so that what happens is contained. The populace has not had the technology by which they can get around, not only because of the negativity and restrictiveness of their culture but because of the isolation in which they've been placed by the Galactic Council and the rest of the Sirius galaxy, which is positive in energy. The planet itself will go critical mass in another few hours from the time of this conversation and, after an extreme rise in heat and volcanic activity, will explode, tragically killing every soul on the planet. It will be extremely traumatic, naturally. The inhabitants will experience passage into the afterlife en masse. There will be no escapees, not one.

They will go for a time as souls into a holding pattern, like at an airport. They will be suspended in animation, so to speak, and their afterlife bodies will look very similar to their living bodies but will be more etheric. However, because of the extreme negativity, they cannot pass through the etheric web that leads to the web of all life. So they will be held in this area and then begin to pass out of this area through a vortex that will take them directly to third-dimensional Earth. They will arrive energetically within their own form and experience a form of reincarnation into their third-dimensional Earth bodies. This is all happening in the cycle of time as played out during this next week of your time.

For you it means a couple of things: There will be some very thin spots in the fabric of time [refer to previous chapter]. The full range of dimensional shift will begin to happen in a more complex way. Places where the energy is exposed to the passage of mortal and immortal beings from one dimension to another (otherwise known as portals) will reactivate. And there will be a major effort by the angelics, by gold lightbeings from all over the universe, to protect the negative Sirian beings during their remanifesting, or reincarnating, on third-dimensional Earth, from accidentally slipping through the thin spots in the fabric of dimension. So it is very important for you to pay attention not only to these thin spots, which are occurring in many places, but also to activity in the portals, many of which you know about; you know where they are. This activity may have multiple effects.

On the one hand, there will be a tremendous energy of angelic and gold-lightbeing and loving being around these portals. This energy is needed to maintain the integrity of the portal, allowing those to pass through the portal who must, and helping those who come near the portal, intentionally or otherwise, stay in their worlds where they are best off. This will help the second-dimensional Sirian beings move to the third dimension and manifest en masse. This extreme case of such a negative group of individual souls passing in its entirety through dimensional time shift into another part of the universe has not been done before. I'm not aware of this ever having been done in your universe, including all dimensions.

There is another situation that is equally important. The angelics who are guarding the portals and the web of life are also trying to keep you in your time from falling through, or at least partially becoming engaged by, the thin spots in the fabric of time. These can open anywhere at any time. By "open" I mean that the structure (the density between dimensions) will become as thin as a thick spider-web that you can see. But a person who leans against it or walks near or through it, unbeknownst to themselves, could become ultradimensional. Ultradimensional in this case is not a positive thing, because you would be not of any dimension — you could become lost in the fabric of time. That is why the beings must stay close; someone has to go through the ultradimensional phase shift with them immediately to bring them back. Otherwise it could take a thousand years to find them. You might be lost indefinitely until someone managed to locate you in the infinite variety of places where you could be.

That's why gold-lightbeings, whom Robert calls Warriors of the Golden Dawn, come from all over the universe to help. There are millions of them here now, each one ready to stand guard over a thin place in the fabric of dimension, each one ready to protect the security and the sanctity of each dimension and what is happening here on Earth. Many of them perform other functions as well. At present there are over five billion people on Earth, to say nothing of animals and so on. And there are many millions getting ready to manifest in third-dimensional Earth from the negative source on Sirius in physical bodies, though not as babies, since they're all coming at once. First-generational negative-Sirian incarnations on third-dimensional Earth will begin when the beings are about one-third into their maturity. This will be their first primordial race of beings; their cycle of birth and death will occur from that point. They will be given their guides and advisors so that they can find their way.

The Need for a Faster Acceleration

As I've stated at length before, you are no longer in third-dimensional Earth (literally 3.0). You have been roughly at 3.37 but you are going to have to make an accelerated, pell-mell move from 3.37 to 3.48 very, very fast. Because as these beings begin to manifest, their energy will affect you even though they're manifesting as beings subject, as you have been, to 50% positive and 50% negative energy on 3.0-dimensional Earth. They will be coming in from a place that has had 97% negativity, so they will bring that negativity with them, adjusting over a period of time to 50/50 polarity. As extremely polarized as they have been, they could not survive an instant shift into 50/50 polarity. They can come to this Earth in 3.0 dimension because there has been 50% negativity, and they can gradually adjust. If you theoretically threw them into a 100% positive, loving place, they would all go insane, and it would then be very difficult to bring them to a point of redemption, meaning redeeming their individuality in a loving fashion. (That is, by the way, the real meaning of redemption. We should be clear on that because the Bible is a little vague.)

So there is a critical function going on right now that is truly affecting you in your dimension. We've got to slingshot you from 3.37 to 3.48 dimensionally. Trouble is, you cannot do that in the week or so that these people are going to manifest. We can slingshot you, but it's going to take 90 days. We can't just go [snaps fingers] like that and shove you, as it were, into this big notch almost halfway between the dimensions, because the intensity would threaten the viability of your race. You can go slowly through the dimensions, but not [snaps fingers] like that, not as a physical being. (As an energy being, yes, but that's another story.)

So you have to go *slowly* to make this next move, and conversely, these entities from the negative Sirian planet have to come *quickly*. They will manifest in 3.0-dimensional Earth within one week. They will come in bit by bit, but within three weeks from this date they will all be manifested during a period where you have thin spots in the fabric of time.

The Biggest, Most Involved, Most Complex Angelic Activity Ever

Thus there is an extreme situation in which the beings of light and the angelics are here en masse. I don't know of a single angelic (not only those fully involved in the angelic work, but even novices who normally have somebody with them at all times) who isn't here right now. Granted, the novices are with their teachers, but they're *here*. This is the biggest, the most involved, the most complex angelic activity that I'm aware of ever having taken place. It's necessary to keep the dimensions from falling into each other; that's a real threat. This threat will decrease as you move through the next 90 days, when you've literally been shoved into the 3.48 dimension. (I'm using these decimal points to delineate your motion between the third and the fourth dimensions.) It has been determined that you *can* be shoved; you're being pulled into the fourth dimension, which is a magnetic way, the feminine way, the gentle, loving way. Because of flexibility in that motion, you can be shoved (compressed a little bit in front of you, as it were) up to the 3.48 mark. This will put enough distance between you and the 3.0 beings in third-dimensional Earth, these negative Sirians, to maintain the integrity of both dimensions on Earth and to keep the fabric of time intact. (When I refer to the fabric of time I'm also referring to the fabric of dimensionality, because you can't separate the two.)

As you reach about 30 days, maybe 45 from today, you will have gotten through the tough part, meaning the extreme fragility of the thin spots in dimensionality. You will have moved through the focus; once you get past 3.41, you'll be in a better state, and the cracks in time and bleedthroughs from the portals that aren't intended to take place will be less frequent. Even though everybody will still be here from other dimensions to help out, they won't have to work so frantically (there's no other term for it).

We've been building this for a while. Some people have been having odd experiences, interdimensional experiences, moments of difficulty in maintaining mental continuity for the past few years. Now it's extremely accelerated.

Be compassionate for a moment for these poor souls (I have to call them that) moving from this extreme situation of 97% negativity, whose planet will be utterly destroyed in a week. The Sirians and the Sirius galaxy will be assisted also in time. They have to put a bubble around that space, because when all the lightbeings, all the angelics who are here on Earth to help out get done, they have to go to Sirius and cleanse that space there. So everybody's working overtime. If you can have some compassion for these beings who are coming, these former negative beings, it would be a good thing. Don't look at them as threatening; they are totally and completely disoriented. They're moving en masse; the entire race is being isolated as you might isolate something in a test tube. They are moving en masse across the universe from one galaxy to another, moving from a planet where they know and understood the way of life. (Granted, it was a terrible, difficult way of life, but they knew it and understood it, and could accept it.) They're moving into something which to them would be true positive. They are not evil. They have been *subjected* to evil. You can understand the difference between a being *being* evil, and being subjected to evil. Many of you have been subjected to evil circumstances, or circumstances of beings who are being evil with you. But the moment you could get away from that, you were relieved, and did not project that evilness.

So these beings have been subjected to an evil system. But now they will have the opportunity to move away from that, and they will appreciate it very much. There will be enough of it so that they can orient themselves (ergo, 50/50 polarity) but there will be enough of the good so that they can make their escape. This is a true redemption of an entire society. It will be a long time before they realize they are not in some form of afterlife. They will be performing functionally on third-dimensional Earth, which is going through major Earth changes even now. Many people in the animal kingdom, certain people, and especially the ants, are very aware of Earth changes at 3.0-dimensional Earth, and are very much affected by it. They have been preparing for the end of the world. You, on the feeling, instinctual level, are being affected just as much, but because your society is dedicated and applied to the pursuit of the mental perception of life, you are not acting on the instinctual feelings you are getting. You have an underlying feeling in your body of something urgent or agitating or annoying or upsetting, which many members of the animal kingdom are acting upon. But you are not acting upon it because you are governed by the rules of society, which tend to be more in the mental areas.

I know it's very complex. But it is all happening at the same time, same moment. As you move gradually away from 3.0-dimensional Earth, you will feel less and less of this extreme situation.

Early Signs of Fourth-Dimensional Terra

I'm not trying to frighten you; I'm trying to explain something that many of you are feeling: a significant conflict between what you are thinking and what you are feeling. In most cases what you are feeling does not have to do with other people in your immediate family and immediate group (some exceptions); it has to do with this extreme and unusual situation. Even now as we speak there are circumstances of weather that are somewhat bizarre — unusual, at the very least. Powerful storms, unusual weather patterns, behaviors in people that seem at times like throwbacks to other times in your history. And other groups of people that seem to be functioning in the future or in some beautiful life that will occur for you in the fourth dimension of Earth.

As we speak, fourth-dimensional Earth (known as Terra) is beginning to influence the plants and animal kingdoms. You as a race of beings cannot help them because you are too caught up in your own manners and mores, values and thoughts. But someone has to help them; someone must work with them and help them to achieve some level of stability, safety and sanctity. This help will come largely from the elfin and fairy worlds and from the Terran goddess Eden (as in the Garden). She is the playmaker of fourth-dimensional Terra (which you know as Earth in the third dimension). She dances into form the loving light of life. Her beauty and her world of beauty support and sustain the animal and plant kingdoms. She appreciates what you can do for the animals and the plants.

Nevertheless, you must also do for yourselves, so we've got themes to represent some form of a conflict: doing for yourself or other human beings versus the animals or the plants. Know that they will be spiritually looked after, that they will even be somewhat physically looked after. Some animals will behave unusually; they may go underground for a time or may seem to disappear. Scientists will say, "They are gone. Where did they go? They are extinct." Many of them will go underground or into deep trenches in the ocean.

Please don't look for them with ultrasonic devices and whatnot. This can further their difficulties in the thin spots in dimension. For those of you who don't know, ultrasonics is a rudimentary means to pass through dimensions; it is a building block. Many people who have heard UFOs, for example, will hear something high-pitched or they'll feel something (whether they note the feeling or not), which means they're experiencing a sound beyond their hearing range from the ship. That is because one of the means of passing through dimensions has to do with ultrasonics. You have to be careful with ultrasonics, because you could accidentally activate a hole in the fabric of time. This is especially important for people in medical clinics: if you're going to use ultrasonic devices, try to use them at the lowest possible setting of energy, should the machine be adjustable, which it ought to be. It might take a little longer, but you'll get the image and the effect you need. If it's for muscle therapy, use it at the lowest possible setting, please.

I'm cramming, as it were, a lot of information into a short space. At a later date I will give you more information. But I need to give you this information now because it is an extreme situation, something you can feel in the core of your being. You can feel it in your heart, you can feel it in your gut, you know something's going on. And I'm not just talking here to sensitive people or New Age people. I'm speaking to everybody, whether you live in a monastery or walk the streets; you can *feel* it. Know that *you're not crazy*; what you're feeling is real. Know that you have help, that you are dearly loved and that you will get through this.

Can you talk about how people's health might be affected, particularly those who have heart problems or any other health issues that you might address?

People with any stress-related condition, such as heart problems, ulcers or anything wherein anxiety or stress plays a part, may be affected. By this I mean that if circumstances existed by which these people had windows of departure to opt to end the cycles of their lives (although everyone is immortal), during this time there is a 10% to 11% or greater chance that this window could be used. People with heart disease or something critical like that could pass in greater numbers through the veil of physical life to etheric life. People with intestinal disorders or such caused or supported by stress could experience increased anxiety. Note to physicians: Encourage these patients in no uncertain terms to practice their stress-reduction techniques without delay every day. You may have to be a bit of a drill instructor — in the kindest possible way, of course — and have to nag them, because they have the potential for experiencing more extreme symptoms.

Also occurring within the cycle of life are injury accidents. If there is always x amount of availability for passage from one life to another into your immortal life and, following that, to reincarnate elsewhere at some time, there will be a 10% to 11% greater possibility that an accident could cause a person to die within the next 90 days or so. Actually, that percentage will decrease about 45 days from the time of this talk to about 8%; within about 60 days it'll drop down to about 5%. When the 90 days are up it should be down to about 1%, and I'm hardly counting that. So from 90 days going forward to about 120 days after this talk, that 1% will have dissipated to almost a zero increase, mathematically speaking, in potentiality for passage through the veil of death.

Health practitioners of all forms, you need to be alert, and it would help you to take greater note of a patient's symptomologies and err on the side of caution. Aggravated symptomology is also certainly possible, yes. In certain conditions it might lead to a deterioration within the integrity of the physical self, which could perhaps lead to complications or further difficulties or conditions. For example, a person could move from a symptomology that can be controlled with the proper medication and lifestyle to a symptomology that might require minor surgery or a brief hospitalization. Medical people: I want you to forget about how annoyed you are with your fellow medical person in some other field, whether because of their field or because of who they are. You're going to need to cooperate. You have all had special training — some of you are extremely specialized. And although this is very valuable in your unique field, because you are so specialized you don't see everything. You don't look for everything, and many times you don't know how to look. It allows you to devote your attention to a specific area, and that's why you specialize. However, you *must* break down the social barriers between medical specialties. You must communicate more. And you must make an effort, chiropractors, to talk to MDs, and MDs need to speak to chiropractors as if they were physicians, which they are, to themselves and to the world. You must make an effort to break down the social barriers from one profession to another and understand that under the umbrella of Caduceus (though Caduceus does not carry one around) you all walk together on the same path. You *must* cooperate for the good of the patient. Thank you. Good day.

29

The End of
Time-As-You-Have-Known-It

Zoosh through Robert Shapiro
September 12, 1995

Now you come to the end of time as you have known it. This is
why I am the end-time historian. Even now as I am speaking, you are
coming to the end of the vibrational time sequence you've been living
in. People have come to a conclusion that time and dimension are
connected — such as third dimension, one time; fourth dimension,
another time — but it is not so. There are many time streams between
the dimensions, and right now your entire planetary, and to some
lesser extent universal, selves are coming to a complete transfer out
of one time stream into another. This situation is causing tremendous upheaval amongst people. For example, you begin something
simple, mundane, something ordinary, like getting dressed to go out
and meet your friend for lunch. In the process of dressing you have
all your clothes laid out on the bed, but you decide to put on
something entirely different and leave the clothes on the bed. Or you
begin to go someplace, driving, walking, bicycling, whatever — and
you go someplace entirely different, not where you were planning to
go. This is evidence of the change of time stream. People have been
overly dependent upon the idea of the change of dimension connected to the change in the pattern of their lives.

This change of time, this speed-up, is causing an immediate
effect that has to do with the collapsing of time. The collapsing of
time does not mean crumpling something into a little ball; rather, it

is like ripples on water. Let us say that the ripply line is time as you have known it (which has been pushed together, hence the ripples), and the time sequence you are now on runs in a straight line above the surface of the main, rippled line. You touch into the time you have known when the line goes through the upper parts of the old rippled time [see diagram]. Thus a person might plan to do something, even something important, but not carry it out, because they feel they have already done it. They feel the effect. You are now at a point where planning to do something, experiencing the results of what you have done and having the feelings, good or bad, of what you have done, all happen in the moment of planning.

Watch for the Delay Factor

People are still adjusting to this, and there is also a slight delay factor. They might say, "I'm going to go see my counselor," and then they think about the issues and what they're going to talk about that day. The more they dwell upon it, the more relaxed they become with the issues, because those issues are being processed in another time sequence. As a result, they don't need to see their counselor anymore, but it takes them a little while to realize that. This circumstance is significant, because it will affect both social and business plans. People who have businesses will need to be alert. Contracts may not be a sufficient means to bring things to you or for you to bring things to others. You will need to constantly observe your client's needs, even when you have the client's name on the bottom line. You will have to observe whether your client has *already* adjusted to what he wanted from you and behaves as if he already has it. If that is the case, you must leap forward and see what he will need *next* — sometimes signing for something you will provide for him. It may mean that you won't have to provide the first thing, but you will have to provide the next thing he would need if he had obtained the first. You can work with your clients in this way, but you will have to stay one step ahead. You will need visionaries, not just salespeople. Salespeople, be alert: you will have to upgrade, as it were, to becoming visionaries, or corporations will have to hire visionaries.

Now on a personal level, individual plans will be affected. For instance, what you plan with another person could be affected by many things, depending upon the cooperation of that person. Say that you and your friend decide to take your friendship to another level and become intimate. You may notice that this not only decreases the anxiety and tension around becoming intimate (if the other person is in agreement with you about it), but you fall into step

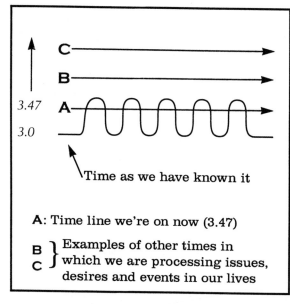

A: Time line we're on now (3.47)

B ⎫ Examples of other times in
C ⎭ which we are processing issues,
desires and events in our lives

and everything looks much better. In this case when you fall into step with your friend, it's as if you've been intimate for a long time and you're old companions already, in the sense of accumulation of experience.

Thus you can see how many things are done within collapsed time, but you do not necessarily apply them in this time sequence alone. You are moving as a society beyond the boundaries of time as you've known it; this is why you've been having so many unusual experiences. Many of you have had bizarre experiences, and many are simply coming into sensitivities, abilities you have in the larger you that have not been available within third-dimensional existence.

A New Capacity to Create on Multiple Levels

As I've been saying, what has been processed by you is being reclaimed by those for whom you were processing it. In the case of the Andromedan linear mind, they are reclaiming it; you don't need it anymore. Does this mean that your mind becomes vertical and nothing more, that you know what you need to know when you need to know it? No! It means also that this instinctual mind (which I'm referring to as the vertical mind) then has the capacity to create on multiple levels. This means that you might be on the A time line, but you have things to process throughout this ripple of time. So you might be processing these things on the B or C time lines; and if things are being processed elsewhere and seemingly accomplished according to the feelings you are getting in your body (though you can't look back and say "I remember doing that"), that's because it's happening up here above the ripples of your current time, in another time dimension.

We have here a circumstance in which you are literally becoming your greater selves as I speak. Many of you will be able to make a giant leap and move beyond the restriction of your third-dimensional personality. You will be able to accept your spiritual gifts, attributes and abilities —not only the god part of you, but the greater part of you in experience, your oversoul, which contains all elements of things you have perfected and accomplished through your many lives.

Others of you will try to hang on to the old time sequence and to your old personality till the bitter end, as you say. I must tell you now that it's not possible. You can try and try again, but linear time, which seemed to have been so fixed in your life, is over. You've moved along far enough to where time is folded up now in ripples, and it's not ever going to go back to being what it was as you have known it.

The Two-Year Preamble and the Next Eight Weeks

Even a five-year-old is affected by this, because that five-year-old child has not only had the preamble to this experience, but for two years before you hit the rippled time effect, you were already feeling some of the vibration from it. Five-year-old children were three years old when they hit that two-year preamble, and now they're in it. But a two-year-old is not going to be affected. To them it will be, "Oh, fine, no problem" because they were born into this cycle. This may not help you now, but it might in the future when they grow up. Then they can guide you.

This cycle, then, is very important for people to know about because it will immediately explain what has been going on. This will become increasingly apparent within the next six to eight weeks. Within the next six to eight weeks [to November 7] many things will occur to you, and I don't mean just thoughts. Issues you have been working on your whole life that are conundrums will seem to work themselves out, and you will not know how! For the life of you won't be able to imagine what happened, why this issue is suddenly worked out and why you can accept it so easily. Perhaps something has been driving you, perhaps you've been avoiding looking at something. Perhaps you've been wanting something very much, but it doesn't seem that you can ever have it. You might suddenly find that you have it, or you might find, for example, that it wasn't ever right for you in the first place because it was a desire stimulated by somebody else, and what you now have or what you have accumulated as a result of this collapsed time effect is much better than what you thought you wanted.

In other words, you are moving through the first veil, often considered the veil of the passage due to death. Although what I'm about to say may or may not come to pass, I and many of my cohorts are rooting for it, and we think there is a good chance (right now it's 40/60, maybe soon it'll be 50/50): Third-dimensional Earth needs to have a purification. The Photon Doctor has been working with Mother Earth and has convinced her that in her third-dimensional version, she must have a major die-off of living beings who are overpopulated.

Now, you as a body of beings are viably moving forward beyond the third dimension, so this is not going to affect those of you who are going with the flow. But those of you who are hanging on desperately to that third-dimensional existence, even though you can't hang on anymore, know now that this hanging on could get you caught up in the purification cycle. I don't think this will affect too many people, but it is possible that the potential disease cycle that could hit your planet in October, November or early December will more likely affect (if all things can be shifted here) those who are rigidly attached to third-dimensional (3.0) existence. This will allow them to move beyond the punishing cycle of what must be done in third-dimensional Earth.

The Purification/Disease Cycle

You as a mass of society are at about 3.47 right now, but those who are hanging on by a thread to 3.0 could be involved in this die-off. On the one hand, that would be tragic for your loved ones and so on; but on the other hand, since you can't seem to let go of 3.0-dimensional Earth, it will let go *for* you so you can continue your reincarnational cycle without delay. For others it's important to understand that this coming disease cycle may not have to affect you all. The disease cycle and the purification (the disease cycle is part of the purification, you understand) are designed to help not only Mother Earth but those who are rigidly hanging on to what was and even what has been for some years. It will help you to move beyond all that has been so that you can experience completely all that will be.

This function of evolution is working for you now on a physical level as well as spiritually and on the feeling plane. It is intended (we hope for this) that if you had had a major disease cycle, as discussed in [Chapter 19], that the impact on your population and the tragedy for those who go on living may be avoided, because you might instead be able to have the experience in other dimensions. The experience on the personal level of those who get the disease and die from it, the experience of all that you go through in that death cycle

—not the suffering but the transformation, the letting go, the seeing what's really important and embracing it and then letting go and moving on —you may be able to get in other dimensional experiences of yourself. For instance, you might have the *physical* experience of the disease in 3.0 dimension and the *visionary* experience that goes with any death-disease in, say (referring to our chart), B and C time lines.

A Dot-Dash Memory

What we have, then, is a circumstance where the evolutionary cycle of your society is now being accelerated so quickly that your linear memory of past events will have a sort of dot-dash effect. You will remember some things well, but there will be huge gaps in your memory at other times. You will arrive suddenly at a decision that's been a conundrum for years —years and years —and you will have no idea how you got there. Suddenly it'll be like, "Oh, this is what I'm going to do," and that's that. There will be no more anxiety about it, no more promises this way and that; it'll just *be* there.

And we are also hoping that because the disease cycle is a portion of what was, it will be possible for your society to go through it en masse on different levels of time so that you do not have, in the 3.47 dimension you're in now, an immediate die-off of one-third to 40% of the human population. I realize it's a frightening possibility that you could even potentially have such a thing in these times, when medical science has created a drug that ought to be able to prevent all disease —interferon. But interferon has a very serious side effect: if you do not continue to take it (at least in its more widely available version, a common cold could kill you, because it essentially replaces your immune system. There is a hybridized version where with only one shot you never get diseases for the rest of your life, not even a tummy ache. But it also greatly interferes with how you experience the dimensional shift. Since so few people are getting those shots, I'm not going to go into that at this time.

I'm holding out a feather of hope here, because I'm trying to say it is possible, especially due to this cyclic effect, that you will find yourself in a circumstance in which you can literally be in more than one place at a time. There will be times (not when you're asleep, mind you) when you are, as far as you can tell, wide awake —maybe doing something, walking, driving —and you will seem to be suddenly aware of your surroundings and notice, "Where have I been for 20 minutes?" Many of you, not all of you, have had this experience before. But now it won't seem to be "where have I been for 20 minutes?" You will be driving along and literally a split second later you will feel totally different, as if you had been somewhere for two weeks, processed something tremendous, and some burden you have been worried about will suddenly fall away from your shoulders. You will drive along feeling relieved, knowing that not only is everything all right, but everything's going to be all right and you don't have to think about it anymore.

In terms of linear time —which you are not really experiencing anymore, but for the sake of your minds —it's going to be almost instantaneous.

It's important to get this information out, because people are already beginning to have these effects. Not only are they seeing things, having visions and having experiences of their greater soul selves through the accumulation of experience and lifetimes (meaning various spiritual abilities and so on), but they are also beginning to have an experience wherein one moment they're terribly worried about something they've been worried about for years, and the next moment [snaps fingers] they're not worried about it anymore.

Now let's examine what's happening in that moment; let's slow it down. It's critically important that you understand this. The older version of you which was worried and was sweating about it unintentionally (something going on for years and years and years) *is that part of you that is hanging on to 3.0 dimension.* Did you know that? That worry —especially anxiety about something you've been anxious about for years and years —creates a tether between you and that 3.0 dimension. So in that moment you —the you that was tethered to 3.0 dimension —simply part company. The anxious you, the worried you, the part of you that cannot let go of 3.0-dimension sequencing, returns to 3.0 dimension (it's critical to understand this) and continues its existence in 3.0 dimension.

But that which you now understand your personality to be, you continue on in 3.47, soon to go up higher. This is it, this is now the time you've been asking about when you said, "But Zoosh, what's happening, where's the evidence of moving between dimensions?" I've given you a little bit here, a little bit there —but this is *critical.* This is where you literally leave the anxious you behind. The you that goes on in 3.47 will feel like you ought to be doing something, and what's going to happen if . . . but it's temporary; it passes. That's the first veil you go through when you're passing out of your physical body in the death cycle (what *you* call death, which of course does not exist). When you pass through that first veil, you still have feelings associated with your life as it has been. But you're already moving past the necessity to act on those feelings. You go through these many veils when your physical body dies, and you continue to go on as a persona, or immortal personality. But here you have a circumstance in which you are, as a society, shifting between the third and the fourth dimension without death, for the most part. Thus you're going through the veils consciously, awake. So of course you're having some extreme situations.

When the living persona has the opportunity to shed all of its anxieties and suddenly finds itself in 3.47 dimension, I'm not saying you will suddenly become carefree, but when you have this experience it is good to try and let go. If you can, take a few days off from work; if you can't, then work. But know that you might no longer be worried or anxious at work; you might not be driven as before. You might not be worried about money anymore, or about deadlines. You might not be anxious about making a mistake on your job or about pleasing your boss.

This does not mean that you suddenly become a terrible employee; it means that the worries and anxieties that were driving you on the job might fall away. You might still be a perfectly good employee — perhaps much better. (Here is a note to management and businesses: Your employees might be changing, but that does not necessarily mean that they will not do a good job. They might do a much better job because they will not be worried about making a mistake, which tends to sometimes cause the mistake through the law of anxious attraction associated with 3.0 dimension.)

These circumstances are critical to understand, as complicated as they are, because now the mass of people are beginning to go through them. Granted, the sensitive people are now going through them first, as I speak.

Seasons to Become More Benign

To understand the cyclic nature of these times, you need to know that the primary function of time now is delineating day and night, as it were. That's it. Granted, the seasons go on, and they will go through a time of more extremes, perhaps, but that will be very short, and then the seasons will become more benign. You won't have such terrific storms. The storms you are seeing now are to some extent the result of what's going on in third-dimensional Earth, 3.0. The hurricanes you are having reach across the ocean and are half an ocean wide, but they may be greater in 3.0-dimensional Earth. They speed over the land and still maintain their structural integrity as they exit the other side. Granted, they're not as strong when they come out the other side, but they're still a hurricane!

What do weathermen think when they see that on the radar? I mention it because some of you might have moments when you see it, you even have evidence on the tape briefly, but it will be fleeting. You see, you will have something taped, and it will be there for a while, but you are moving through the dimension so quickly. You're in 3.47, but you're moving very fast; let's say you're at 3.472 or 3.4721. You might find yourself at 3.4768 at a later date, and you won't have anything on that tape! If you have a videotape of your weather phenomenon, there would be nothing there. You could swear it was there because you remember watching the tape, kind of — but it has a dreamlike quality to it. And everyone else who watched the tape with you feels the same way; it seems like a strange phenomenon you are experiencing together. I'm telling you this because I want you to have landmarks to understand that what I say is true, but it is more important to understand that the 3.0-dimensional Earth is now going through the catastrophic Earth changes predicted in many religious texts and by many sensitive people. It's happening *right now.*

The Destiny of the 3.0-Dimensional Version of You

The critical factor is that the anxious, worrying you separates and returns to 3.0-dimensional Earth to fulfill the destiny it was worrying about, taking the worry and much of your anxiety with it. What happens to *you?* You go on. Because that 3.0-dimensional version of yourself has split off, you are not only able to go on significantly unencumbered with those worries, but that 3.0-dimensional version of yourself accomplishes certain things in that dimension. Granted, it will perish there, but within the functioning of that death it will be able to process certain things that will cause a further expansion of your perception (where you are now in 3.47) as well as a potential fulfillment of certain things you had originally intended to do in your life, which might be achieved. Perhaps it will live in 3.0 for a week regardless of all the storms and volcanoes; perhaps it will live for a month or even eight, ten months, or in some rare cases, longer. It will accomplish a great deal there. It will be very physical there, because it will be a rugged world, almost primitive. But however long it lasts, whatever it does will benefit it — but also you.

I'm not talking about a split personality here. This is not psychological; this is a physical fact. As a society you've moved beyond the need to be in the third-dimensional existence. I have been stating for a long time that you are *done* with the third dimension and that certain things associated with the third dimension, such as anxiety and worry, must be left there. Therefore parts of you are literally *going there* to do it.

Present Consequences

How else will you know when those parts leave? You will know because certain things about you will change. For instance, you've always wanted long pants all your life (I'm trying to come up with mundane things, here, so that you will not feel too dramatic) but suddenly you want to wear shorts or lederhosen and can't imagine a life without them. So you go out and find yourself a nice pair at a local shop that caters to tourists; it's a beautiful pair of lederhosen that you love and wear every day; you even get others to wear them. Suddenly you are a lederhosen person. I mention this because although it's a minor thing — from long pants to short pants, as it were — there could be other, more major things.

Perhaps you have always wanted to do something; maybe you've always wanted to be an artist but you've never quite seen yourself as that. Suddenly you find yourself one day in the art supply store buying canvases and paints and brushes and an easel, the whole works — it's like you suddenly woke up in the store. You remember driving there, but there's a blank space and you suddenly woke up in the store, or felt the need to go to the store, and you went. You didn't shove it away as you had before.

What I'm saying here is that dreams, things that you hope for, wishes — especially those that are benign, beneficial to you and others — suddenly seem to come true! And it's not that they come true because your fairy godmother comes with a wand, places it gently in your auric field and says, "And now, my dear, you shall live happily ever after with the prince," though there is an element of that, granted. It's largely that you move the hurdles out of your way. Most hurdles in your way, you understand, are manufactured by you or by well-intentioned others telling you how life is, in contrast to how life *really* is — in other words, placing their worries and anxieties on you. This often happens regardless of the best intentions — when you are a child, from your parents or adults around you. But now you are suddenly able with one fell swoop to whisk these hurdles aside.

There may be one or two low hurdles associated with something physical in your life. Perhaps you have only one leg; suddenly you decide, "I don't care that they don't make bicycles for one-legged people" and you create one that works for you. You go out and show them how it can be done. You will feel your hurdles easier to leap, and all of the non-hurdles you (or others with the best of intentions for you) have manufactured are just swept aside, and you can do what you have dreamed of. You can move beyond suffering and have a good life.

These things are literally happening. Granted, there will be some people who will experience 3.0 dimension in a version of themselves different from what you have known yourself to be. Although it will be the side of you that is anxious, that worries, it will also be the side of you that is rugged, more primitive. You are moving beyond that and into the time when, should you need an ability, it will be there. You will notice, whether or not you've had it before, that suddenly it is there and you can use it. This is an effect of becoming more whole and complete as yourself.

Why is this change of dimension happening?

Spiraling through the First Veil

It's happening because of the sequence that comes out from the spiral of creation; it has to do with your natural cycle of creation. This is essentially part of the Mayan calendar, though it has unnecessary complications. The Mayan calendar, you understand, is a spiral, as is creation in general. That is why galaxies and other life forms are spiral in shape. Without going into science (which is a religion in search of a God) . . . let's just say it doesn't have to do with ETs.

You have accomplished what you needed to accomplish in the third dimension. You must let it go because you are moving between the veils into what would be the afterlife in the case of a death. You are moving right now through the first veil. Part of you feels slightly motivated, as if you ought to be doing something, but you really do not have the capacity to apply that motivation if it is associated with the past. For instance, "I *ought* to complete my Ph.D.; I'm almost there" — but what has driven you to obtain the Ph.D. is no longer present. Or "I ought to be working in a factory, but I sure wish I could have a Ph.D." Suddenly you find yourself at school; you're accepted. You're no longer in the factory anymore, you've got all the financial aid you need, and you're off and running toward your Ph.D. It works both ways. It is simply that you are now in a ripple of time accomplishing much that you thought you would have to accomplish one step at a time. You are experiencing the skipping of steps, because the steps are being accomplished in other portions of yourself.

So if someone has their usual worries and things keep changing but nothing is happening for them, it's because they are connected with the wrong vibration, the three-dimensional . . .

They're attached to that vibration; they're still motivated somewhat by what's going on in that vibration. But they do not have the tools to apply because they are no longer there; that vibrational self of theirs is in 3.0-dimensional vibration.

The Scene on 3.0-Dimensional Earth

What's going on in 3.0-dimensional vibration? Many of the cinder cone volcanoes around Sedona and Flagstaff are steaming, and some are erupting, not extremely so. There is one just north of the San Francisco Peaks that has a slow lava flow coming down toward the highway. This is not likely to happen where you are, but it's happening in 3.0 dimension. The likelihood of it happening in 3.47 is very slim; it's a chance, but not much, although some sensitive people might smell sulphur in the air or suddenly feel heat, but then it passes.

What about in other parts of the planet? People living up in Greenland, for example, might smell plants, flowers and trees for no particular reason. In 3.0-dimensional Earth, the icecaps would have melted completely. A lot of water is not on the surface of the Earth, and at first the excess goes inside the planet, but rises to the surface later. So they are smelling the landscape, as it were.

Many of you will be affected by this in your career, because your goals ("This is who I am, this is what I do") will change. What you've wanted to be, what you thought you'd love to be but didn't know how you could make a living at it, will suddenly be what you are. You won't have any recollection how you learned to do it, nor will you have any recollection how you got the confidence to do it. *That's the key*: In 3.0-dimensional Earth one gains confidence as a result of what one applies, what one does, what works for one, ergo, one's wisdom. But here it's more instantaneous — suddenly you have the capacity, you have the permission and you seem to have some abilities toward this goal although you are still a novice. This is happening, but not for everybody yet. Because it's happening on an increasing cyclic rate, by the time this is published it will be more apparent.

People will also be affected in their personal lives. For instance, many people are in marriages, for instance, that are not working, who have been together for 20 or 30 years and stay together because they're used to each other, but they have dreams — they wish they could be with some perfect person. Suddenly one day, regardless of their age — they might be 50, 60 or 70, maybe even 75 or 80 — they suddenly look at each other and say, "Why are we bothering with this?" There won't be any anger or resentment, they'll just divvy up their stuff, go out into the world, quickly find the person who is more beneficial for them to be with and carry on from there. It will leave a lot of drama behind, which is necessary for what goes on past the first veil.

Past the first veil violence is not experienced except as a fleeting memory. So why have a big battle after a 25-year marriage that isn't working? Why not just say, "Well, that's it, then," with no recriminations or hard feelings on either side. And no lawyers! ("You take this stuff and I'll take that stuff.") If you need a legal document, you go to some legal aid society ("A divorce? We'll write that up!") and that's that. No lawyers, no courts (lawyers: find something else to do). This is really what's coming! Granted, you're just moving through the first veil, but I can assure you that when you're through the second veil, lawyers, you're going to need to find another job. So I don't recommend that advocates of conflict pursue that avenue too much. If you're a first-year law student, find something else to do.

Much of the political resistance will break down. First we'll see —with the women, for instance —that there will be a coming together. Right now there is this women's conference in China. Women see things more clearly because they've been largely eliminated from the day-to-day political process, so they're not encumbered with as many "shoulds" and back-door deals. Thus they can come out with a document that says, "This is what we believe would be a good thing." Unfortunately, they're allowing themselves to be guided by career diplomats who are necessarily people who have had to make back-door deals. In the next conference they'll get it just right and they'll say, "This is what we believe and that's that —take it or leave it," meaning they will not be attached to people accepting it. They will bring it in as a document to the United Nations, where most representatives are men, and say, "Okay, this is fine." The disenfranchised (the largest group of which on your planet is women) will begin to set up, outside of formal government structures, a social government that says, "These are the rules we feel are valuable to live by." And however vague-looking that is to career politicians, as they are developed these guidelines will become the guidelines of your new society. They will be very simple; they will be associated with what is good to do and what is not good to do.

I give you these examples because they are associated with your daily life, things you can observe now. I will speak more of this in the future, but I have given this so you will understand the extreme change going on around you as we speak. I will talk to you more frequently in the future. Good day.

30

Humanity Pushed/Pulled/Shoved into Null Zone

Zoosh by Robert Shapiro
October 2, 1995

All right. Now you have come into a time-space differential. This time-space differential (which can loosely be described as an area where time and space overlap from one point to another) is what I refer to as the Null Zone. In the Null Zone you do not actually move on the navigational point from the third to the fourth dimension, but you do process. In that sense, you are processing all that is left over from your third-dimensional life. Certain aspects here become critical. Some people will not wish to complete their natural cycle in anything other than the dimension they started. And that is why a few people more than would be natural will end their natural cycle during the period roughly from about three or four weeks ago to . . . I can't put it in sequence in the future.

Well, we're doing this for November. Is this true as of today through October?

As of today. So the factor in the Null Zone is quite extraordinary. You see, you were born into (except those born in the past couple of weeks) the third dimension, where all things third-dimensional work (granted, some work better than others). Now you find yourself on an accelerating journey. From about 3.37 of your shift between third and fourth dimension, you started accelerating also with the implied potential for certain disasters. Many, many individual personalities within the angelics, within your future selves, within a combined total of all of your guides and teachers, which represents millions of beings (and perhaps a larger number if we count past, present and future), all started pushing and pulling and accelerating your pace well beyond what it was even a few weeks ago. This was all a pell-mell rush to get you to the Null Zone.

In the Null Zone a couple of things happen. One, it's like a breathing space. Yes, you're advancing a little faster; you weren't intended to get to the Null Zone just yet. But because of these potential catastrophes and dangers, we had to do something so that the people inclined to extreme behavior would not (as the psychologists call it) act out this extreme behavior, or that the extreme behavior they are acting out would be less impactful on the citizens of your entire world. An example of extreme behavior would be the nuclear explosions being set off by certain political beings of the country of France. French citizens: Do not think I am saying you are bad people. These are a very small handful of people who are setting off these explosions for entirely political reasons – nothing else. This is, nevertheless, extreme behavior, especially because of where they're setting them off. The Polynesian islands is an area intended to be a place of a new continent. This new continent was intended to develop itself over the next few years – now that might be delayed. We are hoping, those of us who reside where I do, that your expedient arrival in the Null Zone might tend to mask the effect of the nuclear explosions so that the rise of Lemuria in this particular area will not be delayed, harmed or otherwise corrupted.

Null-Zone Effects on People

The experience you are having, then, is very odd. Allowing for the time of publication, we'll say that many of you have been having a sensation not only of unpredictable lethargy, but one where things either aren't of interest as they once were, or where you find that the circumstances, neatly arranged on a previous occasion, seem to utterly fall apart when the actual well-laid plans are happening in sequence – or are supposed to be happening in sequence. It's not a good time, then (as you can tell), to be making precise plans. For those of you who are caught up in precise plans such as construction efforts, be it a humble house or a massive high-rise building, you must be very, very clear with your employees. You must urge them to use safety precautions beyond those they normally use, because it would be very easy these days to be distracted by the tiniest thing and inadvertently make a life-threatening mistake, either to themselves or to others. Now, don't be too afraid, because good employees, if they're told that they must pay especial attention to safety and make two trips instead of one, will do so. I know that's going to bring the construction cost up just a little bit, but better to do that than to have the building fall down.

In the Null Zone, what you could do in the third dimension does not work so well, yet what is applied and is effective in the fourth dimension has not come into sequence yet. However, there is one major exception, and that is your dreamtime. You are now experiencing not only the letting go of third-dimensional lessons in your dreams, but you're also experiencing the gradual arrival (or a presymposium experience of fourth-dimensional lessons) of fourth-dimensional realities. You are experiencing dreams that turn into visions and visions that turn into dreams. In this case, a vision takes place when you are awake and a dream takes place while you are asleep. I mention this because the dream experience in the fourth dimension has much more to do with visions. You might fall asleep briefly, then wake up, and the vision continues. Or, fourth-dimensionally speaking, you would have a vision [dream] that is conscious. Dreams now are largely an unconscious experience; in the fourth dimension they are largely a conscious experience, with only a little bit being unconscious. You will remember the dream and make some kind of a well-ordered visionary interpretation out of it; you will be able to understand it.

I tell you this because it's a very good time now to keep some kind of a dream journal. But don't get too caught up in the sights and sounds of potential disasters. Remember, since you all have dream capability, and since the dream universe is real, many of you are processing things in the third dimension, not only for yourselves but as a mass event for many people who cannot reasonably be expected to be processed as an actual circumstance in your physical reality — because if you experienced it in your physical reality, it could be catastrophic.

Balancing Lemuria

For example, the Polynesian area, as I say, is intended to be a continent that I would call New Lemuria. Although it is not exactly where Lemuria was before, we're going to call it New Lemuria because it will rise there as a result of a sequential eruption from a crack in the Earth. It will eventually become a series of high points in New Lemuria (about seven), a volcanically created island. This eruption, if it were to happen in your specific dimension, would totally disrupt your planetary lifestyle. You'd have ash in the air constantly. Now, this *must* occur for 3.0-dimensional Earth to balance it. You are now moving out of that dimension, but there needs to be a balance in 3.0-dimensional Earth so that when you arrive in 4.0-dimensional Earth, the continents there (New Lemuria being one of them there now) will be balanced by its third-dimensional counterpart, its second-dimensional counterpart and its eighth-dimensional counterpart. These balancing counterparts provide necessary physical, emotional, vertical (meaning mental) and spiritual foundations that are absolutely essential for the maintenance, the fluidity (because continental motion is a factor of fluidity) and the integrity of continents above water.

Earth's Return to Sirius Postponed

Now, we've had in the past a circumstance where it was considered that fourth-dimensional Earth might be very much a water planet. But it now appears that Earth will not, in its fourth-dimensional counterpart, return to its galaxy [system] of origin — meaning Sirius. It appears that fourth-dimensional Earth will now maintain its experience of being in your present galaxy for a short time. A short time would constitute no more than (experientially speaking) 10,000 years. It will then most likely return.

This short, fourth-dimensional experience within your galaxy will allow you to complete the problems and issues you were intended to complete before you hit the Null Zone. You were intended to spend longer in the third-dimensional sequence of motion toward your fourth-dimensional becoming, but we have made an attempt (speaking for all of us) to rush you to the Null Zone in hopes (for it is not our ability to create this, because you must create it also) that rushing you to the Null Zone this fast will allow you to skip over potential catastrophic events that have the capacity to eliminate most of the surface population. We'd like to skip over that. So it's a wait-and-see, experiential time for you; we ought to know within two-and-a-half years. If there haven't been any major catastrophes in two-and-a-half years, you will have made it through.

Now, I can't tell you how long you'll be in the Null Zone, because it will depend largely on the progress you make in the dream state. The dream state is your constant link to the fourth-dimensional aspect of your own selves in future Earth, known as Terra. *If you make enough progress in the dream state, then you will come through the Null Zone quickly.* If, on the other hand, you don't make progress very quickly, then you'll go through the Null Zone very slowly.

ELF and Microwave Disruption
from the Secret Government

As an aside, the secret government is attempting to broadcast densifying ELFs (extra-low frequencies) that distract you, give you discomfort. They will attempt to disrupt your sleep state, hoping to delay your progress through the Null Zone. They tried their darndest to keep us from dragging and pushing and pulling you into the Null Zone as fast as we did. But they were unable to prevent it. Once you get over the edge of the Null Zone, you're in it. There's no graduated sequence. Though we got you over the edge into the Null Zone, they're going to continue to broadcast this stuff for a while.

So know that your sleep state might be somewhat disrupted. This is largely in reference to these ELF transmissions, some of which are broadcast by the sinister secret government and some broadcast as carrier waves for communication. I'd say at least 40% of the difficulty in your sleep state now (if not 45%) has to do with microwave transmission, which is a serious disrupter of the sleep state. As a serious disrupter of the sleep state, I might add that it is a considerable antagonist to the immune system.

I don't know if there's anything you're willing to do about that as a society, since you are somewhat attached to your electrical and electronic appliances — to say nothing of your communication satellites and so on. This microwave stuff is really rough for you. It essentially cancels out your immune system's effect in battling disorders in your body, which reproduce their own sequence of events. One example would be, say, cancer. Cancer is an anomaly in which the cancer cell reproduces itself at the cost of its host, eventually destroying both its host and itself. This is happening because the signals that come from the body's electrical immune system to other portions of the body are being disrupted by microwaves, plus the ELF waves.

In any event, this Null Zone is a state of being in which you'll find yourself for a time. Now, a question?

What number are we on between three and four right now?

3.47.

So you're saying that from 8 September to 12 September we moved those ten points that you said would take ninety days?

Yes. As the predictions of your friend [Eileen Nauman] for catastrophic illnesses gradually became more of a real factor, we would either have to jam you into the Null Zone as fast as we could to avoid the potential for catastrophic illness (to say nothing of volcanic eruptions, which are somewhat happening in any event). The only way to decrease the odds was to jam you into the Null Zone, because that tends to soften and dull everything. This is why people's minds are dull, memories are dull, and so on.

Now, this is not to say that these events will not happen, but it decreases the odds of these diseases and volcanic eruptions by a significant proportion.

That's wonderful!

Yes! So our feeling on this side was that it is better to take you to the Null Zone (granted, we cheated a little bit, we put ourselves on the line) and allow your dream states to resolve what you couldn't cover physically, although we knew that some of you would still choose to end your natural cycles before your entrance into the fourth dimension. Now it will happen naturally — or I'd *like* to think it'll happen naturally, without catastrophic illness or some geological catastrophe. There's still a chance for that — granted, it's a significant chance, but it's nowhere near as significant as it was.

Also, giving credit where credit is due, many people are beginning to wake up now. Even in the last four months, a significant number of people are waking up, coming into greater consciousness. And the ascension people (giving credit where it is due) are helping, because they are coming together in their groups and broadcasting all this good energy. And other meditational groups are doing the same thing in their own way. This is all helping people to wake up quicker. You might even say that these groups grease the rail for all of us to run you up into the Null Zone, with all of its inherent risks — meaning that you still have to resolve what you've been through, what you skipped over.

You skipped over about ten or twelve points there, but our belief is that you can resolve it in the dream state. So be prepared for a wild ride in the dream state, but at least it won't happen in your physical life. You might experience some things, too, that are really kind of whacko — meaning that you'll have interactions with people who are famous in your culture, and these interactions could be very strange. But it will allow you, as a result of knowing, to have an impression of who these public people are or were (more likely were, people having passed over) and be able to interpret the dream more easily, because your impression of who they are will be more important in this case than who they really were. Your impression will allow you to create this being as a dream symbol you interact with, and you will be able to understand the dream better as a result of their notoriety, at least in your own mind.

I don't understand the Null Zone. If "null" means "not moving," are we "not moving" at all?

No, no. Motion is in fact happening; "null" means that your motion toward the fourth dimension has stopped – but of course we also rushed you forward. You've covered a tremendous amount of ground in a very short time.

Yes, four days, because there were only four days between those two channelings!

That's right!

The numbers didn't add up.

That's right, so it was, as I said, a pell-mell rush forward in an attempt to avert a catastrophe. So I'd say this: for now, you're not going to be moving any further, it's not going to be a continuing gradual motion. No, you'll just be sitting here in the Null Zone for a while.

Okay, because it was going to take ninety days, what does that do for the next ninety days? Instead of a constant increase in vibration, we may just have to work out what we crashed through, right?

That's really it, you just crashed through a barrier. Some of you felt even in the past few weeks a sudden feeling of disorientation. And this disorientation was so extreme, it actually affected your physical balance in many cases. (That is another reason people need to be very careful in factories and on construction sites where hazard is present.) What I'm saying now does not make what I said before

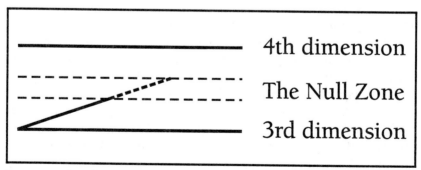

Dimensional Shift. As you ease out of the third dimension you find yourself in the Null Zone where the effects and apparitions of neither dimension are in true toned resonance. What you've learned does not apply – what you've yet to learn is not in effect yet. The Null Zone is like a black hole in applied dimensional lessons. You have to do the best you can as you are guided through it.

null and void; it just gives you the next chapter.

You have to understand that dimensional experiences are time experiences, especially when you're changing dimensions while you are alive, which is pretty unusual. You don't end the third dimension and begin the fourth dimension; there's overlap, and within that overlap probabilities and possibilities become something that you live for a time, and then you jump to another probability or another possibility. All of these things are real. That's why at this time, especially with these overlaps, in your relationships with your country, your family, your state, your city, your wife, your sister, your brother — anything — you can have very odd things take place and then [snaps fingers] they're over right away. You can have good things happen and then "what happened?" — it's gone. You can have things that are uncomfortable happen and then [snaps fingers] it's gone as if it never were there, only you have the memory of it, see?

Now, that's another example of fourth-dimensional experience. In a third-dimensional experience, locked in 3.0, if you had an anomaly in time and were brought back to anywhere within five minutes of that anomaly, you probably wouldn't remember the sequence that you had outside the context of your normal time. You might feel dizzy, you might feel uncomfortable, but you wouldn't remember what took place. You might have a picture, but that's it — not much of a picture at that, just like a snapshot — one moment.

But now, because you're in these overlaps of time, you can have actual sequential experience for a couple of days, and then that sequential experience (as it seemed to be going in a certain direction) is no longer happening. And there's no explanation for it! It's not like "it's his fault" or "it's her fault"; it's just a probability that was a temporary situation, a temporal experience.

Now, don't worry; this isn't going to involve major situations, but it allows us (especially from our side) to be more influential, because we can essentially observe you going through some catastrophe or potential catastrophe, and when you do things in your dream state that allow for certain openings ("you" meaning everybody in the world), and these openings take place, then it is possible, if not probable, that we are able to adjust things from our side and alter that probability to something better.

We're not going to interfere at all if you're doing something that's a good thing, and that probability shifts as a result of dream action to something less pleasant. We won't correct that. We'll only correct it (if we can influence it) if you're doing something very negative and it could get worse. Then we might be able to do that if enough of you have the right dreams.

So now you're in a time when those people who interpret dreams are going to be much more active. You're going to have to account for dreams that are unaccountable, dreams that do not have any relation whatsoever to a person's actual life and are not directly interpretable to that person's individual experience but actually relate to a mass event affecting many people. (Dream interpreters: At this time it might be very beneficial to inform the public about dream symbols and what dreams mean, so that they can have a general grasp of what's going on.)

Can you say who's helping us? Who "all of us" is or was, all of you who are helping on that side?

Good heavens, pick a name, any name. . . . Yes, and many more you don't know. Everybody you've ever heard of plus everybody you've ever forgotten, plus people who've been prepared for years and gone through different incarnations. Many are being called to the other side — spiritual people, people who have good heart, good love; people who had a strong connection with the angelic in this life; people who would normally have finished their natural cycles and come over to the other side. People who would normally have experiential time to have a whole other-side experience, to move on to the next life and so on — if they're the right sort of lightbeings — they're hanging around to participate in this. Even people who have passed over in recent times might be involved in this project in some way.

So be aware, those of you who may have lost a loved one in recent times, that if they were spiritual beings, if they were loving beings (and spirituality here includes religion) especially, they're also likely to be involved in this project, as well as names you know — Jesus, Shiva, and so on and so on.

The Negative Sirius Planet

Can you tell me what led up to the negative planet in Sirius blowing up? Was it just the accumulated negativity?

Oh yes, it was always going to blow up, because planets are very much at the effect of those who live upon them. You know this. On your own planet you have your environmental groups — because even scientifically, the changes caused by all the people living here can be measured. I don't want you to imagine this in a felt experience but *only mentally*: Imagine briefly (no more than briefly) if everybody on Earth was 97% negative. The planet just couldn't take it; it would be a corruption beyond belief. It would short-circuit the entire planet. The planet (meaning the planetary body) couldn't run its natural affairs, and everything good would be transformed into something evil. No; no planet can tolerate that.

Can you help me understand? You've said that the beings there weren't necessarily evil, but they were under the control of and subject to evil; so where was that evil coming from?

I will put a word on it, the evil was essentially *control!* Meaning that those at the top were controlling at all costs every aspect of their citizens' behavior — even controlling their sleep and dreams to some extent. They were able, by attaching electronic devices to the beds the people slept in, to maintain a monitor on what people were dreaming! Not totally, but the beds were wired, okay? If the sleep police didn't approve of what the people were dreaming, they could run a low current through the bed and change it. So the people were forced into being negative so that they could control them entirely. As you know, if people are in a negative space, they are actually much easier to control than if they're in a positive space, because being in a positive space involves creation. Being in a negative space involves destruction and self-destruction. You can easily get people to destroy themselves and others if they're in a negative space.

Okay. Were these controlling beings at the top themselves controlled by someone or something?

I realize that your question really means, was it an evil force?

No, no. I mean, just as on this planet the secret government is sort of a puppet and is controlled off-planet, was there that type of off-world control of . . .

No, no. This negative planet in the system of Sirius had been isolated for so many years by different councils and networks of different planets and so on that there was no chance for any extraterrestrial manipulation whatsoever. The planet was utterly quarantined and isolated. For what it's worth, higher-dimensional aspects of that same planet are still in existence and are benevolent. There was that particular dimension where the planet had to essentially destroy itself in order to maintain some semblance of balance in its other-dimensional aspects. That extreme negative energy was beginning to be a drain on the other-dimensional aspects of the planet.

Okay, so they'll come to 3.0 Earth at 50% positive, 50% negative energy and then eventually work their way back up to the benevolent higher dimensions, then?

That's right. They need to come to Earth because it's going to have a little negativity for them, and they can experience that. And they're moving en masse; they're not reincarnating all over the galaxy, as is normal. They are reincarnating en masse on 3.0-dimensional Earth. That is unheard of, just like what you're doing is unheard of. But something had to be done. You can't have people live whole lives in this extreme situation and expect them to just reincarnate elsewhere and be okay. You've got to have a halfway house for them, and 3.0-dimensional Earth is their halfway house.

But I thought all this time that we needed to help Mother Earth clean up the planet and get rid of all that negativity. So now she's accepted this new burden?

No, she hasn't accepted . . . you have to remember, 3.0-dimensional Earth is not a place you're living in now. It is a place where there are volcanoes, not too extreme, but extreme enough so that these people can stand it. It's a place where there is pollution as you would understand it, but these people can accept that. So you have to understand that what is benevolent to human beings and what isn't benevolent, what is negative to you, is entirely different for them.

For example, 3.0-dimensional Earth, as they are gradually beginning to incarnate there now, is not a place with a great deal of oxygen, and that is essential because oxygen would kill these people! Their bodies are not intended to be bodies of oxygen. You had oxygen so that you could have a shortened life span — I know, you need oxygen to survive, but you don't survive very long here. You understand? *You don't survive very long because you're in school!* Oxygen is basically (talk to any scientist) an oxidizer. It prevents, in the body of a human being, the human being from living too long. You wouldn't want to have a body in school that could live 250 or 1000 years — it's too much! Your soul said, "No, I'll go there for a maximum of 75, 80 years — maybe 100 if I'm having a good life — but that's it. After that I want to go home!"

When the Dimensional Shift Began

When did we leave 3.0 Earth?

You've been away from 3.0 Earth for several years.

How many?

It's hard to measure in your current time; the best I can say is right around 1967.

Oh, that long?

Yeah. But of course, if I measured it from your current time, 1967 was at least several hundred years ago. You see, it's important to mention things like that from time to time, because it's very easy to assume that numbers are a quantity in themselves, when they are really very abstract.

They sound like a relationship!

Indeed! Just threw that in since you're into physics now.

Okay, that's good. One more question: this 40% microwave that's damaging . . .

Your immune system.

Is it simply the microwave that brings TV etc., not the sinister secret government?

Yeah, that's regular microwave, satellite communications, microwave telephone communicatioᴜⱼ and just generally microwave ovens, the works.

Here again, time doesn't make any sense. I can't ask, "When will we arrive at 4.0?" because . . .

It would be totally meaningless. That's why I gave that example of 1967 being a couple hundred years ago, because your sequence of time is totally different. That's part of the reason some people born in third-dimensional Earth just have to end their cycles; it's just too extreme for them. It's a heck of a thing to ask people to stay alive in a passage from one dimension to another; you really have to live all that *stuff* —you know, you're alive and walking and talking, yet you're right in the middle of the astral plane here!

So what is the point? Why did we choose to do that?

It's because you're in Creator school; it's because of material mastery. You needed to see the effects, to experience the consequences of all of your actions as a society, as an individual, as a family and so on. So you needed to have the maximum input of evidence. And one of the best ways to do that is to *live through the experience,* as you know. When someone tells you about some event, it's one thing; but if you live through it, it's entirely another.

31

Reasonable Doubt

Zoosh through Robert Shapiro
October 3, 1995

All right. Zoosh speaking. Now, let me comment briefly on the Simpson case. I have studiously avoided commenting on this case while it has been in the process of adjudication simply because I didn't want to throw my two cents in while all the other cents were blowing in the wind. If you can look at this case as an example of how things work, not how they don't work, then you will be ahead of the game, as they say.

I will explain to you now the basic workings of one of the councils I sometimes interact with. These councils are largely representative of how ideas are passed from the point of creation into some form of experienced reality for various individuals.

The Council of Nine is a group of very wise beings. They are nonphysical from your perspective, but where they exist they experience themselves physically as well as etherically. They are beyond the limits of one or the other; they are all. This is how they are able to make decisions based upon the experience of all beings. They have experienced being every type of being known in their universe, and thus feel they are able to make decisions based upon the full and complete knowledge of all with whom they have interacted.

If an idea is brought to the Council, it is not brought in the form of a witness who presents a case passionately or otherwise; there are no advocates who come in front of the Council; ideas are brought to them through a telepathic means. These ideas are considered by the Council not only mentally but emotionally. They are considered on the basis of all their possible ramifications, what they might do, what they won't do, will it help or will it constrict — all of this. And the ideas must have merit with *all* of the members of the Council, otherwise it doesn't go into application. All members must feel that it has some merit, although each might feel it has a different form of merit. One of them might think it's a good way to test the values and structures of a given society; another might think it is a good application of creation — there's an infinite variety. The main thing is, if they all feel an idea has merit, it is allowed to be applied somewhere to be played out to its completion as far as that society can do so.

An Example: Stress

Let's pick one idea as an example — stress. That's something you all experience. Now, you must admit that stress is, by and large, an unpleasant experience. However, a very small amount of stress does contribute to your motivation to do something. The Council of Nine originally had been given the idea of stress by the Orion Overlord consciousness. This is largely a nonphysical consciousness that was involved in the culmination of the ancient Orion society, which believed then (and still believes to some extent) that stress contributed to the accomplishments of that society. Therefore, the Orion Overlord consciousness put to the Council of Nine the idea that stress might be something worth contributing to another society. Therefore, stress was considered, applied for and granted to your society.

Now, you might say, "But Zoosh, we hardly consider this to be largesse; this kind of grant we can do without!" But you know, really you can't, because a small amount of stress *does* give you motivation. True, a large amount of stress gives you misery, but it also has side effects. So since a small amount of stress is still giving you motivation, this is why you still have stress.

The reason I'm bringing all of this out is this: If an idea has merit, regardless of its side effects, it can be applied and integrated into your polarized society, meaning that *discomfort is being played out here as an applied experience to see if it has any value.* The function of the Council of Nine is to simply apply a creative idea or experience to various other worlds (in this case from Orion, to the Council of Nine, to your world) not only to see if it has value beyond its original experience — it had some value in the ancient Orion system — but because you could take the application.

This is how the Council works: It does not work on the idea of innocence or guilt, as in the Simpson case, but on the principle of something having or not having value. Now, your jury would find Mr. Simpson guilty or not guilty on the basis of the value applied by those words, *guilty* or *not guilty*, to what they heard. In this case the jury system worked very well, because it was not their job to say, "This man is innocent; he had nothing to do with this" or "This man is guilty, and has been an evil man all his life." It was their job to say, "There is a reasonable doubt; a reasonable person could doubt the value of this." Comparing the jury system now to the Council of Nine (you are simply a microcosm of this macrocosm), we can simply say that if a member of the Council of Nine felt doubt that the idea presented to them had value or had merit, the idea would not be applied.

So you see, the jury system works very well, because the defense did not try to say, "Mr. Simpson didn't do this, and didn't have anything to do with it." They focused on the fact that the state had not proven beyond a *reasonable doubt* that Mr. Simpson had done this. This is not an attempt to postadjudicate the case, but rather my attempt to say, "Do you see how the functions of your government were set up by men of vision?"

The United States: A Microcosm of the Councils of Light

The men involved in the creation of your Constitution and in the basic laws and their application in the early years were men of great spirit and vision. It is not known by most people that *80% of your Founding Fathers*, and those who went on to apply what they said for the first 20 or 30 years, *were very spiritual people in positions of leadership.* Not just religious people, but spiritual people, men of vision – and their wives were the same – and they were highly influential.

The United States of America was set up as a spiritual vision designed to be a microcosm of the macrocosmic Councils of Light. It was a nucleus of the idea that the way the Councils of Light work can be applied to an individual government and an individual people (the United States of America). And even with polarity (the Councils of Light do not function in polarity, though they function with the knowledge of polarity) there will be an undying, overall light that prevails. So you might say that the councils (the Council of Nine, the Council of Planets and so on) are equally on trial here, because they're trying to show that the idea of having councils, the basic justice and value and beauty and love of councils, will prevail even in the face of extreme negativity.

So I want you to understand that your system of trial by jury is not a small, insignificant thing. It is not something that is fixed —no, no, no. These people found Mr. Simpson not guilty because the state's evidence was tainted, and also because they had a good reason to doubt that the state's case had value. And when you took the evidence out that was doubtful, it was basically the state saying, "He did it!" and Mr. Simpson and his advocates saying, "No, I didn't." So they decided that that was not grounds to say, "We believe you, Mr. Simpson" or "We believe you, the state," but it was grounds to say, "We have reasonable doubt." That's it; that's all they had to do.

Now, I'm bringing up this "reasonable doubt" and stressing it because it is largely the reason your society exists now. There are many on different councils —even one or two on the Council of Nine —who say that your world has gone far enough with the experiment of good and evil, who say that your world has proven beyond any doubt the inherent goodness of human beings —yes! Even the most evil, the most corrupt human being will (and those close to them can attest to this) surprise you from time to time and do something so good that you'll have a hard time believing they did it. It is this very value, this very goodness within the human being, that has caused various members of all the different councils to state that there is now reasonable doubt whether we should continue with the experiment of discomfort/comfort, of positivity/negativity on Earth. Human beings have shown absolutely, over and over again, that no matter how much negativity they are exposed to, they will not become totally negative. They will always show some example of light.

This is why your world society is now beginning to move to the fourth dimension slowly: you have proved that no matter what the circumstances, light and love will prevail. I hear advocates from the other side saying, "But look at all the wicked things that have been done to people!" and on and on and on, and it's all perfectly valid. Yet the one simple point on the other side is, no matter how grim things get, there still is an underpinning of light and love that all human beings exhibit with some frequency.

So I want you to consider that the Simpson case is not a case of a man who did this or didn't do this. I want you to look at it differently; step back as if you are a member of the Council of Nine and look at it from a distance and say, "Here is a perfect example of people functioning very much like us, the members of the Council of Nine." They felt that this idea of this man being guilty or not guilty was not a factor. They felt that the accusation had reasonable doubt, so they would not consider finding the man guilty. In other words, *the jury behaved very much like the Council of Nine.* Just because an idea has value does not merit its immediate application; we must all feel that its value has been proved. Does this make sense to you?

The Argument That Convinced the Councils

Yes. Will you discuss something about the arguments that went before the sudden push between September 8 and 12 to raise us those ten points closer to the fourth dimension?

Yes. There was a tremendous amount of, not resistance but trepidation (that's the word they want me to use) that at this late date the tried-and-true system of "apply it and see if it works," sink or swim, as it were, should be jumped over. Yet we felt, those of us who prevailed here, "What would be the value to your individual souls to see a glimmer of the value of the higher dimension, compared to what you've been living in, if you did not actually *experience* the higher dimension in some way?" Because your society has already shown that light and love prevail.

Granted, you're not all going to live and die at the same time, but the people on the other side of the issue said, "What if the planet *does* go through a catastrophe? So what if all the people *do* die? They go on even if their bodies die. There is no reason they can't all be herded into one place after death and experience an explanation of what this was all about."

That was a really difficult idea to get around. But we felt (those of us who prevailed) that since you are on Earth to explore material mastery and since you have done spiritual mastery and will do that again, the only way for you to actually see the value in something would be to experience it physically. That is the argument that won the day. To experience the value of something, you have to have *physical* evidence. So it's not only a carrot we're granting you (a reward, as it were, for your hard work) —you get the carrot anyway because you are immortal —but it's an attempt to allow you to have the physical experience of moving through dimensions to something better, of being able to physically, mentally, spiritually and emotionally have the old and restrictive patterns fall away from you, to have the experience of forgetting it (because it's in another world, in the third dimension), and going on into the fourth dimension (or close to it, depending on your cycles and how long you live and so on) as a planetary body of consciousness. Some of you will live to be very close to that.

Our belief was that if you went through this, when you come to the end of your cycle you will not only be able to identify the polarities of the two different worlds, of what was versus what is (the third dimension versus the fourth dimension), but you will also have the physical evidence! I cannot tell you how *much* physical evidence impacts the soul compared to mental thought and theories! You would have the feelings of it all accessible at some level of your consciousness. It was to this exact idea that all the councils said, "All right, then. The idea still has merit." And it was allowed.

So you'll sit in the Null Zone for a while, but it's allowed. And we hope (we cannot guarantee) that the catastrophes and the epidemics and all this business won't happen, because these plans, these corruptions, these happenstances may not have to occur; it has greatly reduced the odds. So, we're hopeful! Let's all stay hopeful.

That's wonderful.

32

The Universe Has Time-Shifted to Preserve the Explorer Race

Zoosh through Robert Shapiro
October 4, 1995

W ell, all right.

Am I correct that this is the most incredible thing that's ever happened to humanity since we came to this dimension?

Well, let's just say that it is the greatest anomaly that you've ever experienced. You know, it's hard to put your finger on what's the best thing or the greatest thing, because there have been so many. But in terms of time anomalies, it's the most extraordinary thing that you've ever experienced as a group – although the shift from dimension to dimension while everybody's still alive is also quite extraordinary . . .

What I'm talking about is the decision to keep five-and-a-half billion beings in their bodies – that's pretty awesome!

It is a major thing. Like I said, it's not an absolute decision, it's a potential. Your friend's predictions still have some bearing, but they do not have the 50/50 likelihood that was approaching – that has been reduced to about one in ten. I feel that that is a worthy risk factor. You might have some small outbreaks, but I feel that what will happen, should these outbreaks take place, is that something will develop that will be quite surprising to the governmental authorities: the worldwide medical computer net will spring into life. Even in places that do not have these facilities, people will fly in bravely to do the work and set up a remote computer station. What governments have been trying to accomplish for years will suddenly be accomplished through the necessity of medical urgency.

In this way the world may have the opportunity to experience not so much a negative, catastrophic epidemic as seeing a worldwide emergency network set up in total cooperation, breaking through all political barriers, and saying "Hey, we've got to stop this. We can do it, we're going to make it happen." That would put the whole thing in a positive light. Granted, there would be some losses, but there would be a major positive effect. It wouldn't be just a catastrophic vortex everybody falls into. disappearing into some other existence. I personally didn't see the value in that. I want you to get every last shred of value here for your experience so that when all is over you'll be able to say, "Well, hey, we did it ourselves!"

September 10, 1995

What was the mechanics, dynamics, physics – how did you move us 10 degrees? When did you move it first?

On September 10th (as you know, the number 10 does have certain mystical value). . . . This was accomplished through extraordinary means. We didn't move the planet. We moved everything else.

Say how.

Well, we're talking well beyond quantum mechanics here. We asked everyone in your known universe – and we have the capacity to do that, my personality and my friends – if they would be willing to experience a brief shift in time-space that would not affect their cultures negatively, but would allow the absorption of Earth and all her denizens into Earth's Null Zone (they all know what's going on here) to avoid a catastrophic end to the genetic experiment on Earth, of which you are all the result (see *The Explorer Race*). They all said instantaneously that they would allow this. You see, if you can't bring the man to the mountain . . .

. . . you bring the mountain to the man.

That's right. So this is how it was done – everything else moved. In this way we were able to cause you to experientially move ahead without forcing the move. If we had moved you ahead . . .

The planet Earth? Are we talking solar system or just planet?

No, if we had moved you, the planet Earth . . .

It would have moved separately from the solar system?

Yes, because it doesn't move separately. The whole purpose of this is not for your solar system; other planets in the system do not need to do anything; they're fine. The crux of the matter is Earth. So Earth is moving dimensionally, not in space but in time.

I see, in dimensional . . .

In the time-dimension. As I said, Earth stayed here . . . ah, a diagram . . .

Yes, a diagram please.

Now, this is not clear but you can describe it to the artist. Here is what Earth was. For Earth to move to the fourth dimension she has to expand. Here is your universe, roughly. I'm putting a circle around it but of course there isn't one. We want to show the universe moving and the Earth staying relatively the same, so since Earth is expanding we need to show that the universe sort of drags her along. This is a spherical view. If you'd rather have a chart, however [drawing again] . . .

So moving to the next dimension is expanding?

Oh, yes.

It's not moving, it's expanding?

Oh, yes. Relatively speaking, fourth-dimensional Earth (Terra) is larger. Just like fifth-dimensional Earth (Terra) is larger. That's basically how it's done, so that the spaces between the molecules are larger. Now, it isn't exactly like that, because obviously that can be perceived and measured, and if you're going to have the dimensions . . .

So the space between the molecules is larger and the vibration of the molecules is faster – that's basically what you're saying?

Basically, yes. It's a little bit more complicated than that, but that's the best way I can put it. Instead of this being a spherical chart, if we can indicate that here's the Earth and here's the universe around the Earth, and the whole universe just goes [he makes cracking sound] like that. . . . The universe moves, it's like . . .

But how can the universe expand us by moving?

At some point the universe moves. This is the fourth dimension; you're not there yet, but we'll put that there for the goal. That's where you're going. Viewing this as a physical chart, the Earth is a marble and the universe is a plate. If the plate moves, the marble rolls. Does that make any sense to you?

Okay, the Null Zone is around where we are now, and the outside is the fifth . . . I'm trying to get a picture that somebody can see. If you have to expand something . . .

If the Earth cannot move to the Null Zone, then the Null Zone must move to the Earth.

So that's what the universe did.

That's essentially it. Instead of the object coming to the mountain, the mountain was literally moved relative to where the Earth was . . .

So we may not have to have a drawing.

I would recommend not, because it's much easier to create your own picture.

I'll let you go on, but what kind of headline do we have here? What is the honest truth? "Council of Nine Allows Genetic Experiment to Continue in Face of Catastrophe"? What headline will sum all of this up?

A moment . . . . What's going on here is that the Explorer Race — you — is given a second chance. The merit of the experiment was proven in discussion with the Nine, amongst others, and it was shown to still have value for you to remain physical. That's it.

Who Was Involved?

Okay, Council of Nine, Council of Planets, what other? Council of Light?

The Interdimensional Council of Focus, the Augmented Orion-Pleiadian-Sirian-Andromedan Symposium —you know, there's thousands here, but I'll just tick off a few.

I just want a sense of how awesome this is.

Yes. The Integrated Conceptual Mind Research Council (this would have to do with the mental powers of the universe), the Library of Consciousness (anything that's ever been thought is there), the Overlords of Creation, the Creator . . . what else do you want?

That's enough. You said "and thousands of others." Were they all telepathic?

Yes, it was all done telepathically in a flashed emergency message, suggesting that they suspend what they were doing for the moment.

. . . and concern themselves with this.

This is how it's done. You can make your own headline, but this is all done because you are the Explorer Race, and the bottom line of the Explorer Race is that they must explore.

To achieve the goals of the Explorer Race, you must be able to explore using all of your senses. Then you can integrate all of the wisdom and knowledge from these senses to form a synthesis of knowledge and wisdom that you can tap for the future. You not only have the physical evidence for yourselves, but when this body of knowledge (which is a synthesis of all beings who go through this time from the third to the fourth dimension) is encompassed, it will eventually be experiential. This means that the races you will help to guide through this experience – the Pleiadians, the Sirians who will come to third-dimensional Earth, and many others who will go through various versions of this –will, because of the physical nature of this body of knowledge, be able to tap into it to the degree that is comfortable to them and feel how you did it, even though what they will do will be different.

It won't be as extreme as your experience in most cases, with the exception of the negative Sirians. For them it will be something like a show-and-tell. It's not enough for you to say to them, "Look, here we are, we did it." There needs to be something they can see, smell, taste, feel, sense (for those who go beyond your five senses) not only the variety of possibilities, but perhaps more significantly, the intent. When a race or a person is going through something, the important thing to that person is why.

How many times have you asked yourself when you were going through something, "Why? Why do I have to go through this?" How often would you have been comforted to know why? You can identify with that. And to have this be physical, synthesized – not only the body of experience but all of the explanations, all of the understandings –would be a wonderful thing for any civilization. They could then, by understanding why for you humans (which is exactly what your historians do now, to say nothing of your anthropologists and so on) and why it was for some other culture, be able to extrapolate why it might be for them.

Had Earth humans all died, as they would have, this would not have been available.

That's right. That understanding would simply have not been available to those other cultures.

So you put that argument forward . . .

That was one of them, yes. It was very persuasive, especially with the Nine, because what they're really into is the application of ideas to one culture, which may benefit all other cultures in some way. So they were very persuaded.

One more key question. The negative Sirians, then, are the next class to use Mother Earth as a school? The next Explorer Race?

Yes, they are. And because of where they're coming from, they will have not only the motivation to achieve higher-dimensional aspirations, but they will really know the down-and-dirty, nitty-gritty consequences of going the other way. They make a very likely replacement for you.

Okay, thank you.

33

Made It through the "Phew"

YHWH through Arthur Fanning
October 4, 1995

So you beings have made it through the "phew."
Well, as a good reporter I'd like the whole story.

Well, it's not over yet, so I can't tell you the end.

Okay. But tell about the fact that we're allowed to still be here, that the people and the planet didn't die, that we got moved up.

You were rescued, in a sense. In truth, what we did, we altered your consciousness here. You are spiritual beings, indeed, lightbeings, and your consciousness creates. You were falling into an arena of overpowering victimhood with regards to many things.

Those many things were disease and earthquakes and floods and things like that?

And more. We shifted, we literally told you what you could not think about any longer. We told you what you couldn't dwell on any longer . . . in one manner, from another perspective, in your light forces. In that command, we allowed you to create a shift in your own consciousness where you saw through the veil. In this I mean, what you say, not physical, yet more; more of your light forces forced their way into your bodies, so you *knew* more. And you knew not to get caught into the magnetics of the thing, we will say that.

Of what thing?

The magnetics of the victimhood. So when you knew that, when your light was there, it was much easier to convince your light it was okay to shift than the ego portions of your personality. That weekend

[September 8-10] we were doing it all over the planet. We were pushing more light into the bodies – that was the purpose of that meditation [done in Chapter 26]: bringing more light into this universal system so that the light, as it forced its way through, would *understand* it does not have to be influenced by magnetics of each environment – that includes thought patterns now, because they are magnetic and electrical in nature. Belief systems. So that is what happened. That was part of my job being sent here, know you? Where your Father says to go, I go, and that is what we did.

Now, it only helped a little bit. It got you over the wall, so to speak over the hump. Yet it is very easy for humans to go into their despair and this, that, and their little whine mode, know you what I mean? Overwhelm[ed], sometimes, by events. Not necessarily by their spiritual nature (I will use that word now), by their god forces. We have spoken of for a long time how you are becoming gods here, how your responsibility is to be caught not up in the drama, be more caught up in your own *becoming*.

Now, one of the things you face when you become is this idea of death, personality loss, persona changing. Somehow you think you're going to be different. Well, you will be, but not as dramatically as you think it will be.

We've spoken of before how it is necessary to forgive, know you what I mean? Everyone! Past, present, future. Not simply words now, not simply words.

I have not only a reputation for being warlike and angry, etc., etc. I have many reputations. One of them is protector. Now, from the perspective of those that I am protecting others from, it would seem that I am warlike. But I deal with the *Will of the Father* (your words now) completely – that is all. I'm not influenced by personality or your wishes, so to speak.

Now, within each, beings on the planet, everyone here, there is a desire to know God, there is that desire. At some level it is there. These shiftings that are going to continue are planned to create that awakening within *you*, each one. I have spoken before that the planet will not be destroyed, that evolution will continue here, that this *is* to be a planet of peace. It is so! It will be so, in your words. It is already so from another perspective.

Now, one of the most difficult phases that you have to go through yet is this idea of manifestation, the power of it, and your place with it. The month of September was the month to . . . we're going to say, learn how to overcome this fear of death, this concept [that] death is an event not controllable by you. Your lightbodies knew this thing, and were . . . well, I will say, you were empowered [with] three to four times of light in your own being, physically, so you could handle the thought forms, the magnetics that were involved in consciousness at that level before the shift. Your month of December is to be a month where the same energies are going to begin to apply to involve the concept of manifestation, to invoke it within you. So you're going to be forced to manifest. Not in your traditional sense. *Really* manifest.

The armadas are great around here now. The councils that are involved are focused here now — many, many. The control of these councils, all of them that are involved here, we're going to say are under my jurisdiction. When I first arrived here I made a statement that was rather outrageous. That is: "It is my planet. I want it back." You're in the process now of becoming into *backness.* [He chuckles.] Everyone is going home. Now, I've told you before I'm very sneaky. All beings are involved in this return, all beings upon the planet, within their consciousness, spiritually speaking — their lightbe-ingness. Now, as the game gets more intense, there are going to be those that will be satisfied to accept a level of understanding where they feel comfortable — what they term their heaven. You are literally moving into superconsciousness. That means you will develop your own heaven, what you *think* it is, and play there until you learn there's more — more, more, more.

These months of your October, November are . . . well, not so much your November (there's going to be a little speed-up there, too) but primarily your October, is a leveling off of the energies we played with in your September. Give you a little break, but be same. In your normal day you will see time shifting. It is more appropriate to say you're realizing time doesn't exist, that it is all one moment. So you could say time is collapsing, or you can say time is stacking. It is a movement to oneness. Now, if you've taken some of the other things I've said before — how there were some beings playing with time, know you, back-forth, back-forth, and we said, "Well, we understand that; we're shifting their scale so they don't know where they're landing" — so we're doing the same with you in one manner, only in what you would term a spiral effect. Know you? An upward thing.

What you're not aware of yet . . . (this is not quite for publication at this time, but I'll say it in a manner so you beings can understand) I've spoken it is my planet, I want it back. And it is known throughout all creation this is so. All those now (because I threw such a fit) throughout creation are helping me get it back because they've seen what goes on here. Now, I've talken to your Father, your Mother, the energies of Source . . . and He has agreed it is okay because it is my fantasy, you see? When that happened, all the beings in the heavens became on my side because they figured if it's okay with the Source, it's okay with them, too.

Well, let us print that, because it relates to what Zoosh said about how all of you went to all the councils and all over creation and all the way to the Creator to get permission to do this.

Let me see . . . I have to see the effect here. What I will say is this: One of the things you don't understand is that I have learned a great deal from my brother Lucifer, indeed? Now I am using some of *his* games to complete here, indeed, to get back things. And I also understand that he had permission, you see, before, in the beginning what you say. So what I did, I say, "Well, he go get permission; me, too!" I got permission. Now that I have permission, I'm not giving it back (from your words)!

This is so dramatic. That's why I'm pursuing this. Humanity would have ended?

As you would know it, indeed, completely. But you would still have thought that you were . . . well, let's put it this way: we've already made a declaration before that it wasn't going to happen that way. There was this setup in a manner to see if you could bail yourselves out. That wasn't working too well. So instead of starting a whole new genetic pool and another game here, somewhere else, we got permission to shift.

So are we beyond the epidemics now?

There'll be a little bit of it, but no big deal. What you have to concern yourself now more with is . . . well, we'll talk about this a little later. There's going to become within humanity aberrations of the physical brain, of the mind, of the thought processes. You've been told that God walks slowly, indeed? Now you're becoming gods. That means you beings must move in a slow, delicate manner. You've been told that competitive behavior, controlling behavior, are going to go, and you still do this thing, you beings on the planet here. With this increase in energy and the increase in your spiritual forces, if you do not practice delicacy, which means the heart chakra open, and compassion (because compassion is a word not only for others, it is for you and your physical vehicle now), because these energies are coming in and they're very . . . how say you? They are energies. They simply come, and it's up to you what to do with them.

It's like you have a glass and you want to get some water, know you? It's much easier to go to a faucet to have your water than it is to hold a glass under a waterfall, know you? Waterfall knock glass right out of your hand. What is happening with these energies is like waterfall, so you have to have your meridians centered and your chakras open so you can handle these things appropriately. The understanding of karma will be realized. Not as dogma of it – the *understanding* of it, that you are now moving into a phase where you are literally creating your karma day by day and facing it the next day by day, so you don't have to die the physical form to play karma, come back, be born. If these things are working the way they are in your bodies now, you can see that this lifetime can be expanded – that you don't have to live your sixty years, die, come back and do another sixty, die, come back – to get the understanding of karmic relationships, nor magnetics, nor thought patterns, nor ecstasy. You can do them now. The only reason you don't is what another thinks, and you allow that to stop you. You will never become that way.

When I first created these sections, sectors, portions of existence, it was to provide arenas, many, for those that were caught in the doubt when Lucifer proclaimed himself – arenas of self-becoming, arenas of lights remembering lights, arenas of ecstasy to learn to understand to overcome this great thing. For you must understand, this explosion, we'll call it, this great force called Lucifer, was doing what he was asked to do, and he did it very well. This has been going on for eons. Now you're at the point of change, within the understanding called the density third dimension, fourth dimension, within that understanding. You are working right through it. So it gives me great pleasure, ecstasy in a manner, to see that my plan worked from eons ago. So it is a completion, in a sense, for I, do you understand? I have made a statement before that I have never been defeated. That's why I be sent in this time – and to reclaim. I have reclaimed. Just the way it is.

Definition of Gravity

Would you agree with Zoosh's assessment that we're at this moment at 3.47, between third and fourth dimensions?

You're talking about the planet itself, or general population?
I didn't know there was a difference.

There is an intermingling now. There are some beings that are playing, literally walking on your planet, playing fifth dimension. It's simply a matter of where you stand in relation to your gravitational forces – that is all [a] dimension is.

Your physical sense of gravity on your planet Earth has no effect upon the body as you play die, indeed? You float through realms, etc., etc., and you understand the ability of thought, indeed, better and your dream state, etc. Indeed? As the harmonics within the Earth's patterns itself changes, then you have an ability to vibrate what you term higher and move into a place of ecstasy, we'll call it. Gravity is literally a force of right angles, ninety degrees. It's not a vertical force, pull you down. It is a ninety-degree shift of thought lowered here that works (you simply forgot that) through the chakras, through your vortices – primarily what you call the pineal system, your crown chakra and your pineal gland. You shift the thought your ninety degrees, you move dimensionally. Body physical moves.

Now there are many . . . you are on a sphere, indeed? Know you? You're on a sphere, the ball, your planet Earth. You are a sphere. Know you how we have done some rather amazing things in our meditations that affect the planet? Literally change the orbit of the Moon; literally create peace; and change what you call the attitudes here what you call within the physical; create fun with meditations. When you meditate and align your being, you may allow yourself to think "ninety degrees," or you would say . . . instead of looking with your eyes this way, you look out the side of your head – that is ninety degrees, indeed, at this level, this physical. You could find yourself in another reality. You could find yourself on the other side of the building. By "other reality" I mean a shifting within your third-dimensional context from place to place. That means you have become a fourth-dimensional being, fifth. Well, fifth is more appropriately using the mind to alter gravity, to understand. It's not really an alteration, it's flying with it. That's fifth-dimensional activity.

There are some beings on your planet now that can do this thing. Do you understand? They need to be able to do it, and create within the collective consciousness the abilities or the thought forms that it can be completed while still physical. Know you? Now, once this has been done, completed by one in this density, it is available to all – but they must tap into it, know you? That is where you get your guru thing, beings going to the guru so the guru teaches you how to tap into, tap into, tap into this, that, the other. The more that do this, the thought form is bigger, so it's *more* available. And then beings have access to it in their dream state and it spreads.

Now I'm going to give you . . . I'm not going to create a distortion here, I'm going to give you my perspective on this 3.4 and 3.7 thing. What is happening is the thought forms available, the size, we'll call it – you beings are into linear – the amount of thought form available is larger than it has been before. More beings practicing their meditations, etc., know you, having their experiences. This gives the *per-ceived* effect of being 3.4 to 3.7, etc., etc. Know you what I mean? If you use your mathematics you are going to create a linear under-standing that will limit you. This is not a mathematical concept. And I'm going to appropriately acknowledge Zoosh here at this time. It is more that you are becoming influenced, you are understanding color —vibrational frequency changing, color, and the sounds that you hear in your body —you're utilizing them. You won't care what the numbers are.

I know, but it's a great way to understand what's happening, to put it in perspective.

That is true. Indeed. But if you allow yourselves to keep focusing on that frequency, you won't allow yourself to understand another frequency. However, it is appropriate to share this information be-cause what it does is, those that aren't even attuned to the possibility of these abilities will allow themselves to be pulled higher by these . . . I'm going to call them fractal components. Little bitty magnets.

Now, what is this song: "We've Only Just Begun," hmm?

Well, thank you —and thank creation, and thank all the beings that we still have something to go on with.

And you, too —don't forget to thank yourself. Indeed? Because it pushes, indeed it pushes. It is taking a while, but the fact that you're doing what you're doing with what you term your magazine, etc., and your books there, you have exposed other beings to these energies, to these procedures, to these becomings, and that made them avail-able within the shift. They were gathered up when we played this thing. Each took part at their level of understanding —nothing was forced. Indeed? And they all shifted, the planet shifted. There were enough to do it.

So that's why I want to get this out. I mean it's so awesome, it's so incredible. The fact that people should just go by and never know that it happened —that's sad, you know? I mean, let's celebrate it, be aware of it.

There's a little celebration be coming up here, indeed. And it's all right because for some it might be disconcerting; they can know they made the first step. There's a much bigger one coming.

Yeah, but we're still here to make it. That's the key.

That is true. That is the truth. But you were going to be here anyway. We would have had to do what we call recycle some of you rather quickly, know you? Quick recycling. In one way that's what happened —you shifted so fast, you didn't know you shifted. A lot of your ego went, got changed. A lot of your personalities changed. Your December is another one. We have a lot of washing to do before we finish your '96, and your '96 is going to be an outrageous year. Remember always that you are gods playing here; you're becoming. And that is the prime purpose here. Know you Zoosh is very excited indeed about the accomplishment, because many thought it couldn't be done. Indeed? Even in their lighthearted conversations many were ready to blow up the planet, indeed, start over. Know you? And that is all right, that is a limited understanding. But we went through that thing. Know you what I mean? They didn't realize who they were dealing with . . . well, he has to keep notes, know you?

Yeah. But it was the soul; he explained it was the concept of the soul — that we need that feeling, the wisdom of it . . .

That is true.

. . . so that other civilizations later could tap into our experience.

Well, that you build the thought form that makes it available so they can overcome this doubt thing caused by Lucifer; that is true. Indeed. That is exactly what was going on. You are the diamond of this experiment here on your planet, you beings. You've been squeezed so hard now, you're becoming brilliant. So you're doing it in this sector, I'll say, so that other sectors will have the information available unto them. And even what you term the Brotherhood of Light, because they will get wisdom from this thing, too, because they haven't been physical, not all of them. Know you? They have the wisdom, the knowing of it, but they don't have the experience. So you get bigger badges.

That's what Zoosh explained, that the mental concept is not the same as the feeling of it. That's what we embodied and that's why we were so valuable.

That is true. And that's why I was sent, because of the name called the protector and other names. The completer, also.

So it happened on the 10th of September, right?

It happened what you would term . . . there was a three-day period of time it was working — four, actually [September 8-11].

So did it start on that Sunday of the meditation [in the intensive]?

It started the Friday night before, and it started pushing, pushing, pushing. Recall you when we worked? And we're still working, know you? Because of the amount of movement and what was done, there was great awe created in the heavens because this has never been done before. You've earned the respect, human here. Now, in one sense you can say it's completed, if you want to stay at that level. That's why I petitioned each one here before. I petitioned others within the councils, because when *you* move, those councils move. Everything is going to move, humanity, when you move . . . *if* they desire to move further, to know more. This is including galaxies you don't even know about. There was agreement; everyone wants to move. Well, we're going to use you as booster rocket. Now, you're going to get it in your December, and that is another reason everyone is watching here. It's not over yet. But you have gone over the hump. You've gone over this big . . . uhm, being at the mercy of events that you seemingly cannot control. You've . . . one manner, become, know you? Become! And you've declared it in your lightbodies.

Prepare for Structural Changes

What can people do to prepare for December?

They would be wise to allow themselves little bit of meditation each day; 10 of your moments sit down and shut up and listen, and attune to your higher self, and your great Mother, I'll call it, that energy. Attune, listen. That does not mean argument. It means listen, because the physical form now and the mental now . . . this is the other thing. The physical form is going to go through some changes. The mental processes now have to be aligned. This is where the distortion is going to come: where you are working to hold thought within a structure that is right now literally in the process of changing. You are then confused and you'll go back to the structure as it be, and it's not there, so you'll try to make it there. And you become even more confused and frustrated and controlled and lost! See? So you have to understand the structure is changing. All of it, all over the planet. And no structure defined yet. So how do you do this? You [be] thought and you move into a flow and let the flow create a structure; and you'll find yourself at peace, what you term in a manner sitting on a lotus flower where nothing bothers you, where you know it's okay. You see?

We've told you before, what you call three to four years before here, and others, [that] your structures are going to change. They are going to come down.

And that's both the walls within us and the institutions outside us, right?

Indeed! Because of the thought processes here. Many, many changes coming upon your planet. There are those that want to hold on, know you, to the old systems. Those are the ones that are going to be in more confusion in these . . . we'll call it months of change.

Now, your September was a great month of change, energywise. *Shift!* Know you? And it's still having an effect. It affected beings that had been studying, more quickly – got it first. Others are going to still get it through October, November; they haven't had it yet, know you? So it's still there, it's not dissipating. Getting used to work with this thing. Your December, more! So then it overflows into your year next. January, it'll be an outrageous month.

So there be a lot of movement now, a lot of power becoming, a lot of christs walking, a lot of beings seeing that it is more appropriate to be centered all of the time, all of the time. That it's easier. And it just be a process of learning this thing, know you? If you move into a place where you're off-center, don't look at others that you be off-center. Simply excuse yourself, take a moment and center, literally. Because what is happening now, there's a great mental energy coming in. The soul knows how to handle it because we've been building these things in you beings that we've been working with. Know you what I mean? *Open the heart chakra. Power.* This [soul] will know, and it be easy for you, for those that I have worked with and for those that have been involved in what you call the meditations and the readings. It'll be easy because you *inwardly* understand what we're doing.

In a moment, move into center, peace. No judgment – none. So there be sort of fun for you. And as you do that each time, you become more power, more power, more power, more power. Because the sixth seal wants to open dramatically in everyone now. Your December is going to create this movement, so you'll see things, what you say "see." And once you start seeing them you'll see the rays, etc., and you have the ability to manipulate the rays. Now, the reason we haven't accelerated this is, you would have taken that ability to manipulate the rays and put it into this old structure. There's not going to *be* a structure. It's shifting! So you're going to allow you to create new, what it is, what be termed your fantasy. You understand? That's what's going on.

Awesome. And the outer structures that are going to change are political, economic, governmental, everything, right?

Whole bunch. All of 'em. Everything. Now, you must remember that when beings have their structures changed, they move into fear, and a lot of those that are in power will become very fearful, very angry, confused; and a frightened tiger, one wounded, is very difficult enemy.

So we're going to have some secret government control and some of the unpleasant stuff that has been talked about?

Well, it's not as much now as it used to be. Know you? Just allow you to become empowered.

We didn't even ask about how the secret government's handling this. I forgot about them. What's happening with that?

They're having a grand time. [He laughs.]

Are they really? Becoming enlightened, huh?

Well, they don't have a choice. They're confused now. Even (you can print this) in their meetings, in their groupings, etc., etc., even those that don't know that they're with those of the secret government, many are being able to have . . . they're being able to see how confused they are in their speech. Their speech is beginning to make *no* sense. All of their inner wisdom . . . how say you? You say, all of the subconscious things they've been hiding, know you, [are] going to start coming out inadvertently, know you? They will say, "I didn't say that; I didn't mean that." It's going to be very public, you'll see it.

That's great.

The Light Inside Will Play Tricks

It *is* great. And they think they be confused, that someone is playing trick on them. It is someone. Be I. Be the light be inside them. Know you what I said, I be there. So they be saying these things that they think are secret, know you?

Right out in public.

What you term "faux pas." There'll be many, many, many.

Oh, that's wonderful!

It is humor. So they're getting moved too. Changes.

Well, that's one good thing. I've been too busy to think about them.

Indeed. It's more empowering not to.

I know. But yet you said I'm supposed to.

It is important to be aware, however.

And let other people know what's going on.

Indeed. Going to get more exciting for everyone. More empowering. Some of you will actually be able to see what your applied thought through the body does. Literally you'll see a fantasy — that's what it is when you're in physical — here, and you'll see it merge with a collective consciousness of collective thought forms (same quality, know you) and then begin to precipitate as an event. You'll see how you do it. You won't have to be out of your body to do this thing. You're becoming overlords in one manner, but beyond that.

Compassionate ones this time.

I'll make sure of that.

Okay. Oh, it's wonderful, it's just wonderful. Okay, what else do the readers need to know?

It is important that they understand how precious their bodies are, this time. And that meditation, even if it's only for five or ten moments a day, sit quiet, meditate on the Father that's within you, and listen. Five moments a day, ten moments, will help you through this thing. The meditation is simply focus on the love of God. It doesn't matter what name you use. Indeed. Focus on the source of love that is that is there within you, focus on that thing. And it'll draw more power, more power, more power, more power, more power. Don't focus on the words or any of this thing. When you use your mantra and you sit in mantra all day, you are using power another developed. You'll get your own mantra. Focus on love inside you, inside you. And so the mantra you get might be the same as another. At least you understand how you got it, do you understand? Indeed, you can tell them that. Tell them that I love them, too.

BOOK MARKET

A reader's guide to the extraordinary books we publish, print and market for your enLightenment.

NEW!
THE EXPLORER RACE

Robert Shapiro/Zoosh

In this expansive overview, Zoosh explains, "You are the Explorer Race. Learn about your journey before coming to this Earth, your evolution here and what lies ahead." Topics range from ETs and UFOs to relationships.

$24.95 Softcover 650p
ISBN 0-929385-38-1

BEHOLD A PALE HORSE

William Cooper

Former U.S. Naval Intelligence Briefing Team Member reveals information kept secret by our government since the 1940s. UFOs, the J.F.K. assassination, the Secret Government, the war on drugs and more by the world's leading expert on UFOs.

$25.00 Softcover 500p
ISBN 0-929385-22-5

POISONS THAT HEAL

Eileen Nauman DHM (UK)

Homeopathy is all that remains to protect us from the deadly superbugs and viruses that modern medicine has failed to turn back. Learn how to protect yourself and your family against the coming Ebola virus and other deadly diseases.

$14.95 Softcover 270p
ISBN 0-929385-62-4

♦ **BOOKS BY LIGHT TECHNOLOGY RESEARCH**

SHINING THE LIGHT

Revelations about the Secret Government and their connections with ETs. Information about renegade ETs mining the Moon, ancient Pleiadian warships, underground alien bases and many more startling facts.

$12.95 Softcover 208p
ISBN 0-929385-66-7

SHINING THE LIGHT
BOOK II

Continuing the story of the Secret Government and alien involvement. Also information about the Photon Belt, cosmic holograms photographed in the sky, a new vortex forming near Sedona, and nefarious mining on sacred Hopi land.

$14.95 Softcover 422p
ISBN 0-929385-70-5

SHINING THE LIGHT
BOOK III

The focus shifts from the dastardly deeds of the Secret Government to humanity's role in creation. The Earth receives unprecedented aid from Creator and cosmic councils, who recently lifted us beyond the third dimension to avert a great catastrophe.

$14.95 Softcover 512p
ISBN 0-929385-71-3

COLOR MEDICINE
The Secrets of Color Vibrational Healing
Charles Klotsche

A practitioner's manual for restoring blocked energy to the body systems with specific color wavelengths by the founder of "The 49th Vibrational Technique."

$11.95 Softcover 114p   ISBN 0-929385-27-6

CRYSTAL CO-CREATORS

A fascinating exploration of 100 forms of crystals, describing specific uses and their purpose, from the spiritual to the cellular, as agents of change. It clarifies the role of crystals in our awakening.

$14.95 Softcover 288p   ISBN 0-929385-40-3

NEW!
THE ALIEN PRESENCE
Evidence of secret government contact with alien life forms.
Ananda

Documented testimony of the cover-up from a U.S. president's meeting to the tactics of suppression. The most complete information yet available.

$19.95 Softcover   ISBN 0-929385-64-0

REACH FOR US
Your Cosmic Teachers and Friends

Messages from Teachers, Ascended Masters and the Space Command explain the role they play in bringing the Divine Plan to the Earth now!

$14.95 Softcover 204p   ISBN 0-929385-69-1

THE SEDONA VORTEX GUIDEBOOK
by 12 channels

200-plus pages of channeled, never-before-published information on the vortex energies of Sedona and the techniques to enable you to use the vortexes as multidimensional portals to time, space and other realities.

$14.95 Softcover 236p   ISBN 0-929385-25-X

◆ BOOKS BY DOROTHY ROEDER

THE NEXT DIMENSION IS LOVE
Ranoash

As speaker for a civilization whose species is more advanced, the entity describes the help they offer humanity by clearing the DNA. An exciting vision of our possibilities and future.

$11.95 Softcover 148p   ISBN 0-929385-50-0

BOOK MARKET

A reader's guide to the extraordinary books we publish, print and market for your enLightenment.

F THE ASCENSION BOOK SERIES by JOSHUA DAVID STONE, Ph.D.

BEYOND ASCENSION
How to Complete the Seven Levels of Initiation

Brings forth new channeled material that demystifies the 7 levels of initiation and how to attain them. It contains new information on how to open and anchor our 36 chakras.

$14.95 Softcover 279p   ISBN 0-929385-73-X

ASCENSION-ACTIVATION TAPES

How to anchor and open your 36 chakras and build your light quotient at a speed never dreamed possible. Scores of new ascension techniques and meditations directly from the galactic and universal core.

ASCENSION-ACTIVATION MEDITATION TAPE:
- S101
- S102
- S103 $12.00 each
- S104
- S105

Set of all 5 tapes $49.95

SOUL PSYCHOLOGY
Keys to Ascension

Modern psychology deals exclusively with personality, ignoring the dimensions of spirit and soul. This book provides ground-breaking theories and techniques for healing and self-realization.

$14.95 Softcover 276p   ISBN 0-929385-56-X

THE ASCENDED MASTERS LIGHT THE WAY
Keys to Spiritual Mastery from Those Who Achieved It

Lives and teachings of 40 of the world's greatest saints and spiritual beacons provide a blueprint for total self-realization. Guidance from those who mastered the secrets in their lifetimes.

$14.95 Softcover 258p   ISBN 0-929385-58-6

THE COMPLETE ASCENSION MANUAL
How to Achieve Ascension in This Lifetime

A synthesis of the past and guidance for ascension. An extraordinary compendium of practical techniques and spiritual history. Compiled from research and channeled information.

$14.95 Softcover 297p   ISBN 0-929385-55-1

HIDDEN MYSTERIES
An Overview of History's Secrets from Mystery Schools to ET Contacts

Explores the unknown and suppressed aspects of Earth's past; reveals new information on the ET movement and secret teachings of the ancient Master schools.

$14.95 Softcover 333p   ISBN 0-929385-57-8

LIGHT TECHNIQUES
That Trigger Transformation

Light Techniques

The Trigger Transformation

VYWAMUS
Channeled by Janet McClure
Edited by Lillian Harben

Expanding the Heart Center . . . Launching your Light . . . Releasing the destructive focus . . . Weaving a Garment of Light . . . Light Alignment & more. A wonderfully effective tool for using Light to transcend. Beautiful guidance!

$11.95 Softcover 145p   ISBN 0-929385-00-4

AHA! The Realization Book
w/ Lillian Harben

The Realization Book

AHA!

If you are mirroring your life in a way that is not desirable, this book can help you locate murky areas and make them "suddenly . . . crystal clear." Readers will find it an exciting step-by-step path to changing and evolving lives.

$11.95 Softcover 120p

THE SOURCE ADVENTURE

THE SOURCE ADVENTURE

VYWAMUS
Channeled by Janet McClure
Edited by Lillian Harben

Life is discovery, and this book is a journey of discovery "to learn, to grow, to recognize the opportunities — to be aware." It asks the big question, "Why are you here?" and leads the reader to examine the most significant questions of a lifetime.

$11.95 Softcover 157p   ISBN 0-929385-06-3

SANAT KUMARA
Training a Planetary Logos

The Story of
SANAT KUMARA
Training a Planetary Logos

Vywamus
Channeled and Edited by
Janet McClure

How was the beauty of this world created? The answer is in the story of Earth's Logos, the great being Sanat Kumara. A journey through his eyes as he learns the real-life lessons of training along the path of mastery.

$11.95 Softcover 179p   ISBN 0-929385-17-9

SCOPES OF DIMENSIONS

SCOPES OF DIMENSIONS

How To Experience Multi-Dimensional Reality

VYWAMUS
Channeled by Janet McClure
Edited by Lillian Harben

Vywamus explains the process of exploring and experiencing the dimensions. He teaches an integrated way to utilize the combined strengths of each dimension. It is a how-to guidebook for living in the multidimensional reality that is our true evolutionary path.

$11.95 Softcover 176p   ISBN 0-929385-09-8

NEW!
EVOLUTION:
OUR LOOP OF EXPERIENCING

EVOLUTION
OUR LOOP OF EXPERIENCING

Vywamus, Djwhal Khul,
The Tibetan, and Atlanto
Channeled by Janet McClure

Vywamus, Djwhal Khul & Atlanto

Your four bodies, the Tibetan Lesson series, the Twelve Rays, the Cosmic Walk-in and others. All previously unpublished channelings by Janet McClure.

$14.95 Softcover   ISBN 0-929385-54-3

$11.95 Softcover 120p   ISBN 0-929385-14-4

BOOK MARKET

A reader's guide to the extraordinary books we publish, print and market for your enLightenment.

◆ BOOKS BY LYNN BUESS

CHILDREN OF LIGHT, CHILDREN OF DENIAL

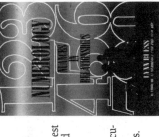

In his fourth book Lynn calls upon his decades of practice as counselor and psychotherapist to explore the relationship between karma and the new insights from ACOA/ Co-dependency writings.

$8.95 Softcover 150p

ISBN 0-929385-15-2

NUMEROLOGY FOR THE NEW AGE

An established standard, explicating for contemporary readers the ancient art and science of symbol, cycle, and vibration. Provides insights into the patterns of our personal lives. Includes life and personality numbers.

$9.85 Softcover 262p

ISBN 0-929385-31-4

NUMEROLOGY: NUANCES IN RELATIONSHIPS

Provides valuable assistance in the quest to better understand compatibilities and conflicts with a significant other. A handy guide for calculating your/his/her personality numbers.

$12.65 Softcover 239p

ISBN 0-929385-23-3

THE STORY OF THE PEOPLE
Eileen Rota

An exciting history of our coming to Earth, our traditions, our choices and the coming changes, it can be viewed as a metaphysical adventure, science fiction or the epic of all of us brave enough to know the truth. Beautifully written and illustrated.

$11.95 Softcover 209p

ISBN 0-929385-51-9

THE NEW AGE PRIMER
Spiritual Tools for Awakening

A guidebook to the changing reality, it is an overview of the concepts and techniques of mastery by authorities in their fields. Explores reincarnation, belief systems and transformative tools from astrology to crystals.

$11.95 Softcover 206p

ISBN 0-929385-48-9

LIVING RAINBOWS
Gabriel H. Bain

A fascinating "how-to" manual to make experiencing human, astral, animal and plant auras an everyday event. Series of techniques, exercises and illustrations guide the reader to see and hear aural energy. Spiral-bound workbook.

$14.95 Softcover 134p

ISBN 0-929385-42-X

ACUPRESSURE FOR THE SOUL
Nancy Fallon, Ph.D.

A revolutionary vision of emotions as sources of power, rocket fuel for fulfilling our purpose. A formula for awakening transformation with 12 beautiful illustrations.

$11.95   Softcover   150p   ISBN 0-929385-49-7

THE GOLDEN PATH

"Book of Lessons" by the master teachers explaining the process of channeling, Akashic Records, karma, opening the third eye, the ego and the meaning of Bible stories. It is a master class for opening your personal pathway.

$11.95   Softcover   200p   ISBN 0-929385-43-8

LIVING THE GOLDEN PATH
Practical Soul-utions to Today's Problems

Guidance that can be used in the real world to solve dilemmas, to strengthen inner resolves and see the Light at the end of the road. Covers the difficult issues of addictions, rape, abortion, suicide and personal loss.

$11.95   Softcover   186p   ISBN 0-929385-65-9

KNOWLEDGE FROM THE STARS

A telepath with contact to ETs, Bateman has provided a wide spectrum of scientific information. A fascinating compilation of articles surveying the Federation, ETs, evolution and the trading houses, all part of the true history of the galaxy.

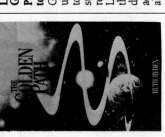

$11.95   Softcover   171p   ISBN 0-929385-39-X

DRAGONS AND CHARIOTS

An explanation of spacecraft, propulsion systems, gravity, the Dragon, manipulated Light and intergalactic motherships by a renowned telepath who details specific technological information received from ETs.

$9.95   Softcover   65p   ISBN 0-929385-45-4

FOREVER YOUNG
Gladys Iris Clark

You can create a longer younger life! Viewing a lifetime of a full century, a remarkable woman shares her secrets for longevity and rejuvenation. A manual for all ages. Explores tools for optimizing vitality, nutrition, skin care via Tibetan exercises, crystals, sex.

$9.95   Softcover   109p   ISBN 0-929385-53-5